KALYĀṆAMITRA

Volume II
Pragmatic Skills for Buddhist Spiritual Care

Monica Sanford

with contributions from

Victor Gabriel
Nathan Jishin Michon
Henry C.H. Shiu
Linda Hochstetler

Kalyāṇamitra
Volume II: Pragmatic Skills for Buddhist Spiritual Care

Rev. Dr. Monica Sanford

Text © by Monica Sanford, 2025
All rights reserved

Book design: Karma Yönten Gyatso
Cover photo: Ekachai Prasertkaew, Shutterstock

Published by
The Sumeru Press Inc.
PO Box 75, Manotick Main Post Office
Manotick, ON K4M 1A2

ISBN 978-1-896559-45-2 Volume I, *print edition*
ISBN 978-1-896559-70-4 Volume II, *print edition*

LIBRARY AND ARCHIVES CANADA CATALOGUING IN PUBLICATION

Title: Kalyāṇamitra / Rev. Dr. Monica Sanford.
Names: Sanford, Monica, 1980- author.
Description: Volume II has statement of responsibility: Rev. Dr. Monica Sanford ; with contributions from Victor Gabriel, Nathan Jishin Michon, Henry C.H. Shiu, Linda Hochstetler. | Includes bibliographical references and index. | Volume II. Pragmatic skills for Buddhist spiritual care.
Identifiers: Canadiana 20200365568 | ISBN 9781896559704 (v. 2 ; softcover)
Subjects: LCSH: Chaplains. | LCSH: Buddhism. | LCSH: Spiritual care (Medical care) | | LCSH: Pastoral counseling (Buddhism)
Classification: LCC BQ5305.C4 S26 2020 | DDC 294.3/61—dc23

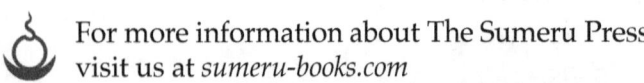
For more information about The Sumeru Press
visit us at *sumeru-books.com*

*To Colin, who takes care of me for reasons I cannot even begin to fathom.
I love you.*

Contents
Volume II – Pragmatic Skills for Buddhist Spiritual Care

Acknowledgments 9
Introduction 11
How to Use These Books 15

Part I: Pragmatic Skills for Every Context

1 Presence 21
Not Being Present 21
Being Present in Meditation & Daily Life . . 23
Being Present in Spiritual Care 26
Being Present for Yourself: Reflexivity . . . 28

2 Listening & Responding 33
Not Listening 33
Listening 35
Responding Appropriately 38
Responding to Difficulty 46

3 Empathy & Compassion 49
The Lexicon of Open-Heartedness 49
The Dark Side: Contagion, Fatigue,
    Trauma, Burnout 52
Cultivating the Four Divine Abodes 56
Connection and Satisfaction 59

4 Spiritual Assessment 63
Existing Assessment Tools and Models . . 63
Buddhist Spiritual Assessment Models . . 68
Creating Spiritual Assessments 72
Charting and Note-Keeping 74

5 Personal & Professional Boundaries . . 79
Confidentiality, Transference,
    Countertransference, & Projection . . . 82
Healthy Boundaries at Work & Home . . . 84
Maintaining Communities of
    Accountability 92

6 Spiritual Leadership **99**
How to Be a Good Follower 99
Models for Leadership 103
Spiritual Authority in Spiritual Care . . . 107
Spiritually Empowering Leaders 111

7 Part I Conclusion & Reflection **115**
Conclusion 115
Reflections Questions for Chapters 1 to 6 . 121
Listening & Responding Exercises 123
Servant Leadership Questionnaire 124

Part II: Pragmatic Skills for Particular Contexts

Introduction **129**

8 Prayer & Ritual
    by Victor Gabriel **131**
Introduction 131
Prayer as Relevant to the Buddhist
    Chaplain 132
Prayer from an Emic Perspective 135
Tibetan Ritual Theory 136
Dynamics of Buddhist Prayer 137
Conclusion 140

9 Interreligious Competencies
    by Nathan Jishin Michon **145**
Personal Interreligious Background . . . 146
Interfaith Consciousness and Definitions . 147
Where Religion and Culture Intertwine . 147
Beginner's Mind and Right Mindfulness . 149
Responsible Learning and Awareness . . 150
Interfaith Rituals 153
Contemplative Practices for
    Multireligious or Interreligious Care . . 155

10 Intercultural Competencies
by Henry C.H. Shiu 157
Dharmic Basis for Intercultural
   Competencies 157
Principles for Intercultural Competency . . .158

11 Practical Psychology for Chaplains
by Linda Hochstetler 167
Introduction 167
Risk Assessment Protocols 168
Homicide Risk Assessments 171
Child Abuse 172
Elder Abuse. 174
Domestic Violence 175
Addictions 177
Mental Health 178
Effective Referrals 179
Non-ordinary Spiritual Experiences 180
Community of Support 180
Potential Barriers. 181
Continuity of Care. 182
General Wholesome Supports 182

12 Privilege, Oppression, & Power 185
Reckoning With the Positionality 190
Case Study: A White Suburban Bubble . . .193
Dealing with Discrimination 196
Working Towards Social Justice 201

13 Part II Conclusion & Reflection. 209
Conclusion 209
Reflection Questions for Chapters 8 to 12 . 215
Ritual Design Exercises 215
New Explorations in Buddhist Chaplaincy 218

Appendices

Buddhist Chaplaincy Programs 225
Case Studies
   Buddhist Spiritual Assessment
     for Charlie. 227
   Buddhist Spiritual Assessment
     for Edith 232
Bibliography. .237
Index 247

Volume I – A Model for Buddhist Spiritual Care

Acknowledgments 9

Introduction: The Four Noble Truths . . . 11

1. What is a Buddhist Chaplain? 15
Chaplains & Spiritual Care 16
Three Stories of Buddhist Spiritual Care . . 23
Constructing Buddhist Chaplains through
   Education, Reflection, & Practice 30
Conclusion & Reflection 35

2. What Do Buddhist Chaplains Do? 39
The Dharma of Spiritual Care 40
Sources of Spiritual Care in the Dharma . . 41
Modern Literature on Buddhist
   Chaplaincy & Spiritual Care 46
Relationships with Teachers and
   Sanghas 51
Integrating through Reflection 53
The Places of Spiritual Care 59
Effective Spiritual Care 68
Conclusion & Reflection 73

3. The Three *Prajñās* Framework 81
Sutta on Learning & Practicing
   Spiritual Care 82
Emergence of the Framework 83
Literature Review of the Three *Prajñās* . . . 85
The Three *Prajñās* Framework of
   Spiritual Care 97
Validating the Framework 108
Conclusion & Reflection 117

4. *Kalyāṇamitra*, or Spiritual Friendship . 121
Literature Review of *Kalyāṇamitra* 123
Stage Four: *Kalyāṇamitra* 135
Implications, Applications, and
   Limitations 137
Conclusion & Reflection 144

Appendices

Appendix A: Research Methods 147
Appendix B: Sources for *Kalyāṇamitra*
   within the Pāli Canon 165
Bibliography 171
Index 183

ACKNOWLEDGMENTS

I would like to offer deep appreciation to everyone who has asked me "When is Volume II coming out?" Your desire for more resources for Buddhist chaplaincy has been my core source of motivation throughout this process. I only wish I could have met your expectations sooner.

I would also like to thank my editor, John, whose patience is indefatigable. He has unfailingly supported the work and my vision for this book.

Likewise, my coworkers in the Office of Ministry Studies at Harvard Divinity School have been a constant source of support. Knowing that I can lean on them gives me the space in my schedule to focus on research and writing. A special thanks to Jonathan, who makes my life so much easier, Teddy and Laura, who support everything I do, and Leslie, Dawn, Lysette, and Gloria, who are my sisters in the work.

I must also acknowledge my many students who constantly inspire and astound me. Thanks to the graduate assistants who have supported my research and writing projects over the past three years, including Keila, Frances, Hongmin, Dana, Tristan, and Alex. Also a special thanks to the students in my courses on "Spiritual Formation on the Buddhist Path" for serving as an indirect source of inspiration for Chapters 4 and 6.

Thank you to Cheryl, without whom I literally would not have my job (which allows me to write books like this), and Janet, Charlie, and David H., who advocated for its creation. Your mentorship, individual and collective, have meant so much to me.

Finally, thank you to my brave co-authors, Victor, Nathan, Henry, and Linda, for your wonderful contributions. Many thanks as well to those who encouraged me to tackle Chapter 12 myself. You advice, admonishment, and guidance are deeply appreciated.

Introduction

*K*alyāṇamitra means good, noble, or virtuous friend. It has special connotations in relation to the Buddhist path. Therefore, I have chosen to translate it as "spiritual friend." A *kalyāṇamitra* encourages us to learn, understand, and practice the Dharma. In Buddhism, Dharma is the greatest gift we can give. The Buddha described himself as *kalyāṇamitra* to all beings in the *Upaḍḍha Sutta* (SN 45.2) because "by relying upon me as a good friend, Ānanda, beings subject to birth are freed from birth; beings subject to aging are freed from aging; beings subject to death are freed from death; beings subject to sorrow, lamentation, pain, displeasure, and despair are freed from sorrow, lamentation, pain, displeasure, and despair." In Buddhist traditions, buddhas, bodhisattvas, gurus, and teachers serve as spiritual friends, leading suffering beings on the path to liberation.

That may seem like a high bar for a Buddhist chaplain to meet. Yet throughout the Buddhist texts, it is also clear that the spiritual friend comes in many different forms, from the most colloquial form of the friend we have known since childhood to the unexpectedly helpful stranger who shows us only a moment of kindness and disappears before we learn their name. Both can be *kalyāṇamitra* so long as they encourage our spiritual growth. Even challenging or paradoxical figures, from beggars to sex workers to trickster deities, have been named as *kalyāṇamitra* if they aid you on your path. In the *Bodhicaryāvatāra* (*Way of the Bodhisattva*), the author, Śāntideva classically aspires to be a lamp, bridge, boat, bed, doctor, guide, or anything that is needed by travelers along the way.

More commonly, *kalyāṇamitra* are those mundane people we meet who serve as moral role models for us, demonstrate the (usually still imperfect) fruits of a spiritual life, guide us towards what is good for us, and, occasionally, introduce us to the Buddhist Dharma. We can find *kalyāṇamitra* in our immediate family, our circle of ordinary friends, our teachers at school, mentors at work, colleagues and coworkers, and even in those we serve. A *kalyāṇamitra* is not always a personal friend in the modern sense of the relationship. In fact, most of the *kalyāṇamitra* in my life have not been my "friends" in this way. For the would-be Buddhist chaplain, our *kalyāṇamitra* play a special role in helping form us into the kind of professional who can offer spiritual care to others by modeling and offering spiritual care to us. Chaplains who themselves have good spiritual friends are better able to become spiritual friends to others. This is the thesis of my first volume in this series (Sanford, *Kalyāṇamitra: A Model for Buddhist Spiritual Care*, 2021, from Sumeru Press). Thankfully, for any aspiring chaplain, we meet many *kalyāṇamitra* among our teachers, classmates, and supervisors during our preparation for chaplaincy.

The Buddhist scriptures also contain a great deal of information on the behavior and qualities of spiritual friends. In the *Mitta Sutta* (AN 7.36) of the Pali Canon, the Buddha describes seven qualities of a spiritual friend.

> A friend gives what is hard to give,
> and he does what is hard to do.
> He forgives you your harsh words
> and endures what is hard to endure.

> He tells you his secrets,
> yet he preserves your secrets.
> He does not forsake you in
>   difficulties,
> Nor does he roughly despise you.
>
> The person here in whom
> These qualities are found is a friend.
> One desiring a friend
> Should resort to such a person.
> (Bodhi, 2012, p. 1022)

This passage has always struck me. In what way does a friend "give what is hard to give?" As a chaplain myself, enduring the suffering of those we serve, maintaining their confidentiality, and not forsaking or despising those in difficulty all seemed clear. But what exactly do I "give" to careseekers? I show up, I spend time with them, I listen, and I pray when requested. But in the face of calamity and death, it can often feel like I've "given" very little.

A possible elucidation to this question was suggested recently by a colleague, Jampa Wang, a chaplain and CPE Educator at New York Presbyterian hospital. In a conversation about healthcare chaplaincy, Jampa mentioned the "Three Types of Generosity" and helpfully sent me a direct reference to Geshe Lhundun Sopa's book, *Steps on the Path to Enlightenment: A Commentary on Tsongkhapa's Lamrim Chenmo, Volume 3: The Way of the Bodhisattva* (2004). A bodhisattva may practice generosity by giving the teachings, giving fearlessness, and through material gifts. Jampa explained that while he very rarely teaches the Dharma in his role as chaplain, he sees his primary gift as that of fearlessness. He helps the patients and families he serves face their difficulties with less fear and anxiety. While we did not discuss in detail how he does this, much sage advice can be gleaned from Buddhist sources.

Generosity, giving, or *dāna* (Pali and Sanskrit) is one of the chief virtues of Buddhism emphasized in all traditions and lineages. In the Pali Canon, generosity is called a "treasure" (AN 7.6) that brings great "rewards" (AN 5.35) to the giver. Even a small gift can have great power (AN 3.57) as it aids us in overcoming the stinginess that is a hindrance to spiritual progress (AN 5.256-263 and SN 1.32). Generosity becomes both a character virtue and a skill to be cultivated:

> These five are a person of integrity's gifts. Which five? A person of integrity gives a gift with a sense of conviction. A person of integrity gives a gift attentively. A person of integrity gives a gift in season. A person of integrity gives a gift with an empathetic heart. A person of integrity gives a gift without adversely affecting himself or others.
> (Thanissaro, 2004, AN)

Giving must be done in a way that harms no one, harbors no ulterior motive, creates no resentment, and, most importantly, that which is given must be appropriate to the recipient. Giving what is needed at the right time requires careful attention and understanding, two qualities that chaplains cultivate deeply in the practice of spiritual care. Giving is also a practice useful to the giver for cultivating nonattachment. This begins through nonattachment to wealth and material objects, like money, food, or possessions. Or it involves nonattachment to time, attention, and effort, such as by volunteering to help others, a generosity open even to those of little means. Giving is an antidote to both material greed and ego-grasping. Robert Buswell describes how "The essential catalyst to cultivation will prove to be, not one of the several important concepts of doctrine and praxis for which Buddhism is renowned, but the simple practice of charity or giving (*dāna*), a specific type of merit-making." (Buswell, 1990, p. 108). Over time, the giver cultivates a nonattachment to self that leads to liberation from suffering.

Because of this chain of causation, giving takes the role of the first of the *paramitas*, or perfections, in Mahayana and Vajrayana Buddhism. Lama Sopa draws from these lineages in his interpretation of Tsongkhapa, that great Tibetan mystic and systematizer of the Thirteenth Century. Tsongkhapa identifies generosity with a state of mind cultivated by the bodhisattvas, one of "disinterested non-attachment to all their possessions and their body" (Tsongkhapa quoting Atisa, 2004, p. 114). It is this state of mind that causes bodhisattvas to be ready, willing, and capable of doing or giving whatever is needed to each suffering being they encounter. Thus, the perfection of generosity is not the complete elimination of worldly poverty, but the perfection of the character of the giver. Lama Sopa describes this as "a consciousness that is willing to give, and the physical and verbal actions that are motivated by this attitude." (Sopa, 2004, p. 255) The mental aspect of generosity is what conveys "reward" or merit to the giver as well as the recipient of generosity. It also strengthens the pattern of generosity, ensuring repetition of behaviors that actively alleviate the suffering of more and more beings. Sopa describes two complementary aspects to the mentality of generosity: 1) non-attachment to material objects, and 2) sincere desire to help others. The first aspect prevents harm to the giver. When one is non-attached, there is no fear in giving "too much"; giving is a joyful activity. The second aspect is also active in compassion and loving-kindness (see Chapter 3) and requires a focus on the other to understand their needs.

Lama Sopa is clear that even though we refer to it as the "perfection" of generosity, we do not all need to be perfect bodhisattvas to practice generosity. Many of us think we can't possibly be so generous as the buddhas and bodhisattvas we read about in stories. Such ideals of generosity may even prompt fear and shame in us. Yet, generosity is often emphasized at the very beginning of our path because it can be practiced even by us imperfect beings. "Just because one does not have the perfect motivation does not mean it is impossible to practice generosity. There are many levels of practice." (Sopa, 2004, p. 256) The goal is to slowly perfect the motivation behind our giving through the repeated practice of giving. We often give with mixed motivations. We want to help others, but we also want some recognition for ourselves and possibly some future reciprocity. "The bodhisattva's practice of generosity," on the other hand, "the perfection of generosity, is giving without any expectation of future reward." This perfection is represented in the common Buddhist practice of dedicating the merit. Lama Sopa continues, "Giving without expectation is more than a simple willingness to give whatever belongs to you; it means that even the merit created from acts of generosity is dedicated to others." (Sopa, 2004, p. 527) Through these simple ritualized acts of giving and dedicating merit we slowly cultivate the perfection of giving as a basis of all our actions in the world.

Tsongkhapa's chapter on generosity and Lama Sopa's commentary are well worth reading in their entirety, but I shall skip ahead to the section on types of gifts to be given. In addition to material gifts and the gift of the Dharma, a third type of gift may be particularly relevant to chaplains, as my colleague Jampa pointed out: the gift of fearlessness. While "fear" is the most visceral form of this emotion, we can expand this idea to encompass forms of aversion that create suffering, including anger, hatred, disgust, embarrassment, shame, anxiety, and more. All of these are manifestations of aversion, of not wanting whatever is happening or whatever we think may happen in the future. Tsongkhapa describes this gift in a very straightforward way as protection from causes of harm such as robbers, tigers, and natural disasters. Lama Sopa describes how we can shelter people from danger: "We start with what we can do; even saving an insect is the practice of giving protection. From small and easy tasks we progress to greater ones." In fact, we begin to protect others from danger when we commit to ethical vows, precepts, and standards. The Five

Precepts of Buddhism and the Chaplains' Code of Ethics (see Chapter 5) exist to protect others from harm, so that they need not fear us. Beyond that, people fear judgement and shame, so approaching them with compassionate and positive regard (see Chapter 3) builds a basis of trust needed for spiritual care.

In the American culture in which I was raised, religion and spiritual matters were not considered a "polite" topic of conversation among strangers. So again, we offer them freedom from fear of social censure or proselytizing and a space where they can openly discuss their spiritual and existential concerns. Moreover, people in difficult circumstances may also hide their suffering, fearing that it is "too much" and will drive people away. They have likely already experienced this first-hand by the time they meet us, so through our equanimity and courage in facing their distress with them, we offer them freedom from the fear that we will abandon them in their time of greatest need.

I believe this last form of fearlessness – the ability to face whatever suffering is taking place with compassion and equanimity – is the special gift of the chaplain. We cannot take their suffering away, but in our willingness to face suffering without fear (or with enough courage to face that fear), we model for them an ability to accept and respond to their situation. In discussing their suffering and their spiritual lives in an open and nonjudgemental way, we help them find some kind of ground from which they can make decisions about their situation that honors what they value most. Many of us have experienced great suffering and know that having someone beside us when we do so, even if they can do nothing about the suffering itself, adds a generous portion to our courage in the face of that suffering. This is the gift of fearlessness. I mean this in the sense of "less fear" (fear-less) or "more courage," not "no fear whatsoever." Even a drop less of fear is worth the effort.

Spiritual care is a generous act. We give our time, energy, presence, compassion, and wisdom to support the spiritual wellbeing of another with no expectation of reward or attachment to an outcome. Of course, we want beings to suffer less. This motivation is essential to the development of compassion. But we must also be willing to give ourselves knowing the outcome is uncertain. The perfections (*paramitas*) begin with generosity. If one can perfect (or simply improve) one's generosity, then one is less prone to become discouraged at the endless pouring out of compassion that this samsaric existence calls for. It becomes an endless opportunity for generosity. The perfection of wisdom calls for seeing our every possession and deed as already belonging to others, to everyone. In this way, according to Lama Sopa, "Whenever someone needs something of theirs, they think, 'OK. This belongs to them anyway.' They feel no difficulty parting with things." (Sopa, 2004, p. 263) Thus, giving to suffering beings becomes joyful and we can sustain our practice through countless lifetimes. We do not have to start in that joyful, selfless place, of course. Generosity is a gradual training:

> In the beginning we do not actually give things away. Slowly and gradually our mental practice will convince us to actually give. We start small, giving only as much as we can without stinginess – perhaps just a few cents or a few mouthfulls of food. Little by little, as we develop the mind, we increase the quantity and quality of our gifts. When one lacks stinginess and feels no hardship in giving, then naturally the physical action of philanthropy will follow. If one's mind is not trained and one crazily gives something away at the urging of others, a little later one may have long and hard regrets. Then that act of giving will be wasted; it even becomes a negative karma. This is not the way to practice. Mental training

– thinking about the faults of stinginess and the benefits of giving – is the key practice in the beginning. After developing the mind one will be happy to give, and then looking back on that action one will be joyful. This doubles one's generosity.
(Sopa, 2004, p. 263)

Different Buddhist teachers may encourage giving first (even in small ways), to habituate one to the act of giving, or to cultivate the mental practice and the actual practice simultaneously. Either way, giving forms the basis of much Buddhist practice.

When you consider embarking upon a career as a chaplain, you should consider those to whom you are giving spiritual care. I do not mean in the mundane sense of who your careseekers are (e.g., hospital patients, inmates, students). I mean, in what ways and to whom is the act of spiritual care a gift? What is it you are giving? What are you able and willing to give? What are you not able or willing to give (right now)? What are you even afraid to give? With what motivation do you embark on this vocation? It's certainly not for fame and renown, nor even for a generous salary (as if!). Do you expect others to thank you? Do you thrive on praise? Do you expect that the work of a chaplain will help you progress on your own spiritual path? Do you want respect for your spiritual attainments or "selfless" efforts? Are you trying to purify some negative karma or generate positive outcomes or better rebirths? Wanting praise, respect, or spiritual progress are all very normal human desires. But consider carefully, how can your practice of spiritual care become an act of generosity?

When I set out to write these books, I knew that I would have benefited from books like these when I was training as a chaplain. If I wrote them for anyone, I wrote them for myself. Thus, I have already been given a great gift in this opportunity to clarify my own thinking on matters concerning my vocation.

Even if no one ever reads them, I have already found my treasure. Nevertheless, if you should read them, I do hope you will be inspired to give those gifts that you are best suited to give. I hope others will find them useful. I cannot live up to Tsongkhapa or Lama Sopa's advice to give without expectation (yet!). These books will not bring me fame or wealth. The field of Buddhist chaplaincy is still very small, after all. I simply give what I am able to give. I dedicate the merit of these works to all the Buddhist chaplains who will provide spiritual care to countless beings (whether they read my books or not). May all beings be swiftly liberated from suffering!

How to Use These Books

This book is the second volume in a series under the name *Kalyāṇamitra*. The first volume presents *A Model for Buddhist Spiritual Care* (2021, Sumeru Press) based on direct research with practicing chaplains. Volume I provides an overview of the spiritual and vocational development of the Buddhist chaplain moving through four stages: self, student, chaplain, and *kalyāṇamitra*. The culminating stage of *kalyāṇamitra* characterizes what happens when we can be present with careseekers in a truly mindful and egoless way, thus providing a model of spiritual care practice for chaplains to aspire to. It is not the only possible model, but it is one that is found throughout all the Buddhist traditions I have thus far surveyed and referenced either explicitly or implicitly by the chaplains who participated in the research. Each stage of the model is further explicated according to the Three *Prajñās* Framework of wisdom developed by listening (*śrutamayīprajñā*), wisdom developed by contemplation or reflection (*cintāmayīprajñā*), and wisdom developed by practice (*bhāvanāmayīprajñā*). Each aspect is then further broken down according to the intentions, tasks, and fruition (outcomes) that characterize it. For example, when listening to develop wisdom during the stage of "self," before we have begun to study, we listen with the intention of finding meaning for oneself, especially in relation to explanations for distressing life events. We may do this (tasks) by reading books or articles, going to Dharma talks, watching videos, or listening to podcasts. Through this process we begin to develop Right Intention and Right View (fruition).

Later on, in the stage of "*kalyāṇamitra*," we may practice spiritual care by seeking liberation from suffering for all beings (intention). As a chaplain *kalyāṇamitra*, we do this by accurately assessing our careseeker's situation and needs to intervene appropriately (task). The fruition chaplains described of these actions includes cultivating positive emotions and values, including relief from suffering, and developing direct insight into important Buddhist truths, such as nonself, emptiness, and interdependence.

Volume I describes this entire arc in more detail, drawing directly on the wisdom of chaplains who contributed to the research as well as the Dharma. Thus, it presents the first overarching set of theories on the topic of Buddhist spiritual care. As such, it can serve as a model or guide upon which to scaffold the pragmatic skills covered in this volume. It also contains many direct examples and stories about the work of Buddhist chaplains, including the challenges they face, that will be useful to anyone considering or starting the vocation.

This book, as a companion, details the tasks chaplains engage in throughout their work. Part I outlines skills that chaplains utilize in almost every situation, starting with presence (Chapter 1), then listening and responding (Chapter 2), cultivation of empathy and compassion (Chapter 3), the process of spiritual assessment (Chapter 4), keeping personal and professional boundaries (Chapter 5), and practicing spiritual leadership (Chapter 6). The concluding chapter of Part I (Chapter 7) provides concluding thoughts, reflection questions, and some exercises should this book be used as a textbook in a training course on Buddhist chaplaincy. The first section of the book is modelled on similar volumes available to theistic chaplains, particularly Howard Clinebell's *Basic Types of Pastoral Care & Counseling* and Rabbi Dayle Friedman's *Jewish Pastoral Care: A Practical Handbook*, both of which I found useful (if, at times, frustrating) in my own education. Rather than drawing on Christian or Jewish sources to elucidate these basic skills, the chapters of Part I provide a distinctly Buddhist presentation, synthesized with the best that modern secular counseling has to offer. Each chapter is written to help readers reflect on your basic motivations before employing each skill, clarify your values and approach, try different things, and reflect on what you have learned from ongoing attempts. In this way, each chapter walks the chaplain-to-be through the intention-task-fruition process outlined in Volume I with respect to each set of skills.

Part II introduces pragmatic skills that chaplains use in some, but not every, situation. This section also introduces different voices to the conversation. Chapter 8 on ritual and prayer is provided by Victor Gabriel, longtime professor and chair of the Buddhist chaplaincy program at University of the West and a Tibetan Buddhist and multireligious practitioner. Chapter 9 outlines interreligious competencies and is provided by Nathan Jishin Michon, a Shingon priest and Buddhist chaplain currently living and working in Japan (himself the editor of two important volumes on chaplaincy: *A Thousand Hands*, 2016, The Sumeru Press, and *Refuge in the Storm*, 2023, North Atlantic Books). Henry Shiu, a professor in the Buddhist track of the Master of Psychospiritual Studies (MPS) program at Emmanual College of the University of Toronto and specialist in Mahayana Buddhism, provides Chapter 10 on intercultural competencies. Finally, Linda Hochstetler, a Vajrayana practitioner, meditation teacher, and a registered social worker with the Ontario Association of Social Workers, provides Chapter 11 with an practical overview of psychological concerns for chaplains.

Unlike the first section, these chapters cannot possibly cover their topics in depth. Each is a brief, but precious, introduction to topics that chaplains-to-be will continue to explore throughout their education and careers. (They could, should, and perhaps one day will, be books unto themselves.) Each includes long lists of further resources. Likewise, my own contribution to Part II, Chapter 12 on how the dynamics of privilege, oppression, and power affect the world we live in and work we do is but a starting point. Chapter 13 serves as a conclusion to Part II, containing a reflective essay, reflection questions, exercises, and some thoughts on the road ahead for Buddhist chaplaincy.

If you are using this volume as a textbook, it is recommended to assign each chapter along with the associated reflection questions and exercises in either Chapter 7 (for Part I) or Chapter 13 (for Part II). The skills are presented in a way that each subsequent skill scaffolds upon the prior ones. If you are reading this volume on your own for your own personal or professional growth, then you may want to jump around to whichever chapter is most relevant to your present circumstances. If you are already working as a chaplain or chaplain intern, it may even be useful to read a chapter before beginning your work for the day or week, and then come back to review it afterward. What was most relevant? What would have been useful? What was missing from the chapter or not as helpful as it could have been? (Do drop me a note and let me know.) I find it endlessly useful to write reflections on my practice of spiritual care. Alternatively, if you don't enjoy the writing process, finding a colleague or friend with whom you can chat about your work can be just as useful (if not more so, because then you get at least two perspectives). The process of articulating what we are doing, why we are doing it, how it went, and setting intentions for next time, can be endlessly edifying. This kind of mindful reflection is likewise a gift that gives twice, first to us as the caregiver, second to our future careseekers (and, third to future generations should we care to publish).

This book is not intended to be a metric of "correct" approaches to Buddhist chaplaincy. In fact, as the first of its genre, it is probably also the worst of its genre. I expect much better scholar-practitioners to learn from whatever mistakes it contains and improve upon the content and format. Let whatever negative karma it generates fall solely and wholly upon myself and may the merit of this volume ripen into liberation from suffering for infinite beings!

Part I
Pragmatic Skills for Every Context

Everything begins with presence. It is only through our presence with people that we can care for them. This may sound so obvious that it can go without saying. However, presence is not simply being in the same room at the same time, just as meditation is not the same as sitting down. Presence requires a particular quality of intention, attention, and response that we can train, just as we train our minds and bodies in meditation. All other skills outlined in this book flow from our ability to be present – listening, responding, empathizing, having compassion, assessing, maintaining appropriate boundaries, and practicing spiritual leadership.

As you will see, many of these skills are presented dualistically – being present versus not being present, listening versus not listening, leading versus following. They are not binary, though they do often appear on a dualistic spectrum. This is because human attention is selective. We find it difficult, if not impossible, to pay full attention to everything happening at once (indeed, doing so often results in diagnosed attention 'disorders'). Therefore, training in presence, listening, empathy, or assessment is also training in attention. As Buddhists, we can see this as a practice of mindfulness. As chaplains, we use our mindfulness in service of particular goals, such as to become attuned to suffering, and to improve particular skills, such as concentration.

Through this mindful caregiving, we develop discernment as caregivers and refine our ability to pay attention to the proper things at the proper times. There is some trial and error involved, and the following chapters will provide a theoretical grounding for this work. The only way to truly hone these skills is through practice. We often begin to practice caregiving in the relatively safe spaces of our classrooms, Dharma halls, and living rooms. At some point, we begin to practice with the careseekers we will serve as chaplains.

In practice, it is important to continuously reflect on our work. We learned about the importance of reflection and reflexivity in Volume I. Practice and reflection bring continual improvement to any skill. Therefore, you may find it useful to return to this book again and again, even years into your work. I hope you will also write chapters of your own and continue to refine the ideas presented here and pass them on to the next generation of Buddhist chaplains.

1
PRESENCE

Not Being Present

Not being present is very easy. Most of us do it most of the time. Whenever we are worrying about the past or dreaming about the future, when we are thinking about someone far away, ruminating on a bad feeling we just can't shake, or enjoying a pleasant fantasy, then we are not present to what is happening here and now. We are not even present to the effects of being mentally and emotionally elsewhere, so it is difficult to see the harm of our mental absence. Sometimes, this kind of thinking is even productive, such as when I'm planning a class I'll teach in the future or reflecting on a conversation I just had with a student to gain some insight. Sometimes being not present is a survival strategy. People who are subject to abuse or trauma often 'check out' to psychologically shield themselves from harm.

In a less extreme example, an engrossing novel can be a blessing while waiting in a doctor's office. There are many reasons not to be present in our lives, not all of them bad. Our attention is selective in useful ways. In this context, when I say 'not present,' I only mean that our attention is not focused on what is happening here and now. Our mind has a wonderful ability to focus our attention so far away from where we are physically present that we can even lose track of our surroundings entirely. When the here and now involves us acting in the capacity of a chaplain with a careseeker, being present, bringing out attention to the here and now and the people before us, is the most fundamentally important thing we can do. This involves both the ability to focus our attention and the ability to overcome our habits of wandering mind.

The habits we have of not being present are adaptive. They help us cope with our daily lives, learn from past experiences, and plan for the future – traits unique among humans (we think). Adaptive behaviors make us more fit for our physical, social, and cultural environment; they help us survive. The trouble is that adaptive behaviors become maladaptive when the context changes. If I am raised by a parent who is needlessly and relentless critical, it may have helped me as a child to learn how to 'tune them out.' However, if my boss is now providing feedback on my job performance and I unconsciously engage in the habit of ignoring an authority figure, this harms my job prospects and relationship with my boss. As an adult, the habit that helped me survive my childhood may now block an opportunity to build better relationships. Thankfully, we can now make different choices, even though being present isn't always easy.

Many of our habits of not being present are established before we even have the language to describe what is happening. Some are reinforced by the rewards we receive for mental and emotional labor. We are praised for being well-organized, despite the obsessive worry that lies behind our perfectionism. We are commended for having a 'cool head,' which is built on years of emotional distancing. Most of us don't have a meditation teacher in kindergarten to show us how to be present. For Americans, in particular, being present is counter to our consumer-driven, hyper-individualistic, instant-gratification culture.

Unexamined, our maladaptive habits can do a lot of damage to us, our personal relationships, and our practice as chaplains. The chaplains I study speak clearly about the negative consequences of not being present with careseekers. Sometimes they felt emotionally disconnected and apathetic, while at other times they felt emotionally overwhelmed and unable to process what the careseeker was sharing with them. At best, we are unable to help the careseeker. At worst, we may harm the careseeker through neglect or unskillful responses.

Koshin Paley Ellison, of the New York Zen Center for Contemplative Care, interprets presence through the lens of the precept against stealing: "Not listening and not being present may be thought of as 'stealing' a potential moment of understanding and healing in our shared encounter" (Ellison, 2016, p. 92).

In addition, the chaplains I study also reported self-harm that comes from not being present, usually manifested in strong negative thoughts and feelings directed inward. They were harshly critical of their inability to be present and connect. The antidote to this, however, is not bitter self-judgment, but self-awareness and self-care. Many chaplains developed practices and rituals, often based on their meditation experience, to help them recenter, return to the present, and connect with careseekers. To be present, we examine the opposite first, because if we can't tell when we're not present, it's impossible to change this ingrained habit.

What causes us to not be present with careseekers? Chaplains I study described at least two general causes (there may be more) – distraction and nervousness – though each can take myriad different forms. Distraction is the presence of intrusive thoughts or emotions unrelated to the present situation. Nervousness is the opposite, an almost obsessive angst about the present situation. Both are forms of anxiety comprised of intrusive thoughts or emotions that limit our ability to perceive and process what is happening right here and now. Anxiety often stems from contextual stressors, such as poor working conditions. These need to be addressed with the proper people at the proper times so that they do not interfere with our ability to be present when working with careseekers. See the section on burnout in Chapter 3 and on healthy boundaries in Chapter 5 for more on these topics. Even as we respond to various sources of stress, we must also be able to focus our attention past the anxiety they create when we are in a caring encounter.

When we are distracted, we may be replaying a difficult conversation from yesterday over and over in our mind or fretting about some news we are waiting to receive. We may even be proactively trying to plan how to handle some problem, but now is not the appropriate time to do that. In some cases, we may be too tired or hungry to summon the mental energy needed to focus our attention and find ourselves daydreaming about our favorite television show while a careseeker with dementia repeats the same story for the third time. We also engage in distraction as a mental safety mechanism when we are psychologically triggered by a situation. That patient dying in the emergency room reminds us so strongly of our brother, we find ourselves reminiscing about our childhood rather than being present with the family's fear, which is now inextricably bound up with our fear of losing a loved one. If this is one of our first experiences at the hospital, it can color future shifts.

The second cause is nervousness, or an inability to relax and accept the present moment just as it is. Nervousness can create an unhealthy focus on doing or saying just the 'right' thing or avoiding the 'wrong' thing. To cope with this, we might create elaborate plans for what to do or say. We walk into places with agendas about how the encounter is going to go, trying to control the situation to avoid any misstep, but this can be just as unhealthy. Ellison returns to the precept against stealing and, in Zen fashion, advises "We may also use this precept by asking ourselves, 'How can I be satisfied with what exists? Can we help the patient and family be satisfied with the current conditions, or must we change something radically?'" (2016, p. 92). We can only help the careseeker be present to themselves to the extent that we are able to be present for them and relatively free from self-involved anxiety. (A level of self-awareness and reflexivity is healthy. One can tell the difference based on the degree to which the self-focus is unpleasant, neutral, or even pleasantly reassuring, as when grounded in confidence and equanimity.)

Buddhism speaks about the benefits of being present and the drawbacks of not being present. I have seen Buddhists use these teachings as a cudgel against themselves and others. I began this section with a discussion of how we develop habits of not being present because, at some point in our lives, those habits served a need. We needn't feel ashamed or embarrassed about that. We simply need to be aware of it. When we learned those habits, they probably weren't the best possible response, just the best of the options we had available to us. If we had known then what we know now, we could have chosen a better response, one based on an ability to be present. But we were a different person then, both figuratively and, in the Buddhist sense, literally. That person was working with the causes, conditions, and knowledge they had at the time and they managed to survive to become this person. We owe them our gratitude for making our practice of presence possible now. Our ability to be fully present with careseekers (and ourselves) may be one of the greatest gifts Buddhist chaplains have to offer. This ability is founded largely (though not entirely) on Buddhist contemplative practices, which is why these practices are so important to many Buddhist chaplains.

Being Present in Meditation & Daily Life

The first English-language book on Buddhist chaplaincy was called *The Arts of Contemplative Care* because of the importance of contemplative practice to the authors. They suggest 'contemplative care' as the Buddhist equivalent to the more broadly used terms 'pastoral care' or 'spiritual care.' (Definitions of these terms are covered in Volume I, Chapter 1.) This is "a kind of care that is informed by rigorous training in a meditative or contemplative tradition" (Giles and Miller, 2012, p. xvii).

Buddhism has a long history of such traditions. For example, Bhikkhu Anālayo notes that the very meaning of the title of the *Satipaṭṭhāna Sutta* can be translated either as "foundation" or "cause" of mindfulness (*sati*) or it can be translated as "being present," "placing near," or "attending" with mindfulness. (This is based on whether the second half of the compound term after *sati* (mindfulness) derives from the noun *paṭṭhāna*, which means "foundation" or "cause" or whether it derives from the verb *upaṭṭhāna* with the vowel dropped, which means "being present," "placing near," or "attending."

Bhikkhu Analayo makes a strong case for the latter, which would change the customary translation of the sutta title from *Foundations of Mindfulness* to something more like *Mindful Presence*. (Analayo, 2003, p. 29-30). As such, the *Satipaṭṭhāna Sutta* is one source of Buddhist contemplative practice that directly trains our attention to be present with a given object, in this case starting with the breath and body, bringing our focus to here and now (though it moves on to other objects in course).

Whether one practices according to the *Satipaṭṭhāna Sutta* or some other source or tradition, meditation or contemplative practices often begin with a somatic component, such as breath, bodily sensations, or sound (particularly important for mantra recitation or chanting), and expand to include awareness of thoughts, feelings, and other objects of mind. What makes a practice 'contemplative' is the process of repeatedly bringing the mind back to be together with (co-) its object. The term 'contemplation' derives from the Latin con- (or com-) prefix and "temple" or place for making offerings. Thus, in contemplation we are offering our attention to something important or sacred. Later it came to mean something akin to uniting the mind with the divine through the direction of one's attention in religious or spiritual meditation. Now it is something much broader. Yet when we consider these meanings we can see the importance they place on what we do with our attention. Thus, many chaplains consider contemplative training the foundation for presence and write that "effective caregiving originates from a rather ordinary quality that can be quite challenging to acquire – true presence, a grounding in the naturally arising reality of the moment" (Giles and Miller, 2012, p. xi). Of course, this begs several questions: 1) What kind of meditative training or contemplative tradition are they talking about? 2) How much contemplative training is enough? and 3) How does contemplative practice help us be present in our own lives as well as our work as chaplains?

I will not address the first question here, as the kind of training we pursue depends a great deal on our lineage. For the second question, I reviewed the way some Buddhist chaplains are trained. While different institutions have different requirements, there are common themes when it comes to contemplative practice. I reviewed the academic catalogs of institutions offering a Master of Divinity degree in Buddhist chaplaincy and a few non-degree certificates to quantify contemplative practice in hours per week either recommended or required.[1] Institutions range from: a) up to two years of required meditation coursework of up to nine hours per week; to b) co-curricular requirements of 9-12 hours per week; to c) no stated course or co-curricular requirements, but numerous electives and extra-curricular offerings.[2] At some institutions, meditation requirements can be met through weekend, week-long, or month-long intensive retreats. All institutions offer electives in Buddhist meditation and other contemplative practices. Buddhist-founded institutions with a strong connection to a single lineage were more likely to have strict curricular meditation requirements. Buddhist-founded institutions that are more ecumenical and diverse have more flexible requirements or no stated requirement, but a clear emphasis on contemplative practice. Institutions that are Buddhist welcoming, but Christian founded and/or Christian normative, such as Harvard Divinity School (Cambridge, MA), Emmanuel College (Toronto), and Union Theological Seminary (New York City), lack such requirements. They may also find contemplative coursework hard to explain or justify to faculty boards or accreditation agencies unused to such forms of instruction. Nevertheless, they all offered contemplative practice in electives and/or co-curricular programs, demonstrating that at least some faculty are aware of its importance and students have a clear interest.

Reviewing descriptions of student life and program learning outcomes indicates that even institutions with no set minimum requirements expect students to engage in some amount of meditation or contemplative practice and many consider this a serious aspect of one's spiritual life. A common expectation with contemplative practice is that, once begun, it becomes firmly rooted in our daily routines and lifelong habits. In schools with course requirements, it seems clear that students are expected to continue their contemplative practice after minimum requirements are satisfied. What we can glean from this simple overview is that while Buddhist chaplaincy training programs vary in the emphasis and mechanisms for ensuring students obtain contemplative competency, they all value it, not only during education but as a lifelong practice.

This brings us to the second question: how does contemplative practice help us be present in our daily lives and professional work? The chaplains I studied resoundingly affirmed the importance of meditation and contemplative

---

1 Please review current year academic catalogues and course requirements when considering a training or degree program as they are subject to change.

2 A table of these requirements and electives can be found in the Appendices.

practices in their life and work.³ Chaplains surveyed and interviewed in later research projects from 2020 to 2022 (Sanford et al., 2022) affirmed this finding by repeatedly describing how their personal meditation or contemplative practice formed an important foundation for their spiritual caregiving. Moreover, their contemplative skills directly affected their ability to reflect on and improve their work. Meditation interacted with wisdom developed by contemplating and practicing, and increased a chaplain's receptivity to wisdom developed by listening through improved concentration.⁴ Meditation and other contemplative practices were listed among the chaplains' sources of knowledge, insight, and wisdom. Overall, meditation was most strongly associated with the ability to be present.

When I began my work as a chaplain, I gained new insight into what meditation and contemplative practice offered me and, through me, what it offered others. As a naturally introspective person, I had plenty of experience being present with myself. The challenge then was being present with and for another person. I desperately needed the concentration cultivated through awareness of the breath to focus and remain aware of the careseeker before me. My own mind was so distracting and my lifelong habit of turning inward became my greatest challenge. Mindfulness enabled me to be present without agenda. Thus, when patterns emerged that connected the present situation to the corpus of human wisdom, I could see the connections between classroom learning and real life. Slowly, I began to see how the life I lived outside of my work predicated the habits I brought into my work. I was finally able to work with these habits and transform them.

Contemplative practice is beautiful in its versatility. Ellison reminds us that while sitting meditation practice is important, "The whole of our lives is a wonderful field of practice. Can we use it?" (Ellison, 2018, p. 223). Contemplative competencies taught via meditation can be practiced in myriad ways: through athletics such as tai chi, yoga, tennis, kendo, or running; through art such as painting, calligraphy, *ikebana*, weaving, or photography; through our relationships, especially with significant others, children, and animals; and, in my case, through walking in nature, knitting, writing, and, occasionally, lucid dreaming. All these activities require us to show up, remain present, and cultivate concentration and mindfulness. In fact, "The mindset that sees certain periods of time as available for practice and others as not is mistaken from the outset. All of us can practice, with everything we do. It is just a question of whether or not we dare do it," Ellison reminds us (2018, p. 223). Meditation is just the beginning. Having a daily meditation practice is important (though I struggle with mine, still). Ellison writes about how when we bring the practice to our daily lives, suddenly meditation takes on a new meaning and we somehow find the time for it. That has certainly been my experience.

Yet I have met chaplains, both Buddhist and non-Buddhist, who provide exceptional care without so much as owning a meditation cushion. Presence, concentration, and mindfulness can be learned in other ways and found in other religious and spiritual traditions. Nor is formal meditation as many Buddhist lineages teach always a universal good. Some may use meditation for spiritual bypassing, as an escape from the difficult aspects of life, or to strengthen their ability to focus on the pursuit of unskillful goals. Concentration must be combined with moral discipline and wisdom on the path. Meditation is not for meditation's sake, nor to increase our sense of spiritual pride. Contemplative practice and meditation

---

3 Only one of those thirteen chaplains I interviewed admitted to having no real contemplative practice before beginning their chaplaincy training; nor did meditation feature strongly for them afterward, though they acknowledged it as a useful tool.

4 See Volume I, Chapter 3 for more on the Three *Prajñās* of wisdom developed by listening, contemplating, and practicing.

are tools for liberation from suffering, our own and that of others. Each of us must develop a regular contemplative practice that suits our needs, supporting us to live better lives and to provide better care as Buddhist chaplains. We must cultivate the habit of showing up and being present in our daily lives if we hope to be present to those who need us most. This is not always easy, because it means being present to suffering as much as to joy and to injustice as much as to care. How we respond to the suffering and social injustice we see (not that it was particularly hidden before) when we practice showing up is the subject of Chapter 12.

Showing up in our own lives isn't always easy or pleasant. The First Noble Truth is the Truth of suffering we all experience – illness, old age, and death; being parted from that which we love; not getting what we want or getting what we do not want. Our lives are full of stress, catastrophe, and pain. Who would want to show up to that? But the truth of the matter is, failure to be present doesn't change the reality of suffering and, in many cases, makes it worse. On the other hand, being present enables us to make the very best choices in bad situations, to process what is happening right here and now, to find acceptance or practice compassion and equanimity. Only when we are present are we able to not compound and perhaps even mitigate the suffering in our lives.

Being Present in Spiritual Care

The chaplains I study report 'being present' as an important aspect – possibly the most important aspect – of spiritual care, and many explicitly referred how presence enabled them to 'connect' with careseekers. Some chaplains used the professional term 'ministry of presence' (common in pastoral theology), but most did not. They frequently reflected on their quality of presence and used presence as an aide to reflection, in that 'being present' entailed being aware of what was going on for later reflection. One chaplain said, "I mean, certainly I reflect a lot on my own presence. Like how much am I paying attention? How much anxiety am I bringing to the room, or distraction, or whatever? I really try kind of before I go into the room to kind of center myself and take some breaths." This chaplain developed practices to strengthen their presence throughout their workday.

Presence has three characteristics: the intention behind it, what one actually does to be present, and the outcomes of being present with and for careseekers (and oneself). (This is another application of the Buddhist paradigm of ground, path, and fruition. (This paradigm appears in Volume I and has been helpful in evaluating the qualitative data collected throughout my research.) Chaplains described the ground or intention as one of goodwill, love or loving-kindness, compassion, equanimity, respect, being openhearted, not preoccupied with doing or saying the 'right thing,' comfortable with silence, nonjudgmental, non-anxious, and having unconditional positive regard, a professional term popularized in spiritual care by scholar Howard Clinebell based on the work of psychologist Carl Rogers (Clinebell and McKeever, 2011, p. 466). One chaplain also described the quality of being non-attached, or being compassionate and "fully there, but I don't bring it home with me." Other chaplains called this having no agenda, not trying to fix things, and having good boundaries. In psychology, getting caught up in the careseeker's perspective or emotions in a harmful way can be described as 'enmeshment,' and will be discussed further in Chapter 3 in relation to empathy. Pastoral theologian Carrie Doehring uses the term "empathic contagion" (2015, p. 41). Chaplains who were present in caregiving situations were compassionate without experiencing empathic contagion because they could observe when they themselves were getting 'hooked' (to use Pema Chödrön's term) by the careseeker's situation.

Words rarely described what they were actually doing while being present. The path of presence has a certain quality, and we know it when we experience it, but it is often hard to specify particular tasks. Many chaplains said they were "just being present," "just be[ing] there," or "showing up," but when those statements are further questioned, chaplains tended to describe practices of attention, focus, flexibility, active listening, eye contact, body language, skillful response, gentle questioning, praying, and noticing and remembering details, even small ones, about the careseeker. These skills are explored in more detail in the following sections of this chapter.

When chaplains are fully present, the fruition or outcome can be positive in almost counterintuitive ways. It doesn't seem like we're doing much of anything, yet careseekers express profound gratitude and undergo amazing transformations. Careseekers reported feeling more peaceful, respected, better connected to their emotions, and better able to make sense of things. They appreciated "someone being there" and experienced moments of levity or joy in otherwise difficult situations. Being present created a sense of connection with careseekers that facilitated spiritual care and healing. Connection became a strong theme in my research and is discussed more in Chapter 3, Empathy & Compassion. Being present and sensing that connection was strongly related to the chaplain's affective state (their emotions) and the emotions they sensed from or shared with the careseeker (their empathy).

Most chaplains spoke about the necessity of emotional self-regulation. They felt it was important to remain calm and equanimous with careseekers, especially when careseekers themselves experienced turbulent emotions. They empathized, would even cry and emote, but not to the degree where it might distract the careseeker or cause additional distress. One chaplain explained, "[My practice] helped me to stay calm, because you hear pretty incredible stories from people, and I can't be reacting to, you know, everything. I think I should be the calm existence in…people's chaotic situations."

Being present with others who are suffering is difficult. Chaplains are there at the moment of dying or when a death notification is given to a loved one. As a chaplain, I have been present with students who share traumatic stories or express a desire to kill themselves. This is not easy, but there is a spiritual grace in being present with another person in such circumstances.

Emotional self-management is important both during encounters and afterward to ensure effective self-care and long-term sustainability. One chaplain I interviewed specifically researched "compassion satisfaction," which is "the inherent pleasure that is experience in being compassion [sic]. So it's a *vedanā*, it's a *vedanā* of feeling, and for me it's been really valuable to notice it and to cultivate it… [as one of the] mitigating factors for compassion fatigue and burnout."[5] Chaplains relied on their Buddhist practice, particularly meditation, for emotional self-regulation, as well as other coping methods, including setting healthy boundaries, self-care routines, social support systems, appropriate consultation, and therapy, as needed.

The final trait that several chaplains repeatedly cited is authenticity. One cannot be present with another if one is trying to be someone else. True presence is that of the authentic self (or non-self, as the case may be). Several chaplains reported anxiety over navigating the new role of Buddhist chaplaincy within a predominantly Christian context. Not only did they deal with all of the same fears of inadequacy, "feeling fake" or "doing it wrong," that I have observed in all chaplains, they were also uncertain whether their religious background would be a help or hindrance, welcome or unwelcome by careseekers and peers. However, as chaplains progressed in their spiritual care practice, they reported overcoming these insecurities

---

5 A vedanā is a sensation that accompanies consciousness and one of the five aggregates that make up what we misperceive as 'self.' See "vedanā" in Buswell and Lopez, *The Princeton Dictionary of Buddhism*, p. 964.

and developing a sense of confidence and sufficiency rooted in authenticity. The more they grew into their identities as Buddhist chaplains, the better they felt about their spiritual care practice and the better outcomes they reported. Some chaplains reported that supervisors and peers helped in this process. For example:

> I made a verbatim presentation on that encounter. The responses from my peer and the supervisor were very supportive. Yeah, and encouraging, because at that time it happened, like almost three years ago, I think. At that time, I was still struggling how to be, say, authentic. Be myself and be a Buddhist at the same time being a chaplain. So, I think, I believe the responses were kind of encouraging me.

Most chaplains reported positive support from their peers leading to greater authenticity, but this was not universal. One chaplain talked about leaving graduate school with a sense of confidence that was then slowly eroded in CPE, where they had to "develop [an] essentially Christian theology for chaplaincy, in order to just function in that environment," only to rediscover their confidence after working for several months beyond CPE residency. After exploring what had not helped them, they shared:

> **Researcher**: What do you think does have a relationship to the quality of the care afterward?
> **Participant**: Being a Buddhist in the encounter. [laughs] Like, practicing in the encounter. Yeah, I think I've had many instances, especially earlier on, where I felt like really armed with some sort of very sound analysis and plan of care, and confidence maybe, and realized like, "None of this is relevant now. They're in a totally, this person's in a totally different place, and I need to adapt to that, and be willing to let go of all of that." And that, I think, is just practice coming in.

This chaplain rediscovered a sense of authenticity as a Buddhist through the positive response they received from careseekers.

These three ideas – presence, connection, and authenticity – were linked throughout the interviews and, in almost all cases, were built on a foundation of contemplative practice. While presence enables a chaplain to see to the needs of another, to be present for and with them, it also enables them to be aware of themselves and reflexively respond to the needs of the present moment.

Being Present for Yourself: Reflexivity

In Volume I, I described reflexivity as the hallmark of the chaplain at stage three in the Three *Prajñās* Framework for Buddhist Spiritual Care:

> At stage three, chaplains and chaplain interns listen with the intention of serving others, but perhaps more critically, they listen with the intention of learning how to serve others. This involves both listening to others and listening to themselves (skills honed during stage two) within the new context of spiritual caregiving. (Sanford, 2021, p. 105)

At this stage, reflexivity is primarily about employing a self-monitoring awareness in our practice of spiritual care so as to become better chaplains. Some people develop this kind of reflexivity without chaplain training. I have observed it in many religious and spiritual leaders, caregiving professionals, and others. Placing it within the stages of chaplaincy development (explained in Volume I) does not imply that is the only or even the best way to develop reflexivity, only that it has been observed in the data among Buddhist chaplains at a particular point in their careers. Reflexivity also has a role to play in our personal spiritual formation, which is where many develop it. We have already explored being present in our meditation and daily life by bringing the skills we learn on the cushion to different tasks off the cushion – washing dishes, gardening, caring for children, or talking with friends. Being present for myself in this way enables me to notice particular habits and patterns in my life and make positive change – that is the role of reflexivity.

For example, the habit I call 'turtling-up' and retreating into isolation in the face of difficult negative emotions or challenging circumstances was no good for anyone, including me. Thankfully, chaplains don't always have the luxury of having a 'bad day' and hiding in their rooms. Strangely enough, on those 'bad days' when I was nevertheless required to do my job and help other people, I felt better. This was the result of compassion satisfaction and a decentering of my self-concern. Neuroscientists have now confirmed the dopamine rush we receive from helping others is the same as we receive from any other pleasurable activity (though I would argue there is more here at work than mere dopamine). My contemplative practice helped me become aware of this and cultivate better habits in my daily life. Now, when I am having a bad day, I go looking for someone to help, even if that just means setting up chairs for an event, lending a sympathetic ear to a friend, or cleaning the kitchen. I do so mindfully, fully engaged with the present moment, rather than my own swirling negative thoughts. (There is a time and place for solitude and rest; self-reflexivity helps us identify when it is healthy and when it is reactively unhealthy.) My relationships have improved with family, friends, and my partner. I am more forgiving and less prone to anger and annoyance at random people for thoughtless behavior. I can see them acting within their own systems of maladapted coping mechanisms. The more I can transform habits like these to be more present within my own life, the more I can be present in my work as a chaplain. But this reflexivity is not merely instrumental.

Reflexivity enables us to be present for ourselves in new ways and it is worth cultivating because, fundamentally, we are worth showing up for. Yes, it can help us become a better chaplain, but that's a bonus. The real magic of reflexivity is in helping us realize that we, too, are a person worth knowing. I have heard Buddhist teachers in America talk about the experience of training Americans in loving-kindness meditation. The meditation typically begins with loving-kindness directed inwards toward oneself. The teachers were surprised to find that Americans struggled with this. We tend to be very self-critical. They adapted their meditation to begin with loving-kindness directed towards our nearest and dearest, then gradually included the self. Kristin Neff, author of *Self-Compassion: The Proven Power of Being Kind to Yourself* (2015), finds self-criticism so pervasive in Western culture that she dedicates entire sections of her book justifying self-compassion and self-kindness against critics who might deride such sentiments as "soft," "namby-pamby," or indulgent. She writes:

> Self-kindness, by definition, means that we stop the constant self-judgment and disparaging internal commentary that most of us have come to see as normal. It requires us to understand our foibles and failures instead of condemning them. (p. 42)

What Neff calls self-kindness and I call reflexivity is about self-understanding and ultimately, wisdom. Jack Kornfield, in *A Path with Heart* (2009), explains that the path of wisdom first involves expanding our knowledge and conception of self before we can begin to dissolve our experience of self into the experience of selflessness. The Buddha's great insight was that humans do not arise as separate beings (nothing does, actually), but rather through the process of interdependent co-arising of various causes and conditions. In the spiritual sense, this can be experienced mystically. In the more mundane sense, it explains why people tell me "You sound like your mother," especially when speaking on the phone. (This enabled me to call myself out sick from school for several days in fifth grade.) I am interrelated to all the causes and conditions that have brought me to this point in my life and understanding them is more important than judging them.

"Yet, these are not our true identity," Kornfield reminds us (p. 199). Fundamentally, what we experience as 'self' is a collection of fluctuating aggregates momentarily giving rise to consciousness conveniently labeled "me," "mine," or "I." Ultimately, reflexivity enables us to see into the truth of *anatta*, or non-self. Let us return to an even older source on this, the *Bodhicaryāvatāra* or *Way of the Bodhisattva* by Śāntideva, who describes all things as empty of inherent existence – and the self is no exception. In fact, the perception of "I" is treated as the primary delusion from which we all suffer, very literally.

8.92
This pain of mine does not afflict
Or cause discomfort to another's body,
And yet this pain is hard for me to bear
Because I cling and take it for my own.

Understanding the self as empty is the foundation wisdom, the understanding of all phenomena as empty. We work hardest to see this emptiness in relation to the self because our self is that to which we are most deeply attached. Śāntideva advocates for a kind of radical reflexivity and the *Bodhicaryāvatāra* is his own reflexive investigation of self and other topics. We can understand the self on the level of the Two Truths, Conventional and Ultimate. From a conventional perspective, it is helpful for me to recognize the various habits and patterns I have picked up from my family, culture, education, and temperament. For example, in my early writing, I had a habit of not naming my emotions. Instead, I used actions and desires to describe what I was feeling. "I wanted to smack him," instead of "I was frustrated." This originates with a familial and cultural practice of emotional repression. From the ultimate perspective, it is helpful to recognize that this is a conditioned response that is ultimately empty and can be let go. From an ultimate perspective, it helps me to know that I have the seeds of buddha-nature within me and true insight is accessible at all times. Thus, I can see this familial habit and decide if and how it serves the present situation (if I'm home for Thanksgiving, it may serve quite well; if I'm delivering a verbatim to colleagues, it will not) and make a conscious choice to use it or not without any unnecessary self-criticism.

Reflexivity develops on a foundation of mindfulness. It is a skill that can be taught, learned, and practiced. In one sense, it is like a background program always running on your mental computer, monitoring the status of the system. In another sense, some contexts call for more reflexivity than others and, sometimes, reflexivity becomes the formal practice of reflection. Spiritual caregiving is one of those times when we need to actively engage our reflexivity. So is learning.

The wisdom developed from listening – *śrutamayīprajñā* – depends on reflexivity to integrate the information we are receiving with what we already know. Making connections between new and existing information is the strongest predictor of retention and future application. This is why we sometimes struggle to retain information on a subject we have never studied before – we don't know what is important or how to connect it with what we already know. As we read books, listen to Dharma talks and lectures, and engage in classroom activities, it is important to engage our reflexivity. How does what we are learning strike us? Highlighting, underlining, and making annotations in the margin are excellent ways to do this when reading. When listening to a talk, we can take notes (during or after), if appropriate. In addition to recording information, we need to be constantly evaluating it against our own experience.

Likewise, when listening to a careseeker, we are reflexively evaluating what they say against our own experience and expertise – not for the purpose of judgement, but for the goal of understanding. (Though we should be wary of over-analysis that interferes with active listening, covered in the next section.) We can do the same with our own experiences. For example, while studying attachment theory, I reflexively evaluated the characteristics of attachment styles against my own experience and, more than that, I paid attention to how I felt simultaneously sad and empowered. I felt sad as I began to suspect I had an avoidant insecure attachment style because that style reminds me of certain negative memories from childhood, but I also felt empowered because the theory had a clear explanation that gave me more control over my life. Now, I can employ that knowledge in my life when I'm relating to my partner, for example, and in my work as a chaplain, such as empathizing with careseekers who have similar experiences.

Reflexivity also provides a strong basis for reflection because it enables us to recollect our internal processes as well as external events. As we learned in Volume I (Chapter 2), reflecting involves recollection and meaning making, it employs various methods to contribute to our spiritual formation. Since I was a teenager, my primary method of reflection has been writing. My writing is often reflexive, exploring both inner and outer experiences. This practice has given me a language with which to understand and describe myself, but it took years to develop. Perhaps reflexivity is new to you, in which case I recommend the meditation practice of 'noting' as a good starting point. Perhaps reflexivity is familiar but articulating your reflexive process is not, in which case I recommend writing (a lot) and sharing with others. By sharing with others, we become better at describing internal processes with clarity and concision.

Sharing also enables us to access perspectives we would not otherwise find. The Johari Window describes various aspects of self-knowledge to which we have access. It illustrates that there are some things about ourselves that are 1) known to us and others, 2) known to us, but not others, 3) known to others, but not ourselves, and 4) known to neither ourselves or others.

	Known by You	Unknown by You
Known by Others	Open	Blind Spot
Unknown by Others	Hidden	Unknown

Reflexivity enables us to enlarge the left side of the window by learning more about ourselves by paying attention to our own experiences, while sharing enables us to enlarge the top half and gain access to our own blind spots (top right quadrant) through the feedback we receive from others. This feedback is not always easy to hear, accept, or integrate, but when it comes from those we love and trust, those we know truly see us, it is often worth the effort to overcome our defensiveness and deeply consider the wisdom of the outside perspective. In Buddhism, awakening is the moment when the lower right quadrant of the window – unknown – disappears as we achieve a complete realization of the nature of self/non-self. (Send me a postcard when you get there!)

2
LISTENING & RESPONDING

Not Listening

As with being present, we must consider the opposite of listening – not listening – to develop our skills as chaplains. As William Miller and Kathleen Jackson (1995) point out, listening is about much more than just being quiet and letting the other person speak – it "is a whole new way of thinking" (p. 32) and open-heartedly integrating what we are hearing to reach true understanding and empathy. Miller and Jackson find this skill so little practiced that they dedicate an entire chapter in *Practical Psychology for Pastors* to "Not Listening" and another chapter to "Listening." Miller and Jackson identify the greatest "roadblock" to listening as "responding with one's own material: one's own views, beliefs, feelings, judgements, opinions, reactions." This isn't always a bad thing, given the level of expertise chaplains amass through their training and practice, but, as Miller and Jackson argue this "is different from good listening" (p. 47). As Buddhists, we should not be surprised that self-preoccupation is the largest barrier to good listening. Indeed, Buddhist teacher Willa Miller (not to be confused with William Miller of Miller and Jackson) illustrates this same barrier in her chapter in *The Arts of Contemplative Care* (2012), saying listening requires genuine curiosity and "We cannot maintain curiosity if we are constantly concerned about sharing who we are and what we know. Good listening begins with letting go of the need to be heard ourselves, in favor of entering the world of another for a time" (p. 285).

Willa Miller, as an American Buddhist lama in the Tibetan traditions, draws on the teachings of Patrul Rinpoche (1808–1887) for three ways not to listen and three ways one should listen. First, do not listen like an upside-down pot into which nothing new can be placed. We cannot listen when we allow inner and outer distractions to prevent receptivity. Inner distractions include our own thoughts, judgements, prejudices, feelings, obsessions, and physical sensations. Outer distractions include sounds, sights, and smells in our environment. Some barriers to listening straddle the inner-outer divide, such as the way our society culturally conditions us to listen or not listen to others within particular social categories based on gender, age, race, and perceived power (for more on this, see Chapter 12). There is only so much we can do about external distractions, but our ability to cope with inner distractions and ameliorate oppressive patterns of prejudice is improved through concentration skills gained in meditation and "aided by curiosity" when "We care to know what the person cares about," writes Willa Miller (p. 285).

When we are not receptive, we miss what the careseeker is sharing. This can lead to asking inappropriate questions (e.g., already answered, not relevant) or offering inappropriate responses (e.g., wrong tone, not helpful). We can sometimes steer the conversation in a different direction than the careseeker intended. Miller and Jackson point to several common responses we have probably all used or witnessed in conversations to distract from what the other person really wants to care about. They start with phrases such as "That reminds me of…," "Well, at least it's not…," "I've seen worse…," and "This one time…." Sometimes we don't want to hear what the careseeker is sharing because it is too painful for us at the moment, so we may subconsciously steer the conversation into different territory. Or we may be feeling neglected and isolated ourselves and seek to use the conversation to get a bit of the attention and recognition we crave. Do any of these sound familiar to you? They're certainly familiar to me. I had to break a lifelong habit of "it could be worse" consoling. For me this is a very effective coping style, but for others it is the exact opposite of what they need. (If they do need it, they'll do it themselves.) Meditation training, reflexivity, and self-care are important practices for turning the pot right side up so that we are ready to listen.

Second, do not listen like a pot with holes. This happens when we listen but cannot retain or understand what is being said. We have all met the person who nods along and appears to be listening and who will say they understand, but then take some action that demonstrates they clearly haven't absorbed a thing we've said. We know how disappointing and frustrating that can be. This happens when we 'listen' but don't connect what we are hearing with our own experiences. We are hearing but not processing. This means we cannot empathize with the speaker and we won't retain what we've heard. Moreover, we won't be able to muster what Willa Miller calls "compassionate responsiveness," which is "an energy of receptivity paired with a willingness to feel" (2012, p. 287).

Let's face it. Some days we just don't want to feel. We've had enough of feeling. We're all tapped out. This manifests in several types of responses outlined by Miller and Jackson. Not only are we not listening or empathizing, but we may respond by ordering the other person around, giving advice inappropriately, lecturing, moralizing, judging, praising, or simply withdrawing (1995, p. 48-50). We might find ourselves using a lot of "should" and "should not" statements. We want to tell the other how to stop feeling what they're feeling (because we don't want to feel it) and get out of their current predicament (because we don't want to be in it). We lose our ability to accompany them as *kalyāṇamitra* (a spiritual friend) through the truth of their experience. We must use our self-awareness to notice when this is happening and take steps to mitigate this process before it results in burnout and shutdown. Not only is a burned-out individual unable to listen and authentically empathize with others, they can poison those around them, which brings us to the third instruction from Patrul Rinpoche.

Finally, do not listen like a pot containing poison that contaminates anything put into it (Miller, 2012, p. 284-290). We must beware of our tendencies to interpret everything through our own lens, whether optimistically or pessimistically. I have a relative who does the latter. We can scarcely have a conversation because everything I say is twisted into a cynical direction I did not expect, and the rest of the conversation is a feeble attempt at course correction. One of the strongest interpretations we have is our often-unconscious attempts to "glorify oneself and vilify others" (Miller, 2012, p. 284-290) or to see the best in things or people we already like and the worst in those we already dislike. This is called confirmation bias and it hampers our ability to be truly open to the careseeker. Our own expectations for who that person is or how we expect the conversation to go (well or badly) can 'poison' the pot. These expectations are often predicated on our own past experiences and by the messages that we have absorbed (willingly or not) from society, such as racist and sexist tropes and stereotypes. Many of these can be enacted unconsciously even in consciously anti-racist or anti-sexist people (see Chapter 12 for more). Wherever our expectations come from, we must first become aware of them and then learn how to hold them very lightly or discard them when necessary.

We will all sit with careseekers we are tempted to morally judge as less worthy than other careseekers. In one situation, I provided care for the victim of sexual assault and, the very next day, for the alleged perpetrator of that assault! As I listened to the second person, I was also carefully listening to myself to assess my own ability to remain receptive and compassionate. Providing spiritual care for perpetrators, prisoners, abusers, addicts, those with personality disorders, mental health struggles, and other people society often categorizes as "failures" can be challenging work as these individuals are no less human, no less in need of care, and, from a Dharmic perspective, no less full of buddha-nature. They have struggled to live meaningfully despite incredibly adverse circumstances, often unrecognized. We are all full of implicit biases about race, ethnicity, gender, culture, ability, age, and so on, that can affect our responses in very subtle and unconscious ways. This manifests in our emotional response (receptivity, empathy) while listening as a subtle judgement of who is worth listening to and what stories or situations are worth our attention. This includes when we ourselves have been the subject of discrimination from others; we may come to expect similar discrimination from certain careseekers. Shedding these expectations and judgements is some of the hardest work we do to become effective chaplains.

Listening

Active, attentive, and empathetic listening is the first task of good spiritual care according to Howard Clinebell, Robert Kidd, and Barbara Breitman, who speaks for all when she writes: "The art of listening is the foundation of all forms of pastoral caregiving" (2013, p. 98). Clinebell, a Christian theologian, relies mostly on secular sources to describe appropriate listening and responding skills, including psychologist Carl Rogers. All affirm that empathic, compassionate, or loving listening are essential for spiritual care. Kidd, also Christian, sees listening as "sacred work" (2012, p. 92-93). Breitman, a Jewish rabbi, sees listening emerging from *kavannah* or sacred intention (2013, p. 102-105). Likewise, Willa Miller, a Vajrayana lama, affirms that it is an effective bodhisattva activity. Koshin Paley Ellison, a Zen priest, describes listening as "one of the most important things contemplative care providers can offer their patients" (2016, p. 238). Steven Kanji Ruhl, another Buddhist author in *The Arts of Contemplativee Care* (2012), bases his practice of listening on his confidence in the buddha-nature of every person (p. 304).

From this we can see that each tradition is in profound agreement on the importance of listening and they describe effective listening in very similar ways (active, attentive, mindful, present, empathic, and so on), yet they have each developed their own theories to explain why listening is so powerful. They connect explanations to religious texts, such as Willa Miller has done for us. We have already examined Patrul Rinpoche's advice on how not to listen (like an upturned pot, a pot with holes, or a pot with poison). Let us now explore how

---

For more information, see the following textbooks on spiritual care:

Clinebell, Howard and Bridget Clare McKeever. *Basic Types of Pastoral Care and Counseling*, 3rd Edition. (Nashville, TN: Abingdon, 2011), 70-77.

Kidd, Robert A. "Foundational Listening and Responding Skills." In *Professional Spiritual & Pastoral Care: A Practical Clergy and Chaplain's Handbook*, ed. Stephen B. Roberts. (Woodstock, VT: SkyLight Paths Publishing, 2012), 93-94.

Breitman, Barbara Eve, "Foundations of Jewish Pastoral Care: Skills and Techniques." In *Jewish Pastoral Care: A Practical Handbook from Traditional & Contemporary Sources*, 2nd Edition, ed. Dayle A. Freidman. (Woodstock, VT: Jewish Lights Publishing, 2013), 98-101.

we can cultivate good listening.

Miller writes: "I had generally been led to believe, if not by words then by implication, that this role [Dharma teacher] wholly entailed teaching the Dharma," but as she set about caring for her own sangha, she discovered another need. Her community needed "a listener and a friend." She explains that even among traditional religious teachers (not chaplains), "They look to us to be heard and seen. They look to us to be acknowledged and loved. They seek to be witnessed. To witness is very different from simply teaching." To witness is a profound act of care. "To witness is to be permeable, to be willing to look and listen" (2012, p. 282-283). Thankfully, the Buddhadharma includes wisdom for listening and witnessing. Let us review how we ought to listen and deeply witness.

We manifest receptivity, empathy, and equanimity that sees all beings as equal in our attention by managing our own barriers to listening, as described above. We do this through three primary strategies. First, we cultivate good intentions, concentration, curiosity, generosity, and selflessness. Concentration, in particular, can be cultivated through meditation. "To choose attention over distraction is a mental discipline," according to Miller, "to stay with what is spoken and not anticipate a future response" (2012, p. 285). I am particularly guilty of finishing other people's sentences for them, especially if they are a slow speaker, a habit I have had to mindfully break. Miller adds that this is aided by the virtues of curiosity and humility. Being genuinely curious about the other person and at the same time humble, "letting go of the need to be heard ourselves, in favor of entering the world of another for a time" (2012, p. 285). When we do this, we engage 'active listening.' This is our ability to connect what the speaker is saying to our own experience; it forms the basis of both memory and empathy. To actively listen we must be willing to feel even negative emotions such as sadness, grief, anger, and suffering. We must also listen for what Ellison calls "the story beneath the story," because "There is often much more being said than what is being verbalized in the moment" (2016, p. 259). We are listening not just to words but to tone, facial expression, gestures, posture, silences, body language, physical signs of health and pain, repetitions, metaphors, idioms, storylines, identity markers, and meanings. The larger social context also plays a role; understanding the social conditions they have endured throughout their life helps us understand their story without the need for them to explain each detail. For example, the events of 9/11 loom large in the minds of those who were old enough to watch it live on the news (or be there in person) and shaped an entire generation. While others were shaped by the Cambodian genocides and experiences of coming to the U.S. as an immigrant refugee, or by the events of the Black Lives Matter Movement, or the 3/11 disaster in Japan. All of these may form the social context that is part of their story, even when never referenced. The story beneath the story is a gateway to understanding and empathy. More about empathy and compassion will follow; suffice it to say active listening engages empathy and compassion.

Second, we reflexively become aware of mental and emotional habits of distancing and distracting, judging and vilifying, and other barriers to open-heartedness. Miller advises us to respect listening as a somatic experience – that is, as embodied, not just something we do with our ears and brain. "Furthermore, when we listen, we can learn to be attentive to how a story we are hearing manifests in our body" (2012, p. 286). Sometimes deep intuitions are hard to put into words and our body reacts ahead of our more developed cognitions. I have learned to be particularly mindful of two forms of embodied experience: 1) intuitions about the careseeker and 2) intuitions about myself. At first, these may be hard to distinguish and they are often entangled. You may notice that you are leaning forward, that you feel a joyful energy that comes from connection or mutual recognition. There is an energy that comes from meeting someone like ourselves in a significant respect, whether it is a shared love of baseball or books. When that recognition is mutual it can deepen our relationship with the careseeker, but it can also derail a caring conversation from the situation at hand. It is always tempting to 'geek out' about a shared experience. The question is, how will you harness that energy to listen deeply to what the careseekers is dealing with right now? At other times you may note tension in your body, leaning back, an uneasy stomach. Your body is sounding a note of caution though you cannot explain why. In some cases, I have later learned that a careseeker was not being entirely truthful or was attempting to manipulate me to be on 'their side' in some conflict. (I am always on 'their side,' while also not being 'against' whomever they are in conflict with.) While I have learned to trust such intuitions, I am also cautious of projection, implicit bias, and transference – phenomena in which we ascribe certain traits to careseekers based on their resemblance to other people we know or our own internalized stereotypes. Our body will often pick up on transference and countertransference well before our mind (see Chapter 5 for more about transference).

Third, we ensure our own needs for being heard and witnessed are met through proper self-care and good relationships with others so that we do not place that burden on careseekers, however unintentionally. Make no mistake, chaplains can and do use those we care for to fulfil our own needs. To some extent there is nothing wrong with this. Compassion satisfaction and a love of the work are good things, for us and for our careseekers. But sometimes, chaplains also use careseekers in ways that are good for us, but not necessarily for them, such as to help us process our own stuck emotions (see Chapter 5 on boundaries for more about this). Gordon Greene provides a powerful example of this in his memoir about CPE, *Facing Suffering* (2019). Greene, a Zen priest, transgresses the boundaries of a hospital patient, placing his need to learn above the autonomy of the patient, and is rightly called out for it by a peer (p. 89-110). At other times, he is brutally honest in his need to process his own grief sufficiently to be able to sit with grieving patients.

Miller and Ellison both advise chaplains to see the work we do as an act of generosity, as *dāna*. "Just as with the practice of *dāna*, the fewer expectations we have when giving our attention the greater the merits," Miller writes (2012, p. 288). Entering a room with an agenda, even the agenda to learn, is a misdirected intention. Learning will happen if we are open to it, but learning often comes about later, through reflection.

Another Buddhist contribution to the art of listening is the mind of nondualism – no listener, no listened to, no act of listening. When we are open and receptive to reality just as it is, active listening is not a practice so much as a natural outcome, according to Miller. In other words, active listening is selfless listening.

Of course, this may seem paradoxical given that I have also advised that as we listen, we listen to both the careseeker and ourselves the caregiver. This (not a) paradox is a manifestation of the Two Truths in action. When we are open and receptive, we are actively listening to all sources, including our own mind, heart, and body. As we do so, we may notice internal thoughts and feelings that need to be dealt with later. Miller refers to this as "flagging" (2012, p. 289) and I have always thought of it as "noting," similar to noting practice in meditation, the habit of non-judgmentally labelling a thought or feeling. Either way, it enables us to set aside that internal process for a moment, return our attention to the object of focus (the careseeker), and then return to the noted phenomenon later. The last step is equally important to our health and wellbeing as a chaplain. Chaplains and others in caregiver roles often experience compassion fatigue and burnout when they neglect this final step and unprocessed thoughts and feelings build up. We can process many of these noted phenomena ourselves and we also need colleagues, mentors, and friends with whom to share them. In other words, we maintain good relationships with the *kalyāṇamitra* in our lives so we can act as *kalyāṇamitra* for others.

We often learn to listen by being listened to. In reflecting on my path to become a chaplain, I remembered an experience from much earlier in my life. I struggled to make friends as a child. I was doing poorly at school and disobedient at home. For a few months in sixth grade, my mother took me to see a child psychologist. Mostly, we played games in her office, and I enjoyed her collection of stuffed puppets. She would ask me questions and we'd talk for a while, but it didn't seem like she was doing anything in particular. I later realized, she was the first adult in my life who listened when I said, "I hate my brother" and didn't immediately tell me I shouldn't hate my brother. (Of course, I didn't hate my brother; I was just 11 years old and frustrated.) She heard and accepted my statement and asked genuine questions. Afterward, she would talk to my mother privately for about ten minutes while I sat in the waiting room. I only saw her for about three months. My parents moved me to a new school for junior high and things got better. I can't remember her name, but I will never forget her. Likewise, I have heard many colleagues relate their first experience of being truly heard and witnessed, often with tears in their eyes. "Listening is so close to love that most people cannot tell the difference," is the saying. (It may originate with David W. Augsburger in *Caring Enough to Hear and Be Heard*, 1982, but others have suggested that he too was paraphrasing an older source.) From a Buddhist perspective, I would argue there need be no difference. Listening is an act of loving-kindness.

Miller's description, based on the teaching by Nyingma master Patrul Rinpoche, shows striking resemblance to Clinebell's description of active empathic listening used to understand and overcome one's own blind spots and obsessions. It also follows Kidd's instruction to stay attuned to the present and Breitman's concern that the caregiver should receive the careseeker's message accurately and take it into their heart. We should allow ourselves to be moved. In all cases, Christian, Jewish, and Buddhist, far more pages are devoted to the art of listening than the art of responding. When we speak of 'listening' it is important to remember that we mean more than simply sitting with ears open – we also mean watching and witnessing. 'Listening' is a simple short form, but the receptivity we bring to spiritual care is whole-body with all senses. (It could also include communicating in sign language or written language, such as via texting.) This is especially important with non-responsive careseekers, as Ellison describes in his hospice work. He invites caregivers to "Watch with me," and

> ...that in watching we should learn not only how to free patients from pain and distress, how to understand them and never let them down, but also how to be silent, how to listen, and how to just be there. As we learn this, we will also learn that the real work is not ours at all. (2016, p. 27)

Responding Appropriately

Daijaku Kinst, faculty at the Institute of Buddhist Studies in Berkeley, characterizes Buddhist spiritual care as responding appropriately to suffering (*Arts of Contemplative Care*, 2012, p. 16). Active listening forms the foundation of an appropriate response. From a Buddhist perspective, an appropriate response is, first and foremost, grounded in Right Speech, an aspect of the Noble Eightfold Path. Jesse Wiens, a Zen communication expert, follows the *Aṅguttara Nikāya* (AN 5.198), which says Right Speech is timely, true, gentle, beneficial, and kind. His chapter in *A Thousand Hands: A Guidebook for Caring for Your Buddhist Community* (2016, p. 31-41) explores how Right Speech is connected to practices of Nonviolent Communication (NVC). I recommend readers review this wonderful chapter in full. While the Buddha advises speech that is gentle and kind, he also makes allowances for "sharp speech" provided it is timely, true, correct, and beneficial. Likewise, with "covert speech" (MN 139.10), which I interpret as information or warnings shared in private, such as when we consult with a chaplain supervisor on a difficult case or are obligated to report an ethical breach to authorities. Thus, speech that is not gentle in tone can be allowed when it meets the other four criteria. We should not mistake an intention of loving-kindness for a kindly tone; the former is about doing what is best for others, not simply 'sounding nice.'

In addition to these five qualities of Right Speech, the Buddha describes several types of speech to avoid, including false speech, divisive speech, harsh speech, and idle chatter or gossip (AN 10.176.4-7). While many Buddhists readily accept the first three, idle chatter offers something of a conundrum as 'small talk' is used in many cultures to initiate conversations among strangers and, while it may sound idle, serves to test the waters – discerning the conversation partner's emotional state, temperament, trustworthiness, and social affiliations – before moving into deeper topics. In my experience, introducing oneself as a chaplain sometimes obviates the need for small talk. Careseekers invest a greater degree of trust and are willing to go to the deep places faster, but this can never be assumed. If a careseeker seems intent on making small talk, it is best to follow their lead and set aside concerns over 'idle chatter.' The Buddha also advises that speech should be unhurried, as hurried speech exhausts the speaker and can be hard to understand.

A speaker should also use the language and idioms of their audience. The Buddha offers as an example six different words for 'bowl' and advises "So whatever they call it in such and such a locality, one speaks accordingly, firmly adhering to that expression," rather than insisting on their own word (MN 139.11-12). Likewise, with careseekers, we demonstrate a preference for their own terms. In Vignette 1 in Volume I, Chaplain A does not use the term 'abuse' to characterize the careseeker's relationship until after the careseeker has done so. In Vignette 2, Chaplain B uses the careseeker's Christian terms in reference to miracles, prayer, and God throughout. In Vignette 3, Chaplain C uses the careseeker's own words to describe how they want someone who 'has their back.' These examples are affirmed as Right Speech in the Pali Canon.

The proper intentions one holds while listening and responding are quite similar, as are the mental disciplines involved, so I will not retread the same ground here. Rather, this section focuses pragmatically on responding by breaking that task down into various types of responses. I recall my own early training as a chaplain involved practicing these types of responses in a triad of careseeker, caregiver, and observer. I found this approach immensely helpful in unlearning my habituated ways of responding and learning a new vocabulary of response. Just as when one first learns music, dance, or sports, one begins with the individual notes or steps or forms, then arranges them to make something beautiful. This level of unlearning and relearning can also be helpful in our practice as spiritual caregivers. Eventually, what at first takes conscious effort becomes a matter of 'muscle' memory that is embodied and reflexive. It will seem awkward and terribly basic in the beginning, but that's okay, because the magic of Right Speech will slowly transform everything you do, say, and even think.

Begin by reviewing the basic types of responses listed in Table 1.1 on the next two pages. Then, consider the example from a spiritual care conversation following the table and identify the types of responses used in this conversation.

\multicolumn{4}{c}{**Table 1.1a Types of Spiritual Care Responses**}			
Type	**Description**	**Examples**	**Warnings**
Silence	Space for the careseeker to explore their experiences; enables active listening; an invitation for the careseeker	Treat the careseeker as your object of focus in meditation; give them your full attention	Chaplains can be anxious to say the 'right' thing; learn to manage your own discomfort with silence and watch for signs of discomfort in careseekers
Nonverbal Cues	Facial expressions and body language signal that we are open or closed to what we are hearing, interested or disinterested, anxious or calm, distracted or focused; cultivate mindfulness of nonverbal cues from the careseeker and from yourself; can be used as prompts to invite the careseeker to continue	Keep a relaxed, open posture without fidgeting; mirror the body language of your careseeker to create solidarity when appropriate. Monosyllables ("Oh?" "Hmm" "Huh" "Mmm") Head tilts / inquiring looks	Nonverbal cues are often unconscious; it takes practice to learn our habits (e.g., tapping foot) and peer observation or reviewing videos can be helpful. Listen to your body during sessions; tension can be caused by anxiety that needs investigation.
Restating	Repeating the careseeker's words verbatim; can be used immediately after or by repeating a key phrase later in the conversation; demonstrates listening and retention; can prompt elaboration of feelings, emotions, and experiences	• CS: "It all feels so overwhelming!" Chaplain: "Overwhelming." • CS: "In the Marines, your guys have your back through everything." Chaplain: [Later] "Like you said, it's important to have people who have your back."	Useful for key words or phrases, not entire sentences; don't overuse — the purpose is to demonstrate listening and comprehension and prompt elaboration through tone (i.e., 'Overwhelming' vs. 'Overwhelming?')
Rephrasing	Simplest form of interpretation; summarizing in one's own words particularly to identify underlying feelings, meanings, issues, and needs; checks for comprehension	• CS: "I don't know what to do." Chaplain: "This is confusing." • CS: "Mom never missed a service." Chaplain: "Church was important to your mom."	Use to clarify the careseeker's meaning, not add meaning from the chaplain; trust careseekers to correct you if your interpretation is wrong
Clarifying Feelings	Clarify for feelings first, before beliefs or behaviors; look for "emotional doorways" and check for understanding; inquire about feelings when careseekers neglect emotions in favor of facts; use their terms for their emotions if given	• "You sound so sad." • "That sounds painful." • "You're angry about…" • "Let's see if I understand…" • "To me, it seems like… Is it?"	When clarifying, don't get overly caught up in trying to understand every detail of the situation (what happened to whom when), seek the emotional effects; trust careseekers to correct you if you name the wrong emotions
Reframing	Reinterpretation in service of a goal, usually to help careseekers see their situation a bit differently; useful to normalize setbacks and responses within the range of human experience, reinforce positive behaviors, or broaden a perspective	• "Sounds like you've made some mistakes. I also see ways you've been remarkably resilient." • "You said this is the third time this has happened. What did you do last time to recover from it?" • "You're not alone."	Don't be Pollyanna; this isn't about putting a positive spin on horrible things. Don't rush to reframe before you understand; this isn't about what meaning you would make if you were in that situation, about you feeling useful, or even about Right View.

Table 1.1b Types of Spiritual Care Responses — Continued

Type	Description	Examples	Warnings
Inquiry	Questions ranging from conversation starters, to clarifying questions, to inquiries about feelings, beliefs, behaviors, meanings, or events; used to learn more or, when appropriate, focus on important subjects the careseeker may have neglected; the goal of questions is to catalyze a careseeker's self-understanding	• "How are things going today?" • "What's on your mind?" • "Since then, how have you been feeling?" • "What does 'better' look like to you? What are you hoping for?" • "Who is supporting you in this situation? Who's in your corner?"	Use sparingly as questions can often change the focus of a conversation; follow the careseeker's lead; learn to be content with the gist of a situation, you don't need every detail; be patient and wait for 'door-opening questions;' avoid leading questions that only have one 'right' answer
Relating	Making connections between the careseeker's situation and stories, traditions, or with the chaplain through self-disclosure; helps careseeker broaden their perspective and consider their goals; demonstrates empathy and solidarity based on shared experiences; can use pop culture or religious tradition	• "I've worked with many students in similar situations, and you may find their experiences useful." • "I have a brother, but I can only imagine what it's like to lose a sibling." • "Your situation reminds me of this story in scripture.... Do you know it?"	Don't overshare, careseekers don't need personal details, and it's not about you; wait for openings that suggest the careseeker is familiar with a particular religious or pop culture reference rather than bringing up things out of the blue; some may be ready to relate their situation to theology/Dharma, but stories can be more accessible
Counseling	More formal process to resolve personal, social, psychological, spiritual, or religious difficulties through directed problem-solving techniques; approaches can be from our traditions (e.g., pastoral counseling, spiritual direction, *dokusan*, etc.) or from social sciences (e.g., brief solution-focused therapy, cognitive behavioral therapy, mindfulness-based stress reduction, etc.); may be brief (1 session) when helping navigate institutional systems, but often multiple sessions	• CS: "Chaplain, what should I do?" Chaplain: "This situation is complex, and I can't tell you what to do. But I can help you work through the problem through some short-term counseling, if you want. First, we would talk about that process and set some goals. How does that sound?" • CS: "I want to report them!" Chaplain: "Let me walk you through the reporting process so you can decide if that's right for you. I support you no matter what."	Be sure that you and the careseeker are clear on your relationship and the goals of the conversations when entering into formal counseling; stay within your scope of practice and only use counseling techniques in which you are trained and authorized; mostly 'takes place' within the context of a longer-term caregiving relationship
Directing	Use of spiritual authority to make requests, suggestions, or directives to careseekers or on behalf of careseekers; strength of directive depends on severity of situation and relationship to careseeker or teammates; spiritual authority can be formal or informal (e.g., respect)	• "I can teach you a simple meditation to do before bed that may help with your sleeping issues. Would you like to learn it? You can give it a try this week, and tell me how it goes." • "I need you to promise me that you won't do anything to harm yourself. If you feel like harming yourself, you're going to call me first. Promise?"	Use sparingly and wisely, usually within the context of an ongoing relationship, especially with careseekers; when using spiritual authority to advocate for careseekers within an institutional system, protect relationships with teammates; informal authority depends a great deal on how you behave with careseekers and teammates on a daily basis

Vignette 4[1]

The conversation takes place between the chaplain, who we will call Chaplain D, and a member of the staff, who we will call Diane, at the institution where they both work. Both Chaplain D and the careseeker are white women in their late thirties. They have a cordial relationship and attend some of the same institutional meetings and committees, but rarely work together directly. They meet by chance in the hallway outside Diane's office and Chaplain D notices that Diane seems upset. Chaplain D asks if she is alright or would like to talk. Diane says she has another meeting in a minute but invites the chaplain into her office and closes the door. Diane sits at her desk and Chaplain D sits in the chair to the side of the desk. Diane begins to cry. Chaplain D sits quietly, leaning forward, and waits for Diane to begin when she's ready.

"I tried so hard to make this project work, but he just won't work with me," Diane says, referencing a coworker. She starts crying and reaches for a tissue. "I really didn't think this would affect me so much."

"I can see that it has affected you a lot," Chaplain D says. They sit together while Diane cries. Chaplain D feels anxious and helpless but allows Diane to express her emotions without trying to fix things.

"I just didn't know what else to do," Diane continues after a bit. "I tried, but he made it impossible. I didn't think I would feel this way." The chaplain surmises that getting so upset at work isn't something Diane usually allows herself. Based on previous conversations, Chaplain D knows that Diane is very conscientious and wants to do her best for their clients.

"I think it says something about your character that you care so much," the chaplain offers.

"I hate feeling this way. I hate this...." Diane dissolves into a sob.

"Weakness," Chaplain D fills in, aware that Diane is normally a calm and assured professional. Chaplain D also considers that she may be projecting.

Then Diane nods.

Chaplain D continues, "I feel the same way about crying, especially at work, even though I know we need to do it sometimes."

Diane turns her body away, at a ninety-degree angle from Chaplain D and says very quietly, "I just want to go home."

Chaplain D feels a moment of panic because she values Diane and the work she does. But she holds on to her own feelings, keeping her face calm and body language open and interested as she waits for Diane to continue. After a few moments, Diane starts to collect herself.

"I mean, I know I just have to go through it, process it. I've been in counseling, and I know it's okay to cry. I just hate the feeling," Diane confesses.

"Yeah, me too," Chaplain D empathizes. "Some people say it's cathartic and all, but when it's happening, it just hurts."

Diane sighs and nods. "Yeah."

"I just want you to know that I'm here if you ever need to chat. As a chaplain, anything we talk about is confidential and private. You can call me or come down to see me anytime," the chaplain tells Diane, sure that she already knows this, but sometimes it's helpful to provide a reminder that chaplains are also there for staff.

"Thanks, Chaplain. I appreciate that. I'll be okay. It will be okay. I know I have some triggers to work through and I appreciate your support," Diane says, drying her eyes.

Another member of the staff knocks on the door just then, so Chaplain D says goodbye and leaves.

Now review the response chart. Then read this vignette again and make some annotations. Consider the following:

1. Where did Chaplain D use the types of responses listed in that chart?

---

[1] Vignettes 1, 2, and 3 can be found in *Kalyāṇamitra*, Volume I.

2. Where does the chaplain employ silence and non-verbal cues?
3. Does she use restating, rephrasing, or reframing and, if so, where?
4. What feelings are being expressed?
5. Does Chaplain D employ inquiry and, if so, where?
6. If they had more time, what do you think a useful line of inquiry might be?
7. How does Chaplain D relate to Diane?
8. Does Chaplain D employ counseling or directing and why do you think that is?
9. When and how should Chaplain D follow up with Diane?

In this vignette, we can see some of the types of responses listed in Table 1.1. Not all of them were employed here and it would be rare to use all of them in a single conversation. You can also compare these types of responses to the vignettes in Chapter 1 of Volume I. What types of responses are used by Chaplains A, B, and C, with their respective careseekers? How effective do you think they are?

As you go about your life, it can be a helpful exercise to see when you can spot the different types of responses, either when using them yourself or when used by others. If it feels too awkward and distracting to do with real people, consider doing it while watching television or reading a book. It can also be interesting to experiment with some of them in low-stakes situations. At a certain point in my training, I remember using more silence in conversations than normal for me. I learned a lot about my classmates, roommates, and neighbors. I began to use rephrasing, reframing, and inquiry with my mother, and it opened new pathways in our relationship. This doesn't mean you should 'chaplain' everyone, just expand your repertoire when appropriate.

To choose the appropriate response, we discern the purpose of the conversation in that moment. Literature on pastoral care contains many ways to understand this purpose. One common Christian paradigm is the healing, guiding, sustaining, and reconciling model of Clebsch and Jaekle (summarized in Ramsay, 2004, p. 4). In surveying Buddhist chaplains, both in interviews and the existing literature, I found six predominant themes that guide the ways we respond to careseekers: 1) witnessing; 2) empathizing; 3) supporting; 4) understanding; 5) assessing; and 6) advising. There could be further research to either expand on or consolidate these categories.

First, bearing witness has influenced chaplain-scholars such as Adele Smith-Penniman, whose 2006 dissertation is one of the earliest on the topic of "Buddhist Resources in Pastoral Care." A Unitarian Universalist minister strongly influenced by Buddhism, Smith-Penniman parallels the Christian concept of the prophetic witness with work by the psychologists Jean Baker Miller and Janet L. Surrey on the ethics of the social witness and then with the teaching of Bernie Glassman, founder of the Zen Peacemaker Order. The ZPO says on their website

> The practice of bearing witness is to see all of the aspects of a situation including your attachments and judgments. ...When you bear witness you open to the uniqueness of whatever is arising and meet it just as it is....
>
> Bearing witness can allow you to eventually come to terms with the most difficult life circumstances. ... In bearing witness, you are actively engaged and embodied, even struggling, with whatever is arising. Sometimes spiritual practices can have a neutralizing effect, flattening feelings rather than stimulating them. To hold to the center is not about becoming a spiritual zombie; it is about living the fullness of your own humanity. You are alive, so be fully alive.[2]

---

2 zenpeacemakers.org/the-three-tenets, 2023

Meditation trains our mind in the stability we need to be an attentive witness and to maintain a stable, open-hearted, curious, and non-judgmental awareness through all life's joys and suffering. Willa Miller writes that "To be a witness involves being really present to others, listening to others, developing the capacity to be in skillful relationship. ...To witness is to be permeable, to be willing to look and listen," (2012, p. 283) primarily at suffering, which is something most people would, understandably, rather not look at too long. Witnesses need not do anything. Indeed, there usually isn't anything we can do. The simple act of being seen and heard by another human being affects people. Most of us can point directly to moments in our own lives when we felt seen and heard and the impact this had on us.

When we witness the joys and sorrows of others, we will inevitably empathize (the second response). We may not empathize with everyone in every situation, but it will happen frequently. Like being seen and heard, being empathized with, or understood at a deep emotional level, has an effect. When we know that others know what it is to go through something similar, this creates a bond. As chaplains, our role is to be aware of and communicate our empathy to others in appropriate ways. We use the responses listed above to communicate empathy, check our understanding, clarify feelings, and allow the careseeker to correct us to draw closer to their emotional experience.

When we witness and empathize, we are also then best able to support careseekers (the third response). There will also be many times when we do not empathize, simply because our experiences are different from those we care for. In these situations, we continue to rely on compassion and loving-kindness to help us discern proper ways to support careseekers. In either case, support is one of the primary functions of a *kalyāṇamitra*. Support takes many forms, from moral and spiritual support to practical resource-based support. Sometimes, careseekers face a major life decision and a chaplain can be helpful in reflecting what they hear with more clarity than the careseekers themselves are able to discern. Ethical and relational dilemmas often come to the forefront, along with matters of faith and belief, during times of crisis. Or careseekers may need more practical support (or both). For example, in a hospital a patient may have been too stunned or embarrassed to ask more questions when the doctor was in the room. Chaplains cannot explain medical diagnoses, but they can help careseekers connect with medical staff and sort through documents. Many healthcare chaplains become conversant in medical lingo and can 'translate' common medical terms, help talk through options, and clarify questions for the medical team. Where I work in a campus environment, I often assist students in navigating the institutional bureaucracy in relation to housing, dining, grievances, and emergency support services.

Many careseekers feel supported simply by being understood (the fourth response). I make a distinction between witnessing, empathizing, and understanding, with understanding coming last because I do not think it is always necessary to fully comprehend a situation in order to help. Witnessing involves seeing another person's distress, regardless of the source. Empathizing may involve shared joy or sadness over a small moment that is part of a larger story. Many resources on pastoral care caution against too many questions. Sometimes we simply won't get all the details and that is okay. However, there are times that careseekers want someone who truly understands their situation. When seeking understanding, inquiry can be a powerful tool, as can simple invitations such as "Tell me more about…" or "It sounds like you are very excited about…" or "I would like to understand more about…" or "I'm not quite clear about…." Checking one's understanding through frequent rephrasing is also essential. Sometimes careseekers want someone to 'take their side.' Chaplains can seek understanding while also being mindful of our role in disputes.

In young people, I find a deep longing to be seen, heard, and understood for who they really are; that is part of their natural identity formation at that stage in life. It can be exacerbated by life as a 'digital native,' connected to the internet and devices sometimes literally since birth. (I often wonder how children will feel about their baby pictures appearing in my friends' social media updates years later.) They have grown up comparing their real, flawed lives to idealized and carefully curated lives on social media. Not only do they feel deficient, they also feel as though they must hide their real selves and therefore that no one really understands them (and perhaps no one does!). When encountering the unconditional positive regard of a chaplain (or a therapist) they may find someone willing to try to understand them for who they actually are for the very first time; this experience can be terrifying and liberating. This can sometimes produce contradictory behavior in careseekers for which the chaplain should be prepared. Patience and not taking it personally can create a beneficial spiritual care relationship even with the most conflicted or contrarian.

As we speak with careseekers, we reflexively assess their spiritual care needs (the fifth response). Assessment is a more professional term for what Buddhists may call *prajñā* or discernment. *Prajñā* is comprised of Right Intention and Right View, both wanting to do good and knowing what would be helpful in this situation. Based on what we observe, we choose ways to respond that are *upaya* or skillful means. This can be done informally through our reflexive responses in the moment or formally. Informal, reflexive assessment and formal written assessments are both part of the chaplain's toolbox. We may also create a formal written spiritual assessment as part of a spiritual care plan. These assessments can be as short as a set of chart notes stating the patient's current spiritual struggle and our plan to check on them again tomorrow or as long as a multi-page case study following a defined model, such as George Fitchett's 7x7 model for spiritual assessment. (See Chapter 4 for more on assessment.) It is important to note here that assessment, like witnessing or empathizing, is both an ongoing activity and a goal of spiritual care.

Sixth and finally, some careseekers will directly request our advice. "Chaplain what should I do?" Before answering such questions, it is important that we gain a better understanding of the careseeker's situation. I often start with a line of inquiry. What have they already tried? How did that work? In the story of their situation, you will often hear of other people they have gone to for help. What did they recommend? What did the careseeker then do or not do and why? As they tell you more, you will begin eliminating certain alternatives they may already have tried. You may be able to reassure them to be patient with what they are already doing (we tend to want immediate results) or eliminate options that aren't working.

We can also begin to discern conflicts between explicit and subconscious goals, which I find at the root of many problems. For example, a student may say that want to improve their grades when their true goal is to avoid their parents' displeasure, revealing the real dissatisfaction is within the parental relationship, not study habits. Conflicting motivations and confusion about cause-and-effect relationships (okay, I got my grades up, why aren't I happy now?) are common sources of struggle. Advice-giving is often about goal clarification more than anything else.

At other times careseekers will ask advice simply from the subconscious motivation to make the problem go away or to make it someone else's problem. They long for a simple path that is easy to follow (as do I!). In such cases, it is up to us to discern if they are the kind of person who could be genuinely satisfied with a spiritual prescription (e.g., chant this mantra, make this offering) or if it is our role to companion them through the struggle.

In cases where I do give advice, usually after a long conversation, I generally preface it with

"I can't say what you should do because each situation is different, but here are some things that I have seen work for others / have worked for me / research tells us works for many people…" and follow it with "What do you think of that?" This emphasizes their agency and your confidence in their ability to discern a path forward.

Responding appropriately involves a combination of understanding and committing to Right Speech, mastering the various types of responses, and discerning the purpose of your response in the conversation you are in right now. This sounds like a lot (and it is!), but remember you have a lifetime of experience to draw upon and are surrounded by peers, teachers, and supervisors who will support you to proactively learn (or relearn) these skills. However, even a *kalyāṇamitra* with years of experience will run into difficult situations that do not seem to have an appropriate response.

Responding to Difficulty

Then the wanderer Vacchgotta approached the Blessed One…and said to him:

"How is it now, Master Gotama, is there a self?"

When this was said, the Blessed One was silent.

"Then, Master Gotama, is there no self?"

A second time the Blessed One was silent.

Then the wanderer Vacchagotta rose from his seat and departed.

Then, not long after the wanderer Vacchagotta had left, the Venerable Ānanda said to the Blessed One:

"Why is it, venerable sir, that when the Blessed One was questioned by the wanderer Vacchagotta, he did not answer?"

"If, Ānanda, when I was asked by the wanderer Vacchagotta, 'Is there a self?' I had answered, 'There is a self.' This would have been siding with those ascetics and brahmins who are eternalists. And if, when I was asked by him, 'Is there no self?' I had answered, 'There is no self,' this would have been siding with those ascetics and brahmins who are annihilationists.

"If, Ānanda, when I was asked by the wanderer Vacchagotta, 'Is there a self?' I had answered, 'There is a self,' would this have been consistent on my part with the arising of the knowledge that 'all phenomena are nonself'?"

"No, venerable sir."

"And if, when I was asked by him, 'Is there no self?' I had answered, 'There is no self,' the wanderer Vacchagotta, already confused, would have fallen into even greater confusion, thinking, 'It seems that the self I formerly had does not exist now.'"

(SN 44.10 "Ananda – Is there a Self?" from Bhikkhu Bodhi's translation, 2000, p. 1393-1394)

We will all face difficult questions and difficult conversations in our roles as chaplains. Most of us will not have the abilities of the Buddha to discern the proper response, though our buddha-nature and wisdom can serve to guide. Within his lifetime, the historical Buddha led many to liberation from suffering, but even he was not able to walk the path for them. Everyone comes to us with their own karma, their own causes and conditions, about which we may know little to nothing. We will face difficult conversations and conflict, including careseekers who reject our services outright. For some, we will be the wrong kind of chaplain. In that case, our responsibility is to nonjudgmentally help that person connect with another chaplain who can support them. Others may not want to speak to a chaplain at all. This may be because they have been harmed by religion in the past or because they associate the presence of a chaplain with bad news, including death. Others may feel they already have sufficient support in family, friends, and their own religious leaders. Sometimes, we can overcome an initial rejection with a brief question or conversation about what other kind of resources or people we could connect them with that would serve better. Occasionally, this can open a door so that they can see our good intentions and become more willing to allow us to help them. Yet we must also be cautious against pushing ourselves where we are not wanted out of our own deep desire to be helpful. We must respect each careseeker's agency.

Even among careseekers who do want spiritual care, and from us, we will face difficult situations and questions we cannot answer. Vignette 2 in Volume I, Chapter 1, includes such an example. Chaplain B assisted a Christian family who wanted to pray for a miracle to heal their mother after a stroke, despite the doctor's terminal diagnosis. Rather than tell the family that such a miracle was impossible, the chaplain engaged them in conversation to learn more about them and their mother, then reframed the idea of miracle in a way that enabled them to cope with the situation. Likewise, students have asked me many questions that I struggle to answer. "Why can't I feel the presence of God anymore?" "Why do I love him if he hurts me so much?" "What happens when we die?" "Will this career make me happy?" As the chaplain, I do not have answers to these questions – not because I don't have ideas, beliefs, or opinions of my own, but because these are not the kinds of questions one can answer for another. These are the kinds of questions that can only be satisfied when one decides on an answer for oneself. If I told a student there is no God, they would be like confused Vacchagotta in the story, knowing that they had felt what they describe as the presence of God before in their life, but that God no longer exists now. Instead, if I talk to the student about their own understanding of God and the role that faith, doubt, and belief play in their life, I can help them to clarify their own ideas and then connect those ideas to resources within their tradition. If they learn that many faithful believers nevertheless spend their entire life without sensing the presence of God, they may develop gratitude for their past experiences and see a path forward from their present situation. The goal is not to give answers, but to help people find their own answers, if possible.

At other times, chaplains may be called upon to mediate conflict, either within a couple, family, or between an individual (or family) and an institution. Hospital chaplains may be called by the nursing staff to deal with a 'difficult' patient who will not provide information or comply with medical directives. In such instances, it is important to remain mindful of our responsibility to the patient first and avoid being instrumentalized 'on the side' of the medical staff. Likewise, with couples or families, our role is to reduce suffering and facilitate understanding. If there must be sides, we are on the side of the most suffering. In a healthcare setting, this can mean putting the needs of the patient ahead of the needs of the family without being 'against' the family. Within institutions we serve as advocates for the needs of careseekers, whether they be patients, students, soldiers, or prisoners. Many prison chaplains prefer to work as volunteers because of the concern that working for the prison will compromise their ability to advocate for the needs of prisoners. When our own livelihood is on the line, we tend to choose our words more carefully, and may feel more inhibited in our responses. I have experienced this as a campus chaplain employed by my university, though I have found that my 'insider' role has ultimately made me more effective at advocating for students. By choosing words that will preserve the personal relationships I have with fellow staff who are in positions to assist, I build long-term trust and social capital. Many institutions will listen more to someone they perceive as an 'insider' than they would to an 'outsider.' Where a chaplain can be most effective in institutional conflicts is a personal decision based on particular situations. Sometimes, it may seem like our advocacy, conflict mediation skills, and good intentions make no difference at all. And sometimes seeds only sprout after a long winter and in places where we never see them. Such difficulties can be frustrating and disheartening. (See Chapter 6 for more about the moral role of chaplains within organizations.)

Here I take wisdom from the Buddha, who could not satisfy all comers, even with his perfect wisdom, and from the Jewish Mishna which says, "You are not obligated to complete the work, but neither are you free to desist from it." (Pirkei Avot, 2:21) There are just some questions we can never answer to the other person's satisfaction. Sometimes there is no comfort to be found from companioning, conversation, or care. Sometimes we can never get an institution to 'do right' by those we serve. The causes and conditions for the reduction of suffering are simply not present and there is little or nothing that we as chaplains can do, except perhaps, try not to make it worse. That does not, however, mean that we give up. We can take satisfaction in the compassion and wisdom we have offered and see each difficulty as a lesson that can serve us well in the future.

3
Empathy & Compassion

The Lexicon of Open-Heartedness

At some point, all of us have had an experience of profound emotional connection, empathy, and compassion. We have seen another person's suffering, felt that suffering as though it were within our own body, and felt moved to alleviate that suffering however we could. We have all shared in the experience of contagious laughter, that fit of giggles that has us swatting the other person and begging them to stop because we know if they keep laughing, we will too. We have looked into another person's eyes and seen that they too know this deep feeling welling up between us both. These experiences may even propel us to become chaplains. They feel deeply meaningful and at the same time almost beyond words. Yet, it is within words that we must at least try to convey them to one another across the pages of time. We scholars have made lives out of words in a feeble effort to convey to those we have never met that which we have all experienced in the physical presence of one another.

Let us begin with two words: empathy and compassion. These terms are related but not identical. Empathy is a larger umbrella term that may include compassion, along with many other experiences. In distinguishing empathy from compassion, Jennifer Goetz and Emiliana Simon-Thomas (2017, p. 6) note that "empathy broadly involves sensitivity to others' feelings," whether these feelings are positive or negative. Research posits two aspects of empathy: 1) the evolutionarily older 'affective empathy' in which we subconsciously experience emotions like those we observe in others; and 2) the more complex and newer 'cognitive empathy' in which we consciously try to understand what another person is thinking or feeling. The former is more automatic while the latter involves greater awareness and effort. Researchers further posit that empathy involves the recognition that the emotions we are experiencing come from the other person as a response to their circumstances and emotional state (Vrticka, Favre, and Singer in Gilbert, 2017, p. 135). Both affective and cognitive empathy can be measured by 'empathic accuracy,' or our ability to correctly assess what the other person is thinking or feeling – an important skill for a chaplain to cultivate.

Empathy for the negative emotions of others is often considered an aspect of and precursor to compassion. That is, when others suffer, we suffer, and so we feel compelled to relieve suffering. However, as Goetz and Simon-Thomas point out, "empathy does not guarantee, nor is it sufficient to engender, compassion. In fact, affective empathy can easily initiate self-focused responses like personal distress," (2017, p. 6) which includes responses that may mimic caregiving but are motivated from our own need to escape difficult experiences. Exposure to suffering does not guarantee either empathy or compassion. When it evokes empathy, it can lead to personal or empathic distress, "in which one is more upset by the others' suffering than concerned for the other," (Goetz and Simon-Thomas, 2017, p. 6). Alternatively, this awareness can provoke disgust or anger focused on the cause of the suffering (not the person who suffers), especially when that cause is perceived as unjust or unfair. An example is when we see police brutality and feel more anger at the police than sympathy for the victim. Likewise, exposure to suffering that simply seems overwhelming and impossible for one to address can produce a 'bystander' effect of protective apathy or indifference.

Non-attachment may mediate the relationship between empathy resulting in compassionate action versus empathy resulting in empathic distress leading to aversive responses (e.g., trying to get someone to stop crying, apathy, and so on). A group of researchers in Hong Kong demonstrated that the Buddhist concept of 'un-clinging,' which they characterize as an aspect of self-awareness, was able to predict the level of stress reduction achieved by mindfulness meditators. To the degree to which meditators did not cling to their experiences, positive or negative, they were able to observe both self and other mindfully and reduce stress responses to experiences (Ng, Chow, Lau, and Wang, 2017, p. 1). Likewise, non-attachment (or 'un-clinging,' if you prefer) or selflessness may mediate between empathy and a skillful (compassionate) or unskillful (distressed and avoidant) response. Chaplains cultivate an ability to accurately empathize with others, act compassionately, discern effective responses, and learn from their mistakes, while simultaneously cultivating non-attachment, selflessness, and equanimity.

Reflexive self-awareness and wisdom (such as into selflessness) are necessary components in developing empathy and transforming it into virtue. Wisdom predicates empathic accuracy. From a Buddhist perspective, a wise person can accurately assess what another is thinking or feeling without necessarily experiencing those states (remaining equanimous). Likewise, a compassionate person acts to alleviate the suffering of others, even when they may not fully comprehend or share that experience. Buddhism describes wisdom, compassion, and sympathetic joy as virtues to cultivate along with equanimity. The latter two frequently involve aspects of empathy, but empathy is not a necessary component in all instances.

Compassion is conceptualized in three overlapping ways from the Western perspective – as an emotion, a motivation, and a disposition. There is no consensus among scholars, but the characterization of compassion as a distinct emotion has recently lost ground in favor of motivational and dispositional understandings, or some combination as both (Gilbert, 2017, p. 6). While compassion shares some traits in common with other identifiable emotions, such as distinct expressions, vocalizations, behaviors, and even measurable physiological and neural responses (Goetz and Simon-Thomas, 2017, p. 4-5), the actual felt experience of compassion can vary depending on the circumstance and the person for whom one is feeling compassion (Gilbert, 2017, p. 6).

Paul Gilbert (2017, p. 6) and others situate compassion as "the motivation to pay attention (on suffering and needs) and the motivation and intention to do something about it." This intentionally caring stance aligns better with Buddhist understandings of compassion. As a motivation, compassion triggers caring for others, which scientists believe is deeply rooted in our need to raise helpless infants and live in a communal society (Goetz and Simon-Thomas, 2017, p. 4-6). Indeed, Buddhist scholar-practitioners Paul Condon and John Makransky point to numerous studies that show "Humans come prepared, through evolution, with innate capacities for empathy and compassion," (2020, p. 1348). Compassion is both relational and biological. The Sanskrit and Pali term *karuṇā* is most commonly translated as either compassion or empathy and defined as "the wish that others be free from suffering" in *The Princeton Dictionary of Buddhism*. *Mahākaruṇā* or "great compassion" is the "primary motivating force that enables the bodhisattva to endure the...path to Buddhahood" (Buswell and Lopez, 2014, p. 424). In other words, compassion is also liberative.

Finally, as a disposition, compassion can be perceived as a personal trait that makes one more likely to habitually experience compassionate emotions and respond with caring behaviors. Those with a compassionate disposition are more empathically sensitive and experience greater joy in helping others. Compassionate disposition can be measured through psychometric questionnaires. It may also have a social dimension, as in, something we learn from our surroundings. The psychologists Jenniver Goetz and Emiliana Simon-Thomas, in their research on compassion, have also associated it with secure childhood attachment (2017, p. 4-6), though more research is needed in this area. Buddhism also teaches the cultivation of compassion through meditation (Buswell and Lopez, 2014, p. 424). Practiced via meditation, compassion can inspire our work as chaplains with those experiencing distress and suffering. These approaches to compassion from the social sciences can enrich our understanding as Buddhists, as we draw on the rich and varied traditions of Buddhism.

Brooke Lavelle provides a helpful overview of the different ways compassion has been conceived in the three branches of Buddhism – Theravada, Mahayana, and Vajrayana. Lavelle writes that while compassion is foundational to all branches of Buddhism, it is not treated the same in all lineages. In Theravadin lineages, compassion primarily supports the development of wisdom by placing the attention on an appropriate subject – suffering. This is explained in Buddhaghosa's *Path of Purification* (*Visuddhimagga*), which describes compassion among the apramāṇas or Four Immeasurables, also known as the *Brahmavihāra*. Liberation itself is achieved through wisdom. In Mahayana and Vajrayana traditions, however, compassion is both a constituent and result of liberation and co-equal with wisdom as a perfection of enlightened beings. These traditions developed further methods of cultivating compassion; for example, the "Seven-Point Cause and Effect Method," "Equalizing and Exchanging Oneself with Others" including *tonglen* (sending and receiving) in the Vajrayana traditions, and guru and deity yoga (Lavelle in Seppälä et al., 2017, p. 19-20) to become aware of the compassion we have received from others and seek to embody ourselves. Many community rituals and chants also invoke the buddhas and bodhisattvas to have compassion for us or generate gratitude for the compassion we have already received from so many. For example, in Pure Land Buddhism, Amitabha's compassion is often a central focus.

Understandings will continue to vary across cultures and be debated and refined among academics, but for the purposes of a Buddhist chaplain, I find two definitions helpful. The first is by Geshe Thupten Jinpa as part of his work with Stanford scholars on the Compassion Cultivation Training (CCT) program wherein compassion has four components. The second is offered by Willem Kuyken and has five components (Gilbert, 2017, p. 7), which overlap with Jinpa's but also add further dimensions important to caregivers. I have developed a composite five-part definition of compassion based on them:

1. Awareness of suffering, whether affective or cognitive;
2. Feeling sympathetic concern as part of a sense of shared humanity or interconnection;
3. Desire to alleviate suffering with an intention of altruistic goodwill;
4. Willingness to help alleviate that suffering to the extent one is able, usually prompting proactive helping behaviors;
5. Ability to tolerate the discomfort of suffering to remain present and engaged, often through cultivation of equanimity, sympathetic joy, non-attachment, and/or selflessness.

Without all five components, our work can result in empathic distress, compassion fatigue, secondary trauma, and burnout. The fifth component involves both the toleration of discomfort and its gradual reduction. As our spiritual practice advances, we can be genuinely present

Components of Compassion	Antithesis
Awareness of suffering	Apathy, burnout, turning away, indifference
Feeling sympathetic concern as part of a sense of shared humanity or interconnection	Judgement, particularly about whether or not someone 'deserves' assistance or sympathy
Altruistic goodwill – intention to alleviate suffering	Empathic distress – desire to make the suffering stop to alleviate our own discomfort
Willingness to help alleviate suffering prompting proactive helping behavior, when possible	Either inaction due to a sense of helplessness OR the need to 'fix' a problem that is beyond our ability, thus prompting unskillful 'busy-ness'
Ability to tolerate the discomfort of suffering to remain present and engaged	Becoming overwhelmed by suffering, secondary traumatic stress, compassion fatigue

for suffering with less aversion, which is itself, to some extent, a form of suffering or discomfort (the *dukkha* of *dukkha*). In part 5, I also caution against the overemphasis on compassion alone, when, in classical Buddhist teaching, compassion is cultivated as part of the four-part construct of the *Brahmavihāra*. The *Brahmavihāra* together can also be protective and support resilience.

The Dark Side:
Contagion, Fatigue, Trauma, Burnout

Neuroscientists have found that many of the key brain areas involved in experiencing our own emotions, particularly pain and suffering, are also activated when we experience empathy in response to another person's suffering. Affective empathy is when we respond to another person's situation or emotional state by feeling what we believe they feel. In other words, we understand that our feelings are in response to the other person. However, chaplains can also experience moments when we are not aware of the source of these emotions (positive or negative). The term for this is 'emotion contagion' (Vrticka, Favre, and Singer in Gilbert, 2017, p. 136) and chaplain-scholar Carrie Doehring calls it 'empathic contagion.'

Empathic contagion occurs "when caregivers feel what care seekers feel without awareness that their emotions have come from the care seeker," according to Doehring (2014, p. 41). Neuroscientists who study empathy point out that this "can occur rather unconsciously without self-other distinction," (Vrticka, Favre, and Singer in Gilbert, 2017, p. 136) which may seem like a desirable thing for Buddhists trying to overcome their egoic and illusory perceptions of self and other. However, from both a psychological and pragmatic standpoint, this is actually quite problematic. Even from a Buddhist standpoint, emotional experiences without awareness or mindfulness can be troubling. How we respond to feelings of anxiety, for example, is quite different depending on

---

For more about the neuroscience of compassion see:

Vrtička, Pascal, Pauline Favre, and Tania Singer. 2017. "Compassion and the Brain." In *Compassion*, 1st ed., United Kingdom: Routledge, p. 135–50.
Klimecki, Olga M. and Tania Singer. 2017. "The Compassionate Brain" in *The Oxford Handbook of Compassion Science*, New York: Oxford University Press, p. 109-120.

whether or not we need to soothe our own anxiety or remain present and attentive to someone else's anxiety. Awareness predicates *upaya*, or a skillful response. Moreover, research has demonstrated that empathic contagion often triggers empathic distress, which interferes with compassion.

Empathic distress (sometimes also referred to as 'personal distress') "is an aversive and self-oriented emotional response to the suffering of others," (Vrticka, Favre, and Singer in Gilbert, 2017, p. 137). It is characterized by protective withdrawal from situations of suffering or maladaptive behaviors that mimic caregiving but are actually aimed at 'fixing the problem' for one's own sake, rather than for the good of the careseeker. I have never met a chaplain who did not experience a moment of trying to 'fix' things to alleviate the discomfort they experienced at another person's suffering at some point in their career. These lessons are inevitable, but it is also important to learn how not to repeat them too often. Empathic distress has also been linked to aggressive behavior, such as less cooperation, higher competitiveness, and a need to 'punish' misbehavior in others (Klimecki and Singer in Seppala, 2017, p. 118). We can see this in the human tendency to judge others experiencing misfortune (they 'got what they deserved'); in some sense this is a mechanism to cope with our own discomfort and sense of powerlessness.

Psychology has investigated various antidotes to empathic distress, most of which focus on cognitive strategies to reduce the negative aspects of the experience, such as reframing. Research has also validated the Buddhist view that compassion (together with the other *brahmavihāra*, though these are less well researched) is also a positive way of coping with other people's suffering. Compassion does not mitigate the negative aspects of the experience, but rather engages counteracting positive aspects, including positive emotions that come from altruistic helping behavior. Neuroscientists find that compassion triggers areas in the brain associated with affiliation (relationships) and rewards (feeling good). However, they also stressed that "empathy/empathic distress (i.e., negative emotions) and compassion (i.e., positive emotions) can be experienced simultaneously while being exposed to a suffering person" (Vrticka, Favre, and Singer in Gilbert, 2017, p. 141). Which experience dominates determines the overall emotional character of the encounter. Thankfully, Buddhist compassion training has been shown by these same scientists to effectively counteract empathic distress.

Even with training, skilled chaplains and others in professional caregiving roles, such as first responders, may still experience compassion fatigue, secondary traumatic stress, and burnout in response to repeated experiences of emotional contagion and empathic distress, especially when combined with negative contextual factors. Just as our body requires both exercise and rest, as well as a good diet, our hearts and minds need a balanced set of emotional experiences and the nourishing support of good relationships. Chaplains should take steps to protect themselves from compassion fatigue and surround themselves with people who can notice and ameliorate the symptoms. It is not a question of if we will experience this kind of fatigue, but rather when.

Compassion fatigue is the depletion of empathy, and emotional strain resulting from working with distressed and traumatized careseekers. Compassion fatigue is similar to secondary traumatic stress and burnout, but has both a quicker onset and shorter recovery than burnout (Doolittle, 2015, p. 183). Some researchers, such as Oliver et al. (2018, p. 72) identify secondary trauma and burnout as two dimensions that combine to result in compassion fatigue, but other scholars treat the three as distinct if overlapping constructs.

Secondary traumatic stress was identified in the 1990s as stress caused by interpersonal interactions between a caregiver and traumatized careseekers (Galek et al., 2011, p. 633).

It is sometimes also referred to as 'vicarious trauma.' Secondary trauma can result in normal stress responses, including physical and mental exhaustion. However, it can also deeply challenge one's core value system or fundamental worldview (Galek et al., 2011, p. 633). This is why it is important for chaplains to undergo a lengthy period of spiritual formation and discernment during their education and early training and to retain relationships with *kalyāṇamitra* in their ongoing work. Negative experiences can manifest as secondary traumatic stress (STS) due to repeated exposure and chaplains can develop symptoms similar to PTSD, including intrusive thoughts, flashbacks, nightmares, disillusionment, sense of isolation, and emotional distancing.

Secondary traumatic stress can manifest quickly, sometimes even after a single encounter, but its likelihood increases with repeated exposure to traumatized individuals, often over years, and especially when the caregiver also has a personal history of trauma. Some studies have indicated that younger women are more susceptible to secondary trauma (Galek et al., 2011, p. 637-8). This may be an artifact of higher rates of traumatization and lower sense of overall safety among women due to the prevalence of sexual and gender-based harassment and assault within modern society. Trauma therapists with higher levels of education (doctorates vs. master's degrees) seem to experience less secondary trauma, but the mechanisms for this is unknown. Galek theorizes that: a) more education may enable caregivers to develop a more nuanced and stable worldview, received better supervision, or developed better ways of managing therapeutic boundaries; or b) the therapist's perception of the effectiveness of their education may affect their feelings of efficacy (Galek et al., 2011, p. 645). Likewise, the long process of formation for chaplains can be protective and continues after formal education is completed and credentials are achieved. While secondary trauma is less related to contextual factors, organizations can reduce its prevalence by ensuring appropriate caseloads (not overloading caregivers with trauma victims as compared to other careseekers), creating a sense of safety and security in the workplace, and through ongoing educational programs (Galek et al., 2011, p. 633).

Burnout is a related condition identified by Pines and Maslach in the late 1970s as a psychological problem among the caring professions (Galek et al., 2011, p. 633). Experiences of burnout have three primary components (Galek et al., 2011, p. 633): 1) emotional exhaustion; 2) depersonalization, which is a psychological defense mechanism to create distance between the caregiver and careseeker by viewing careseekers as 'objects' rather than individuals and prevent empathic contagion and distress; and 3) sense of ineffectiveness and loss of motivation. Burnout shares several symptoms with depression but is distinct in a lack of anhedonia, or the reduced expressiveness, typical of depression. More importantly, burnout is directly job-related and does not persist when people leave their jobs (Doolittle, 2015, p. 182-183).

Early theories attributed burnout to the stress of helping those in need and some internal factors do correlate to burnout, but (unlike secondary trauma) ongoing research has shown that workplace factors play a much greater role (Galek et al., 2011, p. 633). Burnout can occur in almost any profession and does not require frequent or intense interactions with people in need, but seems most prevalent in caring professions. Burnout can build up very slowly, sometimes taking years to manifest, and is therefore often harder to recognize among other normal personality shifts. Among chaplains, burnout has been correlated to several factors.

First, burnout appears more common among those who base their self-esteem on a deep need to be appreciated for helping others, which may partially explain its prevalence in caregiving professions. Idealistic expectations about our ability to help others can also exacerbate compassion fatigue, secondary trauma, and burnout. This has been found both among congregational clergy as well as chaplains, who arguably have less 'control' over the situations where they work and what their careseekers experience. Chaplains may subconsciously and habitually sacrifice their own needs to feel helpful and appreciated. This pattern may be deeply rooted in childhood family dynamics. Chaplains may then experience burnout when they do not feel effective or appreciated. Over-functioning is common among helping professionals, who tend to internalize blame for ineffectiveness rather than looking towards external factors such as unrealistic workloads, institutional barriers, or a lack of rewards, (Galek et al., 2011, p. 633-7) despite the outsized role such factors have been found to play. This combination of high expectations, negative self-assessment, and lack of outside positive reinforcement contributes to burnout, but is not the only factor.

Second, a sense of identity fusion with the 'system' in which one works (low self-system differentiation), such as a school or hospital when that system is 'uncaring' or actively impedes one's effectiveness, is a major contributor to burnout. Some studies have noted that those with a strong need for external validation are particularly vulnerable in hospitals, which are highly bureaucratic, demanding, and have low reward systems. On the other hand, another study found that "chaplains who perceive that they are well-integrated into the healthcare team suffer less burnout and compassion fatigue" (Doolittle, 2015, p. 192 citing Yan & Beder, 2013). Institutional indifference can be countered by a strong team of colleagues.

In religious vocations, the sense of identity we draw from our traditions can both sustain us and leave us vulnerable to burnout when those communities, sanghas, and institutions let us down. We have seen much of this in recent years in sanghas rocked by scandals of sexual misconduct. In studies of Protestant ministers, those who differentiated between work and home life, kept a healthy balance by taking time away from work and time for oneself, maintained supportive relationships outside the church, had mentors, and exercised regularly tended to experience lower burnout, better functioning, adapted to change, and maintained a healthy spiritual life of their own (Doolittle, 2015, p. 190). However, this kind of differentiation is not always encouraged in Buddhist sanghas, particularly for clergy. More study on finding the right balance is needed within Buddhist contexts.

One thing we can do is look at our sanghas, communities, and institutional workplaces for the third factor that contributes to burnout: system characteristics. Recent research demonstrates that this may, in fact, be the primary source of burnout and thus the key mechanism for its prevention and alleviation. System characteristics conducive to burnout include autocratic administration, rigid hierarchy, low status within an existing hierarchy (such as chaplains in hospitals where medical staff have priority), lack of autonomy, little appreciation, or low rewards (including low salary), few/no promotion opportunities, lack of support from supervisors or other social supports, high caseloads and understaffing (Galek et al., 2011, p. 635-6). A 2013 study of over 2,000 VA chaplains found that those who reported poor collaboration with other mental health teammates and lower support had higher levels of burnout (Doolittle, 2015, p. 185, citing Yan & Beder's 2013 study). We can advocate to change these systems and, when change is not possible, take active steps to protect ourselves and our colleagues from systemic harm, often through staff care that is part of a chaplain's role.

Some personal factors are protective. A 2005 study (Flannelly et al.) of 343 clergy involved in Ground Zero responses following September 11, 2001, found that CPE training appeared to limit burnout and compassion fatigue and improve compassion satisfaction (Doolittle, 2015, p. 187). Age, years of experience within a profession, and social support outside the work environment (i.e., family, community), also seem to be protective, but are often insufficient to overcome systemic factors.

In other words, more self-care cannot solve burnout in a toxic workplace. Institutions often invest in self-care programs such as mindfulness, relaxation, or even life coaching for employees as though burnout is a personal problem (and personal failing) rather than a systemic problem rooted in the institution. Chaplains therefore have a responsibility not only to themselves, but to care for their fellow staff and the careseekers they all serve by advising the institution as to the suffering it causes. In Christian chaplaincy this is called "prophetic voice" in reference to the (often unwelcome) advice Biblical prophets offered to kings and rulers. In the Buddhist scriptures we find numerous instances of the Buddha advising kings and nobles regarding behavior that perpetuates suffering in their domains. Chaplains thus serve the role of a moral compass within institutions, particularly on topics such as these.

Cultivating the Four Divine Abodes

Compassion and empathy in Buddhism are aspects of a construct known as the Four Divine Abodes or *Brahmavihāra*. The English terms/concepts do not map neatly onto individual correlates; therefore, it may be more useful to consider the four abodes in their totality as inseparable components for the openheartedness that chaplains need. The abodes are: (Sanskrit / Pāli)

- *Karuṇā* – compassion or the desire to alleviate suffering, one's own and others
- *Muditā* – sympathetic joy or the delight in other's happiness
- *Upekṣā / Upekkhā* – equanimity or impartiality
- *Maitrī / Mettā* – loving-kindness, goodwill, or the desire for happiness, one's own and others

The Divine Abodes are cultivated through states of meditative absorption, as principal virtues, and as counteragents to unwholesome states. Compassion specifically counteracts harmfulness; loving-kindness counteracts hostility; sympathetic joy counteracts dissatisfaction and envy; and equanimity counteracts craving in both its aversive forms (e.g., hostility, anger) and attachment forms (e.g., sensual pleasure, pride). The Divine Abodes become *apramāṇa* or "boundless states" when applied to all beings during meditation (Buswell and Lopez, 2014, p. 143). Thus, equanimity can refer both to one's ability to remain stable within stressful and emotionally turbulent situations as well as one's ability to apply the other abodes (compassion, loving-kindness, and sympathetic joy) to all beings without exclusion, including the 'difficult' people in our lives and even those we may consider 'enemies.' The abodes balance one another, and it is important to both understand and practice them together. For example, compassion and its focus on suffering must be balanced with experiences of sympathetic joy. The desire to seek happiness must be balanced with non-attachment to the transitory causes of that happiness.

While the definition of the Four Abodes stresses their contemplative underpinnings, Condon and Makransky argue that the first foundation for the cultivation of compassion and empathy is secure relationality – that is, a sangha in which one finds these qualities modelled and supported. This matches with my findings that chaplains who have *kalyāṇamitra* of their own are more able to act as spiritual friends to others (see Volume I). We often discuss the importance of giving compassion to others as chaplains, but Condon and Makransky also point out that we ourselves have been the recipients of compassion and loving-kindness from countless others of the past and present. Every time we generate the thought of compassion for all beings, we are also encompassed by those who include us in their conception of all beings (2020, p. 1352). Far from merely an abstract recognition, secure relationality can only be established through ongoing personal relationships with others, past and present. These relationships inform what Condon and Makransky call an "unlimited secure base" (2020, p. 1346) – a psychological and emotional felt state that we can recall at will in order to draw upon our own compassionate resources for caregiving work.

Condon and Makransky have spent the past few years developing Sustainable Compassion Training (SCT). This training includes contemplative practices of receiving, sending, and deepening a felt sense of compassion and loving-kindness. One begins "by recalling a simple moment of caring connection from any time in one's own life…and then reinhabiting that moment to reexperience oneself as seen and loved within it (2020, p. 1353)." One repeats this process, recalling other moments, and learns to dwell in that feeling. This is especially useful for individuals with insecure attachment who have learned to dismiss moments of love and care from others as unreliable or insincere (Condon and Makransky, 2020, p. 1354).[1] Studies have found that individuals with insecure forms of attachment can have difficulty extending and sustaining compassion for others and experience lower compassion satisfaction (Goetz and Simon-Thomas in Seppälä et al., 2017, p. 5-6). Likewise, I found that it is difficult for Buddhist chaplains to act as spiritual friends to others if we lack spiritual friendships of our own. Unfortunately, as Condon and Makransky note, many Buddhists, in addition to having troubled relationships with parents and primary caregivers (a cause of insecure attachment), also have looser relationships to their Buddhist sanghas for both personal and cultural reasons.

---

[1] For more on secure and insecure/avoidant attachment, see this brief overview of "Adult Attachment Theory and Research" from R. Chris Fraley at the University of Illinois at Urbana-Champaign: http://labs.psychology.illinois.edu/~rcfraley/attachment.htm

Many of the foundational practices in traditional Buddhist communities include relational elements embedded in ritual practices of refuge, devotion, and service to community. Relational elements include taking refuge—in other words, finding a safe place—in the love, compassion, and wisdom embodied by Buddhas, bodhisattvas, teachers, and other accomplished practitioners (sangha), offering service to them and receiving their blessings. These practices form a basis for generating a similar power of love, compassion, and wisdom that would encompass many other beings. Through the lens of modernism, these devotional relational practices were perceived as superstitious or mythological accidents or "accretions" of Asian culture. Moreover, these cultural "accretions" have been perceived as deviations from the original essence or core teachings of the Buddha, which were construed through a modernist lens as more exclusively rationalistic and individualistic. (Condon and Makransky, 2020, p. 1347)

SCT is then both a training in compassion and a recovery of this aspect of Buddhist wisdom. Relationships with teachers and sanghas is essential for Buddhist chaplains to create the "unlimited secure base" that we need to extend empathy and compassion to others and practice the brahmavihāra in our caregiving work.

Moreover, SCT aligns with western psychological research to help overcome inner barriers to compassion such as "lack of a secure base, aversion to suffering, feeling alone in suffering, and reductive impressions of others" (Condon and Makransky, 2020, p. 1346) that have been identified by social scientists. Early research on SCT from eight-week trainings with adults has demonstrated encouraging findings, but it is too soon yet to definitively prove SCT can overcome these psychological barriers from the perspective of the social sciences. As Buddhists, we find support within the Dharma for these ideas.

There are many contemplative trainings and techniques for the cultivation of the Four Divine Abodes, such as SCT. Several of the authors in *The Arts of Contemplative Care* describe the importance of cultivating and applying the abodes. According to Mikel Monnett, the Buddha taught compassion as the foundation of all actions (2012, p. 106). Robert Chodo Campbell describes the deep compassion within the act of bearing witness (2012, p. 80). Kristin Deleo describes how compassion may seem deceptively simple, but it is not easy, and provides a basic meditation to cultivate it (2012, p. 244-251). Cheryl Giles summarizes Phadampa Sangye's instructions to Machig Lapdronma (through Pema Chödrön's commentary) for cultivating compassion, particularly to overcome racism and other forms of prejudice (2012, p. 46-51). If we have attended a teaching or retreat, it is likely we have experienced a guided meditation on loving-kindness or compassion and, if not, these can easily be found online. The point is not, however, to experience them once, but to integrate these contemplative techniques into our regular practices, our caregiving, and our social lives as Buddhists in whatever way works best for us. Many traditions have prescribed and ongoing training regimes to do just that.

Others are adapting contemplative trainings for secular audiences (which is even creating an analogous vocabulary within the social sciences around "compassion-based interventions" or CBIs), following in the footsteps of John Kabat-Zinn and his adaptation and popularization of mindfulness via the secularized practice of Mindfulness-Based Stress Reduction (MBSR). New secular forms of *Brahmavihāra* training include:

- Loving-Kindness Meditation (LKM) and Compassion Meditation (CM) studied by Kabat-Zinn and others since the early 1990s; LKM has been recently (from 2008) studied for its effects on a variety of psychological conditions and emotional states
- Mindful Self-Compassion (MSC) training developed by Kristin Neff's team at the University of San Diego around 2003 and the shorter Self-Compassion for Healthcare Communities (SCHC) training developed in 2019–2020
- Cognitively-Based Compassion Training (CBCT) developed by Lobsang Tenzin Negi's team at Emory University in 2005
- Sustainable Compassion Training (SCT) developed by John Makransky's team at Boston College in 2007 and subsequently adapted by the Mind and Life Institute (mindandlife.org) and Courage of Care Coalition (courageofcare.org)
- Compassion Cultivation Training (CCT) developed by Thupten Jinpa's team at Stanford University in 2007
- ReSource Project developed by Tania Singer's team at the Max Plank Institute for Human Cognition and Brain Science in Leipzig, Germany, in 2010
- Cultivating Emotional Balance (CEB) training developed by Paul Ekman's team at University of California, San Francisco in 2010–11

The theoretical underpinnings of these protocols are drawn from a combination of Buddhist teaching and positive psychology. Their effectiveness is being validated through randomized controlled trials, physiological measurements, and psychometric instruments. It is yet to be seen if secular contemplative training for compassion, loving-kindness, or equanimity will face the same criticism as secular mindfulness training or serve as a corrective to some of those self-same criticisms. What we do know is that modern social science is, by and large, validating what Buddhism has taught for more than two thousand years – qualities like mindfulness, compassion, and equanimity are useful for living a good life and helping others, and can be taught and cultivated over time.

Connection and Satisfaction

While compassion has both positive and negative qualities and working in and around suffering exposes chaplains to certain risks, it also provides clear rewards, including experiences of connection and satisfaction. Again, we can explore these concepts both in the Dharma and the social sciences. Empathic connection is referred to in various ways in social sciences literature, including under the term 'empathic concern' where it is defined as an "other-oriented emotion elicited by and congruent with the perceived welfare of a person in need," (Batson in Seppala et al., p. 28). However, this definition does not seem to truly capture the energy, power, and even joy found in the kinds of connections described by chaplains. A related concept called 'compassion satisfaction' was identified by social scientists about 20 years ago as a protective factor against compassion fatigue. Buddhists are already aware of the benefits of compassion both to oneself and others. In the Buddhist model, compassion and wisdom are interconnected through the realization of suffering, non-self, emptiness, and interdependence. These Dharmic concepts do not fit neatly into social scientific models of compassion fatigue resilience, which will not be discussed further in this section. Instead, I will focus more here on the positive benefits Buddhist chaplains reported from empathic connection with careseekers and then consider compassion satisfaction through a Buddhist lens.

The chaplains I interviewed all repeatedly stated that presence helped them connect with careseekers. "If I'm not totally present, I'm gonna lose that connection," one chaplain said. The concept of connection developed complex dimensions as interviews progressed. In relation to being present, it refers to the connection between two people, specifically the chaplain and careseeker(s). It could be as simple as having a conversation that both parties are interested in having. One chaplain described how connecting with careseekers "felt like magic and I didn't have [to] work so hard [scoffs], which is odd." Many chaplains associated connection with joy, even in traumatic circumstances. Daniel Siegel identifies this as a 'resonance' and writes that "From a positive psychology perspective, the resonance around a negative emotion might lead to the positive emotional experience of being cared for by another, and caring for another, even though they became connected through a negative emotional state initially" (Fredrickson and Siegel in Gilbert, p. 208). In other words, though the circumstances in which chaplains and careseekers meet may be distressing and traumatic, experiencing a caring connection during that time can be positive for both.

Chaplains understood that connection also had a spiritual dimension. During their conversations with chaplains, people connect with their deeper selves or things greater than themselves, such as God, the divine, or the big existential questions of the universe. The big questions that all people ask "break down all labels and barriers," according to one chaplain. Even non-theist chaplains could empathize with careseekers' sense of connection with God because the chaplains had their own sense of connection with something larger than themselves, though they may not call that thing 'God.' In these instances, being open to mystery or not-knowing helped Buddhist chaplains empathize with careseekers who felt connected to things the chaplains did not personally experience but could imagine. One chaplain likened connection to "the yoga idea of union versus separation or isolation." The latter, to them, was a form of suffering.

Other chaplains interpreted connection as a byproduct of interdependence or emptiness. We connect with others because we are, in fact, not separate from them. Any sense of separation is a delusion that perpetuates suffering. In this respect, connection had a soteriological function for several of the chaplains I spoke with. One described it as being "beyond words," a phrase often used to describe *prajñā*. Connection takes on an aspect of wisdom when viewed as a function of interdependence or emptiness. One chaplain talked about connecting with careseekers on the basis of a shared buddha-nature, of not being fundamentally different from others, and being interdependent. (*Prajñā* has already received a fuller discussion in Volume I, Chapter 3.)

Some chaplains talked about having strong connections with people in their past, particularly teachers, mentors, and *kalyāṇamitra*. They attributed their ability to connect to careseekers now as arising from this prior experience. This implies that empathy, compassion, presence, listening, and connection are learned skills commonly acquired through direct experience and modeling. We know what it feels like when someone is truly present with us, even in our darkest hours, and the felt sense of that connection enables us to replicate it in our own spiritual care work.

Empathic connection goes beyond empathic concern (which is solely individual) and occurs when both the chaplain and careseeker mutually recognize they are sharing the same emotional experience. Jean Baker Miller and Irene Pierce Stiver refer to this as "mutual empathy" and call it "the great unsung human gift" (1997, p. 29). Miller and Stiver emphasize that western psychological paradigms often mistakenly prioritize independence – physical, mental, emotional, financial, and social – over dependence, which is pathologized, as in, for example, 'co-dependent' relationships. As Buddhists, we recognize that while a certain amount of self-care and self-reliance are helpful, independence itself is fundamentally illusory. We are all dependently co-arising with everyone and everything else all the time. Moreover, the *kalyāṇamitra* model resonates with Miller and Stiver's "model of psychological development within relationships, in which everyone participates in ways that foster the development of all the people involved, something we might call 'mutual psychological development'" (1997, p. 17). This also resonates with Condon and Makransky's cultivation of a secure relational base as the origin of empathy and compassion. Miller and Stiver's work, based on the study of women's psychology, carries many lessons for all people, including the recognition that mutual empathy can be mutually empowering as it enables careseekers the safe space in which to recognize, explore, and more fully express their emotions (1997, p. 29-30). As a result, the careseeker experiences a sense of empowerment to act and create change, sense of worth, greater sense of connection and more desire for connection which can lead to better use of social supports and resources, and what Miller and Stiver refer to as "zest" in emotional connection, which "feels like an increase…in vitality, aliveness, energy," (1997, p. 30-34), or the "magic" described by one of the chaplains I interviewed.

Unfortunately, sometimes it can be extraordinarily difficult to connect with people, especially across vast personal differences. For some chaplains, empathy comes easily, while for others it is more elusive. Remember that empathy is based on what we perceive the careseeker feels, while empathic connection is based on the confirmation from the careseeker that our perception is accurate. Empathy, then, is largely based on imagination. When we get it right, a strong, genuine, healing connection is formed. When we get it wrong, we call this 'projection.' We project our own feelings onto the careseeker based on how we think they ought to feel or how we ourselves might feel in a similar situation. When we proceed carefully and are open to correction, projection can be manageable. However, when we strive ahead too quickly, certain we know what someone else feels, we can cause harm. Compassion helps us remain mindful of this possibility, and it comes with benefits of its own, even when empathy is tenuous.

Compassion satisfaction is defined as the good feelings we get from helping others. Oliver et al. defines compassion satisfaction as the "positive feelings about the ability to help other people (2018, p. 72)." I question the sufficiency of this definition in the work of a chaplain, who often, in fact, cannot materially 'help' other people yet may nevertheless describe satisfaction from simply being with other people in their time of need. A 2013 study of 2,017 VA chaplains found high levels of compassion satisfaction and low levels of compassion fatigue and burnout in comparison to other helping professions (Doolittle, 2015, p. 185, citing Yan & Beder's 2013 study).

A 2008 study (Ekedahl and Wengstrom) compared the existential coping mechanisms of chaplains and nurses in hospitals and found that chaplains used a broader array of coping strategies "including 'reconstruction,' where the patient and the event are understood within the context of the sacred" and noted that this kind of coping had both personal and professional dimensions (Doolittle, 2015, p. 188). In other words, the meaning we make from our work has an impact on our satisfaction, sense of efficacy, and resilience in the ongoing work of accompanying people in times of suffering. While few studies on compassion satisfaction in chaplains have been completed and none on Buddhist chaplains as a group, studies of Protestant clergy have found that practices including acceptance, active coping (concentrating on what one can change rather than what one cannot affect), and positive reframing were associated with a greater sense of accomplishment (Doolittle, 2015, p. 190). Likewise, confidence in the efficacy (personal or cosmic) of prayer has been positively correlated to good mental health in Christian clergy (Doolittle, 2015, p. 190, citing Turton and Francis, 2007). Students need to undergo spiritual formation to develop their understanding of where they stand and how they personally make meaning of the situations they will encounter as a chaplain before and as they begin to encounter them. CPE can be very helpful in this process. Once in professional practice, chaplains should continue the process of spiritual maturation, professional education, and maintaining supportive relationships.

Satisfaction also comes from a sense that we are making a positive impact and from appreciation from colleagues and careseekers. Compassion satisfaction is more likely in a supportive working environment and can protect us from compassion fatigue, vicarious trauma, and burnout (Stamm, 2005, Barr, 2014, p. 17-18;). While a supportive workplace can encourage compassion satisfaction, it also helps chaplains to cultivate *kalyāṇamitra* and support systems beyond their immediate professional environment. Chaplains need to maintain a professional support network both within and beyond their work settings, regularly consult with that network, and seek ongoing supervision (Doolittle, 2015, p. 194 summarizing Weaver's 2002 recommendations). Likewise, the personal is professional and chaplains must maintain healthy family relationships and cultivate family support systems (Doolittle, 2015, p. 194 summarizing Weaver's 2002 recommendations). Their work will affect their family and their family will provide a stable support base for their work.

Compassion directed towards oneself is related to our sense of compassion satisfaction in our work. In a study of clergy, Barnard and Curry found that higher self-compassion predicted overall satisfaction with their work and lower emotional exhaustion (2011, p. 156). The researchers found that "clergy who are high in self-compassion, i.e., kind towards themselves during times of stress or failure, see themselves as connected with others, and are able to hold their worries in mindful awareness without ruminating, are less likely to experience burnout" (2011, p. 159). The regular cultivation of self-compassion is thus linked to compassion satisfaction and overall work satisfaction.

Every year the Boston marathon sees thousands of athletes, professional and amateur, run 26 miles from the suburbs to the heart of Boston, one of America's oldest cities. Crowds line the entire 26-mile course to cheer them on. I have never had the urge to run a marathon. It appears arduous, even torturous. Yet, thousands of people train for months or years to complete the task, often encouraged by running groups, partners, coaches, and their families. They experience immense satisfaction as a result, often returning year after year. And they also accrue health benefits that lead to a long and happy life. Likewise, while the work of walking with others through some of the darkest times of their lives can be incredibly stressful, it can also be incredibly rewarding. Chaplains train for years and those who develop a deep well of compassion, loving-kindness, sympathetic joy, and equanimity, also with a robust support system of fellow *kalyāṇamitra* around them, return year after year to continue the work. We experience both immense satisfaction in that work and advance along our own spiritual paths towards awakening.

4
Spiritual Assessment

Existing Assessment Tools and Models

Modern 'spiritual assessment' began in the 1970s as chaplains in healthcare responded to the empirical demands of medicine and the bureaucratic demands of business and government. In other words, chaplains were pressured to document what they did and how it benefited careseekers. This is not to say that chaplains have never evaluated their work, only that assessment as a formal practice by that name came about due to the causes and conditions of the modern context. Chaplains developed models for spiritual assessment that have since spread to other disciplines, such as nursing and social work. See Wendy Cadge's 2015 article, "The Evolution of Spiritual Assessment Tools in Healthcare," for a good history of this development. These models, though perhaps spurred by outside pressures, can be useful to any chaplain. The idea of assessing someone's spiritual condition exists within many world religions. Buddhism's emphasis on the spiritual path (*marga*), its various stages, and the metaphor of the Buddha as a physician and the Dharma as medicine with clear 'antidotes' for particular afflictions, may make it particularly suited to the practice of spiritual assessment. (*Marga*, according to the *Princeton Dictionary of Buddhism*, is a "term that derives in part from the view that the means of achieving liberation from suffering have been identified by the Buddha, and he himself has successfully followed the route to that goal, leaving behind tracks or footprints that others can follow." Various Buddhist schools have developed numerous complex staged models of *marga* or path in relation to states of mind, spiritual progress, and practices (Lopez & Buswell, 2013, p. 532).) Before exploring the potential for Buddhist models of spiritual assessment, let us first look at some models from other religious traditions and secular sources currently being used by chaplains.

Ruth Stoll's Guidelines for Spiritual Assessment of 1979 was one of the earliest attempts at a structured spiritual assessment tool within a medical setting. The assumptions of the model are immediately evident in the first part of the assessment on the "Concept of God or deity." Nevertheless, this framework did provide a helpful starting point. It included categories for "sources of hope and strength," "religious practices," and "relationship between spiritual beliefs and health" (McSherry, 2010, p. 58-59). We see a Christo-centric understanding of religion in the emphasis on 'belief' as the defining feature of a tradition, rather than practice or community. From this early example, McSherry describes a spectrum of spiritual assessments ranging from informal inquiries into religious belief to detailed spiritual histories. Along this spectrum, McSherry (2010, p. 57-65) identifies six main methods of spiritual assessment:

1. Direct method in which caregivers ask direct questions about "religious or spiritual beliefs" in order to determine "spiritual needs;"
2. Indicator-based models that look for characteristics of spiritual distress, sometimes to make a spiritual "diagnosis;"
3. Audit tools that attempt to assess the effectiveness of spiritual care provided and if it has met spiritual needs;

4. Value clarification using easy-to-administer Likert-scale questions;
5. Indirect methods including observation;
6. Acronym-based models such as FICA and HOPE that are focused and easy to remember.

When choosing a model, chaplains should understand who developed the model for use by which type of practitioner. Models come with built-in assumptions. For example, spiritual assessment models designed for nurses are intended to reveal if the patient has religious beliefs or practices (such as dietary restrictions) that would impact medical care or if a referral to a chaplain is warranted. Models designed for social workers assume that they will be used as part of longer-term, goal-oriented therapy. The hazard with models for chaplains is, of course, that they have been developed with a largely theistic outlook, often by and for Protestant Christians. As most North American careseekers are, in fact, theistic and largely Christian, this can be useful. However, these models can create interpretation challenges for the Buddhist chaplain and may not be suitable for non-theistic or non-Christian careseekers.

Howard Clinebell describes assessment within the process of spiritual counseling, usually conducted within a congregational (i.e., community or sangha) setting, in which the caregiver meets with the careseeker one-on-one (or with a couple or small group) for a limited number of sessions, usually four or five. This kind of assessment matches the direct method from McSherry's typology, since the counselee has sought out the spiritual counselor for their expertise in religious and spiritual matters. In this model, assessment is the first stage in a collaborative process of evaluation, strategizing, and contracting to meet the needs of the careseeker. Clinebell recommends answering five basic questions:

1. What kind of help does the careseeker request?
2. What is the nature and urgency of the current crisis or problems and are they recent or chronic?
3. What are the dynamics of the careseeker's social context?
4. What strengths, hopes, resources, goals, and relationships does the careseeker bring?
5. Does the careseeker need short-term crisis care, decision-making assistance, long-term supportive care, or specialized psychotherapy? (Clinebell, 2011, p. 81-83)

In the latter case, the spiritual caregiver, unless they are also a psychotherapist, should refer to

---

Acronym-Based Assessment Models

FICA - See: Puchalski, Christina, "The FICA Spiritual History Tool: A Guide for Spiritual Assessment in Clinical Settings," The GW Institute for Spirituality & Health, 1996 & 2022, https://gwish.smhs.gwu.edu/sites/g/files/zaskib1011/files/2022-08/v2_fica_pdf_2_final_updated_6.29.22.pdf; Borneman, Tami, Betty Ferrell, and Christina Puchalski, "Evaluation of the FICA Tool for Spiritual Assessment," *Journal of Pain and Sympton Management*, vol. 40, issue 2, August 2010, p. 163-173.

HOPE - See: Anandarajah, Gowri and E Hight, "Spirituality and Medical Practice: Using the HOPE Questions as a Practical Tool for Spiritual Assessment," *American Family Physician*, vol. 63, issue 1, 2001, p. 81-89; Whitehead, Ishbel Orla et al, "Discussing spiritual health in primary care and the HOPE tool—A mixed methods survey of GP views," PLoS One, vol. 17, issue 11, 2022, online, https://www.ncbi.nlm.nih.gov/pmc/articles/PMC9642893/

a known network of community contacts.

George Donovan's chapter on assessments in *Professional Spiritual & Pastoral Care: A Practical Clergy and Chaplain's Handbook* (2012, p. 44) provides basic guidance for chaplains in a medical setting, including overcoming their preferences to simply listen and 'be there' for the patient. Assessment can be difficult for chaplains who may feel like they do not have enough information about a patient, insight into their situation, or a 'right to make judgments' about them. However, assessment is important to the care process when conducted with the best interests of careseekers at heart. Based on McSherry's typology, Donovan's form of assessment relies primarily on indirect methods, as the chaplain makes observations based on a careseeker-led or semi-structured conversation. If appropriate, the chaplain may also use an indicator-based model, audit tool, or value clarification scale depending on the situation, but these are infrequently used in crisis care or single-visit care.

Donovan recommends assessing for three elements: 1) relationships and connectivity; 2) meaning and purpose; and 3) degree of understanding of their situation and congruence of responses to their situation. In other words, does the patient understand their medical situation and are they making decisions about it that match their values and beliefs? This can be challenging for patients and families in stressful situations, especially since medical staff are not always trained to explore meaning and values as they relate to medical decisions. The very process of assessment can help patients uncover information about their own values and needs they may not even have realized. (We see an example of this in Vignette 2 in Volume I, chapter 1.) When conducting assessments, Donovan provides the four L's. Chaplains should ask themselves what they are *looking* for and what *language* would help explore that topic. They should then consider what those conversations *lead* them to think and what they could *learn* that might be of benefit. Donovan provides examples of questions related to the four L's in several charts (2012, p. 45-56). Donovan also provides a list of ten 'shalt nots' for writing a spiritual assessment (2012, p. 58), including an admonition not to confuse assessment with the provision of religious services or confuse assessment tools with spiritual goals.

Donovan's chapter is followed by a chapter in the same volume on spiritual care plans, by Roberts, Donovan, and Handzo. The authors consider the process of spiritual assessment and the design of a spiritual care plan to be separate but related activities. Spiritual care plans are created by chaplains in medical settings and integrated into the overall care plan for a patient. Some goals of a spiritual care plan can be fulfilled by anyone, such as by providing kosher food, while other activities should only be performed by a chaplain, such as spiritual interventions (Roberts et al, 2012, p. 62-64).

Since spiritual assessment is not the exclusive domain of chaplains, we must interface with nurses, therapists, and social workers around the practice of spiritual assessment and the goals of the spiritual care plan. Sometimes this is done through charting and note keeping (see section below) and sometimes through formal multidisciplinary team meetings to discuss patient care. In non-medical settings, chaplains may also seek anonymous consultation with other clinicians (such as when a careseeker presents with mental health symptoms but resists a mental health referral) or formal permission from the careseeker (usually a signed form) to coordinate care with their other caregivers. In such cases, it can be useful to conduct a structured spiritual assessment that can be shared with other clinicians.

A comprehensive model for spiritual assessment is George Fitchett's 7x7 framework, explained in his 2002 book *Assessing Spiritual Needs*. Prior to presenting his own model for assessment, he reviews nine other approaches to assessment (Fitchett, 2002, p. 12-14):
- Implicit assessment, which is similar to McSherry's indirect method;

- Inspired assessment grounded in divine revelation;
- Intuitive assessment relying on the 'gut feeling' of the chaplain;
- Idiosyncratic assessment using personal ad hoc diagnostic schema;
- Assessments based on traditional pastoral acts (e.g., prayer, chanting);
- Assessment based on normative pastoral stances, such as beliefs about how the careseeker needs the chaplain to behave: e.g., compassionately;
- Global assessment that is applied to all careseekers without distinction;
- Psychological assessment, which is similar to McSherry's indicator-based method;
- Explicit spiritual assessment such as Clinebell's direct method.

Fitchett's own 7x7 model guides the chaplain to make a detailed written account of the careseeker's 1) medical, 2) psychological, 3) psychosocial, 4) family systems, 5) ethnic and cultural, 6) societal, and 7) spiritual dimensions, then details the last dimension more fully to account for 7.1) belief and meaning, 7.2) vocation and consequences, 7.3) experience and emotion, 7.4) courage and growth, 7.5) ritual and practice, 7.6) community, and 7.7) authority and guidance (Fitchett, 2002, p. 42). Thus, it reviews seven holistic dimensions and seven spiritual dimensions to yield the 7x7 name.

Fitchett defines spiritual assessment as both a process and a product concerned with uncovering and describing the "dimension of life that reflects the need to find meaning in existence and in which we respond to the sacred." In this definition, Fitchett purposefully does not distinguish between spirituality, religion, faith, and belief, nor between assessment and diagnosis (2002, p. 16-17). Assessment is important to Fitchett because it informs action, communication, contracting, evaluation, personal responsibility, quality assurance, and research, and can also serve as "the touchstone of a profession's identity" (2002, p. 20-22). In a short section on the "theology of spiritual assessment," Fitchett proclaims,

> The emphasis on the importance of assessment is rooted in the conviction that revelation about the divine nature and foundation of existence is continuing and that it proceeds through person; as the Quakers are fond of saying, "There is that of God in everyone." (2002, p. 22)

Fichett's model is general enough for use by non-Christians, though clearly it remains laden with theocentric, psychological, and Western cultural assumptions. At the same time, there is an analogous position within Buddhism that because the Dharma reflects the way reality actually is (not just the teaching of the Buddha), the Dharma is applicable in all situations with all people. Therefore, spiritual assessment provides insight into Dharma via our observations of others.

From my experience using the 7x7 model, the main drawback is that it is cumbersome and not intuitive. As a Buddhist chaplain, the 7x7 model feels foreign. It is not how I normally think about spiritual problems. Therefore, I must make a conscious effort to adopt and then interpret the model's aims back into my own frame of reference. (Sometimes doing things that are not intuitive can be helpful in forcing us to examine our subconscious assumptions.) Understanding the careseeker's needs from their point of view can enable empathy and wisdom to blossom. However, most careseekers don't express their needs in the manner of the 7x7 model either. Therefore, we must inevitably 'translate' what the careseeker expresses twice, first to fit into the model and then again through the lens of our own experience and expertise as Buddhists. Donovan alludes to this in his four L's. The language we use to elicit information from the careseeker should be capable of serving its intended purpose.

For example, we would not ask "What is

your epistemological framework?" but we might ask "How do you come to know that?" or "What leads you to that belief?" when trying to understand spiritual experiences or the sources of particular ideas, such as from religious upbringing. Likewise, the language we use for thinking and writing about careseekers plays a role in how deeply we understand and empathize with their concerns. Unfamiliar language can distance us from the felt experiences of our careseekers. For example, I do not directly empathize with an experience of 'essence of divine love within all creation,' but I can create a bridge to that experience when I consider my own experiences of *pratītyasamutpāda*, or dependent co-arising of all phenomena. Therefore, in assessing this careseeker, I might talk about a sense of 'oneness with…' to find a bridge between them and myself. I am aware that these feelings, concepts, and meanings are not the same, but similar enough for a felt recognition that is critical in forming a supportive relationship between caregiver and careseeker. I can recognize and affirm the need for and power of transcendent experiences, however described. Thus, I learn (another of Donovan's L's) what may be of benefit by coming as close to the careseeker's experience as I can while remaining grounded in my own worldview.

The entire foundation of spiritual assessment is based on the assumptions of Kluckholn and Murray's 1948 formula that persons are in some respects like all others, like some others, and like no other (Lartey, 2003, p. 15). The universalizing impulse, that people are like all others, allows the chaplain to assume that they can effectively deal with universal spiritual concerns through shared empathy. The categorizing impulse, that people are like some others, helps chaplains determine what bridges need to be built, if any, between themselves and the careseeker. The individualizing impulse drives the assumption that spiritual assessment is, in fact, both necessary and useful to understand the unique position and needs of each person. After all, if all people were the same or easily categorizable, detailed spiritual assessment would hardly be necessary.

It is interesting to note that the formal practice of spiritual assessment emerged at the same time as post-modern theories and methods of spiritual care and pastoral theology (e.g., communal contextual and intercultural methods, feminist and liberation theologies, and so on) when caregivers could no longer rely on blanket assumptions to diagnose and treat spiritual ills. The post-modern movement recognized the subjectiveness of experience and sought to recover previously marginalized voices and stories. It also enabled the diversification of the spiritual care professions and the recognition that new voices may have something unique and valuable to offer even to the most established professionals.

Buddhist Spiritual Assessment Models

This section contains two potential models for Buddhist spiritual assessment. I write 'potential' as these models are new and relatively untested beyond the applications of their authors. One is my own invention and the other comes from a colleague at the University of Hong Kong based on his work in Buddhist-based counseling and psychotherapy. The tools provide Buddhist caregivers with ways of performing assessments of interfaith careseekers within the framework of Buddhist psychology and philosophy. The purpose is not to conform careseekers into a Buddhist mold or assign them Buddhist spiritual goals, but rather to help the chaplain better understand the careseeker's circumstances, worldview, goals, and how best to assist them.

The assessment process benefits from a psychological framework and lexicon deeply familiar to the chaplain. By crossing back and forth between the careseeker's worldview and the chaplain's lexicon, new possibilities for spiritual care emerge. While this may seem strange at first, it becomes more familiar with repetition. This conceptual movement is similar to the work of secular caregivers, such as in the medical field and mental health professions, who regularly use specialized language to describe situations. Specialized language forms the basis of expertise in many disciplines. It helps caregivers clarify concerns and focus on areas for appropriate interventions. They may rarely communicate with the careseeker in the language of their discipline, instead favoring common terms for ease of communication (e.g., 'heart attack' rather than myocardial infarction). Likewise, the chaplain uses specialized spiritual and religious language to understand common human problems and translates their expert knowledge into the careseeker's perspective during interactions.

The first template for Buddhist spiritual assessment (my own development) proceeds from two recognitions. First, spiritual assessment frameworks should be as explicit about their foundations as possible. For example, some frameworks guide the chaplain to consider the careseeker's religious "beliefs" or "relationship with God" as if these were: a) common to all careseekers; and b) of equal importance to all careseekers or in all spiritual care settings. In fact, neither is true. Nevertheless, these spiritual assessment tools have performed fairly well in predominantly Christian American culture. As the profession of chaplaincy expands to include Buddhists and others, and as the population of non-Christian careseekers continues to expand, new tools are needed.

The second recognition is the inevitability of our subjective perspectives. As a Buddhist chaplain, I naturally flow between my own understanding and the careseeker's understanding of the situation. For example, when a careseeker says she just can't let go of her deceased husband, Buddhist teachings on impermanence, attachment, and suffering immediately come to mind. If the careseeker is not herself Buddhist, I may never mention these teachings to her, preferring to work within her existing worldview. However, when assessing her spiritual state, spiritual needs, and a possible plan of care, my own perspective necessarily informs conclusions. I may, for example, believe that acceptance is an important step in her bereavement process. While this would be congruent with the findings of social science and other religions, I cannot help but think about it in terms like *anicca* and *saṃsāra*. Moreover, while essentially Buddhist, I also believe this understanding to be broadly beneficial.

The main risk and point of legitimate criticism for such a spiritual assessment tool is that it amounts to a silent imposition of the chaplain's religious tradition on the careseeker and may bias their plan of care in directions not preferable or beneficial to careseekers with different worldviews. This risk is always present, however, regardless of which assessment paradigm is used (Christian, secular, or Buddhist) or the worldviews of the caregiver and careseeker involved, including when chaplain and careseeker share a religious tradition. The risk increases when assessment tools are applied with unexamined assumptions, which is why the first recognition (explicit foundations) is so important.

The framework for the first assessment model is based on classical Buddhist teachings that are psychosocial in nature and can be useful lenses into common human experiences without imposing cosmological or metaphysical worldviews. Suffering, for instance, is a common human experience. When working with Buddhist careseekers, Buddhist interpretations of the causes of suffering may come more to the fore, whereas with interfaith careseekers, it may be helpful to explore their self-understanding of what causes their suffering. Likewise, the pursuit of happiness or reduction of suffering is a common human goal and while Buddhists may define it in certain ways (i.e., enlightenment, *nirvana*), the format of the assessment does not dictate that as the only conceptualization of spiritual happiness. While based on the Buddhadharma, the framework has been adapted in various ways to the context of modern, interfaith spiritual care.

A Buddhist Spiritual Care Assessment Framework

1. Describe the nature of suffering (*dukkha*) – What is causing the careseeker physical, psychological, emotional, social, financial, or other kinds of distress? What is their situation? How do they think, speak, and act in relation to it?
2. Determine the immediate causes (*samudaya*) of the suffering, using the three roots as guides:
   - Attachment (*lobha/rāga*) – What does the careseeker want, expect, or hope for? How do they go about pursuing their desires? What happens (or may happen) when they can or cannot achieve their desires?
   - Aversion (*dosa/dveṣa*) – What does the careseeker avoid, fear, dislike, or hate? How are aversive emotions affecting their thoughts, speech, and behaviors? What impact does this have on their situation?
   - Ignorance/Delusion (*moha*) – Where does the careseeker expression confusion or ambiguity? Where do they contradict themselves? Is their assessment of their present situation realistic (especially in relation to medical diagnoses)? What maladaptive coping mechanisms are they exhibiting, including religious or spiritual beliefs that may not be supporting them well?
3. Discover what it would look to reduce suffering and, if possible, bring about joy (*nirodha*) – What are their immediate and their 'big picture' goals – physical, psychological, professional, and/or spiritual? What brings them joy and happiness, even in difficult circumstances? What are their strengths, supports, positive qualities? What does 'salvation' or 'liberation' or 'satisfaction' look like to them?
4. Co-create a path (*magga/marga*) to that place relying on:
   - Words that encourage joy, consolation, or healing (*sammā-vācā/samyag-vāc*);
   - Actions that relieve suffering and increase happiness (*sammā-kammanta/samyak-karamānta*)
   - A revised or renewed sense of life purpose or meaning (*sammā-ājīva/samyag-ājīva*);
   - Supportive refuges (*ratana*) such as social networks and communities (*sangha*), spiritual resources (e.g., books, videos, podcasts, music, art; *dhamma/dharma*), and mentors, teachers, leaders, clergy, or role models (*buddha*).

Buddhists will naturally see a strong resemblance to certain classical teachings, though some meanings have been broadened. Pali and Sanskrit terms have been supplied so that the foundations of the tool are clear, but they need not be applied rigidly during its use.

A Buddhist chaplain will see in this in this framework echoes of the Four Noble Truths, Three Unwholesome Roots, three parts of the Noble Eightfold Path (*śila*), and the Three Refuges. As the chaplain becomes familiar with applying this framework, she will become skilled at using it informally during the caregiving encounter but may still benefit from a complete write-up occasionally. It is possible that one might also be tempted to believe this is a problem-and-solution focused framework. In a basic sense, that is exactly what it is. However, in a broader sense, it describes the ongoing work of a lifetime (or many lifetimes) through an iterative process of change, learning, and growth.

One must be careful not to move the careseeker through the framework too swiftly, but merely to hold it in mind, listening to the careseeker without agenda as they set the pace. The chaplain then reflects on these aspects as they share with their care team in relation to this assessment tool. It may take time for the second or third aspect to emerge, perhaps several conversations. This may not be possible in some acute care or emergency situations. Achieving the fourth aspect, co-creating a path towards a better place, may be limited or partial. If a chaplain sees a careseeker for a single visit, as is common in hospitals, their intervention may be limited to words of consolation (e.g., a prayer or well-wishes) or a supportive social presence (brief refuge within a momentary sangha of two), without any longer-term plan.

When writing a spiritual assessment, describe in as much detail as possible the nature of the careseeker's physical, psychological, spiritual, or relational suffering. This spiritual assessment framework is not intended to serve as a formal interview. The chaplain should come to understand these items gradually through organic conversation focused on careseeker concerns. When information is not uncovered during the normal course of a conversation, the chaplain may use their inquiry skills, however, this model is not intended to be applied by systematically going through the questions above with the careseeker. It is not a survey instrument. The questions should prompt reflection in the chaplain on an appropriate care plan. Unlike some other spiritual assessment tools, this tool is not intended to be used by other chaplains or multidisciplinary staff, such as nurses or social workers. Once completed, a Buddhist chaplain may share their assessment, or portions thereof, with appropriate colleagues for a team approach to care. Two examples of completed Buddhist spiritual assessments are provided in the appendices, one of a Buddhist careseeker and the other of a non-Buddhist careseeker. Readers may wish to review these in detail and discuss with peers or classmates if possible.

The second Buddhist assessment tool was developed by Kin Cheung "George" Lee of the Centre of Buddhist Studies at the University of Hong Kong. The assessment method summarized below is described in detail in *The Guide to Buddhist Counseling* (Routledge, 2023). Lee and I recognize a common goal in our work: the reduction of suffering, whether achieved through spiritual care or psychotherapy. Both of our assessment models begin from this common assumption. Lee's theoretical model of Buddhist counseling recognizes that suffering arises from a combination of internal and external causes and conditions. Helping the careseeker understand these conditions can lead to a reduction in suffering, primarily through cultivation of self-awareness, subsequent non-attachment, and effective action. In other words, careseekers can change the conditions of their own lives (internally and externally), accept what they cannot change (such as the actions of other people), and learn how to tell the difference. This combination of awareness, non-attachment, and effective action has proven beneficial for Lee's clients, both Buddhist and non-Buddhist.

Lee draws on his own experience as a psychotherapist as well as other studies in the development of his assessment tool and overall approach. For example, faculty at the University of Hong Kong conducted a study with 415 participants to determine if the primary mechanism for the reduction of stress experienced by mindfulness meditators was self-awareness or 'un-clinging.' The effectiveness of mindfulness meditation for stress reduction is well established, but the exact psychological mechanisms behind this are less well understood. Researchers in the West may be hesitant to test hypotheses based directly on Buddhist psychology out of concern for conflating a 'religious' teaching with a purported secular academic discipline. The team in Hong Kong took this important step, recognizing that Buddhist psychology is not based on a metaphysical or cosmological doctrine (though it does interact with them), but on the careful observation of the human mind. As such, testing at least some of its theories empirically should be possible and they devised a strategy to do so. They found that while increased self-awareness was reported by meditators, un-clinging served as the primary mechanism for stress reduction. They concluded "Un-clinging, but not awareness, can distinguish meditators from non-meditators. Lastly, based on the Buddha's mindfulness discourse, a path analysis model illustrates that the effects of un-clinging and awareness on stress reduction are mediated by emotional intelligence and non-attachment." (Ng, Chow, Lau, and Wang, 2017, p. 1)

What this tells us is that it is not sufficient for someone to become aware of the causes of their suffering, they must change how they relate to their suffering on both an inner level – such as through the cultivation of non-attachment to external circumstances and un-clinging to internal ego or self-identity – and an outer level, such as through pragmatic actions and new choices. Lee draws on this research in formulating his assessment model and therapeutic approach.

Lee's assessment tool divides the causes and conditions causing suffering into categories to help the therapist and client better comprehend the situation and decide on a course of action. These categories are:
- Internal conditions: "intrapsychic elements and cognitive tendencies," "characteristics of self, views, states of mind, and habitual patterns of thought."
- External conditions: "conditions outside of the mind, and various conditions of a client's lived system, subsystems, and interactions between them," body, history, demographics, family, and culture (p. 71).

Lee explains that

> The internal conditions and external conditions are interdependent in nature and mutually influential to each other in a spiral manner: how an external condition of environmental impacts play a role in fostering the internal conditions of self-notion and view of the world while such constructed notions and views affect one's interactions with the environment, thereby eliciting certain responsive conditions in the environment. For example, a boy growing up in poverty (external condition) develops a low self-esteem as he sees himself as a "less-than" (internal condition) when compared to his classmates. This poor self-image makes him shy, timid, and afraid of voicing out his needs and this presence made other classmates further reject him or tease him (external condition). As a result, the external reinforces and concretizes boy's self-notion of being a "less-than" (internal condition). (p. 71-72)

We can see similar dynamics in the two sample spiritual assessments presented in the appendices. (They are not presented in full here, as they are each quite long. You may wish to go to the appendices to read them before proceeding, but I hope you will still be able to get the gist from what is presented here.)

In the assessment for Charlie, the careseeker perceived the relationship between his mother and stepfather as deeply unsatisfying (external condition). He then resolved to avoid a similar relationship in his own life (internal condition), which led him to seek out relationship partners with whom he experienced a high degree of passion (external condition). However, this volatile energy mix eventually resulted in conflict and dysfunction, leading to breakups that left him feeling bereft and alienated (internal condition).

In the assessment for Edith, conflict with peers (external conditions) led to feelings of insecurity and self-doubt, to which the careseeker responded through ego-clinging ("I'm so great") and anger at 'unfair' standards (internal condition). This, in turn, only fueled a spiral of negative conflict and hindered any opportunity for reconciliation with the peer in question (external condition) resulting in further frustration (internal condition). These kinds of dynamics can take time to unearth in conversation with careseekers.

In the psychotherapeutic application, Lee's assessment process takes place during an intake interview of 60-90 minutes, covering six items: "(a) client's reported concerns; (b) assessment of internal conditions; (c) assessment of external conditions; (d) assessment of habits; (e) assessment of potential risks; and (f) preliminary case formulation" (p. 72). Lee provides a case study to illustrate how this interview might proceed. The case includes a series of questions about family background, social relationships, challenging experiences, education and work, notion of self and views, and habits of mind. It also includes risk assessment, if needed, for things such as suicidality. It is important to recognize that therapy and spiritual care are different in several ways. Chaplains do not often conduct formal intake assessments or contract with careseekers to work on specific issues over multiple scheduled visits (though some chaplaincy settings may support ongoing care). However, the theoretical framework behind the assessment model – uncovering the interconnected causes and conditions contributing to a careseeker's suffering – can still serve as a useful tool even for chaplains with limited careseeker visits. Specifically, focusing on the dynamic interactions that cause of suffering can provide useful information that we may be able to reflect or reframe for careseekers. By bringing these causes into their awareness, we empower them to make conscious choices about how they wish to address them, providing a source of empowering support for their own spiritual growth.

Creating Spiritual Assessments

At this point we may wish to step back a moment and consider some examples of spiritual assessment within the scriptural traditions of Buddhism. I use the term 'assessment' in the broadest possible sense here, as in the methodical evaluation of a situation and the application of knowledge, expertise, discernment, wisdom, or judgement to suggest an appropriate course of action. Likewise, I use 'spiritual' in the broadest possible sense to include existential, ethical, emotional, relational, and religious concerns that would fall within the chaplain's scope of practice. Examining instances of spiritual assessment within the Buddhist canons may suggest how we can go about creating our own spiritual assessment paradigms consistent with our understanding of common human crises and contexts.

In the *Sunakkhatta Sutta* (MN105), the Buddha describes to his disciple Sunakkhatta how one with knowledge of the spiritual path may aid others in understanding that path. He likens himself to a doctor who pulls a poison arrow from a wound, treats the wound, draws out the poison, and then gives instruction to the patient for the care of the wound until it heals. Furthermore, he explains the purpose of the simile:

> Sunakkhatta, I have given this simile in order to convey a meaning. This is the meaning here: 'Wound' is a term for the six internal [sense] bases. 'Poisonous humour' is a term for ignorance. 'Arrow' is the term for craving. 'Probe' is a term for mindfulness. 'Knife' is a term for noble wisdom. 'Surgeon' is a term for the Tathagata, the Accomplished One, the Fully Enlightened One.
> (Ñāṇamolī and Bodhi, trans., 2001, p. 867)

Thus, from this simile and its explanation we find the Buddha himself translating the Dharma between the language of a layperson and a spiritual expert. We find him practicing a form of spiritual diagnosis and treatment using the spiritual tools of Buddhism to aid another in healing from suffering. This simile uses a medical model, which was very different in the Buddha's time. Chaplains today do not make formal diagnoses in the way of doctors, psychologists, or other clinical professions. However, we do use our discernment in relation to spiritual matters, as the sections above describe.

Another example we can draw from is the consideration of the Five Hindrances and their antidotes as described in the *Connected Discourses on the Factors of Enlightenment* (SN46.2, SN46.51, and SN46.56). I explore this teaching with an example from my role as a campus chaplain working with students. The five hindrances are listed as the desire for sensual pleasures, ill will, sloth and torpor, restlessness and remorse, and doubt. They are typically applied within the practice of meditation. By applying them in meditation, we may become adept at applying them in life. The fourth hindrance, restlessness and remorse, is described as proceeding from an unsettled mind, something we can all relate to in this anxiety-fueling age.

When working with students, I would often find our conversations bouncing from one anxiety to the next. Small things, like an assignment due at the end of the week, would ricochet off larger existential crises like trying to sort out if they even wanted the career their studies led towards, about which they lacked the experience to make an informed decision. Trouble getting along with their roommate would trigger a shame attack and leave them feeling unworthy of meaningful relationships, casting their dreams of marriage and a family into doubt. As in meditation, the first step is to learn to recognize the hindrance, in this case when one is becoming trapped in an anxious spiral. Once was identified, we could work together to find activities that helped students settle the mind, develop concentration, equanimity, a sense of calm, and an ability to self-soothe in times of distress. They needn't be Buddhists or on the path to enlightenment to benefit from the identification of a 'hindrance' and development of an appropriate response.

Likewise, the seven factors of enlightenment can be helpful; they are mindfulness, discernment, energy, rapture, tranquility, concentration, and equanimity. If we examine the factor of tranquility as an antidote to the restless and remorseful anxiety described above, we see that it is divided into tranquility of body and tranquility of mind, linking the physical and relational with our cognitive and affective experiences. A commentary on this section by Soma Thera further elucidates that tranquility is enabled through certain preconditions, including good food, a safe place to live, and avoiding restless people in favor of calm people. We can explore these conditions in the life of the student. Are they experiencing food insecurity? Do they feel safe with their housemates? What are their media consumption habits like? Young adults often need a little help considering how to secure their own physical wellbeing and many find that once this is accomplished, other anxieties seem more manageable. However, in some cases, anxieties persist and require more affective and cognitive interventions, such as therapy or contemplative training.

From these two short sections of the Pali cannon – the simile of the arrow and the explication of the Five Hindrances and Seven Factors of Enlightenment – we may already see models for spiritual assessments emerging. In this space, I encourage all Buddhist chaplains to consider what resources from your tradition of Buddhism may be useful in guiding spiritual assessments with the kinds of careseekers you work with. Perhaps there is a sutta, sutra, tantra, or commentary from your tradition that outlines how to discern spiritual needs, frames spiritual stages, describes barriers to spiritual progress, or methods of spiritual support? We might also include artistic representations, such as the Ox Herding images, mandalas, or the Elephant Taming picture. Perhaps the Five Hindrances work well with students but may not be as effective in a healthcare setting. What models might be more appropriate in prisons or the military?

When creating your own spiritual assessment model, there are several pragmatic goals:
- Can you remember and easily draw upon this model during spiritual care?
- Is this model comprehensive and holistic enough to account for the careseeker's entire situation?
- Is this model detailed and diverse enough to encompass a wide variety of circumstances?
- Can you translate this model into general language both to aid the careseeker and communicate care plans with a multidisciplinary team?
- Can you apply this model to a wide diversity of careseekers without imposing a Buddhist cosmological, metaphysical, or soteriological frameworks on non-Buddhist careseekers?
- Does this model support your ability to understand and discern the current (subject-to-change) 'state' of the careseeker on spiritual and religious matters in relation to their context, identify existing causes of wellbeing or suffering, and suggest potential interventions to improve wellbeing and reduce suffering to the extent possible?

Hopefully, you will be able to develop a model wherein the answers to all the above questions are 'Yes.' When you do so, I encourage you to extensively test your model and then publish your findings to assist your fellow Buddhist chaplains.

Charting and Note-Keeping

Keeping accurate records of spiritual care encounters is an important aspect of a chaplain's daily work. Chaplains in health care settings enter notes into medical charts or record keeping systems. Healthcare charting may require the entry of a single option from a multi-choice list, such as for religious identity. Some systems allow for longer narrative notes. You may decide to keep longer notes in your own fashion provided they also meet the institution's standards for secure record keeping and privacy. Chaplains in non-medical settings may have no record-keeping requirements and, in fact, may be actively discouraged from keeping notes accessible to employers or supervisors to protect the anonymity and confidentiality of their careseekers. Nevertheless, it can be useful for the chaplain to devise a habit and a system of note-keeping.

Note-keeping benefits the careseeker, multi-disciplinary teammates, and the chaplain. First, it provides a clear record of the chaplain's activities and the careseeker's primary concerns. This avoids duplication of effort and eases the referral process. Second, it outlines care provision plans for both the chaplain and other team members, noting such things as the need for particular religious implements, food, gender-specific care needs, and support for spiritual and religious activities (e.g., being assisted in ablution before prayer). Some of these can be provided by the chaplain directly, while others rely on the cooperation of the team. Third, this practice documents the outcomes (if any) of interventions and monitors for efficacy, both in relation to this careseeker and to be potentially aggregated for future research. Fourth, it aids in establishing a common language around spiritual care provision that the entire team can use when discussing the needs of careseekers. This common language, reinforced through repetition, ensures that other members of the care team can make clear requests to the chaplain on behalf of careseekers. Even in situations without shared notes, it is helpful for the chaplain to have a record to review for their own purposes so that they can follow up with careseekers at appropriate points and refresh their memory before subsequent visits.

I have found it helpful to keep a basic taxonomy of spiritual care close at hand to aid in making concise and accurate notes. A group of chaplains within the Advocate Health network published a taxonomy for spiritual care in 2015 based on review of electronic medical records, chaplain focus groups, and a meta-review of literature on spiritual care interventions and taxonomies. The authors grouped 100 items according to their intended effects, methods, and specific interventions.

Creating a hierarchy of information in notes is useful. A narrative chronology about an encounter as it happened can be a tempting default. Chaplains are often trained to do this when writing clinical cases or verbatims. However, for notes, I recommend using a hierarchy of information that places the most important information in the first paragraph or as bullet points, followed by elaborations or longer narratives. Especially since it can take time to build trust and rapport and the most important information may come near the end of the conversation. For example, in relation to the case of Charlie, Chaplain C's first note may start out like this:

- Setting: Self-initiated visit by appointment with 'Charlie' on [Date], known from Tuesday PTSD meetings and Friday AA meetings, past three months.
- Careseeker: White, hetero, cis-ender, ex-military enlisted, single college student, 28-years-old, good health; ex-Protestant Christian, now Buddhist, no local community; family history of abuse (father), divorce, remarriage (mother), younger siblings.
- Actions: Established caring relationship and identified areas of concern: adaptation to civilian life, relationship struggles, recent breakup; in conversation, reinforced coping mechanisms, offered support, and made referral to local Tibetan Buddhist community.
- Follow-up plan: verbal check-in at next PTSD meeting; monitor for possible transference re: sibling-like relationship to chaplain.

(See Appendix and Vignette 3 in Vol. 1, ch. 1.)

Chaplain C may then make more detailed notes by expanding each of the main sentences above into its own paragraph, starting with how she knows Charlie and the behavior she has observed from him in three months of support group meetings, an outline of what she understands about his religious and spiritual beliefs, and sections detailing each of the identified areas of concern, along with his family history. Writing longer notes helps solidify information in memory, while review of the bullet points prior to their next meeting may be sufficient to then recall the full depth of information found in the longer notes (if not, those notes can be reviewed).

Finally, our private notes include our responses to the careseekers and our unanswered questions, which there will almost always be. For example, Chaplain C may use her notes to reflect on Charlie's habit of calling her "sis." What does a sibling relationship imply to Chaplain C, who has younger brothers, but perceived a feeling of ambiguous discomfort to being called "sis?" What does it mean for Charlie? He has sisters, but they are all significantly younger than him, while Chaplain C is about ten years older than Charlie. Chaplain C might expand on her note about potential transference and countertransference in order to surface her subconscious assumptions and feelings and monitor subsequent conversations. These notes should not be included in a medical chart, but can be useful for Chaplain C's own learning, developing a spiritual care plan for Charlie, or when seeking consultation with other professionals.

While using a hierarchy of information to start notes, longer-form notes help people understand their identities and relationships through the stories they tell about themselves. Likewise, we understand others through the stories we tell about them. Chaplaincy narratives capture a complex interplay of the experiences of the careseeker and the chaplain, both the stories they share with us and the way we respond to those stories. I find narratives useful when attempting to clarify areas of confusion, whether in reference to the careseeker or my own responses. I often write my way into greater clarity by articulating and reviewing what is happening. This practice aids processing my own difficult or unclear emotions. You may find other uses for reflective narratives.

In our example, if Chaplain C's next meeting with Charlie is soon, it may be sufficient to read just the top paragraph of her notes. Sometimes, chaplains may not see a careseeker again for a long while. If Charlie were to reappear in a year, for example, Chaplain C could then rely on her comprehensive narrative notes to bring herself back up to speed before chatting with Charlie again. 'Outsourcing' our memory, which is not always the most reliable, is a conscientious practice. It demonstrates to the careseeker that we care enough to 'remember,' or, at least, to carefully write and then read a set of notes to remember for us. Writing a note like this, including longer sections suggested here, should take an experienced chaplain about 10-20 minutes. It may take a bit longer for a novice chaplain to develop the knack, so plan your appointment calendar appropriately.

The Chaplaincy Taxonomy

Intended effects	Methods	Interventions	
Aligning care plan with patient's values	Accompany someone in their spiritual/religious practice outside your faith tradition	Acknowledge current situation	Facilitate closure
Build relationship of care and support	Assist with spiritual/religious practices	Acknowledge response to difficult experience	Facilitate communication
Convey a calming presence	Assist with spiritual/religious practices	Active listening	Facilitate communication between patient and/or family member and care team
De-escalate emotionally charged situations	Collaborate with care team member	Ask guided questions	Facilitate communication between patient/family member(s)
Demonstrate caring and concern	Demonstrate acceptance	Ask guided questions about cultural and religious values	Facilitate decision making
Establish rapport and connectedness	Educate care team about cultural and religious values	Ask guided questions about faith	Facilitate grief recovery groups
Faith affirmation	Encourage end of life review	Ask guided questions about purpose	Facilitate life review
Helping someone feel comforted	Encourage self care	Ask guided questions about the nature and presence of God	Facilitate preparing for end of life
Journeying with someone in the grief process	Encourage self reflection	Ask questions to bring forth feelings	Facilitate spirituality groups
Lessen anxiety	Encourage sharing of feelings	Assist patient with documenting choices	Facilitate understanding of limitations
Lessen someone's feelings of isolation	Encourage someone to recognize their strengths	Assist patient with documenting values	Identify supportive relationship(s)
Meaning-Making	Encourage story-telling	Assist someone with Advance Directives	Incorporate cultural and religious needs in plan of care
Mending broken relationships	Encouraging spiritual/religious practices	Assist with determining decision maker	Invite someone to reminisce
Preserve dignity and respect	Explore cultural values	Assist with identifying strengths	Perform a blessing
Promote a sense of peace	Explore ethical dilemmas	Bless religious item(s)	Perform a religious rite or ritual
	Explore faith and values	Blessing for care team member(s)	Pray
	Explore nature of God	Communicate patient's needs/concerns to others	Prayer for healing
	Explore presence of God	Conduct a memorial service	Provide a religious item(s)
	Explore quality of life	Conduct a religious service	Provide access to a quiet place
	Explore spiritual/religious beliefs	Connect someone with their faith community/ clergy	Provide compassionate touch
	Explore values conflict	Crisis intervention	Provide Grief Processing Session
	Exploring hope	Discuss concerns	Provide grief resources
	Offer emotional support	Discuss coping mechanism with someone	Provide hospitality
	Offer spiritual/religious support	Discuss frustrations with someone	Provide religious music
	Offer support	Discuss plan of care	Provide sacred reading(s)
	Setting boundaries	Discuss spirituality/religion with someone	Provide spiritual/religious resources
		Ethical consultation	Respond as chaplain to a defined crisis event
		Explain chaplain role	Share words of hope and inspiration
		Facilitate advance care planning	Share written prayer
			Silent prayer

Table reprinted with permission from the authors. The article explaining the development of this taxonomy can be found at https://www.ncbi.nlm.nih.gov/pmc/articles/PMC4397872/. Massey K, Barnes MJ, Villines D, Goldstein JD, Pierson AL, Scherer C, Vander Laan B, Summerfelt WT. "What do I do? Developing a taxonomy of chaplaincy activities and interventions for spiritual care in intensive care unit palliative care." *BMC Palliative Care*. 2015 Apr.

5
Personal & Professional Boundaries

Confidentiality

A friend gives what is hard to give,
and he does what is hard to do.
He forgives you your harsh words.
and endures what is hard to endure.

He tells you his secrets,
yet he preserves your secrets.
He does not forsake you in
    difficulties,
nor does he roughly despise you.

The person here in whom
these qualities are found is a friend.
One desiring a friend
should resort to such a person.
(AN 7.36)

Trust is one of the most important characteristics of the connection between chaplains and careseekers. As *kalyāṇa-mitra*, we are trustworthy companions on the spiritual path. We witness people at some of their best and worst moments, when they are full of anger and despair. These moments can be very hard to endure. The harsh words of a careseeker railing against the universe, the doctors, their family, society, and, sometimes even at you, the chaplain, can be very difficult. People often say things in the presence of a chaplain they would never say to anyone else, due to powerful emotions and the deep need to be known and witnessed. As chaplains, we honor the careseeker and the stories or secrets they entrust to us.

Confidentiality is the root of trust. This trust can facilitate remarkable transformations in careseekers. Much of the trauma we carry comes from betrayal of trust when we needed care – childhood needs unmet, confidences not kept, violence where affection should have been. Ongoing loss of trust leads to lifelong anxiety and stress, especially for those subject to systemic oppression, living in a society that is fundamentally untrustworthy when it comes to their safety, basic needs, or human dignity. Chaplains play a role in ameliorating these situations at the levels of the person, institution, and society – first and foremost by being trustworthy caregivers. Chaplains can offer safe refuge amid uncertainty and life transition. This is true regardless of whether a careseeker is naturally open and trustworthy or secretive and distrusting. Neither is a reflection on the chaplain, as such attitudes and behaviors are established in response to life circumstances long before we ever meet the careseeker. Regardless, our obligation to maintain confidentiality and be worthy of trust remains.

One of the ways we maintain trust is by disclosing exceptions to confidentiality intended to preserve life. Disclosing exceptions at the appropriate time preserves trust and honors the agency of the careseeker by providing them with the ability to make informed decisions about what to share. Exceptions may vary slightly from state to state and institution to institution, so be sure to carefully research your location and institution's guidelines for "mandated reporting," including who is a "mandated reporter" or "responsible authority" in what context, what they are mandated to

report, and to whom. In general, mandated reporting exceptions to confidentiality cover the following situations:
- Neglect or abuse of a child or dependent adult (i.e., an adult or elder with developmental differences or cognitive impairment who is under legal guardianship of another)
- Imminent threat of suicide, homicide, or gross harm to self or others

These situations must be in the present. For example, when working with college students, I advise them that any abuse they suffered as a child will be kept entirely confidential, as will abuse they may currently be experiencing as a legal adult. However, if they have younger siblings or elderly dependent relatives still living in the abusive home, I will report that to the proper branch of child or adult protective services. It is not our responsibility to be certain that abuse or neglect is occurring. We are obligated to pass on reasonable suspicions to the proper authorities for investigation to protect members of our society who are least able to protect themselves.

Likewise, if a student had contemplated suicide sometime in the past, that remains confidential. However, I will ask a series of questions to ascertain imminent risk of suicide. There are many helpful resources for evaluating the level of urgency in suicidality, from "I've occasionally wondered what it would be like if I weren't here anymore" to "I have the means to kill myself and I am going to do so today." It is crucial to refer careseekers experiencing suicidality to mental health professionals or, if they will not take the referral, to gather as much information as possible and seek anonymous consultation. In some cases, psychiatric detainment may be necessary. (See Chapter 11 for more guidance.) When the threat of suicide (or homicide) is imminent, chaplains are mandated to get help and preserve life. Disclosing exceptions to confidentiality includes disclosure of when those exceptions are enacted unless you believe doing so would put the careseeker further at risk, such as by accelerating plans for harm. When making a mandated report, sometimes the best way to do so is in the form of an in-person referral to mental health resources. As a college chaplain, this might mean physically walking with a suicidal student to the campus mental health center or staying with the student wherever they are until other caregivers arrive to take them to a treatment facility such as a hospital.

It can be reassuring for careseekers to understand that while I must disclose their situation to other professionals to get help for them, those professionals are likewise bound by a circle of confidentiality.[1] Nor does disclosure mean I share every detail they have shared with me. Exceptions to confidentiality are not blanket; they are narrow, specific, and need-to-know. Further details, such as sources of past trauma that led to feelings of suicide, remain the careseeker's to disclose (or not) to others. The size of the circle of confidentiality depends very much on the context of care. Confidentiality in a hospital, prison, and college setting are very different. The chaplain plays a different social role within each institution, and each has different legal frameworks for confidentiality. It is important to understand local law, institutional policy, and best practices for sharing information within your setting.

Many situations require maintaining confidentiality from other caregivers, while also allowing for opportunities to anonymously consult. A consult can involve sharing specific information about a careseeker to receive the opinion of another chaplain or professional without disclosing the careseeker's identity and limiting information only to that which is necessary for the purposes of the consult. Requesting permission from the careseeker to

---

1 In the college context, this means reassuring them that parents are only notified with their explicit consent, so long as the student is a legal adult. It can also mean helping them make that phone call to their parents, if they choose.

seek an anonymous consultation is advisable, but not strictly necessary so long as identity remains private and information remains within the circle of confidentiality. This framework allows chaplains (including student interns) to receive feedback to improve their skills, to consult with multi-disciplinary teammates on concerns that may be outside a chaplain's scope of practice (such as screening for suspected mental health or medical conditions), and for chaplains to receive support when dealing with secondary trauma and stress. In other words, chaplains need a confidential support system just as much as careseekers do.

Sometimes careseekers may entrust us with a secret we feel it is harmful for them to keep, yet still falls within our circle of confidentiality. For example, when counseling young adults in new relationships, I may feel that it is absolutely vital for them to communicate well with their romantic partner, including sharing how the partner's actions harm them (even accidentally) or when a past incident is affecting their current relationship. Understandably, many young adults are hesitant to do this. We should never try to diminish the potential consequences, tell them "it will be alright," or make them feel bad or dishonest for keeping a secret. We must respect their agency and insight into their own lives and relationships.

This can be very hard to do when counseling students in abusive relationships, for example. We must, therefore, carefully monitor our internal response as we listen to their stories and consider what we can and cannot hold. As Emma Justes points out in her book *Please Don't Tell*, "reaching the point of burnout…is not a good way to determine how much we can carry" (p. 56). (See Chapter 3.) During the conversation with a careseeker, you must monitor how your discomfort with the secrets they share and your agitation for them to "tell someone" or "do something" causes you to respond. No matter how strongly we believe it would be helpful for the careseeker to disclose the information to someone else, we must respect their confidentiality and agency.

Sometimes family members or other staff may expect us to disclose information we are not able to share. Those who see us as congregational clergy may expect us to share far more than is typical in a chaplaincy setting. Within a religious community, members often share information about who is ill or injured, looking for work, going through a divorce, or experiencing a disaster. Clergy may coordinate community support, resources, and prayer. In such settings it may even be difficult for the chaplain to ascertain who already knows what and what information the careseeker considers private or public. Chaplains must follow the standard of explicit consent from the careseeker about what may be discussed and with whom. Just because a family member, community member, or teammate already has some information about the careseeker's situation does not authorize you to discuss that situation with them or share what you know about it. You can lend a sympathetic ear to their concerns about the careseeker and affirm other individuals' caring impulses.

Dealing with explicit requests from family members can be especially tricky. Spouses will want to know what you discussed with their partner, especially if there are problems in the relationship leading to suspicion or distrust. Even refusing to answer the question due to confidentiality can often only serve to 'confirm' in the mind of the questioner whatever it is they suspect. The best option in these scenarios is to advise the questioner to discuss the issue with their family member. You can use your chaplain skills to empathize with their anxiety without explicitly addressing their questions while also nudging them in the direction of better communication patterns with their family.

Parents are a special case as they often have overwhelming concern for their children. In medical settings they also have final responsibility and authority for medical decisions. In the college setting, it often takes parents a while to adjust to the notion of their children as adults. For the last 18 years they have expected to know everything about their children from the professionals their children interact with. As a college chaplain, I reassured young adults "I won't call your parents," and then fielded phone calls from parents wanting to know about their adult children. When working with minors, it is important to establish clear expectations around confidentiality early, particularly for adolescents. With adolescents, this should be one of the first topics of conversation when all parties are present. Then you may address it again privately with the (minor) careseeker, because children often won't acknowledge they withhold anything from their parents for fear that the parents might force them to share it. Details of conversations can remain confidential. Information shared with parents may be mostly limited to what the parents can do to help their child in the current circumstances. Sometimes the best thing a parent can do is give their child a trusted adult other than themselves to talk to.

As an adult who once received the services of a child psychologist (around age 11), I can tell you that this is a rare gift parents can provide their children. It still took me several weeks of careful testing to ensure my therapist was a 'safe' person to receive my true thoughts and feelings. She became a refuge for me because she did not have the reactionary emotional responses that my parents displayed at my more negative thoughts and feelings. "I hate my brother," became a frequent refrain in therapy, whereas I had learned to suppress such sentiments around family who would admonish me for them. Rather than scold me, my therapist asked me more about my frustrations and we talked about both the annoying and good qualities of my brother. This allowed me to both vent my (overstated) feelings towards my brother while also considering ways to relate to him that were more constructive. She never disclosed the exact nature of these sentiments to my parents, but rather shared ideas for how they could help both of their children feel equally heard and valued and learn to relate to one another in better ways. My brother and I now have a good sibling relationship.

Transference, Countertransference, & Projection

We have already seen an example of transference and countertransference in the Vignette of Chaplain C and Charlie shared in Volume I and expanded upon in the section on Spiritual Assessment. (See the appendices for Charlie's assessment.) Charlie, our former member of the military, referred to Chaplain C as 'sis' during some of their conversations, prompting Chaplain C to reflect on the nature of both Charlie's transference and her own potential countertransference. Transference is when careseekers repeat patterns of feelings, attitudes, and behaviors from prior relationships in their relationship with the chaplain. When Charlie went to see Chaplain C, he repeated the pattern of relating to a female sibling because he himself had sisters who had cared for him during moments of difficulty in the past. Countertransference is when the chaplain plays into this role and repeats their own patterns of feelings, attitudes, and behaviors from their past towards a careseeker. Chaplain C has brothers, but unlike Charlie, she is aware of the psychological phenomena of transference and countertransference, so she monitors herself to ensure that she relates to him in a healthy way, as a chaplain and careseeker, rather than as siblings.

Transference and countertransference can be positive or negative. They often involve powerful subconscious emotions. Transference can be triggered through emotional intimacy. Chaplains witness events and careseekers share stories that they might only otherwise share within the context of their closest family or romantic relationships. The empathy and kindness that chaplains offer may only have been previously experienced in the careseeker's close relationships. The phenomenon of patients falling in love with their therapists is well documented in life and dramatized in fiction. Chaplains do not always interact with careseekers in the long term, especially in health care settings, but some places, like schools, prisons, or the VA where fictional Chaplain C works, can involve relationships with careseekers that last years. In these contexts, it is especially important for chaplains to be vigilant. Chaplains can acknowledge the feelings careseekers have while recognizing the feelings aren't really about them, the chaplain. Rather the careseeker is enacting a previous pattern or, in some cases, attempting to 'heal' or 'fix' an older relationship using the chaplain as a proxy.

As a campus chaplain working with young adults, I would experience this as either approval-seeking behavior or 'rebellion' from young adults relating to me as a parental figure. By demonstrating concern for them, I was cast in the role of a parent they could then please, perhaps in ways they felt unable to please their own parents. Alternatively, I was the parent from whom they had to establish their independence to become an adult. In either case, bringing these patterns into the open by gently asking the student about their parents or other authority figures in their lives helped them surface and recognize the patterns of behavior on their own, without naming it explicitly. This is what some therapists refer to as a "corrective emotional experience" (Roukema, 2003, p. 228). Meanwhile, I remained self-aware of whatever countertransference I was experiencing. Since I am not myself a parent, like Chaplain C, I would notice this most frequently as older sibling feelings and behavior towards students. While a little sibling-like joking can help create a sense of connection and ease with students, we cannot fully enact the social role due to our responsibilities as a chaplain. This is one of the reasons that throughout my books, I refer to the paradigm for Buddhist chaplains using the Sanskrit term *kalyāṇamitra*, rather than the translation of good or spiritual friend. The latter might encourage countertransference in which the chaplain behaves towards the careseeker as they do towards their personal friends, which would not be appropriate. Working with transference and countertransference can be aspects of psychotherapy and other forms of counseling, but this is not the goal of spiritual care. Chaplains should be aware of how they occur but should not seek to use transference or countertransference to meet therapeutic goals outside our scope of practice.

How does one know if countertransference is occurring? We should remain vigilant for emotions that seem out of proportion to the circumstances, either that come on too fast or too strong. Self-reflection or a conversation with a colleague can help clarify the sources of these emotions, which are not caused entirely (or even mostly) by the present situation, but by earlier experiences and relationships in the chaplain's life, often ones that are emotionally charged or unresolved. These unexplained strong emotions can be alarming or confusing. They may result in distress or even ethical problems and poor boundary-keeping. This is one of the reasons why chaplains spend so much time and energy examining their own life and past relationships in preparation for their entry into the profession. It is also why we ourselves need to maintain a network of *kalyāṇamitra* to turn to when (not if) new experiences surface. A neutral observer can often help us clarify aspects of our emotional experience we are too close to see clearly.

A related concept is "projective identification," sometime simply called 'projection.' This occurs when careseekers ascribe their own present feelings to the chaplain. For example, a careseeker who is wary and combative may feel that spiritual care is ineffective. Rather than identifying their own dissatisfaction, they project that dissatisfaction onto the chaplain who is "not helpful." In another example, if a chaplain is assisting someone experiencing a deep and painful loss, the careseeker may try to avoid dealing with their sadness by labelling the chaplain 'a downer.' Often, this can be very hurtful to hear as a chaplain, discouraging and distressing, especially if we believe what the careseeker is saying. Perhaps we really are not helpful or too depressing? Conscientious chaplains take this kind of feedback seriously. Yet we must also ask ourselves, what does this kind of feedback tell us about the careseeker's emotional state? Could this be more about what they are feeling that what we, as chaplains, are saying or doing?

When we recognize projection as it occurs, we can use this feedback as information to understand the careseeker's emotional experience. It often makes sense in the context of their situation or what we know about their background. Someone who has been repeatedly hurt or betrayed by others will be on the lookout for people who say they want to help but who then cause harm. It would be understandable if they became so resistant to care that nothing a chaplain could do would be 'helpful.' When this happens, the best we can do is witness and reflect what emotions we are observing in the careseeker back to them in the hopes that they learn to identify with their own emotional experience, rather than projecting it onto others. We can also offer the careseeker's agency back to them by admitting that while we don't intend to be 'unhelpful' or 'a downer' (quite the opposite) that may happen sometimes, so what in this situation would they find helpful or positive? What is their goal and how can we help them meet it? Finally, as with transference, projection is more about the careseeker than the chaplain. Given a different chaplain, the same patterns will likely repeat. And just as we should be on the lookout for countertransference, we should also be on the lookout for defensive responses (e.g., frustration, hurt, anger, anxiety, and so on) in reaction to careseeker projection. When (again, not if) we experience defensiveness towards a careseeker, it is a good idea to check in with ourselves and our own *kalyāṇamitra* for perspective.

Healthy Boundaries at Work & Home

> no
> is a necessary magic
> no
> draws a circle around you
> with chalk
> and says
> i have given enough.
> (McKayla Robbin, "Boundaries," from *We Carry the Sky*, 2016)

Boundaries are important for the chaplain (and our families) and the careseekers we serve. But what precisely do we mean by 'boundaries?' What are the benefits of healthy boundaries? What boundaries are we responsible to maintain and respect both professionally and personally? How can we set and monitor boundaries? How do we respond when boundaries are crossed or violated, by ourselves or others? And if boundaries are so useful, why do we fail to maintain them? In this section I will cover common ethical guidelines for professional boundaries and personal boundaries for our own wellbeing. Professional boundaries concern the appropriate use of professional power for the benefit and protection of those in our care, first and foremost. Personal boundaries are part of appropriate self-care and enable us to remain physically, mentally, emotionally, and spiritually healthy enough to pursue our work and enjoy our lives.

To understand boundaries, we must first talk about power. Boundaries establish guidelines for the safe use of power within relationships. We all have power, which the Faith Trust Institute defines as "the sum of one's resources," including financial resources, knowledge and expertise, social privilege, relationships, and personal qualities. Power enables us to change our circumstances as we desire (this includes when we desire things on behalf of others). It can be seen as positive, or simply as neutral, until and unless the change we desire is contrary to someone else's desires or their basic needs. Then power can become oppressive. Power can be used to benefit others and ourselves, to harm both others and ourselves, or to benefit one at the expense of another. Professional boundaries ensure we use power to benefit those in our care and do not use it in harmful ways. Personal boundaries ensure we don't harm ourselves or allow ourselves to be harmed for another's benefit. Of course, these distinctions are not all neat and tidy; there is a lot of overlap. Chapter 12 provides a more detailed overview of power, including the social dynamics of inequal power distribution due to race, gender, and so on. If you are new to the idea of having power, it may benefit you to read the first sections of chapter 12 before proceeding.

Sometimes, as people and as chaplains we may feel that we have very little power. Yet we still have more power than those we serve in most contexts, so we must wield it responsibly. There are many ways to wield power. We associate power with strong verbs like directing and commanding, but there is also power in witnessing, supporting, advising, inspiring, asking, modelling, and teaching, as well as in advocating, resisting, refusing, and helping. All of these actions require some amount of power to be effective. There are many types of power, such as professional power, personal power, and spiritual power. (See Chapter 12 for more.) For now, we will focus on professional power as it relates to maintaining professional boundaries followed by spiritual power as it relates to our role.

Professional power is conveyed by our status as chaplains and, for some of us, as Dharma teachers or clergy. The distinguishing trait of any professional is an advanced education and expertise that enables us to help others fill needs they cannot fulfill by themselves. Because we are not able to fulfill all our own needs, this creates vulnerabilities. We must go to a professional, but we are rarely capable of judging if what the professional is doing is in our best interest due to our lack of knowledge. We've all probably had an experience with doctor or lawyer or mechanic who told us we needed to do something for reasons we didn't quite understand, but wanted to trust, so we all know that feeling of vulnerability. This situation creates an asymmetry of power between the professional and those they serve. This also entails an asymmetry of responsibility. Those with more power have more responsibility. Doctors take an oath to do no harm. Ordinations often involve oaths or vows, as my own did, to benefit others. These rituals and traditions recognize that the professional is responsible to protect those they serve. Maintaining healthy boundaries is a key mechanism in protecting others and it also protects ourselves.

As chaplains, we also have unique forms of power associated with our role, which I will call 'spiritual' power (you may prefer a different term). The concept of spiritual power deserves a much longer treatment, but I will only briefly summarize here in relation to our main discussion on boundaries. Spiritual power has two aspects: who we are (or aspire to be) and how we are viewed by others. As a chaplain, we have undertaken certain spiritual commitments or vows, received an extensive education, followed a religious or spiritual practice, possibly experienced mystical or revelatory states, cultivated moral virtues, and developed wisdom or insight however limited it may sometimes seem to us (speaking mostly for myself, here). Then there is how we are viewed by others, which may be a realistic or completely unrealistic assessment. Either way, how others view us as a 'spiritual' person can also convey (or sometimes mitigate) power. They might perceive us as closer to divinity or enlightenment, as an authority on spiritual matters or religious tradition, as a moral guide, worthy of trust, or as a representative of a larger tradition about which they have certain perceptions. Some people may associate negative qualities to those they deem 'spiritual people.' A hospital patient may decline a visit because they are 'not religious' or 'don't believe in God' or have a negative perception of religion. In that case, how we are viewed can limit our power in that relationship, though it may not affect who we are. This reminds us that power is always relational and dynamic, changing from one situation to the next. However, our responsibility for maintaining healthy boundaries remains constant.

At this point, you might be reading along and thinking this doesn't really apply to you because you don't feel like you have much power. That's very normal, especially if you are still a student. You are probably reading this because you want to serve others in some way, not because you want to accrue power. That's good. But please recognize that not feeling powerful is not the same as not having power. We can and do have power, even when we don't feel like it. I sometimes revert to feeling like that awkward little girl who brought home report cards full of F's, hated church, and was more likely to be found alone up a tree than in a large group. Yet I am still the Rev. Dr. Monica Sanford, an ordained Buddhist minister, chaplain, scholar, and an assistant dean at the oldest ministry school in the nation. Yes, it still feels surreal sometimes, but I must recognize the power I have in order to use it in the best interests of those I serve. We may experience many internal struggles with power, including fear of power and feelings of powerlessness. (See Chapter 12.) The key point here is that the ethical use of power requires the recognition of power. It is hard for us to use power responsibly if we don't want power or deny that we have power.

Ethical use of power is predicated on appropriate professional boundaries. Marilyn Peterson's book *At Personal Risk: Boundary Violations in Professional-Client Relationships* (1992) provides a basic overview of professional power, risk, and boundaries appropriate to chaplains, religious leaders, and many other kinds of professionals. Boundaries are limits that allow for a safe connection within relationships according to Peterson (1992, p. 46). Boundaries have many benefits, including protecting and reducing risk to: 1) those we serve; 2) ourselves; 3) our institutions and employers; and 4) our profession and tradition, in that order. They also make power more easily recognized. Healthy boundaries can empower others by avoiding over-functioning and doing for others what they can and should do for themselves.

Boundaries can be physical, mental, emotional, sexual, material, financial, or temporal. For example, we can set a mental boundary about sharing personal information, a physical boundary about being touched, or a temporal boundary around hours we are available to work. A boundary is about limits we set to our own behavior, not about controlling others. (Of course, if someone is harming us, we should tell them to stop immediately and use whatever means we have to protect ourselves.) This is true for both professional and personal boundaries. We can rarely directly control how other people behave (though we can use our power to influence others), but we can decide how we will respond to their behavior, especially when it is transgressive, harmful, or disrespectful. In a situation where we have more power, we bear the greater responsibility for setting and maintaining boundaries through how we choose to behave. In a situation where we have less power, someone else (another professional, perhaps) may bear greater responsibility, but we can still set personal boundaries and monitor that they are respected.

Boundaries are specific to both context and role. A behavior that may constitute a boundary violation in one context may not in another. For example, kissing your spouse in your home is generally not considered a boundary violation, but when a Spanish soccer official spontaneously kissed a player during a match, he was subsequently banned for sexual assault.[2] Boundaries can be communicated, negotiated,

---

[2] Dunbar, "Spanish soccer official who kissed unwilling star player is banned for three years," AP News, October 30, 2023.

navigated, crossed, and violated. Boundaries need to be communicated to others to be effective. People cannot respect a boundary they do not know we have. Sometimes, a boundary only becomes clear to us when it has been crossed (or nearly crossed). Therefore, it is important to consider our boundaries in advance and plan when and how we will communicate them. In some cases, we need to negotiate boundaries that are mutually acceptable to different parties and enable both to safely meet their needs. These boundaries are then continuously navigated in relationships, sometimes crossed, and sadly, sometimes violated.

There is a difference between a boundary crossing and a boundary violation. There may be times when boundaries limit us from doing what is truly helpful in a novel situation. A boundary crossing is a behavior that is different from previously established norms, but ultimately helps those being served. For example, you may work with a student or congregant for years without any physical contact, but following a sudden death in the family, offering a hug at the appropriate time may be beneficial. A boundary can be safely crossed when the behavior serves to renew trust and strengthen the relationship because it is in the other person's clear best interest. Sometimes it can be appropriate to cross a boundary to prevent greater harm, such as when we must break confidentiality to prevent someone from committing suicide. However, when we cause harm by not respecting appropriate boundaries, this is called a boundary violation. Even if we act in what we believe is the other person's best interest, it is the consequences that define whether or not the behavior is a violation. If the other person is harmed, we must recognize that a violation has occurred and act appropriately to make amends and initiate healing, if that is possible. Denying the violation because "that was not my intention" only delays or makes reconciliation impossible. Depending on the harm caused, it may help someone to hear our good intentions, but sometimes it may not. Either way, it can't change the behavior in the past.

Boundary violations involve behavior outside of established professional norms, harm those being served, betray trust, destroy the relationship between the people involved and sometimes between the person who is harmed and the organization or institution they are part of. This is because boundary violations are not in the best interest of the other person; rather they serve the self-interest of the professional, the person with more power. According to Marilyn Peterson,

> Boundaries are the limits that allow for a safe connection based on the client's needs. When these limits are altered, what is allowed in the relationship becomes ambiguous. Such ambiguity is often experienced as an intrusion into the sphere of safety. The pain from a violation is frequently delayed, and the violation itself may not be recognized or felt until harmful consequences emerge.
>
> Boundary violations are acts that breach the core intent of the professional-client association. They happen when professionals exploit the relationship to meet personal needs rather than client needs. (1992, p. 75)

Sadly most of us have already experienced boundary violations in our lives. Nevertheless, it is often hard to distinguish between a crossing and a violation at first. Different people may interpret the same behavior very differently based on their background and context. What is harmful to one may be helpful to another. Moreover, people often respond to boundary violations by distancing themselves from their emotions, claiming it's not a big deal, or even denying that it was a violation so they don't feel victimized. Sometimes when people finally report a violation, they are asked "Why didn't you report this sooner?" even though the harmful consequences of boundary violations don't manifest until much later. A behavior need not have extreme consequences to be a clear boundary violation. While we may experience uncomfortable, unpleasant, or disagreeable behavior from the professionals in our lives from time to time this does not always constitute a boundary violation. For example, my dentist often causes me discomfort and pain and my doctor sometimes uses words I don't understand, but these actions are in my best interest, a normal part of professional practice, and don't create a breach of trust.

There are three basic causes of boundary violations:
- Being unaware of or unwilling to recognize our own power
- Trying to meet one's own needs through relationships where we have power (coercion) – we need to fulfil our needs elsewhere
- Complying when others, including those we serve and the institutions where we work, initiate boundary violations

We have already covered the first cause in our discussion of power and Chapter 12 provides more resources to help chaplains recognize and understand power differentials in relationships with careseekers. The second kind of violations are often prompted by the professional's needs, which impose a second agenda on the relationship of which the person they are serving may be unaware. This can cause confusion, ambiguity, and, eventually, a lack of trust in the professional who is not acting in the other person's best interests. In some cases, the professional may not even be fully aware of this second agenda. Therefore, it is important for us as professionals to self-monitor our own needs and how they can, will, and do color our relationships with those we serve. Thinking to ourselves that we don't have needs is very dangerous. It's much safer for those we serve and ourselves to recognize, "Oh, I'm feeling a little lonely and this person would make a great friend, but I'm not here to be their friend; I'm their chaplain," or whatever our role is. Being aware of that need for friendship is what helps us prevent the need to from turning into a boundary violation. Maintaining appropriate personal boundaries as a form of self-care can also aid in ensuring our needs are met outside our relationships with careseekers, limiting risk to them.

Third, sometimes those we serve may try to initiate a boundary violation, such as by flirting or offering services to curry favor. There are many books documenting the phenomenon of people falling in love with their pastor, therapist, or spiritual teacher and trying to initiate a romantic relationship. Relationships that involve the potential for idealization of the person in authority alongside a sense of intimacy, such as with a therapist you tell your darkest secrets to, often experience this kind of transference dynamic. There are also more mundane ways that people might try to violate boundaries, such as by offering to babysit a teacher's children in hopes of a better grade. These are still boundary violations even if they are initiated by the more vulnerable party in the relationship.

It is always the responsibility of the party with more power to maintain healthy boundaries. This responsibility will lie with you in most circumstances, even as a chaplain intern still in training. When a boundary violation is initiated by a careseeker, it is our responsibility to clearly state what behavior is and is not acceptable and define the role and responsibility we have in the relationship. This is primarily to protect the careseeker, but it also protects the chaplain. Chaplains occasionally receive inappropriate requests from careseekers, ranging from lewd sexual comments to requests for money to insistence that "only you," the chaplain, can help them with their problem when they are clearly in need of a referral to mental health or other services. In all cases it is important to remain calm in the moment, respond clearly and decisively to the careseeker to communicate and enact your boundary (including removing yourself from the situation as needed), attend to your own emotional state and spiritual needs (including needs to express anger at inappropriate behavior or engage in self-compassion meditation to self-soothe), possibly report the incident to appropriate teammates, and make appropriate referrals. (See Chapter 11.) We can also, when able, continue to cultivate compassion and loving-kindness towards the careseeker, even in instances where the careseeker's behavior is harmful and we decline to visit them again. Cultivating compassion for the suffering that prompted their inappropriate behavior preserves our capacity to enter new caregiving situations with equanimity and address our own responses self-compassionately.

Let us be turn now to the subject or romantic and sexual relationships. To be clear, dating and sexual relationship with careseekers, congregants, students, employees, or those over whom we have direct (or even indirect) power are prohibited because people in those circumstances are never free from (as least implicit) coercion and cannot meaningfully consent. Don't date within an organization where you are in a role of leadership or authority, whether as a chaplain or religious teacher. Many Buddhist teachers have violated this stricture and created much harm within their Buddhist communities.[3] Avoiding romantic relationships can be tricky for those of us who may serve small communities or work in small towns and nevertheless want to find a partner who is equally committed to a spiritual path, particularly within our own tradition. For everyone who successfully manages to find a partner this way, there are dozens of stories of harm both to the potential partner and to the community or organization as a whole. Whether or not you are a chaplain or Dharma teacher or clergy member within your tradition, the book *Sex and the Spiritual Teacher: Why It Happens, When It's a Problem, and What We All Can Do* by Scott Edelstein (2011) can be an illuminating read.

It may at this point sound like the situation is very fraught and healthy boundaries are hard to maintain, but there are some good guidelines, and, in fact, most professionals manage to have fulfilling careers and personal relationships. In response to the dangers of boundary violations, Peterson proposed a relational model of professional care that is equally appropriate for chaplains.

> The structure of the professional-client relationship derives from a relational model of care in which professionals are charged to: (l) establish and maintain trust through their willingness to engage fully and respectfully with their clients; (2) take charge by accepting their authority and setting the tone and direction that keep the work focused and task oriented; (3) create and maintain a safe environment by establishing clear boundaries; and (4) define for us the behaviors that are necessary to fulfill our expectations by keeping us mindful of our power to effect our own decisions, aware of our responsibilities for ourselves, and cognizant of the need for feedback in the give-and-take that keeps the process between us healthy and current. Operating within a relational model imposes a natural constraint, in that it pulls professionals to remain sensitive to the power differential. (Peterson, 1992, p. 48)

It is crucial to empower those in our care to provide input about their expectations and receive clear communication from us about how we will meet (or not meet) those expectations within particular healthy boundaries. We must

---

[3] See, for example, "Will Sanghas Learn from the Scandals in the Buddhist World?" by Wendy Joan Biddlecombe Agsar in *Tricycle*, January 28, 2019, or "Breaking the Silence on Sexual Misconduct" by Willa Blythe Baker in *Lion's Roar*, n.d.

also be willing to hear and even directly encourage feedback from them on how well we are meeting their needs and expectations. This may be challenging at first because they may lack the language to even describe what they need, but through our relationship, we can empower them to articulate themselves in specific and appropriate ways. Encouraging and accepting feedback well is part of what establishes and maintains trust and respect within the relationship. And we should encourage them to also seek care outside of their relationship with us. This can be done through clear chains of reporting, referral to other kinds of professionals, creation of mentoring programs or peer groups, and cultivation of caring community so that the person in authority is not the sole or dominant form of care. The next section will further consider communities of accountability and how they help us maintain healthy professional boundaries as well as meet our own needs for personal wellbeing.

As mentioned above, one of the primary causes of boundary violations is trying to meet our own needs through the relationships we have with careseekers. Good personal boundaries can provide a solid basis for self-care that can help ameliorate this risk. Personal boundaries can be more individualistic based on your needs and situation. When setting personal boundaries, we have a variety of choices about how to maintain our wellbeing, and there are a few common ways to transgress personal boundaries. Take the time to get to know yourself and experiment. Discovering what works for you is an ongoing and self-compassionate process. Setting personal boundaries is a compassionate activity both for yourself and those you serve.

What is a personal boundary and how is it different from a professional boundary? Personal boundaries tend to be more individual and less guided by professional ethics and norms, but still share some common features with professional boundaries. A personal boundary is a guideline we set to maintain our own physical, mental, emotional, social, spiritual, and financial health. This is important because: a) we are worthy of living a healthy and happy life; and b) we must maintain our own health to serve others. Even if 'b' were not the case, 'a' still applies. 'B' only applies to us because we have chosen a vocation in caregiving. This means that everyone has the right to set boundaries simply because they are likewise a human worthy of living a healthy and happy life. Recall that a boundary must be clearly communicated and consistently enacted to be effective. The way we communicate our boundaries is just as important as what the boundaries are. When entering a new relationship, personal or professional, we should have an early conversation about boundaries and expectations and then revisit the topic regularly. When a boundary is crossed or violated, we immediately restate the boundary and refer to the past conversations.

Let's consider some examples of personal boundaries. Some boundaries only affect our private behavior. For example, early in college I learned that I would become so immersed in reading novels I often neglected all other work. Therefore, I limited reading fiction to breaks between semesters. Some boundaries are expressed through how we manage our time and make ourselves available to others (or not), including through electronic mechanisms. For example, when I review my weekly calendar, if a day already has a certain number of meetings scheduled, I will block out the remainder of the time for solitary work so that no one can schedule another meeting. As an introvert, spreading out social interaction helps maintain my energy levels. Likewise, many people choose not to respond to work email outside of work hours. Again, this is not about controlling other people's behavior. As Olivia Vizachero[4] pointed out in an Instagram thread on the topic "You can't email me on weekends" is not a boundary. A proper boundary is "If you email me on weekends, I will not respond until Monday."

---

4 @thelessstressedlawyer

This is a clearly communicated boundary about your own behavior that others can rely on. Some boundaries are about how we will respond to disrespectful or harmful behavior from others. For example, if someone speaks to you in a vulgar or hateful manner, it is acceptable to say, "If you continue to speak to me that way, I will leave," and then do precisely that, whether this person is a stranger, family member, careseeker, or colleague. A boundary is not a demand or a threat – it is a behavior you take to maintain your own wellbeing. While we cannot control others, we can request they behave appropriately, and we can remove ourselves from harmful situations.[5] Sometimes we feel guilty about setting boundaries because it often means not doing what other people want us to, but when we reframe boundaries as both a form of self-care that we are worthy to receive and a professional obligation that helps us meet our responsibilities as chaplains, then we can see their value.

Finally, if boundaries are so vitally important, why do they feel so hard to maintain sometimes? As mentioned earlier, the three primary reasons for failing to maintain professional boundaries include being unaware of power differentials, trying to serve our own needs, and complying with others who initiate boundary violations. These reasons apply to all kinds of professions, but they may feel too abstract or theoretical to easily identify in our lives and work. For chaplains, specifically, there are several root causes that I have observed in myself and the colleagues with whom I work and research that may feel more immediately recognizable.

- We mistake a 'boundary' for getting other people to do what we want. This allows us to shift blame for whatever stress we feel from ourselves to the other person (who may genuinely have been acting badly, but we can't control them).

- We do not recognize where we need a boundary or what a healthy boundary may be for a given situation. Paying close attention to our stress levels and emotional responses can provide clues about where we might need to set a better boundary.
- We have set an unrealistic boundary. We have probably all met someone like this (someone who won't attend any meeting before 10 am or refuses to meet for longer than 30 minutes on any topic), but we like to think we'd never become that person. Peers can provide an important check on our expectations.
- We do not clearly communicate our boundaries to others. It is important to clearly define how you will respond to certain situations in unambiguous language.
- We do not remain consistent, especially when others make demands on our time, attention, and effort. If people learn that what we actually do is not consistent with what we say, they will use that to their advantage. (Children are particularly adept at this!)
- We feel guilty for setting boundaries, as though we are behaving selfishly. Unhealthy family, workplace, or social dynamics can inculcate and reinforce this feeling and normalize a lack of boundaries or frequent transgression of boundaries. In this case, it can be hard to set a boundary that goes against the 'norm,' but it becomes even more important to do so if we expect to continue functioning in that environment long-term.
- We feel bad when we fail to keep boundaries and consider giving up altogether. We won't find the right balance for our boundaries on the first try and should use this as an opportunity to pay attention to what is happening and adjust as needed.
- We feel helpless and that other people will continue to disrespect us regardless of

---

5 We can and should ask people to stop doing what is harmful, forcefully if needed; that is still a request, not a boundary in the technical sense we are using it.

how we respond. This can be particularly difficult for people experiencing systemic oppression such as racism, sexism, ableism, and for members of minority religious groups (including the non-religious). Rely on your social support system during these experiences and ask for help from others to change the culture. If able, remove yourself from such situations when no change appears possible.

- We try to live up to unrealistic expectations, including heroic ideals in religious rhetoric. Buddhism has idealized altruistic behavior, selflessness, practicing "like your hair is on fire," and even feeding one's own body parts to a starving tiger. These messages should be used for inspiration – to give us energy – not to exhort us into unhealthy ways of being or feelings of guilt.
- We feel a sense of urgency around the work or that there is just so much to do that we don't dare slow down to rest or care for our own wellbeing. Those of us who have taken bodhisattva vows have literally vowed to save infinite beings. It is important to recognize that suffering is part of the nature of *saṃsara*. Even if we work 24/7 (which is not physically possible), we will not change *saṃsara*. Adding to our own suffering through overwork is not useful to anyone.
- We use caregiving to meet egoistic emotional needs that should be met in other ways. Caregiving can be very rewarding, but it should not be the primary basis for our sense of self-worth. Our work may provide a sense of efficacy we lack in other areas of our life, in which case we need to give attention to those other areas to achieve a healthy balance.
- We do not respect our scope of practice (as chaplains) or feel more competent than we actually are to help people suffering with physical or mental illness. It is important to remain accountable to other chaplains, multidisciplinary teammates, our *kalyāṇamitra*, and professional mentors in our practice of spiritual care.
- We do not experience ourselves as powerful because so much in our lives feels beyond our control, so we do not understand the impact even a few words or a simple deed can have on another person. We may think what we do doesn't matter very much, but it may matter a great deal to someone who relies on us for care.
- We feel an urgent need to progress on our spiritual path and see chaplaincy as an aspect or means to make spiritual progress, which in turn will alleviate our suffering and bring peace and happiness. While chaplaincy is a spiritual vocation, it should be undertaken by those willing and able to prioritize the needs of careseekers when providing care. We should cultivate our spiritual practice in multiple ways outside of chaplaincy as well as during our work.

Do any of these situations or feelings sound familiar to you? If so, take some time to carefully consider what is happening and seek support from your *kalyāṇamitra* and professional mentors to create and maintain a healthier boundary in that area of your personal or professional life.

Maintaining Communities of Accountability

Social mammals, like humans, are evolutionarily adapted to form groups. Thus, isolation (as distinct from solitude) leads to pervasive anxiety, including feelings of insecurity and uncertainty. Many Buddhist chaplains report a feeling of isolation created by being the only Buddhist at their workplace and lacking connections to other Buddhist chaplains. Feeling alone can lead us to the assumption that we need to be able to do everything ourselves. In the setting of chaplaincy, this leads to over-functioning and operating beyond our scope of practice, knowledge, competencies, and personal capacities. It also hides our mistakes from potential oversight and limits our ability to learn from them. When we feel like we must 'do it all' while simultaneously knowing we cannot, this creates tremendous anxiety and danger both for ourselves and our careseekers. The antidote for this condition is the confidence and security (refuge, even) we received from relationships and communities we can rely on. They correct us when we make inevitable mistakes and keep us safely connected and supported.

The Buddha created the monastic sangha to fill this role. The monastic sangha relied on the support of laypeople for their every physical need, from daily food to lodging and medicine. Simultaneously, the members of the sangha supported each other, including physically such as when a member was ill or injured and could not go to collect their own food or needed bodily care. They also supported one another mentally, emotionally, and spiritually, as *kalyāṇa-mitra* on different stages of the path, and relied on their spiritual teachers for this same kind of support. The monastic sangha supported laypeople with teachings and rituals. To maintain harmony in the community, the Buddha created systems of accountability for the monastic sangha. The Vinaya, or monastic code, includes complex rules for how to confess mistakes and adjudicate disputes.[6] Traditionally, monastics met together once every two weeks to confess and review violations of the monastic rules by members of the community and decide how to respond. This continues to the present day.

Most chaplains are not monastics but can still learn from the example of the sangha. To whom are we accountable? Most importantly, we are accountable to our careseekers, but because careseekers are often experiencing distress or crisis they are the least able to hold us accountable. Nor should we consider them

a source of support in that way. We must recognize that while we feel responsible towards our careseekers, a power differential places us in the position of institutional authority. No matter how much we might like to cede this authority to empower the careseeker, they are rarely in a position to hold us to account and, even when able, they should not need to do so in addition to whatever burden they already carry. Certainly, we are accountable to our employers or supervisors at the places where we work or volunteer. They have been actively tasked with taking responsibility for us. Yet most of our work takes place beyond their observation. They have empowered us with a great deal of trust. Therefore, when we make mistakes or fail to provide adequate care, it is left to us to bring this to their attention and seek out their guidance or support.

The lesson I take from the example of the sangha is that rather than only being accountable to other individuals within hierarchical relationships, it can benefit all to create communities of accountability. In a community of accountability, members are mutually accountable to one another. Though hierarchy may still exist, it ultimately becomes the responsibility of the community to support one another through difficult periods. The goal of this kind of accountability is not to find and punish wrong-doers (though the modern justice and penal system may give the impression that this is what accountability is), but to help those who make mistakes or fail in their responsibilities to redress the situation in such a way that it is possible to remain in relationship and for the community as a whole to flourish. Relational healing is the goal of this kind of accountability. The rules of the Vinaya are aimed towards this goal – the flourishing of the community and, in the community, the preservation of the Dharma.

Likewise, where is our community of accountability? Some workplaces can operate in this fashion. The chaplain may help nurture this kind of organizational culture. But that is not always the case. Some workplaces are

---

6 See for example, "Chapter 12: Community Transactions" in *The Buddhist Monastic Code II: The Khandhaka Rules*, translated and explained Thanissaro Bhikkhu (Geoffrey DeGraff) of Metta Forest Monastery, freely available on accesstoinsight.org.

too high pressure, disconnected, transitory, or toxic for communal sentiment to develop. In these instances, chaplains must look outside our workplaces for our community of accountability. That could be our Buddhist community or sangha. However, many Buddhist chaplains report that their Buddhist communities know little about their work as a chaplain and thus would not be able to hold them accountable in that regard. It may be possible for the chaplain to change that situation by sharing their work with their community (while maintaining appropriate careseeker confidentiality) and encouraging community support and accountability. Some workplaces require endorsement from a religious community for a chaplain on the premise that the religious community will serve exactly that function. Chaplains who are ordained are accountable to the teachers, lineages, and communities who ordained them, but ordination responsibilities may be separate from their role as a chaplain. Many Buddhist chaplains report innovative ways of creating their own communities of accountability within various peer groups made up of Buddhist chaplains, interreligious chaplains, or interdisciplinary caregivers. Chaplains who complete CPE training will have some idea of how an interreligious community of accountability functions through their interactions with their peer cohort and can draw on this experience when considering their ongoing needs. Chaplains who receive Board Certification or licensure remain accountable to their certifying bodies through formal structures.

Recall that a key finding of the first volume in this series is that *kalyāṇamitra* need *kalyāṇamitra*. In Volume I, Chapter 4, I shared my research with Buddhist chaplains (and my personal experience): "Through being accompanied by spiritual friends, one begins the process of developing confidence in the Dharma, diligence in one's practice, and a sense of support from a community of practitioners that fuels one's practice to go deeper." (Sanford, 2021, p. 140) I reiterated this conclusion again: "Inversely, chaplains who struggle in spiritual care and find it difficult to facilitate reflection for others will need the guidance of strong role models who can accompany them through reflection and build their skills. I have chosen to characterize this as the behavior of a spiritual friend, or *kalyāṇamitra*." (Sanford, 2021, p. 143). One of the primary functions of our *kalyāṇamitra* is to 'admonish' us and 'point out the faults and deeds of Mara' (Conze, 1994, p. 88). In other words, our *kalyāṇamitra* hold us accountable.

Scholar-practitioners Paul Condon and John Makransky point out that relational security serves the starting point for compassion training and other forms of Buddhist practice in their 2020 article "Recovering the Relational Starting Point of Compassion Training: A Foundation for Sustainable and Inclusive Care." Concerned by the 'modernist' presentation of "meditation as an autonomous, self-help practice," Condon and Makransky's response is "centered on relationality that is derived from the integration of diverse areas of psychology with contemplative traditions," (p. 1346) particularly Buddhist traditions. Traditional Buddhist practices, they point out, help "practitioners learn to become an extension of the field of care in which they are held: to love others as they are loved, to know others as they are known, and to hold others in the wisdom and compassion in which they are held by their spiritual community" (p. 1347-8). Accountability can likewise be modelled. To the extent that we witness accountability within our communities, we can enact accountability within our own work, and through our demonstration of accountability we encourage like behavior in others who witness it. To the extent that our communities lack accountability or fail to hold us (and each other) accountable, we may struggle to enact accountability within our work as chaplains.

Accountability is a hallmark of professionalization. All professions develop mechanisms for holding their members accountable. Inasmuch as chaplaincy is a profession and Buddhist chaplaincy as subgroup within that profession, we must likewise hold ourselves accountable, both to the wider inter-religious profession of chaplaincy and to our lineages of Buddhism. The Association of Professional Chaplains developed a Code of Ethics and Standards of Practice, which states that "In becoming a member of the Association, one affirms this Code and holds oneself accountable to it. Membership implies agreement to participate with integrity in any process of the Association to hold oneself or other members accountable to this Code, and to accept the Standards and judgments of the Association" (item 100, p. 1). The Code also includes language holding the Association as a whole accountable to its by-laws and policies. The APC Standards of Practice begin by drawing on similar standards for nurses when they state that they "are authoritative statements that describe broad responsibilities for which practitioners are accountable, 'reflect the values and priorities of the profession,' and 'provide direction for professional… practice and a framework for the evaluation of practice'." (APC, p. 3, quoting the American Nurses Association's Nursing: Scope and Standards of Practice.)

Likewise, the Canadian Association of Spiritual Care (CASC) publishes and regularly updates a Code of Ethics and Professional Conduct that "Provides a mechanism for professional accountability" (spiritualcare.ca). The Code of Ethics comprises chapter 5 of a larger policy manual that includes standards of Professional Practice (chapter 3), as well. Section C.1 of the CASC standards of Professional Practice lists the constituencies to which chaplains are held accountable, including:

> Certified Professionals are accountable to all of the following:
> 1.1. The persons with whom they work (students, clients, patients, and members of faith communities);
> 1.2. Appropriate workplace standards and authority;
> 1.3. Workplace colleagues;
> 1.4. Their own faith community; and
> 1.5. CASC/ACSS. (CASC Manual, p. 15)

Thus, chaplains must consider and maintain not just one, but several overlapping communities of accountability.

Moreover, the CASC Manual has an appendix of "Competencies of Spiritual Care Practitioners and Psycho-Spiritual Therapists (2011)" which includes the following language:

> 3. SPIRITUAL AND PERSONAL DEVELOPMENT
> Continues to develop and maintain personal and professional growth, awareness and self-understanding and makes oneself appropriately accountable.

Further information on Codes of Ethics and Standards of Practice

Association of Professional Chaplains Common Code of Ethics
   https://www.apchaplains.org/wp-content/uploads/2022/05/Common-Code-of-Ethics.pdf
Association of Professional Chaplains Standards of Practice
   https://www.apchaplains.org/wp-content/uploads/2022/05/Standards-of-Practice-for-Professional-Chaplains-102215.pdf
Canadian Association of Spiritual Care Code of Ethics and Professional Conduct
   https://spiritualcare.ca/about-casc_acss/casc-acss-code-of-ethics-and-professional-conduct/
Canadian Association of Spiritual Care Policy & Procedure Manual
   https://spiritualcare.ca/members/manual-2/

3.1. Engages in ongoing theological/spiritual reflection.
3.2. Nurtures and utilizes own spirituality with integrity.
3.3. Identifies and integrates areas of need and interest regarding continuing education in development of areas of own personhood, religion, spirituality and meaning.
3.4. Identifies and utilizes personal and professional support, consultation and supervision.
3.5. Evaluates clinical practice, identifies strengths and weaknesses, set goals and modifies practice accordingly as necessary.
3.6. Consults with other professionals and spiritual care and counselling colleagues when appropriate.
3.7. Engages regularly and holistically (body, mind, spirit) in self-caring practices. (CASC Manual, p. 43)

In other words, not only do we 'make ourselves' accountable to others, we are also accountable to ourselves for our own ongoing development. We maintain this accountability to ourselves by continuously engaging in reflection, nurturing our spirituality, integrating new learning into our work and spiritual lives, seeking support from our *kalyāṇamitra*, evaluating our own work and asking others to do likewise, seeking consultations, receiving feedback, and taking care of our mind, body, and spirit. Accountability is about more than to whom we report or how we make amends for mistakes. It is fundamentally about our own ongoing wellbeing.

Sometimes we may find teachings and metaphors in the Dharma that valorize solitude and spiritual autonomy. For example, the *Khaggavisana Sutta* (SN1.3) states:

For a sociable person
there are allurements;
on the heels of allurement, this pain.
Seeing allurement's drawback,
wander alone
like a rhinoceros.

One whose mind
is enmeshed in sympathy
for friends & companions,
neglects the true goal.
Seeing this danger in intimacy,
wander alone
like a rhinoceros.

The *sutta* continues for quite some time, listing many dangers on the spiritual path and advising the practitioner to "wander alone like a rhinoceros" to avoid them. The *sutta* is warning us against falling in with bad company and, should no good company be available, it is preferable to seek solitude. This poem also serves to create the aspiration necessary for a layperson of ancient India to leave home to become a renunciant, a radical and frightening proposition at a time when most people lived and died within walking distance of their birthplace. However, good company is available to us today in the form of our fellow Buddhist chaplains and *kalyāṇamitra*. As the Buddha advised Ananada in the *Upaddha Sutta* (SN45.2), "Admirable friendship, admirable companionship, admirable camaraderie is actually the whole of the holy life." While some Buddhist practices involve intense periods of solitude, from a few days to the three-year retreat of the Tibetan traditions, these periods are always preceded by intense preparations within communities that then support the retreatant throughout their practice period, followed by return to a community afterward. While solitude plays an important role in spiritual development, this is not the same as 'going it alone' in one's work as a chaplain. Teachings valorizing independence must be balanced alongside other teachings on the importance of accountability, appropriate student-teacher relationships, and community support.

6
SPIRITUAL LEADERSHIP

How to Be a Good Follower

An often-overlooked aspect in the field of leadership studies is the role of the follower. Even though there are far more followers than leaders and most of us will be followers before we become leaders, research has focused on the glamours of leadership. Since none of us start there, this chapter doesn't start there either. (Even the rare *tulku*, selected from a young age to become spiritual leader, will spend many years as a student first.) In fact, this chapter spends only one of its four sections on leadership models. The literature of leadership studies is mostly related to leadership in a business or political context, yet there is a sub-discipline focused on leadership in the humanitarian, non-profit, religious, and spiritual spheres.

Rather, this chapter focuses on the peculiar role of chaplains – a person educated and qualified for spiritual or religious leadership working within an institution wherein we are rarely 'the leader' of those we serve, whether careseekers, teammates, or the institutional administration. In *Chaplaincy and Spiritual Care in the Twenty-First Century*, McClure and Theil state "Chaplains are in a unique position to leverage such organizational change. They are in the organization (hired by or volunteering in it) but not of it (belonging instead to a religious/spiritual/existential tradition). Their moral perspective is larger than the organization's" (2022, p. 196). Many chaplains serve dual roles as clergy, leaders, or Dharma teachers, but a good number are also laypeople with no defined role within their community or sangha. They are, nevertheless, spiritual leaders as well as what Joanna Elizabeth Crossman and Brian Crossman define as 'spiritual followers,' which is explored below.

'Followership' is the counterpart to 'leadership' and its scholarly study mostly comes to us from the perspective of organizational management, business, and the social sciences. A library search of 'followership and Buddhism' turns up very little, but, as with other topics discussed in these volumes, that doesn't mean Buddhism has nothing to say on the topic. Buddhist hierarchical relationships are typified by the teacher-student paradigm. We can find hints of what it means to be a good follower in advice related to being a good student. Some advice seems universally applicable, while

---

Further information on Spiritual Leadership

Religious Leadership edited by Sharon Callahan (Sage Publications, 2011)
The Future of Religious Leadership: World Religions in Conversation edited by Alon Goshen-Gottstein (Lanham, 2016)
Servant Leadership and Followership: Examining the Impact on Workplace Behavior edited by Crystal Davis (Palgrave MacMillan, 2017) or
The Palgrave Handbook on Workplace Spirituality and Fulfillment edited by Satinder Dhiman, Gary Roberts, and Joanna Elizabeth Crossman (Palgrave MacMillan, 2018)

other advice is clearly contextual. We can also consider cultural norms for leaders and followers in Asia and in North America, about which there is an emerging academic literature, though I shall not review it here. Taken together, we can derive guidance for how to be a good follower. This section condenses that guidance into considerations for chaplains in our unique contexts and points towards more information should you wish to delve further into the topic. First let us consider Buddhist advice on how to be a good student before we explore what it means to be a spiritual follower and how both may apply to our role as a chaplain.

In his *Great Treatise on the Stages of the Path to Enlightenment*, Tsongkhapa enumerates both the qualities of a skillful teacher and those of a skillful student. In chapter 4 about "Relying on the Teacher," Tsongkhapa quotes earlier sources:

> Āryadeva states in his *Four Hundred Stanzas* (*Catuḥ-śataka*):
> It is said that one who is nonpartisan, intelligent, and diligent
> Is a vessel for listening to the teachings. (2014, p. 75)

Tsongkhapa then elaborates via his own commentary: "Āryadeva says…that if you have all these qualities, the good qualities of one who instructs you in the teachings will appear as good qualities, not as faults" (2014, p. 75). In other words, a capable student will be able to recognize what they may learn from a teacher, including how they may learn from the teacher's mistakes, thus transforming even faults into lessons. When students lack these qualities "the influence of your own faults will cause even an extremely pure teacher who instructs you in the teachings to appear to have faults" (2014, p. 76). Some people are simply not presently open to learning or change, even if they should have the best teachers. Tsonkhapa further illuminates Āryadeva's three qualities. Being "nonpartisan" means you do not take sides and strive to remain unobstructed by your own biases, including the bias of being attached to one's own religion and hostile to others. Within the student teacher relationship, Tsongkhapa quotes the Bodhisattva Vows of Liberation (*Bodhisattva-prātimokṣa*) "After giving up your own assertions, respect and abide in the texts of the abbot and master" (2014, p. 76). A student should also be intelligent, meaning they are able to distinguish between 'correct and counterfeit' paths. Being open to the views of the teacher does not mean abandoning one's own judgement. When listening to a teaching, one must be able to distinguish between a good explanation and a bad one. Finally, a student must be diligent and willing to work. To these three qualities Candrakirti's commentary adds two more. The good student remains focused when listening and respects the teacher. They demonstrate this respect by discarding the teacher's bad explanations while retaining their good ones (2014, p. 75-77), again demonstrating the role of one's own discernment.

A student-teacher relationship, whether between monastics or laypeople, is different from a leader-follower relationship or an organization-employee/volunteer relationship. Yet there is still applicable guidance here. As a follower, we must be willing to follow, just as the nonpartisan student is willing to learn. We must be open to adopting the mission, vision, and values of the organization while at the same time using our natural intelligence and educated judgment to determine if they are worth following. In some cases, we may feel that the organization has gone astray from its mission or the implicit purpose through which it could serve society. Or perhaps we cannot endorse the purpose of the organization at all, though we can find meaning for our work within that organization. In all cases, we must be willing to follow the policies and procedures of the organization and the dictates of its leaders to the extent that our work becomes possible. When we cannot, then we may choose to object, attempt to correct, or depart from the organization. So long as we choose to remain, we should do so with dignity, respect, and diligence towards our work.

This extrapolation of followership is similar to Joanna Elizabeth Crossman and Brian Crossman's definition of 'spiritual followership:'

> The spiritual follower, holds him or herself accountable to a higher power or force, defined and inspired through a personally, culturally and socially constructed spiritual paradigm that in turn influences and motivates responses, actions and decisions within an organizational context. Whatever the source of that inspiration, it defines and binds the follower to a sense of meaning and purpose and tends to draw on virtues such as, courage, integrity and honesty. The spiritual follower is empowered, confident in maintaining a balance between loyalty to a leader and an ethical approach to serving the common good. They work to be of service to a leader and the community, and advise those stakeholders to the best of their ability, expertise and knowledge, even when advice will probably be considered as unpalatable. Spiritual followers will withdraw their support for a leader where leader direction or actions have the potential to compromise the health and well-being of others, and also what is deemed financially responsible or ethical. The spiritual follower is mindful that personal health and well-being sustain optimum performance but does not seek out acclaim, or material recognition, for its own sake, in order to satisfy the ego.
> (*Palgrave Handbook of Workplace Spirituality and Fulfilment*, 2018, p. 460-461)

Comparing this definition to the conceptions of chaplains in Part 4: Organizational Competencies in *Chaplaincy and Spiritual Care in the Twenty-First Century* as well as Tsongkhapa's qualities of a good student, we may find that the Crossmans' conception of 'spiritual followership' is an ideal description of one role of Buddhist chaplains. The chaplain, according to McClure and Theil "hold[s] forth a moral vision larger than any single organization," (2022, p. 196) that may also be understood as the Crossmans' "higher power or force" (2018, p. 460). This vision/higher power, drives "motivation to create a more just, compassionate, and flourishing world," (McClure and Theil, 2022, p. 195) that "motivates responses, actions, and decisions" (Crossman and Crossman, 2018, p. 460). The Crossmans describe how the spiritual follower's value system promotes "an ethical approach to serving the common good" that includes service and advice "even when advice will probably be considered as unpalatable." McClure and Theil reference this same idea via the Abrahamic conception of "the chaplain's prophetic role – the commission to speak truth to power" (2022, p. 196) demonstrating that chaplains must have a "concern for ethics" (2022, p. 196) at an organizational level as well as an interpersonal one.

As with Tsongkhapa's student, spiritual followers must apply themselves to discern 'correct from counterfeit paths' and 'good from bad explanations,' only committing to those worthy of their respect after a long period of observation (this is enumerated in later in Chapter 4 of *The Great Treatise*...in reference to seeking a teacher) and be willing to "withdraw their support for a leader where leader direction or actions have the potential to compromise the health and well-being of others, and also what is deemed financially responsible or ethical," (2018, p. 461) per the Crossman's definition. But perhaps the aspect of the Crossman's conception of the spiritual follower that makes it applicable not only to chaplaincy at large, but to Buddhist chaplains specifically, is the final sentence: "The spiritual follower is mindful that personal health and well-being sustain optimum performance but does not seek out acclaim, or material recognition, for its own sake, in order to satisfy the ego" (2018, p. 461). Though the Crossman's may not be aware of the full implications of their statement for Buddhists, this conception of followership places nonself or egolessness at the center. The spiritual follower is not interested in the eight worldly concerns (gain and loss, pleasure and pain, praise and blame, and fame and disgrace; see AN8.6), particularly the acclaim they may receive in the workplace. While the spiritual follower practices sufficient self-care, or as Śāntideva advises "So pay this body due remuneration, / And then be sure to make it work for you" (verse 5.69), as chaplains we are also willing to strive to "sustain optimum performance" (Crossman and Crossman, 2018, p. 461) in the care we provide.

The Crossmans' definition for spiritual followership exists within a broader conception of what constitutes followership as a whole, which, according to Zoogah, can be understood as a rank (subordinate), person (aligned with goals of organization or leader), role (enacted behaviors), state (influenced by a leader), process (endorsing leaders), or capacity (sharing mutual influence). Regardless of how followership is understood, it is always relational, existing between a leader and follower or between and organization or community and an individual member (Zoogah, 2014, p. 6-8). This relational nature is also highlighted by McClure and Theil when they share a definition of leadership provided by Lee Bolman and Terence Deal: "**leadership** is situational (dependent on organizational, environmental, and/or historical context), **relational** (a relationship between leader and followers), and **distinct from position** (not synonymous with authority or high position)," [emphasis original] all of which could also easily be said of followership (through with reference to subordinate rather than high position), and "It is a subtle process of mutual influence that fuses thought, feeling, and action to produce cooperative effort in the service of the purposes and values of both the leaders and followers" (McClure and Theil, 2022, p. 195-196, quoting from Joan V. Gallos, Using Bolman and Deal's *Reframing Organization: An Instructor's Guide to Effective Teaching*, 5th ed., p. 194). We will return to the concept of leadership below, but it is clear from this definition that followers likewise exercise considerable influence on the path of an organization, which is why, according to McClure and Theil, "the chaplain needs to be knowledgeable and skilled in creating change in organizations in the direction, ultimately, of global flourishing," (2022, p. 196) whether the chaplain is acting in the role of a leader, follower, peer, or caregiver.

As both followership and leadership are relational constructs, Zoogah presents a definition of 'strategic followership' that includes ways in which the follower 'invests' in their relationship with leaders within their organization. As chaplains, most of our time and energy is spent with careseekers. Yet in order to provide the spiritual care they need, we must also strategically invest in relationships with colleagues and institutional administrators who are capable of making decisions that affect the quality of the care we provide. Zoogah describes 'strategic followership' as "the systematic process by which a follower, in enacting an impactful role, strategically discerns the value of his/her interaction with a leader, and behaves in a way that yields short-term and/or long-term meaningful outcomes for significant organizational constituents." (2014, p. 8) In other words, chaplains who invest in good relationships with their leaders or supervisors create tangible long-term benefits for their careseekers and organizations. The ways in which followers do this are not haphazard, but rather carefully considered, proactively chosen, and evaluated for their effectiveness in relation to specific goals – hence, strategic followership. As a chaplain, I have been both an administrator and a supervisor of other chaplains, as well as a direct report to various supervisors and follower of institutional leaders. I have created value for my managers by finding ways to 'make their job easier.' For example, while leading the spiritual life department at a large university, I created policies to streamline previously haphazard approval processes, saving time for decision makers above me to approve the outcomes of those processes. I developed ways to assess and report program effectiveness that helped my managers look better to their managers. This work did not directly involve student needs, but made more resources available to support student-focused programs in the long run. Zoogah describes this as "The support followers provide to supervisors or leaders frees up psychological and social resources of the latter" (2014, p. 10) by understanding their strategic goals, helping them look good to the organization, and by demonstrating interest in their lives as people. Zoogah proposes three features of strategic interactions between followers and leader/managers: 1) they solve problems; 2) they sustain relationships; and 3) they advance the organization as a whole (2014, p. 9).

In some cases, this does not always mean following a manager/leader; sometimes it means correcting or resisting a leader who is ineffectual or bad for the organization. Zoogah writes that "The restorative behaviors of followers in dysfunctional relational situations are also significant. It is not unusual for followers to undermine leaders when the latter are not effectual." (2014, p. 9) So while strategic followership is enacted through the relationship between the follower and leader, the follower's ultimate allegiance remains with the organization or community, per Zoogah. In the case of the chaplain, as we have seen, their ultimate commitments may, in fact, transcend the organization and include an evaluation of the organization's role in and contribution to (or not) the world. Thus, spiritual followers, strategic followers, and chaplains may resist the ways that institutions harm careseekers. Chaplains in for-profit health care organizations share stores of this nature. Chaplains working in corrections, the military, or law enforcement may find themselves in even more precarious situations. Tsongkapa (partially quoting from the *Cloud of Jewels Sutra*) even advises that within the student-teacher relationship, in which disloyalty is strongly admonished even in the face of a harsh or demanding teacher, the student should "Engage in virtuous actions in accordance with your masters, but do not act in accord with their nonvirtuous actions" (2014, p. 82) and "'do not act in accord with the gurus' words with respect to nonvirture.' Therefore, you must not listen to nonvirtuous instructions" (2014, p. 86). A student should not comply with harmful instructions from their guru, whom they regard (per the Vajrayana paradigm) as a living buddha. Likewise, a chaplain as a follower should not comply with harmful organizational practices, policies, or instructions from managers, leaders, or supervisors. Whatever paradigm we choose, followership can and should be just as thoughtfully enacted as leadership. Moreover, through our actions as virtuous followers, we can demonstrate a type of moral leadership to careseekers, teammates, and the leaders and administrators of our organizations.

Models for Leadership

Regardless of our job description or position in the hierarchy, chaplains are symbolic leaders because of the way we are perceived by others, according to Barbara McClure and Mary Martha Theil in their introduction to "Part 4: Organizational Competencies" in *Chaplaincy and Spiritual Care in the Twenty-First Century*. We carry 'symbolic power' (regardless of how, or even if we use that power) that people respond to in different ways, including with resistance, respect, and indifference. Their responses are based on enculturation and transference (as discussed in the prior chapter) rooted in the person's prior experiences with religious leaders (McClure and Theil, 2022, p. 196).

We must also be prepared to act as leaders when called upon. Buddhist chaplains operate as moral, visionary, empowering, strategic, and servant-leaders (Thanissaro, 2018). McClure and Theil describe how the standards of practice in North America specify leadership and organization management as key skills for chaplains, but note that "In practice, most chaplains and chaplain educators today have not been taught to understand how organizations function or how to contribute to their positive change," such as through leadership roles (2022, p. 195). The authors seek to rectify this gap with three chapters on 'organizational competencies' for chaplains, which are recommended reading. This section discusses some of these paradigms and connects them to Buddhist approaches to leadership. As usual, there is no dedicated literature on this topic (yet!), so we must synthesize a perspective on leadership for Buddhist chaplains from literature on leadership studies (mostly in other contexts), religious leadership and chaplaincy (mostly non-Buddhist), and Buddhist leadership (mostly in the context of Buddhist communities, rather than chaplaincy settings).

Let us begin with a defining leadership as the ability to influence another person to do something, particularly something they would not otherwise do, that contributes to the goals of the organization or community. Leadership derives from the human ability to influence one another "to behave in a transformative way" (Zoogah, 2014, p. 10). Spiritual leadership then, might be understood as the ability to influence another person not only to do something, but also to be or become something (namely, a better version of themselves). Thus, it is not merely behavior that is transformed, but the person themselves, and, with them, the organization, community, or society at large. This definition may sound somewhat autocratic, like we try to get people to do things they resist using some kind of power over them. However, leadership can be much more subtle than it is often portrayed in television dramas. As a chaplain, we sometimes describe our work as 'making space' for something to happen that might not otherwise have happened and 'inviting' careseekers to feel, think, and reflect in a way that they aren't otherwise prompted or welcomed to do. This is sufficient to meet the definition of 'leadership,' even when gently and graciously enacted. The second half of the definition 'contributes to the goals of the organization,' may also seem a somewhat odd turn of phrase for a chaplain – except in this case, one of the goals of the organization is the spiritual wellbeing of the careseeker. McClure and Theil also describe how chaplain leadership is unique in this sense because "Their moral perspective is larger than the organization's" (2022, p. 196). Thus, not only do chaplains exercise leadership with careseekers, they also exercise leadership within organizations to help the organization (or community) be a greater benefit both towards those it directly serves (careseekers) and the wider world (society). Chaplains "hold forth a moral vision larger than any single organization," one that is "grounded in their religious/spiritual/existential tradition" (2022, p. 196). Chaplains both meet and go beyond many secular definitions of leadership.

Within the field of leadership studies, which is primarily concerned with leadership in business, government, and politics, but has recently broadened its interest to include non-profit and religious or spiritual concerns, there are four types of leadership theories: 1) trait theories try to understand the personal qualities of leaders, as in, who leaders are; 2) behavioral theories attempt to describe what leaders do; 3) situational theories explore how leaders adapt to different contexts and how those contexts determine what types of leadership will succeed, and; 4) congruence theories attempt to demonstrate how successful leadership finds the right fit between a context and the particular strengths of a leader. McGonagill Associates has developed an *Annotated Bibliography on Leadership* (2008) that describes these categories and the various types of leadership theories and scholars that contribute to each.

Buddhist leadership theories do not fall neatly into any of the four categories; all four can be found in various places within the Dharma. The spiritual formation of the leader, their personal virtues such as compassion and wisdom, and their own awakening may fall into trait theories, while the precepts and ethical behaviors to which they commit themselves, particularly among monastics, fall into behavioral theories. The Buddhist concept of upaya or skillful means also features prominently in Buddhist discussions of leadership and serves as a situational theory. Finally, we could explore congruence theories through the lenses of karma and the interdependent co-arising of sufficient causes and conditions that enable a particular leader to succeed in a particular context. From this brief overview we can see that the Dharma is rife with guidance on leadership.

Phra Nicholas Thanissaro in the *Journal of Buddhist Ethics* provides us with another comparative typology, in which he explores nine specific secular leadership theories for their applicability to Buddhism, including ethical, symbolic, charismatic, visionary, servant, facilitative, strategic, and path-goal leadership, as well as management theory (2018, p. 119-145). I will not explore all these here, except to say that Thanissaro demonstrated evidence of each within Buddhist contexts. He also explored some of the differences in leadership style between various forms of Asian Buddhism and since Buddhism has come to the west. For chaplains, I find that almost all of these types of leadership (and even management) apply at different times. I will assume that chaplains understand their role as ethical leaders (explored in Volume I of *Kalyāṇamitra* in relation to the spiritual friend as 'moral exemplar'). McClure and Theil explain symbolic leadership and subsequent chapters in Part 4 of *Chaplaincy and Spiritual Care in the Twenty-First Century* describe strategic, path-goal, and other forms of leadership well. Thus, the remainder of this section focuses on Buddhist chaplains as facilitative and visionary leadership. The final section of this chapter touches on servant leadership, which has had a strong impact on leadership in religious contexts in the west.

The word facilitative derives from the root 'facil' which means 'to make easy.' Thanissaro describes a facilitative leader as one who helps the group to solve problems and achieve common goals by providing their expertise on various subjects. As chaplains, our familiarity with religious traditions and spiritual, existential, ethical, and emotional concerns enables us to offer language, questions, and ways of thinking to our careseekers and teammates. The basis of an academic field or profession often lies, at least in part, in expertise in the use of descriptive language. Sometimes, as in the case of legal or medical jargon, this language can become almost impenetrable. A chaplain's job works in the opposite manner, to make language for spiritual, religious, ethical, and emotional concerns accessible. In chapter 2, we discussed skills of listening and responding. A careseeker may spend thirty minutes circling around what they want to convey, struggling to find the words. The chaplain helps by reflecting what they've heard using terms from our discipline. For example:

- A bereaved spouse talks about how their family is not sympathetic: "It sounds like you're experiencing disenfranchised grief – where you're not allowed to grieve in front of others." To which they respond, "I never heard it called that, but you're right, that's what it is."
- A Christian addict catalogs all their misdeeds and wonders if God hates them: "Most Christian traditions believe in an omnibenevolent God – one who loves you no matter what." To which they respond, "I didn't know that."
- A student describes spaces they enjoy compared to those they don't: "It sounds

like you're an aesthetically-minded introvert." To which they respond, "Yes!"

This is not to say we reduce people's problems to easily catalogued terms, but by sharing this language with them, we normalize their experiences, empower them to understand and describe their spiritual lives in new ways, and help them explore what they are going through by finding other resources that use these terms. Likewise, we can use this same expertise when making chart notes or having conversations with teammates. With a team, we may also serve as the expert on religious practices and cultural customs related to physical care, such as appropriate food, providing ritual objects, the timing of holidays, contact with opposite genders, or moving the body after death. Knowing about these concerns in advance makes it easier for both the care team and careseeker. We operate as leaders in the sense that we offer these services proactively according to our own judgement as to when they are needed (though we also respond to questions or requests) and being directive when appropriate.

A chaplain also serves as a visionary leader. McClure and Thiel describe how "Chaplains are moral leaders, holding forth for an organization a vision of just and sustainable communal thriving rooted in their religious/spiritual/existential traditions." (2022, p. 193). Organizations often suffer from too little vision, driven by budget constraints, profit margins, massive bureaucracies, and a too pessimistic view of difficulties that prevent the organization from striving to be better when better is entirely possible. The visionary leadership of the chaplain is called upon to both put challenges into a larger perspective and motivate people to do better using an inspiring vision of the future.

In addition to holding a vision for an organization, Buddhist chaplains in my research also describe their role as holding a vision of hope on behalf of careseekers, sometimes even when the careseekers themselves cannot hold their own hope. Holding out hope for the careseeker was identified as a practice of wisdom by Buddhist chaplains I study – an outcome of their Right View and contained in the Third Noble Truth that states the cessation of suffering is possible. Sometimes that which we are hoping for on their behalf is not necessarily awakening as Buddhists understand it, but physical healing from illness or injury, a safe and successful future, communion with God in heaven, forgiveness from family, a less stressful job, or any host of other possible goals – all of which can be understood as a way to reduce suffering and increase happiness and equanimity in the present moment. This is not to say that our vision is always perfectly aligned with that of careseekers, who can, at turns, be both overly pessimistic and overly optimistic (sometimes in the same person from one minute to the next). Careseekers may envision for themselves a life that is difficult or impossible to obtain, such as unearned success or miraculous healing, or exceedingly unlikely, such as everyone hating them or never being able to recover from an injury or setback. Sometimes our role entails holding a vision for what is possible (or realistic), not simply for what is most desired or most feared and helping the careseeker recognize that for themselves. This vision comes, at least in part, from our expertise working with people going through similar situations, our education and training, and our spiritual formation within our religious traditions.

Visionary leaders inspire others, which broadens leader's influence well beyond those they technically 'lead,' 'supervise,' or 'direct.' Visionary leadership operates indirectly on those around us, especially when combined with symbolic and ethical leadership. Thanissaro describes the visionary leader as one able to "inspire extraordinary levels of achievement in followers through an inspiring vision…and empower others to enact the vision," (2018, p. 128). When a positive vision is persuasively communicated, people feel empowered to pursue it on their own, which is exactly what we hope for as chaplains. In Buddhist communities throughout history, Thanissaro connects vision to leaders who are "perceived as having attained or the potential to attain enlightenment or the ability to induce such experiences in followers," (2018, p. 128). (Don't worry if you, like me, have yet to attain enlightenment or induce others to it; while chaplains reported some level of spiritual practice as the foundation of their caregiving ability, awakening was not listed as a prerequisite.) In other words, sometimes the way the chaplain is present – calmly or empathetically or unwaveringly ethical – can be sufficient to inspire a new vision of how things can be for others.

Spiritual Authority in Spiritual Care

The term 'spiritual authority' in chaplaincy originates from the Christian concept of the vocation as a 'calling' from 'God.' According to Joel Graves in *Leadership Paradigms in Chaplaincy*, "Chaplains are second chair leaders in one sense, because they support leaders above them in almost every organization they serve. But their authority does not come from someone above them; it is not delegated down, like it is for second chair leaders. Chaplains derive their authority directly from God. It is pastoral authority" (2007, p. 100). According to this, those who have been called by God to work as chaplains have also been invested with authority from God to do that work. In fact, many theistic traditions, including Christianity, Judaism, and Hinduism, perceive the chaplain as an 'instrument' through whom the divine works or flows. This divine will is what transforms the care that the human chaplain provides into 'spiritual' care and makes it a sacred act. Thus, some theists have gone so far as to state that all spiritual care ultimately comes from God or gods. This may seem challenging for the Buddhist chaplain, particularly if one does not perceive oneself in relationship with or as an instrument of divine or supernatural forces. Nevertheless, Buddhism has it's own understanding of spiritual authority, usually referencing forms of spiritual attainment, cultivation, or awakening.

There are at least four sources of spiritual authority in Buddhism. First, there are forms of spiritual authority in Buddhism that derive from supernatural forces. For example, Vajrayana traditions view certain individuals as the incarnations of bodhisattvas on Earth, such as His Holiness the Dalai Lama as an incarnation of Avalokiteśvara. Also, Buddhists whose location, family, sect, or lineage is under the protection of a deity or supernatural being may appeal to that being for help or guidance. Likewise, many Buddhists appeal to their deceased ancestors for guidance. Such relationships may be perceived as a source of spiritual authority or they may not.

Second, authority in Buddhism can derive from spiritual attainments. Thanissaro, whose typology of Buddhist leaders was discussed in the prior section, categories visionary leaders in this way. According to Shenpen Hookham, spiritual authority was vested first in the Buddha by way of his enlightenment. The Buddha later confirmed spiritual authority in those of his disciples in whom he likewise affirmed the awakened mind (p. 46). As Buddhism became an institutionalized religion with settled monasteries, authority was vested in a clear hierarchy based on seniority and appointment to positions. Thus, third, Buddhist authority is also conferred by institutions. At the same time, some monastics continued to wander, as the Buddha had, or live in seclusion, prizing spiritual authority based on direct realization. According to Hookham, the tension between authority that is bestowed by an institution (such as through endorsement) and that which is achieved by the individual practitioner, who may then attract their own disciples, (2010, p. 46-47) has provided a vital source of energy for the various Buddhist traditions for over two-thousand years. Should authority be only institutionally based, it runs the risk of becoming perfunctory, stultifying, and corrupt. On the other hand, should authority be only based on the declaration of a 'realized' individual, it runs the risk of becoming delusional, megalomaniacal, and also corrupt. The twin sources of authority thus keep one another in balance. In theory, institutions should bestow authority on those they recognize as realized and the type of lifestyle fostered and passed down by the institutions should enable individuals to become realized.

The fourth form of spiritual authority in Buddhism is also the one most recognized by secular colleagues – expertise. Most Buddhist chaplains have a least some advanced education in Buddhism, religion, spirituality, and psycho-social wellbeing, as well as a grounding spiritual practice of their own. In traditional Buddhist societies, almost all religious expertise was invested in the monastic community as only they had the time and resources to dedicate to study and practice. (Hookham explores some interesting exceptions in his book *The Guru Principle*, 2018.) Now, such opportunities are more readily available to laypeople through broad literacy, more free time (compared to subsistence farmers), and more educational opportunities within both academic institutions and the Buddhist organizations themselves. Likewise, more laypeople are able to engage in contemplative and ritual practices. Hookham points out that

> A model is emerging [in the West] that is not the two-tiered model of monks and laypeople …but more like the original pattern of wandering yogins surrounded by their disciples. The difference tends to be that these days the heads of [Tibetan Dharma] centers are often appointed by heads of monasteries in Asia.
>
> The forest renunciant model is reminiscent of the Christian desert fathers who were hermits on the edge of society, outside the institutional hierarchy of the priesthood. These fathers were the ones who were the spiritual guides, and even the people in the priestly hierarchy would go to them and recognize their spiritual authority, even though the fathers were not ordained. The desert fathers' authority derived basically from their reputation. This is similar to the way Tibetan Buddhist tradition has always operated and still does today. (2018, p. 47)

This is also similar to the way chaplains operate – outside the religious institutions and their embedded hierarchies but doing the important work of spiritual guidance that elicits respect from their community, whether the chaplain is ordained or not.

Hookham sites a three-fold model posited by Reginald Ray of spiritual authority vested in monks, laypeople, and "yogins" (2018, p. 47) – chaplains, whose work does not neatly fit into the category of a traditional monastic or layperson (though they may be either), may come closer to the category of "yogin" or exist in an as-yet emerging fourth category, given that we do not collect disciples the way yogins often did. Rather, chaplains cross paths with people in some of the most distressing moments of their lives, walk with them for a time, and then part ways, hopefully leaving those they meet better off for having had company for a while. Hookham laments the lack of scholarly attention paid to yogins, without whom "I believe our tradition would be spiritually lost, even spiritually dead." Likewise, I lament the lack of attention paid to chaplains, without whom I believe our tradition would be, if not lost or dead, certainly less socially and spiritually relevant. Buddhist chaplains play an important role within the institutions where we serve and also within our Buddhist communities, where the spiritual realizations we learn via our work can be shared with our Dharma brothers and sisters, our *kalyāṇamitra*.

Thus, the loving-kindness and compassion that leads to our caregiving experience and the wisdom we derive from it forms a unique basis of our spiritual authority, a combination based on attainment, expertise, and a fundamental outlook. Henri Nouwen, in this famous work on chaplaincy, *The Wounded Healer* (1972), likewise found multiple sources of the chaplain's spiritual authority: "First, personal concern, which asks one man to give his life for his fellow man; second, a deep-rooted faith in the value and meaning of life, even when the days look dark; and third, an outgoing hope which always looks for tomorrow even beyond the moment of death" (1972, p. 71). While Nouwen conceived of faith, meaning, hope, and the moment beyond death in characteristically Christian ways, we can, as Buddhists recognize that we to affirm the value and meaning of life, hope for cessation of suffering, and look to an ever-changing future. This outlook in and of itself can become a source of spiritual authority.

The question remains: what do we do with our so-called spiritual authority? Primarily chaplains use their spiritual authority to empower others in a search for meaning, purpose, and values. We can draw from the model set by the Buddha for examples. Hookham examines the Kalama Sutta and Canki Sutta for how the Buddha engaged people in dialogue (2018, p. 53). Dialogue is also the standard model for a careseeker-chaplain relationship (though chaplains may also care for non-verbal careseekers). The Buddha often engaged people through questioning, helping them uncover and understand their own dilemmas in reference to their own existing wisdom. Hookham points out that even when the Buddha gave directions or advice, he never insisted on obedience or submission. "He can show us the path, but it is up to us to follow it. It is our responsibility to decide whether to follow that path or not" (2018, p. 53). These relationships were based on trust. Without trust, no guidance is possible, though companionship and comfort may still be offered.

As a chaplain, we work to ensure that we are trustworthy people so that our careseekers may trust us, but we cannot require or assume their trust. Some careseekers may immediately invest their trust in us as a symbol of institutional and spiritual authority, others will wait to know us better as persons, and some may never trust us at all. Trust can be beneficial to the caregiving relationship, though not always in the way we assume. Rather than expect the careseeker to invest their trust in us, we can invest our trust in them as experts in their own lives, equipped with the wisdom and spiritual resources they need to see them through whatever situation they find themselves in. This is what we mean when we say that we 'empower' careseekers with spiritual authority over their own lives.

Two common uses of spiritual authority include: 1) validating beneficial spiritual experiences of careseekers; and 2) challenging harmful beliefs, theologies, or delusions. Tim Ford, a Buddhist chaplain, provides a clear example of the former from working with careseekers of different religious backgrounds:

> The responsibility of a spiritual care provider is not to shape or influence this journey, but simply to recognize its profound power. By naming the authentic spiritual presence found in any moment of relationship, the patient's previously held spiritual beliefs are validated by the chaplain's symbolic spiritual authority, regardless of denomination. The only things that change are the words and concepts that the patient uses to communicate this awareness.
>
> I recall one patient who reacted to hearing his terminal diagnosis by "curling up in a spiritual ball trying to wait through all the blows that were landing." He described being in that place like being in a dark womb wherein he found a singular

luminous presence. Following "the light of that presence" led him back into the world again with a remarkable amount of humor, grace, and acceptance. As I shared with him my admiration and gratitude for being able to witness his journey, he in turn shared his admiration and gratitude for my ability to appreciate it. What happened next is difficult to describe, but our mutual respect for the profound power we saw related in one another led to a sort of feedback loop that ended with both of us deeply moved, weeping, and almost literally glowing.

...As a chaplain, I journey with my patients to the very depths of meaning in their lives and then invite them to apply that meaning to the present moment. Ultimately, the healing comes in companioning them on this journey, not championing any one form of dogma over another. What authority and gifts I offer are not as a Buddhist but rather as a human being with deeply held beliefs. I believe that enlightenment, waking up to increasing depths of spiritual truth, is possible in the midst of trauma and grief. I believe that finding enlightenment in dark times is not only healing but transformative. When faced with the power of what this kind of spiritual growth can do, I frankly do not care what words you choose to describe it; I am comfortable lifting prayers in whatever language is best understood by my audience.
(2012, p. 658–659)

Ford describes not only how he validates the beneficial experiences of careseekers, but also articulates how his companioning them is a deeply human act, one that enables him to witness amazing moments of transformation that, in turn, help him wake up to the truth of reality, which is its own source of spiritual authority.

An example of second use of spiritual authority – to gently challenge careseeker's less beneficial beliefs – is provided in Vignette 2 in Volume I in which Chaplain B helps the daughter of a careseeker suffering from a stroke to reframe the idea of 'miracle.' Rather than praying for miraculous healing, the chaplain suggests to the daughter "Well, you know, sometimes the miracles we want – we want Mom to get better – we want her to stay here with us. And, you know, sometimes the miracle is Mom being with God. Maybe that is part of it; it's also like a miracle." Chaplain B wasn't sure how the daughter would react. He couldn't be certain they had built enough trust through their brief interaction. However, he had reason to believe that the daughter already had a Christian faith she could trust and that she trusted the strength of her mother's belief that she would be reunited with God in heaven. Later, the daughter found Chaplain B again and said to him "We have to let Mom go. This miracle is, you know, God. We respect this miracle of her being with God and she's lived a good life, and we give her to you. Will you come pray with us again?" This kind of challenge is not an imposition of the chaplain's 'better judgement,' but an opening to suggest new opportunities, ask questions that lead down different pathways, or remind careseekers of things they have already said about what they believe and value that apply to the situation in ways they might not have expected.

Just as chaplains can use their spiritual authority with careseekers in either of these two ways, they can also use their spiritual authority within the organizations, institutions, and communities where they work in similar ways. I have sometimes found it necessary to do this as a college chaplain and have explored similar experiences with chaplains in other sectors. The chaplain's spiritual authority within an organization enables us to wield power not through direct hierarchical relationships, but via influence, perceived altruism, and moral authority. Influence is primarily wielded through personal relationships with other staff that must be tended and invested in over time. For example, verbally supporting someone who wants to improve a program or procedure, even when the change has no direct impact on our work, invests in our relationship with that person and builds a 'stock' of trust that can be called upon later. Reciprocity is a strong human instinct. When we later call upon that stock of trust to be used for altruistic purposes, such as to aid the careseekers served by our organization, we enrich that trust rather than depleting it. Finally, as McClure and Theil note, a chaplain's moral vision is often larger than that of their organization and can challenge the organization to do better, particularly in relation to social justice. As chaplains we are obligated to notice, confront, challenge, and help organizations heal from the systemic oppressions of racism, sexism, agism, ablism, heteronormativity, religious discrimination, xenophobia, and other forms of harm.

Some of the most satisfying work I did as a college chaplain always involved the positive use of spiritual authority in changing institutional structures in the direction of equity, inclusion, and welcome for all students and staff. I knew such work would outlast my presence on those campuses. For example, even as I am writing this book, the kosher kitchen I advocated for finally opened for business on my previous campus! Being able to feed Jewish and Muslim students (since what is kosher is also halal, except alcohol) good food on par with that available to all other students is crucial for their ability to live on campus (required for freshman of that institution) and get a good education. If it means that I, as a Buddhist chaplain, need to memorize Jewish dietary rules, holiday calendars, and daily Muslim prayer times, then I am more than happy to do that work. It enabled me to speak to my colleagues with authority about how to accommodate and support all students, and particularly those most often overlooked and overburdened by systems not designed for them. Sometimes spiritual care is accompanying someone through a period of crisis and distress and sometimes it is having budget meetings with dining services administrators – both require the chaplain's spiritual authority to be effective.

Spiritually Empowering Leaders

We may think we cannot be leaders or have spiritual authority because we are just 'ordinary' and have no spiritual realizations ourselves. Hookham believes "there is a lot that ordinary unenlightened people can do to protect and validate teachings and validate one another's experience and understanding, as long as they remain clear about what they are in a position to judge and what they are not." (2018, p. 56) In Western sanghas (including both lay and monastic members), Hookham notes that people in recognized positions stand for "the particular vision, values, and ethos" of the place and thus "have a special responsibility" to identify when that vision and ethos is being embodied by others or not (2018, p. 56). Likewise, as chaplains we have a responsibility to embody in ourselves and recognize in others an ethos of spiritual care, regardless of whatever realizations we may or may not possess. That is something that any ordinary person can do. We also have a special responsibility to continue to work and practice to deepen our spiritual knowledge for the benefit of all beings. We deepen our knowledge while also remaining able to clearly state what we do not know and be open to learning from others. Hookham describes this as "the only qualification that really matters in a [Buddhist] teacher" (2018, p. 56) and could likewise describe a chaplain. According to Ford, "The chaplain's job as a religious person is to develop his or her own faith to the point where they can relax or surrender their beliefs enough to join another person in theirs" (2012, p. 658-659) Our religious practice is for our own wellbeing. To the extent that it enables us to be present, receptive, reflexive, compassionate, and equanimous, then we can explore the beliefs and practices of others from that stable ground even during moments of deep suffering or sublime joy.

One Buddhist lens we can use to think about our role is that of *dāna* – generosity or giving. What we give to the careseeker is our presence, witness, and care. Carl Rogers called this 'unconditional positive regard.' Ford, a Buddhist chaplain, shares

> In my tradition, there are levels of generosity beginning with material gifts, then the gift of fearless presence, and culminating in the gift of Dharma or Truth. What I aspire to give to the world in repayment for all it continues to give me is simply that Truth. What I am beginning to understand is that the truth is not a statement of religious fact but rather a level of participation in what is before us all the time. To stand with another and simply compassionately speak to the depths of what is present, even if it that is death, is to embody the truth of every religion. (2012, p. 658-659)

This distinguishes the work of the chaplain from that of the Dharma teacher, who may be called upon to actively teach the Buddhist version of that 'Truth' to others. Rather, chaplains embody our understanding of that truth in how we are present, and we continuously seek that truth in every moment that presents itself to us through our work with careseekers. We likewise empower careseekers to find and articulate their own fearless presence and their own wisdom or truth. While we can influence and accompany that process, we do not control it.

Leadership paradigms often operate with assumptions of power and control. The leader has power and is in control. The leader makes decisions that followers carry out. In the mid-twentieth century, many scholars and leaders realized that not only was this not always a good model for leadership, but it also wasn't realistic in many settings. Servant leadership was first described by Robert Greenleaf in the 1970s based on his work in Christian religious communities. He defined it simply:

> It begins with the natural feeling that one wants to serve, to serve first. Then conscious choice brings one to aspire to lead. The difference manifests itself in the care taken by the servant—first to make sure that other people's highest priority needs are being served. The best test is: Do those served grow as persons; do they, while being served, become healthier, wiser, freer, more autonomous, more likely themselves to become servants?[1]

By becoming servants, we also become leaders. The goal of servant leadership is ultimately to make the leader obsolete by transforming and empowering those served to be able to achieve their own goals without the leader. This is the same goal as that of a teacher or a chaplain – ultimately to make themselves unnecessary to the continued health, functioning, learning, and growth of those served.

Over the last fifty years, servant leadership has been studied and documented in numerous contexts, from for-profit companies like Home Depot and Southwest Airlines to non-profit and religious settings. Roberts and Hess-Hernandez review 29 separate theories of servant leadership for their article "Servant Leadership Behavior: Leadership Development Implications" (2018, p. 371-375). The authors derived five primary dimensions of servant leadership attributes from their overview of the literature including: servanthood motivation, stewardship

---

[1] Greenleaf, p. 4, quoted in Barbuto & Wheeler, 2006, p. 301.

mission, character, reasoning abilities, and spirituality. Barbuto and Wheeler examined many of these same theories in their development of a Servant Leadership Questionnaire, condensing 11 original dimensions (calling, listening, empathy, healing, awareness, persuasion, conceptualization, foresight, stewardship, growth, and community building) into a five-part measurable scale including altruistic calling, emotional healing, wisdom, persuasive mapping, and organizational stewardship. Many of the terms used in describing these dimensions sound like the attributes of a chaplain (Buddhist or otherwise). Servant leadership has been positively associated with both the role of a chaplain and that of a Buddhist leader.

The literature on Buddhist leadership likewise coalesces around a series of similar leadership dimensions, some representing personal attributes and others representing behaviors. They include moral and ethical excellence (Thanissaro); mental and emotional self-discipline, knowing oneself (Sriburin); warning against being a leader while spiritually immature; spiritual attainment (Thanissaro) and spiritual 'experience' (Findly, Tsomo); altruism (Sriburin) such as via compassion and loving-kindness for the benefit of beings, kindness, compassion, and wisdom (Tsomo); ability to teach the Dharma (Sriburin), expertise in Dharma (Thanissaro), and competence (Findly, Tsomo); empowering others (Sriburin), being inspirational (Thanissaro), and the 'ability to inspire confidence' (Findly, Tsomo); ability to choose the 'proper' time for one's efforts (Sriburin), strategic view (Thanissaro), and knowing the community or organization (Sriburin, Thanissaro). This list can likewise be condensed into five primary dimensions: 1) spiritual and ethical maturity (relative to those served); 2) personal virtues grounded in altruistic motivations; 3) knowledge of and ability to share the Dharma; 4) ability to empower and inspire; 5) strategic vision and organizational competence. The characteristics of a servant leader correlate to most of these.

Empowering others is a key attribute of each conceptualization, which is captured under the term 'stewardship' in the secular studies of servant leadership. From Buddhism, Sriburin uses the example of the Buddha sending his 60 disciples out to share his teachings as an instance of empowerment. In so doing, the Buddha affirmed their ability and conferred a responsibility upon his disciples to benefit others. Committing to empowering careseekers is crucial because of, as Richard Coble and Mychal Springer note, the imbalance of power within institutions where chaplains work, including between chaplains and careseekers. Institutional, symbolic, moral, and religious authority is invested in the chaplain. Power confers simultaneous ability and responsibility. Chaplains must choose to use that power wisely and to influence others to do likewise. Coble and Spring write: "…the chaplain has the opportunity – and, in fact, the obligation – to empower the patient by reiterating the importance of her spiritual health and experience" (p. 174, in Cadge and Rambo) in the face of the ways institutions often disempower careseekers. Patients in healthcare can be disempowered by the behavior of doctors and other medical staff, who wield great expertise and authority in medical

Roberts & Hess-Hernandez's Dimensions	Barbuto & Wheeler's Dimensions	Buddhist Leadership Dimensions
spirituality	altruistic calling	spiritual and ethical maturity
servanthood motivation	emotional healing	personal virtues & altruistic motivation
character	wisdom	know & teach Dharma
reasoning abilities	persuasive mapping	empower & inspire
stewardship mission	organizational stewardship	strategic vision
		organizational competence

settings, in addition to impersonal and often bureaucratic rules and policies. Prisoners are literally and legally disempowered in prisons and jails. Military members exist within a strictly codified hierarchical power structure with more of them at the bottom than the top. Students face disempowerment in educational institutions as the least educated, youngest, and often poorest members of the community, reliant on the good opinion of their teachers and supervisors to succeed. In many ways, those we primarily serve are the least empowered in any context where we serve. Sometimes our colleagues also suffer from disempowerment due to stratified hierarchies and burdensome bureaucracies that prevent them from doing their best work on behalf of careseekers.

Though we may not see ourselves as high on the 'food chain' of our organizations, we are nevertheless invested with a certain amount of power that we are obligated to use and, whenever possible, to give away to others who need it most – thus fulfilling another act of *dāna* or generosity. One of the ways we can do that is simply by recognizing the importance of careseeker's spiritual, religious, philosophical, moral, and existential dilemmas and concerns. By giving focused attention to this area of their experience, we legitimate it to the careseeker, our colleagues, and the institution. Using our skills and expertise to give language, voice, time, energy, and space (sometimes literally through the management of chapels) to spiritual concerns, we empower others who want to take these concerns seriously but may hesitate because it was 'not my job.' We model, for our colleagues and institutions, a wise, compassionate, and generous presence wherein giving power to others does not in the least diminish our own power, but rather magnifies the ability of each person to live into their best self. Thus, we fulfil the model of servant leadership and its call for all people to be both servants and leaders. We also fulfil the Buddha's charge to his 60 disciples, our many-generations-past-great Dharma grandparents.

7
Part I Conclusion & Reflection

Conclusion

Start by showing up. Then listen. Then care. Because you care, you are obligated to learn. Develop your expertise and use it to better understand where people are, where they want to go, and how to get there. Respect them and also respect yourself. Recognize and use your ability to serve, lead, and empower others. That's the gist of it. Like so many other things in life, simple rarely means easy.

When working with new chaplains, some anxieties surface repeatedly:

- "The amount of suffering the world scares me. How am I supposed to do anything useful at all?"
- "What if I say or do the wrong thing?"
- "I have no idea what this person is going through. How could I possibly help?"
- "Who am I to think I know what is good for this person?"
- "I'm so tired and yet there is so much I still need to do. How do I carry on?"
- "I'm not special. I don't have 'authority.' How can I be a leader?"

Knowledge can be conveyed, skills can be learned, wisdom can be developed. We can study texts, sample practices, meditate for days, go to workshops, learn conflict mediation and how to identify trauma and family systems theories. We can practice what we will do and say in role playing with our peers and pour over case studies full of heartrending examples. But there are two things in the education of a chaplain that cannot be rushed. They take the time they take. And the two are interrelated. They are spiritual formation and spiritual authority. This volume of pragmatic skills has not focused on these very much, though I hope both have appeared as a subtext. Spiritual authority is part of spiritual leadership, discussed in the prior chapter. It is largely predicated on spiritual formation of the chaplain. Volume I of this series provides an overview of the stages of spiritual formation of a chaplain, from self to student to chaplain and, ultimately, to kalyāṇamitra. Yet Volume I is primarily a descriptive work (I state that it may be prescriptive, but more research needs to be done). Throughout both volumes, I urge readers to seek communities, sanghas, teachers, and their own kalyāṇamitra – this is the ground where spiritual formation takes place. Yes, it can also happen in the curriculum of a certificate or degree program, but coursework is a limited substitute for community. Some programs (See Upaya Zen Center or Maitripa College) act more like full Buddhist communities than others (See Harvard Divinity School or University of the West). All have their merits.

Prioritize your own spiritual formation, which involves transformation of the whole person through: 1) religious practices; 2) intellectual study and knowledge building; and 3) relationships. First, religious practices in Buddhism often (but not always) involve contemplative practices, particularly meditation. Some Buddhist lineages, such as Chan, Zen, and Insight, start with meditation, while others may build up to it following preliminary practices such as giving, precepts, study, chanting, and prostrations (the later two can also be done in a contemplative fashion). Pure Land traditions may de-emphasize meditation in favor of devotion, prayer, and recitation, yet contemplation is not entirely absent there either. The purpose of all such religious practices is to establish discipline, tame the mind, and develop focus. This corresponds to Right Mindfulness and Right Concentration on the Noble Eightfold Path. Buddhist chaplain training programs may do this through coursework, practicums, or co-curricular offerings. In most cases, the expectation is that these programs build or supplement, but do not replace, a personal practice commitment.

Second, spiritual formation is intellectual and involves the acquisition and integration of knowledge, including the study of Buddhism and secular topics relevant to caregiving. Buddhism includes an entire genre of literature on spiritual formation, though it does not use that term. Rather, it uses am emic Buddhist term: path or *magga* or *marga*. The Eightfold Path in Pali is *Atthangika-magga* and in Sanskrit it is *Astangika-marga*. The path can be found in the words of the Buddha starting with his very first *sutta* (*Dhammacakkappavattana Sutta*, SN56.11), wherein he explicitly listed the spokes of the Eightfold Path, to his final words (*Maha-parinibbana Sutta*, DN16), wherein he described factors of enlightenment and the fruits of a moral life, among many other topics. The path has been the topic (and title) of numerous foundational commentaries, such as the *Path of Purification* by Buddhaghosa, the *Lamp for the Path to Enlightenment* by Atiśa, *Advice for Travelers on the Bodhisattva Path* by Candrakīrti, *Letter to a Friend* by Nāgārjuna, *The Way of the Bodhisattva* by Śāntideva, the Oxherding pictures and their numerous commentaries in Chan and Zen Buddhism, *On the Endeavor of the Way* by Dōgen, and the entire lamrim genre in Tibetan Buddhism, notably *The Great Treatise on the Stages of the Path to Enlightenment* by Tsongkhapa and *The Jewel Ornament of Liberation* by Gampopa. All these works have now been translated into English along with numerous classical and modern commentaries. Oxford Bibliographies has produced a helpful overview article on "*Mārga* (Path)" by Pierre-Julien Harter, last updated in 2021, that lists these works and many more.[1] Path texts provide not just practical instructions for the formation of students within their lineages, but also an overview of the path with its theoretical, ethical, psychological, and philosophical foundations. Many quote extensively from earlier works, establishing a line of thought going back hundreds or thousands of years, and many are in direct conversation with one another and other lineages of Buddhism, though they may be separated by centuries and continents.

Modern path literature is still being produced, in such works as *A Path with Heart*, by Jack Kornfield, chapter "VII. The Path to Liberation" in *In the Buddha's Words* by Bhikkhu Bodhi, several chapters in *Black and Buddhist* edited by Cheryl Giles and Pamela Ayo Yetunde, *Lectures on the Ten Oxherding Pictures* by Yamada Mumon Roshi, parts of *The Three Pillars of Zen* by Philip Kapleau Roshi (particularly the Oxherding pictures and the enlightenment letters), *Untangled* by Koshin Paley Ellison, *Be the Refuge* by Chenxing Han, and *Dreaming Me* by Jan Willis, just to name a few. Some of the modern literature takes on the tone of memoir or autobiography not seen in the classical texts, yet nonetheless narrates a path experience that can be even more compelling for its personal nature. In a course I taught at Harvard Divinity School in 2023, we examined the classical path literature side-by-side with the modern works. Students found reading the two together to be far more illustrative than reading either alone. Within the course, we also 'sampled' various religious practices described in the texts. Along with other forms of study, having intellectual knowledge of the path itself can prove catalytic to transformative religious practices. Several students were inspired to seek out local Buddhist communities that could support ongoing practice, which brings us to the final aspect of spiritual formation – relational.

---

1   DOI: 10.1093/OBO/9780195393521-0242 or go to oxfordbibliographies.com

Third, despite the romanticism of the lone wandering ascetic or solitary cave dweller, most spiritual formation in Buddhist happens in and through the relationships one develops with ones' teachers and fellow students. The role and relationships of *kalyāṇamitra* have already been extensively covered in Volume I, so here I shall more directly consider the teacher-student relationship relying on advice from one of the path texts mentioned above (and in Chapter 6), *The Great Treatise on the Stages to the Path to Enlightenment* by Tsongkhapa (also known as the *Lamrim Chenmo*).

Tsongkhapa's *Great Treatise* is explicit about the qualities one should expect to find in a person capable of teaching the Dharma to others. It lists ten qualities in Chapter 4 "Relying on the Teacher." These are:
1. Disciplined
2. Serene
3. Thoroughly pacified
4. Surpasses one's students
5. Energetic
6. Knowledge of scripture
7. Loving concern
8. Knowledge of reality / selflessness
9. Skill in instruction
10. Not dispirited

The text then goes on to further explain these qualities:

> With respect to what Maitreya said, "disciplined" refers to the training in ethical discipline. ...
>
> "Serene" refers to having accomplished the training of meditative concentration. Meditative concentration is a mental state in which the mind remains peacefully withdrawn. This is achieved by means of a reliance on mindfulness and vigilance in your ethical discipline, turning away from wrongdoing and engaging in good activities.
>
> "Thoroughly pacified" refers to having accomplished the training of wisdom. This is done by specifically analyzing the meaning of reality in dependence on meditative serenity, wherein the mind becomes serviceable. (p. 71-72)

We can see a clear connection between the definitions of these first three qualities and the three-fold categories of the aspects of the Noble Eightfold Path: moral discipline (*sila*), meditation (*samadhi*) and wisdom (*prajñā*). Before one can teach, one must first follow the Eightfold Path. Tsongkhapa explains the most important prerequisite for one who is going to teach the Dharma:

> This is a great instruction. You will not transform your mind without being certain about this. Without that certainty, no matter how extensively you explain the profound teachings, these very teachings often serve to assist your afflictions, like a helpful deity becomes a demon. (p. 67)

What afflictions are they talking about here? Principally pride. We can become very proud of our own knowledge and the work we have put in to attain it. This can manifest as arrogance. We have all probably experienced bad teachers at some point in our lives. The arrogant or egotistical ones can be some of the worst. Teachers are not free of afflictions until and unless they attain full enlightenment. Until that time, these afflictions can manifest in our motivation and methods for teaching, as well as other areas of our lives. Tsongkhapa provides instructions for things teachers should contemplate before delivering a teaching to serve as an antidote to some of these afflictions, only some of which are described later in this lecture. Then he continues to explain the prerequisites:

> ...Thus, those with intelligence should work at this way of successfully

hearing and explaining the teachings and should have at least a portion of these qualifications every time that they explain or listen to the teachings. This is the most important prerequisite for teaching these instruction. (p. 67)

How far along you are in your own practice and what 'portion of qualifications' you possess before beginning to teach is determined largely by your audience. Who are you teaching? Elementary science teachers don't need a strong grasp of quantum physics, but college physics professors certainly do. But both teachers should have some grasp of the subject matter through their own experience.

However, practicing the Dharma is not the same as being able to teach the Dharma. Without practice, no teaching is possible at all. Yet, while some amount of spiritual attainment is the prerequisite, it is not itself sufficient to make a great teacher.

Some aspects in the above list of ten qualities are good to obtain for oneself, including discipline, serenity, pacification, knowledge of scripture, knowledge of selflessness, and the quality of surpassing one's own students. The remaining four aspects are what make one qualified to teach: 5) that one is energetic and delights in others' welfare and learning; 7) a pure motivation free from personal gain that is rooted in loving concern for one's students; 9) skill in instruction that enables others to understand; and 10) that one never becomes dispirited or tires of repeating the Dharma to answer students' endless questions. Qualities 5, 7, and 10 all have the characteristics of altruism. Quality 9 affirms that teaching is a skill to be learned and an altruistic teacher will make the effort to attain it through the study of pedagogy and curriculum design. Tsongkahapa advises teachers to

> Cultivate love for those who have gathered to listen. Give up jealousy that fears the superiority of others; the laziness of procrastination; the dispiritedness of being tired due to explaining something again and again; praising yourself and listing the faults of others; stinginess with regard to explaining the teachings; and concern for material things such as food and clothing. Then think, 'Just this merit from teaching in order that others and I attain buddhahood is a favorable condition for my happiness. (p. 64)

Tsongkapa describes how the merit from teaching is conducive to our happiness as teachers. I myself can vouch for this. Teaching is my favorite part of my job. I am never happier or more energized than when I am teaching, even in tough classes with lots of critical students. That work makes me a better scholar, person, and practitioner. Of course, Tsongkhapa is writing for a very different audience, though his advice remains relevant today.

The Tibetan tradition is notable for the emphasis it places on the role of the guru in the student-teacher relationship. In recent years, many highly publicized abuse scandals have made us wary of the risks of such relationships. In his book *Wise Teacher, Wise Student* (2000), Alexander Berzin explores some of the reasons this happened and how Buddhist teachings can be used as resources to prevent and rectify such situations in the future. We must remember that texts such as *The Great Treatise* were intended for fifteenth century Tibetan monastics (mostly monks) who were studying under a learned master as part of an advanced curriculum. Yet, even in Tsongkhapa's time the faults of teachers were recognized and *The Great Treatise* deals with them directly. Part of Tsongkhapa's text is dedicated to questions and answers, anticipating objections to descriptions of teachers that seem too perfect on paper and not feasible in real life. One such question is about how much one should compromise if one finds a teacher who has most, but not all of the ten qualities.

> The guru who helps you to achieve liberation is the foundation of your deepest aspiration. Therefore, you who wish to rely a guru should understand these defining characteristics and strive to seek one who has them. …Therefore, accept as the defining characteristics of a guru a minimum of one eighth of all the defining characteristics set forth here, combining those that are easy to acquire with those that are difficult to acquire. (p. 74-75)

Even highly realized masters are still human beings and, short of reaching enlightenment, remain imperfect and subject to afflictions. Nevertheless, they deserve the respect and gratitude of students.

Does this mean we should meekly accept the imperfections of our teachers? On the contrary, Tsongkhapa emphasizes how the student-teacher relationship relies on the judgement of both the teacher and the student for its success. Students do not abdicate their discernment or moral responsibility to their teachers. The devotion that Tsonkhapa's student should show to their teacher is quite different from the attitude we in the west have towards teachers in general and even towards spiritual teachers. The passages in *The Great Treatise* can be startling to read and most of us will probably see the potential for abuse created through the extreme reverence of teachers, who are treated as the personification of the perfect enlightened buddha. The attitude towards one's teacher is, in effect, more about training the mind of the student to let go of egoic preoccupation and surrender fully to the spiritual practice, than it is about the teacher themselves. Just as the attention towards the breath in meditation is about training the mind, not about anything particularly special in the breath. Part of the efficacy of this attitude is that it serves to make one receptive to the teachings.

However, Tsongkhapa also balances this reverence with realism. The responsibilities of the teacher towards the students are extensive and clearly laid out. This advice is important for both teachers and students to know. Teachers should demonstrate four consistent behaviors. First, they should show generosity by giving material things. This responsibly comes from a period in which students lived in their teachers' households, where they were also clothed and fed. This may be less relevant in modern times, but teachers should continue to show care for their students' material welfare. Second, teachers should use pleasing speech to arouse interest and faith. There are two types of pleasing speech, including "worldly customs," wherein the teacher must be polite, caring, and inquire after the welfare of students (disrespect and verbal abuse should not be tolerated); and speech that presents the Dharma for students' benefit. It is the students' comprehension that defines the quality of the lecture, so no teacher can get away with blaming the student for failure to grasp material poorly explained. Fourth, the teacher should set students to "work the aims" (aka practices) appropriate to their level that they can accomplish. This, of course, means the teacher also has to be able to discern the students' spiritual level and what practices are appropriate for their particular circumstances.

Setting a task that is too easy will create complacency and disinterest. Setting a task that is too difficult will create frustration and lead to giving up. To set an appropriate task, they must know each student quite well. Finally, teachers must behave consistently to serve as a role model. To do this, they must stay one step ahead of their students in their own spiritual practice. *The Great Treatise* demonstrates responsibilities teachers must fulfil towards their students if they truly want them to succeed. An effective and sufficiently practiced teacher will be fully capable of behaving in these ways. Abusive teachers, while they clearly do occur, betray these responsibilities.

When does one begin a student-teacher relationship? According to Tsongkhapa, students should observe the teacher for a long time, looking for the right qualities in them before committing to becoming a disciple. A qualified teacher will be unconcerned by this and encourage students to observe for as long as necessary to feel comfortable or choose a different teacher who may be better suited to their needs. Likewise, the teacher must assess the student to ensure they are ready before becoming a spiritual mentor. The teacher must be certain the student understands what mentorship entails and that they (the teacher) have the right qualities to support this particular student. Abuses and misunderstandings occur when these things are not done. Berzin provides a commentary on when one should become a student in a dedicated mentor-disciple relationship. Despite the characterization of the relationship as the "root of the path," it does not need to be the first step in one's spiritual journey, according to Berzin. In fact, it is better if the student arrives with some level of knowledge and maturity and takes time to evaluate the potential teacher before committing to such a relationship.

> ...before building a relationship with a spiritual mentor, seekers need to recognize and acknowledge the suffering in their lives and to develop the wish to overcome it. In other words, they need a rudimentary level of 'renunciation.' In addition, they need knowledge of the Buddha's teachings about what to practice and what to avoid in order to reduce and eliminate the suffering they wish to overcome. Only then are seekers ready to establish a serious relationship with a spiritual mentor, to help them achieve their goals.
>
> ...seekers also need initial interest in becoming Buddhas for everyone's sake.
>
> ...developing a Mahayana motivation of bodhichitta presumes at least a beginning level of safe direction (refuge) in the Buddhas, the Dharma, and the highly realized Sangha community.
>
> ...for the necessity and propriety of taking safe direction and developing bodhicitta before establishing a disciple-mentor relationship.
> (p. 34-35)

It is acceptable for seekers to only understand these aims at an intellectual level to start, rather than at an experiential or 'visceral' level, as Berzin puts it. The deeper understanding will result from their practice with their mentor. Berzin also writes that is important to set realistic expectations for this relationship and, for Westerners in particular, to understand that your teacher is not your therapist. He outlines several key differences, largely around how personal problems are dealt with (or not) within the student-teacher relationship and advises that one should only seek out a spiritual mentor when one is already emotionally mature and psychologically stable. Seeking a teacher to help one "fix" intractable personal problems is not advisable. One should choose a role model one strives to emulate to fundamentally transform one's life, including on an ethical level. Students retain their moral agency. Tsongkhapa also clearly states that students should not commit transgressions even if their teachers instruct them to do so. Allegiance to a teacher does not supersede one's own judgement or responsibility.

Once you have found a good teacher, then you should show the kind of respect and receptivity Tsongkhapa describes in Chapter 5 of *The Great Treatise*. Respect has three aspects. First, we recognize that the teachings are rare and beneficial because they lead to wisdom and liberation. This generates a sense of gratitude and willingness in the student. Second, we follow the practice instructions without arguing.

(I am not very good at this one.) Third, we do not look for excuses to disrespect the teacher, such as lapses in discipline or poor appearance. Receptivity is described using two metaphors, the first being the metaphor of the pot which was also conveyed in Chapter 2 of this volume on listening skills. Do not listen like an upside-down pot by not paying attention. Do not listen like a dirty pot with a bad motivation that leads to misunderstandings. And do not listen like a leaky pot that forgets everything it hears before putting it into practice. The second metaphor is that of the sick person who listens to their doctor without arguing, cherishes the medicine their doctor provides, and follows the doctor's orders completely. This is how a student remains receptive to a teacher. We should enter into student-teacher relationships with our eyes open, knowing what the guidelines say, understanding the criteria, and also watching for the exceptions, taking on the responsibility to use our own judgement and the responsibility for our choice when to rely on the teacher's judgement.

As Buddhist chaplains, we will probably have multiple student-teacher relationships. One of those may be the kind of mentor-disciple relationship that Tsongkhapa and Berzin describe, though this is not a universal feature of all Buddhist traditions. We may be fortunate to know and learn from many different Buddhist teachers, both within face-to-face relationships and from sources like public talks, books, articles, podcasts, and videos. We will also likely have teachers in the formal contexts of classroom education, either in higher education or some kind of certificate or workshop program, where we learn spiritual care and other chaplaincy skills. Chaplains' relationships with teachers are often bifurcated in this way, between the teachers of their personal practice lineage on the one hand and their chaplaincy or academic teachers on the other. Some chaplaincy training programs attempt to integrate the two, while others establish clear boundaries between them. The student-teacher relationship comes with very different expectation in either instance (Buddhist or academic), yet relationships in both contexts are an important aspect of one's spiritual formation and should be recognized as such. Chaplains' academic teachers may not acknowledge, understand, or even want a role in the spiritual formation of their students, especially if they are teaching on some clearly defined subject or discipline, such as history or textual study. Meanwhile, chaplains' teachers in the traditional Buddhist context may not feel a great deal of responsibility for their student's spiritual formation but struggle to grasp its relationship to work as a chaplain, with which they may be unfamiliar. The student should carefully discern how each type of teacher can and does (whether the teacher wants to or not) affect their spiritual formation (often positively, but sometimes negatively). Critically, students should seek out those teachers clearly interested in and able to supporting their spiritual formation. Just as Tsongkhapa advised that spiritual formation is the prerequisite of any teacher, it is also the prerequisite of any chaplain.

Reflections Questions for Chapters 1 to 6

1. Was there a time when you noticed a habitual pattern that you have as it was happening and were able to reflexively observe your own internal response and outward behavior? If so, what was that like? What insight, if any, did you gain from your experience? How did that subsequently affect future experiences or behaviors? If this has never happened, can you imagine what it might be like? Describe it.
2. Can you remember a time when you felt truly heard or witnessed? Think back, consider the first time you might have experienced this as a child or a young adult. What was that experience like? Who were you with? How was different and why does it stand out in your memory?

What happened after that experience?
3. Think back to a time when you felt like you connected with someone on a deep emotional or spiritual level. How well do you feel you understood one another in that moment? What made you think or feel that way? What did the other person say or do that resonated with you and vice versa? Do you feel like the other person felt a similar connection to you and, if so, why? What was it, for both of you, that made that moment possible? What effects did that moment have on your future relationship with that person and on your own life (and the other person's, if you know)?
4. Go to the Sustainable Compassion Training website – sustainablecompassion.org – and select a guided meditation under the audio, video, or text section of the website. How does this meditation resonate with you (or not)? Do you experience resistance to it and, if so, why do you think that is? Where is that resistance rooted? How easy (or difficult) is it to generate the felt sense of compassion or loving kindness? What is your 'doorway' into these feelings?[2]
5. Using the Buddhist Spiritual Assessment outline, write a spiritual assessment of yourself. Choose a troublesome topic or problem in your life and describe the nature of that dukkha, the causes as understood through the lens of the three unwholesome roots, what an ideal outcome would look like, and some ways you could achieve that outcome. Then consider, was this process helpful for you? Did you gain any new insights into your situation or see new potential courses of action? Why or why not? If you had to do it again, what would you change about this assessment model?
6. Using the taxonomy for chaplain activities in Chapter 4, write a brief 'chart note' of a recent interaction or conversation with someone. It does not necessarily need to be a caregiving interaction. How might you summarize that interaction in a sentence or two? If none of the items on the taxonomy apply, feel free to make up your own, such as "told a joke" or "exchanged sports scores" or "updated project timeline." How succinct can you be without losing too much detail? What details can be omitted while still conveying essential and actionable information to a third party? It may be useful to write your note and then start crossing out sections until you arrive at the essential information.
7. Consider a time when you felt like your personal or professional boundaries were transgressed. Consider how you had communicated (or not) your boundary and the action you would take in relation to it? Did you follow through on those actions? Why or why not? How did that experience affect you physically and emotionally? How did it affect your life or work? What did it take to recover or regroup from that experience? What did you learn as a result? Would you do anything differently now and, if so, what?
8. To whom are you accountable? To what organizations, institutions, communities, or individuals are you accountable and in what concrete ways do you enact or express this accountability? Consider drawing this as a mind-map or chart. How does that accountability feel, either positively or negatively (or mixed)? Does it help or hinder your work and spiritual growth and how so? What would be an ideal and supportive system of accountability for you, in your view? How is that different from your present situation?
9. How do you see yourself as a leader,

---

2   The Center for Mindful Self-Compassion also offers a number of guided meditations that may also be useful for this exercise at centerformsc.org.

if at all? How have you been a leader in the past, if at all, and how is that related to your work as a chaplain? Does being a leader feel comfortable or uncomfortable and why? How might you, as a chaplain, relate to other leaders within your organization? How might you 'lead' people over whom you have no direct authority (or who technically have authority over you?
10. What is your source(s) of spiritual 'authority'? Consider carefully where you feel a deep sense of confidence or stability or refuge? Where is that foundation and how do you feel when you stand rooted there? When and where do you feel confident (if at all) using your authority? Can you think of a time when you were the expert and were able to use that expertise to help someone? What was that like? What is it like when this 'authority' is challenged or rejected? How does it affect you and how do you respond (skillfully and unskillfully)? How can you embody your authority in a way that serves as a place of refuge for both yourself and others, even if they don't recognize or accept that authority?

Listening & Responding Exercises

The following exercises are intended to help readers practice the responses in Table 1.1 in Chapter 2. They are best done with a partner or, better yet, in a triad. Each group assigns the following roles:
- **Speaker**: the speaker will respond to the prompt below either from their own personal experience or as part of a role play in which then invent a scenario (the latter is recommended when material may elicit a strong emotional response not appropriate to a classroom setting)
- **Responder**: the responder will listen to, watch, and observe the speaker and then reply using one of the assigned response types from Table 1.1 (this may include 'silence,' and, in such a scenario, consider how you are nevertheless communicating using body language, facial expression, eye contact, etc.); two rules guide this exercise:
  o Do not attempt to come up with your response in advance; listen only while the speaker is speaking, with your full attention
  o When you respond pay attention to a) how the speaker reacts to your reply and b) how you feel internally about your reply
- **Observer**: (optional, but encouraged) the observer observes both the speaker and the responder throughout the entire exercise, including what is said, tone, body language, facial expression, etc.; the purpose of the observer is not to judge either the speaker or responder or offer advice on what they should or should not say or do, only to share what they have observed with both at the conclusion of the exercise. For example, it may be helpful to use the following prompts:
  o "When the speaker said X, I observed that the responder reacted by [smiling, frowning, glancing down, etc.]"
  o "When the responder said Y, I observed that the speaker reacted by [crossing their arms, nodding, relaxing their shoulders, etc.]"
  o "When the speaker said X, they sounded [afraid, angry, questioning, happy, etc.]"
  o "When the responder asked Y question, it made me wonder [had they had a similar experience?; did they understand the term the speaker used?; etc.]

Once roles are assigned and understood, choose among the prompts below for a scenario and then select a response type to practice. Remember, that the responder should reply to the speaker only using the response type being practiced. If there is an observer, they may note when the responder deviates for the sake of the learning exercise. (Such as, "You were practicing asking questions, and you did so three times. Then I noticed when you said X, it sounded more like a statement than a question.") Once you begin the exercise:

1. The speaker shares based on the scenario prompt
2. The responder replies based on the response type
3. The observer shares based on what they have observed: body language and facial expressions, perception of emotions in each party, connecting thoughts and ideas (skip if there is no observer)
4. The speaker shares how they internally reacted to the responder's reply in this order: bodily sensations, feelings or emotions, thoughts and ideas, questions (to be shared, but not immediately answered)
5. The responder shares how they internally reacted to the speaker's initial sharing: bodily sensations, feelings or emotions, thoughts and ideas, questions (to be shared, but not immediately answered)
6. The observer then poses one question to the speaker (their own or from the respondent) to answer and one question to the respondent to answer (their own or from the speaker)
7. The group may then engage in more natural dialogue to learn more or seek to answer each other's questions

Finally, after each exercise, it may be useful to reflect either privately or with your group about not just the type of response you used, but it's ultimate goal. Recall the six purposes of a spiritual care response described in Chapter 2. What is the purpose of your response: 1) witnessing; 2) empathizing; 3) supporting; 4) understanding; 5) assessing; and 6) advising? Some combination of these? What does the speaker need at this moment? Discussing this with your group can be fruitful, because the speaker, responder, and observer may all come to different conclusions. And each could be right! There is often no one 'right' way to respond. What the speaker thinks they needed at the outset may be very different from what actually helps. Or they could offer the responder an important correction. A responder with a different set of life experiences may be able to bring that discernment to the conversation that the speaker appreciates even if they could not have predicted. The observer may notice things that neither the speaker nor the responder perceived. This conversation can be very enriching.

Servant Leadership Questionnaire

The Servant Leadership Questionnaire (SLQ) was developed by Barbuto and Wheeler in 2006. It involves a self-assessment and rating by two or more people familiar with your leadership behaviors, particularly people who work with you or whom you directly supervise.[3] The questionnaire measures five scales:

- **Altruistic calling**: deeply motivated to serve others, placing others' needs ahead of their own, and being willing to work hard and sacrifice to help others
- **Emotional healing**: sensitive to the emotional needs of others, trusted by others in times of distress and trauma, capable of helping others process and heal on an emotional level
- **Wisdom**: perceptive about what is happening in a given situation, able to understand cause and effect and predict the consequences of actions, able to realistically assess future possibilities and likelihoods

---

[3] You can download this open-access questionnaire for free at https://training.hr.ufl.edu/cxuf/2021/presentations/day-2/2.2.5_ServingGatorNation_Handout.pdf or by searching for "Servant Leadership Questionnaire" in your browser search bar.

- **Persuasive mapping**: able to inspire and persuade others to pursue a compelling vision for themselves and the organization or community to which they belong
- **Organizational stewardship**: believes that the organization or community to which they belong has a moral obligation to contribute to society, able to build community, and moves others to make a positive difference

Complete and score the self-assessment. Does your score on any of the scales surprise you? Why is that? Ask a couple of friends, classmates you have worked closely with, coworkers, or people whom you supervise to complete the rater forms. Consider asking several people to do so and submit them anonymously, such as by leaving forms in an accessible location and accepting paper returns in your mailbox. Score the rater forms. Does your score on any of the scales differ significantly from your self-assessment? If so, why do you think that is? Be aware the developers of this questionnaire found that leaders often rate themselves higher than others did in relation to altruistic calling (perhaps because only they can truly know their own motivations?), while rating themselves slightly lower than others on all other factors, on average (though there was significant variation across their original sample of ten leaders).[4]

---

[4] For more information see: Barbuto, John E. and Wheeler, Daniel W., "Scale Development and Construct Clarification of Servant Leadership" (2006). Faculty Publications: Agricultural Leadership, Education & Communication Department. 51. https://digitalcommons.unl.edu/aglecfacpub/51

Scenario (for Speaker)	Response (from Respondent)
Grief: Your loved one has just died after a protracted illness. You feel sad that they are gone, but glad they are no longer suffering. You also feel conflicted and guilty about these feelings.	**Silence**: No verbal responses; maintain a calm and open affect
Fear: You have received a diagnosis of a life-threatening illness. It is treatable, but the treatment is long and arduous. Most people recover, but many do not. You are afraid not just for yourself, but for your family, which includes young children. You have always had ambiguous ideas about what happens after death, but now you feel like you urgently need to know one way or another.	**Nonverbal Cues**: Use facial expressions and body language to signal openness, interest, curiosity, concern, and empathy; practice non-verbal ways to prompt the speaker to continue sharing
Frustration: You have been working for a company for six months and you feel like your boss and coworkers don't really care about your ideas. Sometimes they interrupt or ignore your contributions in meetings. You're frustrated and don't know what to do about it. You're trying to respond ethically, but worry you might lose your cool.	**Restating**: Repeating the careseeker's words verbatim; can be used immediately after or by repeating a key phrase later in the conversation
Conflict: You have received a job offer in another state. Your significant other of five years does not want to move, even though they recognize this could be good for your career. They work remotely and can live wherever they like, but have never their home city before, while you have moved several times. You are frustrated and angry while also trying to understand and reassure them.	**Rephrasing**: Simplest form of interpretation; summarizing in one's own words particularly to identify underlying feelings, meanings, issues, and needs
Depression: Over the last year you have lost interest in everything. You have a hard time getting out of bed and frequently skip classes or work. The future seems so bleak you wonder if anything is worth the effort anymore. You are starting to think life really doesn't have any meaning or purpose.	**Clarifying Feelings**: Clarify for feelings; look for "emotional doorways" and check for understanding; inquire about feelings when careseekers neglect emotions in favor of facts; use their terms for their emotions if given
Dread: You have been dating someone for six months and it is going very well. However, you recently had your first argument. You have had several bad relationships, including abusive ones, in the past and you start to worry this one will also turn out bad. You feel yourself starting to pull away and are torn between love, shame, and fear.	**Reframing**: Reinterpret to help careseekers clarify, provide language and terms, see their situation differently, or become away of new options and choices
Transcendence: Last week you went camping with your friends. Late at night, you went out to see the stars and were filled with this overwhelming feeling of joy and connection you can barely describe. It only lasted a few minutes, but it's changed how you see everything in your life and has you asking some hard questions. You don't know what it was or what do to about it, but you have a strong sense that it was good.	**Inquiry**: Respond only with questions ranging from conversation starters, to clarifying questions, to inquiries about feelings, beliefs, behaviors, meanings, or events
Questioning: You were raised in a conservative religious tradition you never questioned before and usually enjoyed. Since you have moved away for college, you are meeting all kinds of different people. They've asked you some questions about your tradition you don't feel you can answer very well. You've started to wonder if your tradition really makes much sense at all and you feel guilty and ashamed, but you can't stop thinking about it.	**Relating**: Make connections between the careseeker's situation and stories, scripture, traditions, psychological tools, or with the chaplain through self-disclosure
Choices: You've had a fulfilling career and you're ready to retire from your current job, but you don't really feel like you're 'done' yet. You can't imagine just relaxing all day or travelling. You want to do something useful and fulfilling while you're still healthy and able, but there are so many good things you could do, you're having a hard time deciding what that should be.	**Counseling**: Help resolve personal, social, psychological, spiritual, or religious difficulties through directed problem-solving techniques; attempt to apply an approach you have learned or seen done elsewhere, such as from our traditions (e.g., pastoral counseling, spiritual direction, dokusan, etc.) or from social sciences (e.g., brief solution-focused therapy, cognitive behavioral therapy, mindfulness-based stress reduction, etc.)
Balance: You broke up with your long-term partner six months ago and since then, you know you've been drinking more than usual. Last night, you drove into a ditch on the way home. No one was hurt, but you scared yourself. You think you may need help but don't want anyone to find out because it could ruin your reputation and career.	**Directing**: Use your spiritual authority to make a clear request, suggestion, or directive

Note: The scenarios and responses above can explored line by line or mixed and matched. Or speakers can be given the freedom to invent a scenario of their own, to which the responder replies using a pre-defined response type.

Part II
Pragmatic Skills for Particular Contexts

PART II

INTRODUCTION

Every situation is different. It seems like an obvious thing to say, but how we ought to respond to those differences can often feel far from obvious, particularly for new chaplains. There are some things we want to bring to every situation, like presence and compassion. Another thing we need to bring is flexibility, willingness to learn, and a basic knowledge of what kinds of situations we may face and what some of our options are. That is where these chapters come in. Of course, they are not exhaustive. In fact, each chapter is just a starting point to begin considering a much broader topic.

The first prayer I ever offered in any capacity as a spiritual caregiver was for my professor who went into the hospital while I was still in my MDiv program. He was an Episcopal theologian, so I recited the Lord's Prayer, which I hadn't said in over a decade and yet still knew by heart from a childhood spent in the United Methodist Church. Sadly, the first ritual I organized was his memorial held a few weeks later at the university where he helped establish only the second MDiv program for Buddhist chaplains in North America (then; now there are a dozen or so). These two situations drove home the importance of prayer and ritual in my work as a chaplain and their power to affect those suffering from illness, death, and grief. After living most of my adult life devoid of prayer or ritual, this unanticipated reintroduction solidified my dedication to perfecting these skills. The first two chapters provide entry points for ritual and prayer in both Buddhist and interreligious contexts from two colleagues who likewise attended that too-soon memorial, Victor Gabriel and Nathan Jishin Michon. Gabriel helps us consider how prayer and ritual nurture both caregivers and careseekers and then provides a model for ritual prayer from the Tibetan Buddhist tradition. Michon describes the dynamics of interreligious ritual and prayer for Buddhist chaplains, including a consideration of how his own background (as, like me, a white American convert to Buddhism) influences his approach to prayer.

The following two chapters come from colleagues at the first educational program for Buddhist chaplains in Canada, which can be found at Emmanuel College of Victoria University within the University of Toronto. The Canadian context has important differences from the U.S. context even as the basic needs of careseekers remain very similar. Henry Shui begins with an overview of intercultural competencies important for anyone providing care within a multicultural society such as those found in Canada and the U.S., with increasingly diverse multi-generational immigrant populations as well as existing and marginalized indigenous groups. Linda Hochstetler, brings the lens of a dual-trained social worker and chaplain to her chapter on risk assessment and referral protocols for individuals facing mental illness or significant psychological distress from situations such as addiction or suicidality. In such cases, chaplains can function as part of an interdisciplinary care team comprised of psychological, spiritual, and medical professionals. In such cases, chaplains can function as part of an interdisciplinary care team comprised of psychological, spiritual, and medical professionals. Triaging for such concerns and making effective referrals was often part of my work as a college chaplain, including, when necessary, walking students over to the counseling center or supporting counseling staff during times of crisis, such as notifying a student far from home of a death in the family. Working as a team was critical to the support of careseekers during such situations. While not every careseeker needs mental health support, every chaplain will need to be able to identify warning signs and make referrals.

Finally, Chapter 12 concerns a topic that does affect almost every situation we find ourselves in as chaplains, sometimes in subtle ways and sometimes in obvious and infuriating ones. Racism, sexism, ableism, classism, homophobia, transphobia, religious prejudice, and other forms of oppression are endemic within modern society. Even when we as individuals strive to take anti-racist, anti-oppressive, and liberatory actions, we are often caught within structures and systems which perpetuate inequality in sneaky ways. The first step in addressing the unjust distribution of power within society is to recognize power dynamics, including the forms of privilege that we ourselves hold and the types of oppression to which we ourselves are subject. This chapter prompts chaplains to reflect on their own positionality within society using my own life as a case study, then provides some all-too-brief starting points for how to understand discrimination at multiple levels, and work towards social justice as inseparable aspects of spiritual care. Buddhist values, such as equanimity and compassion, demand our response to social inequality. At the same time, other Buddhist concepts, such as non-self and emptiness, have been used by some to spiritually bypass urgent work for social justice both within Buddhist communities and society as a whole. This chapter directs readers to a plethora of resources on these topics. As with every chapter in this section, it can serve as a starting place but certainly should not be the end of your education on these important topics.

8
Prayer & Ritual
by Victor Gabriel

Introduction

This chapter is about Buddhist prayer voiced by the Buddhist community, for the Buddhist care-seeker, and by the Buddhist chaplain. There are many ways that this chapter can be written, many different lens and voices that can be highlighted. I have decided upon a bricolage of lenses and voices centering on three issues: prayer as relevant to the Buddhist chaplain, prayer for an emic perspective, and the dynamics of prayer. The chapter will consider formal or informal Buddhist prayer. Readers wanting to read about interfaith prayer, for example, where prayer is requested by a non-Buddhist care-seeker of the Buddhist chaplain, are directed to read any of the resources listed in the breakout box near the beginning of this chapter. A breakout box at the end of the chapter contains resources for further information on topics related to Buddhist prayer.

At this juncture, it is helpful for me to reflect on my social location/intersectionality. I am a Tibetan Buddhist priest from a mixed ethnic (non-Tibetan) and religious background who grew up in Singapore. I lived mostly with my Asian grandparents who held formal Buddhist services twice a year at our home. I remember the excitement, the hustle and bustle associated with these services, the drone of the Theravāda monks, and the bell, drum and cymbals that accompanied the Chinese Mahāyāna monks' chants. I remember being taught to pray by my grand aunt (my grandmother's eldest sister) at the age of four. She knelt beside me, shaped my hands into a lotus and whispered into my ear. She told me to speak to the Buddha and our family dharma protector as I would a friend. I hope this chapter will convey to you the wonder, joy, contentment, fulfillment, and gratitude I have felt throughout my life journeying with prayer.

This chapter draws primarily upon my experience with Buddhist prayer, and my training/formation in the various lineages of the Tibetan Buddhist tradition. This chapter is not meant to be exhaustive or prescriptive. However, there will be places where I will consider the contributions of other Buddhist traditions and scholarship around prayer. I would have loved to cover Buddhist prayer more thoroughly within the three main divisions of Buddhism: Theravāda, Mahāyāna and Vajrayāna; with their major and minor regional traditions, for now this must remain a book project for the future.

Generally, this chapter is grounded upon the Religious Studies dictum of "Remembering the Past, Evaluating the Present and Envisioning the Future," which is part of the Standards of Accreditation for graduate theological degrees of the Association of Theological Schools. Occasionally, when we engage in this conversation around Buddhist prayer, we hear that chaplains of other religious traditions and even some Buddhist chaplains assume that since Buddhists do not have a creator being, there is no one to address prayer to, or that prayer has no place within Buddhism, or that prayer is useless. This chapter will explore the issues around to whom Buddhists address their prayer to, the place of prayer in Buddhism and the efficacy of prayer and healing.

This conversation about Buddhist prayer, may echo the discussion around the "Two Buddhisms" debate, that is, what is Asian Buddhism and what is Western Buddhism (Hickey, 2010, p. 1-25). This quick, messy and unnuanced categorization may assume that Asian Buddhists pray, and that Western Buddhists do not pray. The very definition of Asian Buddhists and Western Buddhists is itself challenging. Additionally, when we consider who is doing this classifying, the implicit and explicit bias that one kind of Buddhism is considered better or superior or more authentic to the other, then this categorization becomes alarmingly problematic (Cheah, 2011; Arai and Trainor, 2022).

This categorization centering the white colonial (Christian) gaze can prevent contemporary Buddhist chaplains from drawing upon the rich spiritual resources of their Buddhist past. This colonial gaze, often patriarchal and Protestant-normative has led to the valorization of monastic practice as more authentic than lay practice, meditation as more authentic than prayer and ritual; even though lay domestic practices emerged early in the Buddhist tradition. In this chapter, I hope to offer resources within our Buddhist past that can be of benefit to the contemporary Buddhist chaplain.

Prayer as Relevant to the Buddhist Chaplain

In this section, we consider how prayers fulfill the two benefits: for the benefit of self and other, here, for the benefit of the chaplain and their care-seeker. We will consider how prayers nurture the chaplain's spiritual health, and how prayers benefit others – the performance of private and public rituals and prayers.

For self: Nurturing the Chaplain

The tone of this section will differ from the previous sections; in this section I will take a more informal and collegial tone. I will highlight three simple practices that nurture the Buddhist chaplain from among the many that different Buddhist traditions can emphasize. These three are: setting a motivation, rejoicing/aspiration, and dedicating merit. I will also introduce a short prayer for the Buddhist chaplain.

The practices that follow are not prescriptive but derived from the teachings of various Buddhist masters. You are encouraged to modify them to suit your circumstances. If you are not familiar with these practices in your daily life, I invite you to try these prayer exercises for 40 days. If you happen to encounter a break in the 40 days, just resume the practice. Decide how long you will pray/practice each day. Dzongsar Khyentse Rinpoche, in *Not for Happiness*, recommends that lay persons practice two hours a day in various contemplative practices including prayer (2012, p. 44-46). Decide what time is conducive for you to pray. You may prefer to practice earlier in the day or later at night. Experiment for yourself and see what fits for you. You can do one of these practices or all three if that is what you like. Perhaps try one for 40 days and then move to the next practice.

Set your motivation. Setting your motivation is a practice of setting your intention and reminding yourself of your reason for practice/work (Khyentse, 2012, p. 55-56). It can be used before the practice of prayer, before you begin your chaplain work, and before you begin your day. If you are going to pray daily, try to set a different motivation each day. Your motivation can be wide or narrow as you wish. An example of a wide motivation is "Today as much as possible, I will be of benefit and service to as many beings as possible" or "Today as much as possible, I won't harm anybody." An example of a narrow motivation is "Today, I want to help at least one person in some small way" or "Today, if I feel annoyed, I will count at least ten breaths before I say anything." See which motivation is from your heart. Do not judge yourself or your heartfelt motivation. The traditional advice is to always make the highest and best motivation possible, but sometimes this can feel inauthentic for us. In aligning with our chaplaincy values of meeting our care-seekers where they are, we too must meet ourselves where we are.

Next, is a prayer for the Buddhist chaplain that I found helpful:

> May my understanding of all healing arts, especially in the texts and practices of chaplaincy, increase and benefit beings.
> May my ministry of presence bring comfort and connection.
> May whatever I say be beneficial and insightful.
> May all ordinary and supreme powers be bestowed on me, I pray!

This prayer is inspired by a prayer for traditional Tibetan medical doctors. One can imagine the Buddha or Medicine Buddha surrounded by various healing and chaplaincy texts, the texts dissolve into five colored lights which dissolve into our five chakras and we feel empowered.

The second practice is rejoicing. Rejoicing is the practice of being joyful over the virtuous activities of holy beings and ordinary beings. Rejoicing is related to sympathetic joy, wherein we connect with the joy others exprience. From the Seven Limbs, rejoicing is the fourth limb and is also related to the practice of making aspirations. Lama Zopa states if we rejoice over our own virtuous activities, we double our merit (Zopa, 2018). If we rejoice in the merits that a bodhisattva collects in one day, we will get half their merit; if we rejoice in the merits of a buddha, we will get one-tenth of their merits. These fantastical numbers given by the received tradition represent the power of rejoicing in transforming and nurturing our mind states.

Rejoicing over our own virtue can take a form that looks like a prayer, for example, "How wonderful it is that I have accumulated so much merit in the past, I am making in the present, and in the future." I have found this practice so central in my ministry. I spend a few minutes at the end of the workday to rejoice in whatever merits I may have made, and I finish with a meditation on emptiness. We can rejoice over the virtue and merit of various buddha, bodhisattvas, living teachers as well as ordinary people – the various people who work to benefit their families, who work hard to achieve their goals, the work of first responders, and so on. A form of this prayer can be: "I rejoice in the virtue and merits of hospital chaplains in the past, present, and future."

Related to the practice of rejoicing is the practice of making aspirations. A prayer of aspiration is the wish to do more and be more. An aspiration is a hope to do a positive act in the near or distant future. An aspiration comes from an open mind that acknowledges limitations while not being self-critical. An aspiration makes our mind state lighter, broader than when focusing on just our ordinary concerns. An aspiration can be broad or narrow. It is best to reflect on what is going on for us at the moment. A broad aspiration can be "May I benefit all beings today like the buddhas and bodhisattvas of the past, present, and future." An example of a narrow aspiration is "May I have assistance at my job today." You may like to add the words "for the benefit of all beings" to an aspiration for yourself (Khyense, 2012, p. 53). For example, "May I be blessed with strength today for the benefit of all beings." This allows you to transform a narrow aspiration to something broader.

The final practice is the practice of dedication. Dedication is found in many Buddhist traditions. Dedication is the practice where we direct the positive energy of what we have done to a particular cause. The received tradition encourages us to dedicate our practices to two main purposes: the enlightenment of all beings and flourishing of the dharma. Often the long life of our teachers is glossed with the dharma's flourishing. We can dedicate after any meritorious activity like our prayers, our contemplative practices, our work, our efforts in benefiting our families and communities. A common dedication prayer is below:

By this virtue may I quickly
Attain the state of Guru Buddha, and
Lead every being without exception,
To that very state! (Wangdu, 2020)

FOR OTHERS: PRIVATE/PUBLIC RITUALS & PRAYERS

In considering the benefit of others, I will introduce you to these resources for public prayers and rituals.[1] There are four books on *paritta* and *sutta* chanting as well as *dhāraṇī* and *sutra* chanting exceedingly helpful to my ministry. The first is *The Energy of Prayer* by Thiền sư Thich Nhat Hanh. In Appendix I, Thây provides meditation exercises, and in Appendix II he provides prayers and *gāthās* for the chaplain and their care-seekers. Thây highlights two elements for effective prayer; the first is the connection between the one who is praying, and the other is the one who is prayed for (Nhat Hanh, 2006, p. 42-43). The second is what Thây calls the energy of prayer. This energy comes from contemplative practices of love, mindfulness, concentration, and wisdom; without these, Thây states that "our prayer is just superstition" (Nhat Hanh, 2006, p. 44). Prayer, in Thây's opinion, is the out-growth of our own personal cultivation.

The next book is *Not for Happiness* by Dzongsar Khyentse Rinpoche. It is a book about the traditional "Preliminary Practices" within Tibetan Buddhism. Here, they comprise taking refuge, arousing bodhicitta, Vajrasattva purification, mandala offering, *kusali* practice and guru practice. These practices can be done for oneself or adapted to be used with others. Rinpoche speaks of the Three Noble Principles of Practice that are for him, the foundation of Buddhist practices. They are: arousing bodhicitta, awareness of non-duality, and dedicating. These elements have been addressed in our chapter. Rinpoche ends this book with advice for more advance practitioners and anticipates how the spiritual journey may look like further on.

The third book is *Pearls of Wisdom*. It is a two-volume English and Chinese bilingual book of prayers by Venerable Master Hsing Yun (2003).The Master notes that in traditional Chinese Buddhism, prayers were highly formal and "required a certain cadence to recite them correctly" (Hsing Yun, 2003, p. 8). With candor, Master Hsing Yun describes his own formation in Buddhist prayer. He began by praying for himself, next he moved to praying for people within his circle, then after turning forty, he began praying for "world peace, for wealth and strength our nation, for safety and happiness of our society, and for liberation of all beings" (Hsing Yun, 2003, p. 9). When he entered his fifties, he experienced another transformation and he prayed "let me shoulder karmic hinderances and sufferings for all beings…, let me put the great compassion of the Buddha into practice" (Hsing Yun, 2003, p. 10). The reader is invited into the Master's spiritual journey and how this prayer journey might look like in the future for us.

Volume I of *Pearls of Wisdom* provides prayers for various rites of passage, prayers various circumstances like for children who suffer abuse, for warmongers, for those who suffer from violent tendencies, for one's birthday, for self-confidence, among others. Volume 2 comprises prayers for various careers (including sex workers), prayers for a Buddhist wedding ceremony, 9/11 commemoration, and for the consecration of Buddha statue, among others. I am always touched by the compassion of Venerable Master that shines through the words of these prayers. In using these prayers, I have found that in some contexts, these prayers are too long; however, they can be adapted easily.

In the Theravada tradition, there is the practice of recitation of *paritta* (Saddhatissa in Kalupahana, 1991, p. 125-137). *Paritta* are scriptural texts (*sutta*) that have been canonized by the tradition as having healing powers when used in the relevant situations. Mahinda Dee-Galle (2022) in his study of *paritta* has made an excellent summary of past scholarship and

---
1 Noticeably absent in this chapter are sadhanas, liturgy of prayers that are centered on identification with various teacher and Buddha figures.

highlighted current issues. The final book, I want to introduce is a book of *Paritta* by Venerable Sumitta (2016). Venerable has helpfully provided chants for daily devotions, protective parittas, healing parittas, contemplative *gāthās* and funeral chants. His introduction to *paritta* is comprehensive and illustrates the different ways that the Theravada tradition has understood the power of these *parittas*.[2]

The use of *dhāranī* and Mahāyāna sūtras that function like paritta has been noted previously in this chapter. These *dhāranī* and sūtras were recited sometimes with additional visualizations/imagination. Common in the use of spiritual care are the *Great Compassion Dhāranī, Medicine Buddha Dhāranī, Crown Parasol Dhāranī, Heart Sūtra, Medicine Sūtra, Golden Light Sūtra, Great Cloud Sūtra, Diamond Sūtra, Lotus Sūtra*, and others (van Schiak, 2020, p. 68-80).[3]

Prayer from an Emic Perspective

Types of Prayer

We now step back from the dynamic of prayers and consider the types of prayer and ritual theory. This section can be explained through etic and emic perspectives. Catherin Bell (2009) notes with irony the failure of the etic perspective because in seeking to be scientific and objective, the lens often used was one that perpetuated the white colonial gaze. The discussion that follows takes an emic perspective within Tibetan Buddhism. A common classification of prayer follows the liturgy of the "seven branches" or "seven limbs." (Skt. *saptāṅga*; Tib., *yenlak dün*). (This is not to be confused with the equally popular "Seven Line Prayer" which is addressed to Padmasambhava.) In the Tibetan Buddhist tradition, liturgy of seven limbs is believed to have been taught by the Buddha.

The Seven Limbs are also found as elements within Śāntideva's (c. 700 CE) *Way of the Bodhisattva* (Skt. *Bodhisattvacaryāvatāra* or *Bodhicaryāvatāra*, Tib. *byang chub sems dpa'i spyod pa la 'jug pa*), a foundational text for Buddhist chaplaincy. The seven limbs are: refuge and prostration, offering, confession, rejoicing, requesting for teachings, requesting the dharma, requesting the teacher to remain, and dedication. These seven parts can further be seen as seven types of prayer (Berzin, n.d.). A common form that the Seven Limbs takes is given below:

> I prostrate to the glorious assembly.
> I offer all possible appearances of the
>   five desirable objects.
> I apologize for all the sins I have
>   committed in the three times.
> I rejoice in all virtuous activities.
> I request [that you, Buddhas and
>   Bodhisattvas] to turn the wheel
>   of the teachings according to the
>   needs of all beings.
> I supplicate you [Buddhas and
>   Bodhisattvas] to remain with us
>   and forsake parinirvana.
> I dedicate all virtue which I have
>   accumulated for the enlightenment
>   of all beings; may all sentient
>   beings become Buddha.[4]

Lotsawa House (https://www.lotsawahouse.org/), a virtual library of Tibetan Buddhist translations gives 48 types of prayer in its practice section. These can be mapped on to the Seven Limbs as seen in Table 8.1 on the next page.

From this extensive but not exhaustive list, we can see the connection between the seven limbs and different types of prayer found

---

2 A collection of *paritta* is also available from Access to Insight (www.accesstoinsight.org), an online Theravada library.

3 84000 (84000.co), an online Tibetan Buddhist canon translation project offers a curated selection of scriptures that were chanted for well-being. I have used this resource with great success.

4 (Dudjom, 2016)

Table 8.1: Seven Limbs and Types of Prayer listed by Lotsawa House	
Seven Limbs	**Types of Prayer**
Refuge and Prostration	Averting Obstacles, Bodhicitta, Longevity, Windhorse (Lungta), Magnetizing, Pilgrimage, Sickness and Healing, Taking Refuge, Wealth and Prosperity, Transference (Phowa)
Offering	Chod, Fasting Ritual, Fire Offering, Mandala Offering, Incense Offering, Torma, Feast Offering
Confession	Confession, Samaya, Saving Lives
Rejoicing	Aspiration
Requesting for teachings	Descent of Blessings, Empowerment, Guru Yoga, Meditation, Mind training, Mindfulness, Foundational practices, Retreat, Six Perfections, Sleep and Dream
Requesting for the teacher to remain	Calling the Guru from Afar, Consecration, Fulfillment, Guru Prayers, Lineage Prayers, Masters' Long life prayers, Swift Rebirth, Turning back the Dakini's Summons
Dedication	Auspiciousness

within the Tibetan Buddhist tradition. The types of prayer and mapped on the general themes of the Seven Limbs. It must be noted that all Tibetan Buddhist prayers, whatever their type are preceded by refuge and bodhicitta prayers.

Also noted and with reference to our previous discussion about the nature of refuge and compassion, the tradition has classed prayers that seek to protect from suffering like prayers for healing, for wealth, and for magnetizing resources with refuge. This is because the general theme of refuge is the idea of seeking protection from various sufferings.

Tibetan Ritual Theory

The Tibetan Buddhist tradition offers a seemingly simple emic ritual theory: "the preliminaries, the main practice and the concluding activities" (Trinlae, 2018, p. 108-110). Within these three main sections are various subsumed ritual activities. This simple categorization belies the fact that each section involves a change of the individuals' mental state, a change in their relationship with their body and their environment. When we speak of this ritual theory, we move from informal prayers to formal prayers/ritual.

We will illustrate this ritual theory using Stephen Beyer's excellent and detailed analysis of the *Four Mandala Offering to Tārā*. Formal ritual/prayers are different from informal prayers because they are not spontaneous and they are often written by a Buddhist saint; here the *Four Mandala Offering to Tārā* is attributed to the Buddhist saint, Lama Atiśa Dīpankara Śrījñāna (982–1054 CE) (Beyer, 1973, p. 171-172). There is a place for informal personal prayer in these formal rituals. Whereas, in the text given above for contemporary students, the place for informal prayer is noted, in prayers such as the *Four Mandala Offering* usually the place for informal prayer is not apparent but is known by its traditional practitioners. There is a lineage of transmission for the formal ritual/prayer, in our example the *Four Mandala Offerings to Tārā* have been formally orally transmitted from Lama Atiśa to the contemporary practitioner.

In the Tibetan Buddhism, Tārā is the embodiment of the *Prajñāpāramitā*. Here, *Prajñāpāramitā* means the direct experience of the interdependence of all phenomena and the attainment of non-abiding *nirvana*. This means that the received tradition considers Tārā to be the activity manifestation of the Buddha's realization (Shaw, 2006; Wilson, 1996), hence, an important energy to supplicate. The mandala that is offered four times during the ritual is a representation of the Buddhist cosmology and represents an offering of ourselves and whatever we can possibly imagine since beginningless lives. The mandala can be represented by a ritual gesture (*mudra*) or built up ritually with a four-tier tray filled with grain (and sometimes precious stones) (Khyentse, 2012, p. 151-171).

Next, we consider the parts that make up the three main sections. The Preliminaries consist of Refuge, Bodhicitta, Four Immeasurables, Self-Generation, Purifying the Inner Offering, and Purifying the Outer Offerings (Beyer, 1973, p. 176). The Main Practice consists of Imagining the Merit Field, Homage, Offerings to the Merit Field, Seven-Limb Prayer, Mandala Offering, and Prayers to Achieve the Desired Goals. This is followed by three more units of mandala offerings. Each unit includes Homage, Offering to Tārā, Seven Limb Prayer, Mandala Offering, Refuge, Bodhicitta, Requesting Prayer, Praise to the 21 Tārās, and Final Request. In the first unit, Praise to the 21 Tārās is recited twice; in the second unit, the Praise is recited three times; in the third unit, the Praise is recited seven times and includes a Prayer of the Benefits. The Concluding Activities consist of Offering the *Torma*,[5] Offerings, Praise, Final Prayers, Confession of Faults in Recitation, Requesting to Remain, Dedication Prayer, and Verses of Auspiciousness.

The individual practitioner moving through prayers/meditations in the Preliminaries transitions from an ordinary being to imagining themselves to be Tārā through the meditation of emptiness, later enacting Tārā's activities of purifying and blessing the offerings and the environment. In the Main Practice, the individual practitioner while as Tārā makes praises and offering to themselves, giving themselves tremendous confidence to overcome their concerns and achieve their aims. In this practice, the Praise to the 21 Tārās functions as a mantra. This relationship between deity practice, mantra, and healing is explored in other works (Gabriel, 2014; Shaw, 2022; Copp, 2014; Yeshe, 1987; Blofeld, 1977). In the Concluding Activities, the individual practitioner amends any mistakes made in the ritual, abides in their imagination as Tārā and dedicates the energy of the practice to all who are in difficult situations.

The spiritual outcomes of the *Four Mandala Offering to Tārā* presupposes that the individual practitioners have been privy to the inner explanations of the practice. However, as Bhikshuni Trinlae (2018, p. 111) notes, those who are untrained and "even the naïve casual observer, could benefit from a simple devotional perspective toward the liturgy because of the virtues associated with devotion." In her groundbreaking work, Bhikshuni Trinlae has found these elements of psychospiritual transformations from the field of spiritual care present in the ritual of Amitāyus. These elements are: trustful belonging in the universe, moments of transcendence, flow-emersion experience, emotional well-being, source of inspiration, meaning and purpose in life, and nourishing self-concept. These elements are found in the Four *Mandala Offering to Tārā* and many other Buddhist rituals.

The simple emic ritual theory of the preliminaries, the main practice, and the concluding activities lead the practitioner in the development of these psychospiritual transformational elements that support emotional well-being and growth. This can another area of fruitful research.

Dynamics of Buddhist Prayer

Refuge

This section on the dynamics of Buddhist prayer begins by reflecting on its foundations. The received tradition positions refuge and compassion as the foundations of Buddhist prayer. Refuge and compassion discussed in the context of Buddhist prayer can be further be explained in terms of the two truths: conventional truth and ultimate truth. Conventional truth is the ordinary way we perceive things. While, ultimate truth is the way things truly exist, seen through the lens of non-self, beyond the conception of self and other, beyond conceptual and linguistic conventions.

---

5 Ritual cake embued with the our aspirations.

This lofty perception, the received tradition believes, is not inaccessible to ordinary beings but can be glimpsed through Buddhist meditative analysis (Gyamtso, 2001, p. 15-17).

Within the realm of conventional truth, refuge (*śaraṇa* in Sakscrit; *saraṇa* in Pali; Tib., *kyab dro*, or, *kyab su drowaba*) is seen as the confessional statement and gateway to Buddhist practice. In fact, most formal Buddhist prayers begin with refuge. In the practice of refuge, an individual affirms that they want to abandon *saṃsāra*, attain enlightenment by relying upon the Buddha, Dharma, and Sangha (the Three Jewels, *triratna* in Sanskrit and *ti-ratana* in Pali); that is, by relying on the Buddha, his teachings and those who have completed their Buddhist training (Tsongkhapa, 2000, p. 177-207; Loden, 1996, p. 159-192; Orgyan, 1992, p. 57-64). A common Tibetan Buddhist refuge prayer reads:

> In the Buddha, Dharma, Sangha,
> I take refuge until enlightenment.
> By the merit created by generosity
>   and so forth,
> May I attain Buddhahood for the
>   benefit of all beings.[6]

In discussing the praxis of refuge, Dzongsar Khyentse states that Buddhists are those who accept the Four Seals: a) all compounded things are impermanent; b) all emotions are dissatisfying; c) all things have no inherent existence; and d) nirvana is beyond concepts (Khyentse, 2007, p. 3). Dzongsar Khyentse makes the argument that refuge is training in accepting and finally embodying the Four Seals.

When we take refuge, we begin to grow in the realization of the Four Seals. From the practice of this prayer, its conventional truth, we can see how its contemplative aspect is a bridge to its ultimate truth. The contemplative aspect, the feeling of refuge or sanctuary, the feeling of being in a safe space, the feeling of being accepted without judgment by relying on the Three Jewels and training in the Four Seals will lead us to enlightenment, the ultimate truth of this practice. (The reliance on the Three Jewels is the causal refuge and the attainment of enlightenment is the resultant refuge.) The practice of refuge demonstrates the connection between conventional truth and ultimate truth of refuge. Refuge and many prayers in the Tibetan Buddhist tradition are accompanied by relevant visualizations or imaginations. For example, in refuge we are taught to imagine ourselves in a beautiful grove with the Buddha seated on a teaching throne held up by eight fearless lions (Zopa, 2002).

Traditionally refuge is taught in the context of five dimensions: 1) Causes for going for refuge; 2) objects of Refuge; 3) way of going for refuge; 4) stages of training in refuge; and 5) meditation on taking refuge (Loden, 1996, p. 159). For the purposes of this chapter, I will focus only on two dimensions: the reasons for taking refuge and the objects of refuge. The discussion around these two elements speak to why we as Buddhists pray and whom we pray to.

The tradition gives three reasons for going for refuge. We take refuge: to protect us against suffering found in the three lower realms; to protect us against the suffering of all *saṃsāra*, that is, the suffering of all six realms of existence; and finally, to achieve enlightenment for all beings (Loden, 1996, p. 160-161). The common traditional view is to see the six realms as actual realms of existence. They can also be seen as psychological states of intense anger, miserliness, ignorance, greed, jealous and pride respectively (Trungpa, 1992). In the context of this chapter, we go for refuge to protect ourselves from all suffering, to protect our minds from intense psychological states, and to achieve enlightenment. It follows that we can pray to protect ourselves from all forms of suffering as well as to achieve enlightenment.

Next, we turn to the 'objects of refuge' or whom we pray to. This section can be explained

---

[6] Access to Insight, "Threefold Refuge," https://www.accesstoinsight.org/ptf/tisarana.html

from the perspective of conventional truth and ultimate truth. In terms of conventional truth, we take refuge in Buddha, the teacher, Dharma, his teachings, and Sangha, the community that has realized these teachings. The qualities of the Three Jewels are extensively explained in the tradition (Pabongka Rinpoche, 2006, p. 354-384). Just focusing on the qualities of the Buddha, the Tibetan Buddhist tradition provides extensive lists from which we can summarize four main qualities: the Buddha has freed himself from all dangers; he knows how to free others from danger; he is compassionate to all; and he works for the benefit of all (Pabongka Rinpoche, 2006, p. 357-359). Thus follows that the Buddha is a worthy object of refuge and of prayer. (In the Theravāda tradition, the chant "Iti pi so" captures the qualities of the Buddha according to the Buddho editors in *Dhajagga-paritta Chant*.)

In terms of ultimate truth, we seek refuge in the Buddha's mind, also known as the "wisdom truth body" of the Buddha (*dharmakaya* in Sanskrit). The "good qualities [of the Buddha's mind] are to be understood as the 21 divisions of unsullied primal awareness, the ten powers, the 18 unique qualities, and so forth" (Pabongka Rinpoche, 2006, p. 364). More accessibly, this pure nature of the Buddha's mind, is one that we share (Tsadra Foundation). This pure nature is known as our buddha nature (Tib. *kham/rig*), which has two aspects – the developing potential and the natural potential (Loden, 1996, p. 175). The developing potential expresses itself in the virtuous minds that we share. The natural potential is our lack of inherent existence. In context of Buddhist prayer, when we pray, we connect to the Buddha's pure mind, his wisdom truth body as well as our own buddha nature. The act of prayer begins as a conventional truth and ends as an (expression of the) ultimate truth.

COMPASSION

Having addressed why we pray and to whom we pray, in this next section, we turn to the second foundation of Buddhist prayer – compassion. Compassion not only refers to this prayer, but also the mental attitude or feeling that underlies this prayer. Compassion (Skt. *karuṇā*; Pali *karuṇā*; Tib. *nyingjérje*) and its corollary, loving kindness (Skt. *maitrī*; Pali *mettā*; Tib. *jampa*) can explained in terms of conventional truth and ultimate truth. Compassion is defined in the Buddhist tradition as the wish to free ourselves and others from suffering and its causes; while loving kindness is defined as the wish to provide happiness and its causes to ourselves and others (Sera and Newland, 1984, p. 35-54). Often in formal Buddhist prayer, the section on compassion follows the section on refuge. In the Mahāyāna, compassion is often glossed with a prayer of bodhicitta. The Dalai Lama states that "real heart of the Mahāyāna is loving kindness and bodhicitta" (quoted in Yeshe, 2003, p. 56). An example of a prayer of compassion is given below:

> May all beings have happiness and
> the cause of happiness.
> May they be free of suffering and the
> cause of suffering.
> May they never be disassociated
> from the supreme happiness which
> is without suffering.
> May they remain in boundless
> equanimity, free from both
> attachment to close ones and
> rejection of others.[7]

There are many Buddhist practices to train in compassion and loving kindness. (Practices like the Four Immeasurables or Four Sublime States, Seven-Point Cause-and-Effect, Exchanging Oneself for Others, Ten Deeds of a Bodhisattva, and Bodhisattva Vows, and so on.) Here I want to highlight the conventional truth of compassion in terms of the four types of giving (Tib. *jinpa nam shi*): we give to others material objects, dharma, protection from fear, and love.

---

7 Dragpa, "Four Immeasurables."

When we pray for ourselves and others, we enact these four types of giving for ourselves and others. Another way of expressing conventional truth of compassion is through the three types of compassion (Tib. *nyingjé sum*). This is compassion directed to all suffering beings, compassion directed to those who have yet to understand impermanence, and compassion directed to those who have yet to understand the lack of inherent nature in all phenomena. Our compassion is directed from gross materiality to those who have yet to understand the subtle nature of reality.

This subtle nature of reality is the pure nature of mind, that we mentioned above. In the Tibetan Buddhist tradition, this pure nature expresses itself as compassion energy (Tib. *tukjé rje*). This is also the ultimate aspect of compassion. This ultimate aspect of compassion is the reason why the Buddha remains available to us for prayer and why ultimately, we pray. When we pray, we touch our ultimate pure buddha nature and over time we become that pure awake compassion. Both the conventional truth and ultimate truth of compassion encourage us to hold prayers for ourselves and others with compassion.

Conclusion

In this chapter, I have provided three frames to consider Buddhist prayer: prayer as relevant to the Buddhist chaplain; prayer from an emic perspective; and the dynamics of prayer. In the first section, we considered practices of motivation, rejoicing/aspiration, and dedication as personal practices. In the section on prayer for others we looked at a few resources for prayer and ritual for the personal use of the chaplain and for their care-seekers. In the second section, we considered a Tibetan Buddhist ritual theory and types of prayer. In the third and final section, we considered refuge and compassion.

I am humbled to have been asked to write this chapter on Buddhist prayer. It is vast topic and I hope I have managed to give readers a glimpse of the different perspectives to begin to think about this topic There are many traditional and contemporary ways to think about Buddhist prayer and this is but a few of many ways. In my chaplaincy teaching career, I have witnessed a shift in how we teach Buddhist prayer, from one under the colonial graze to finally one that centers Asian perspectives and interests. I hope this chapter will contribute to a fruitful conversation about Buddhist prayer and its place in the formation and ministry of Buddhist chaplains.

This chapter was completed on Vesak 2023. In the writing of this chapter, our pet cat, Johnny HeartThief, passed. I would like to dedicate whatever merit that arose from the writing of this chapter so that all Buddhist chaplaincy schools flourish and that all beings may attain full enlightenment, especially to our loyal furry companions.

More Information

For more information on specific topics explored in this chapter, see the following resources:

Aspiration: For extended discussion, see Jamyang Khyentse, "King of Aspirations," https://dharmatranscripts.wordpress.com/2017/02/19/the-king-of-aspiration-prayer-transcript-of-talk-given-by-dzongsar-khyentse-rinpoche/.

Compassion: Reginald Ray, *In the Presence of Masters*, p. 96-101

Deity Practice: For extended discussion on Deity Practice, the practice of imagining ourselves as a Buddha, see Padmasambhava and Chokgyur Lingpa, *Dzogchen Deity Practice: Meeting your True Nature* (Leggett, Ca: Rangjung Yeshe, 2016); Bstan-pa'i-ñi-ma and Zhe-chen R.-tshab P.-'gyur-med-rnam-rgyal, *Vajra Wisdom: Deity Practice in Tibetan Buddhism* (Boston: Snow Lion, 2012); 'Jigs-med-gling-pa, R.-byung-rdo-rje, Orgyan-'jigs-med-chos-kyi-dbang-po, and 'Gyur-med-tshe-dbaṅ-mchog-grub. *Deity, Mantra, and Wisdom: Development Stage Meditation in Tibetan Buddhist Tantra* (Boston: Snow Lion 2006); and Kong-sprul, B.-gros-mtha'-yas and Sarah Harding, *Creation and Completion: Essential points of Tantric Meditation* (Boston: Wisdom, 2002).

Deity Practice & Healing: Victor Gabriel, "Embodying Generosity: A Comparison of Buddhist and Feminist Views of the Body in the Chöd Ritual," PhD diss., (University of the West, 2014), 147-152; Miranda Shaw "Buddhist Practice in South Asia" in *Oxford Handbook of Buddhist Practice*, eds. Paula Arai and Kevin Trainor, (New York: Oxford University, 2022), 29-33; Paul Copp, *Body Incantatory: Spells and the Ritual Imagination in Medieval Chinese Buddhism* (New York: Columbia University, 2014); Thubten Yeshe, *Introduction to Tantra : Transformation of Desire* Boston: Wisdom, 1987), 136-142; John Blofeld, *Mantras: Sacred Words of Power* (New York: E.P. Dutton, 1977).

Four Mandala Offering: An abbreviated *Four Mandala Offering to Tārā* for contemporary students, Shantideva Center, "Pujas and Practices," https://shantidevanyc.org/wp-content/uploads/2020/03/four_mandala_chittamani_tara_c5.pdf

Healing: For the relationship between prayer and healing, see Ann Ameling, "Prayer: An Ancient Healing Practice Becomes New Again," in *Holistic Nursing Practice 14*, 3April 2000: 40-48.

Merit: For extended discussion, see https://www.lamayeshe.com/article/dedicating-merit; Lobsang Wangdu, "Tibetan Dedication of Merit Prayers," https://www.yowangdu.com/tibetan-buddhism/dedication-of-merit-prayers.html

Motivation: For extended discussion, see Thubten Zopa, "Motivation in Daily Life," https://www.lamayeshe.com/article/motivation-daily-life; Thubten Chodron, "Importance of Motivation," "https://thubtenchodron.org/2019/05/significance-intention/.

Refuge: Theravada perspective: Bhikkhu Bodhi, "Going for Refuge and Taking Precepts," and Thanissaro Bhikkhu, "Refuge," https://www.accesstoinsight.org/lib/authors/bodhi/wheel282.html and Thanissaro Bhikkhu, "Refuge," https://www.accesstoinsight.org/lib/authors/thanissaro/refuge.html; Mahayana & Vajrayana perspective: Reginald Ray, *In the Presence of Masters*, p 51-60

Rejoicing: For extended discussion, see Lama Yeshe Wisdom Archive, "Site Search Rejoicing," https://www.lamayeshe.com/search/rejoicing.

Ritual Theory: <u>Buddhism</u>: Lozang Trinlae and Padma-dkar-po, Kun-mkhyen pad-ma dkar-po's *Amitāyus Tradition of Vajrayāna Buddhism: Contemplative Text, Phenomenological Experience, and Epistemological Process* (Kathmandu: Vajra Books, 2018), 108-110. Bstan-pa'i-ñi-ma, and Zhe-chen Rgyal-tshab Padma-'gyur-med-rnam-rgyal, *Vajra Wisdom: Deity Practice in Tibetan Buddhism* (Boston: Snow Lion, 2013), 13. Stephen Beyer, *Cult of Tārā: Magic and Ritual in Tibet* (Berkeley: University of California, 1973) 170-226. This Tibetan Buddhist ritual theory can be mapped upon Theravāda and Mahāyāna liturgical forms with certain observations, but this would require a longer discussion. <u>Critical analysis</u>: For a critic of the popularization of ritual theories, see Catherine Bell's work *Ritual: Perspectives and Dimensions* (1997).
<u>General</u>: Etic ritual theory described by Arnold Van Gennep, *Rites of Passage* (1961).

Seven Limbs Prayer: For extended discussion on the Seven Limbs Prayer, see Pha-boṅ-kha-pa Byams-pa-bstan-'dzin-'phrin-las-rgya-mtsho, *Liberation in the Palm of Your Hand: A Concise Discourse on the Path to Enlightenment* (Boston: Wisdom, 2006), pages 150-213. The subsection

"Petitioning the Merit Field" can be included in Refuge section, while the subsection "Requests to Lineage Lamas" can be included in Requesting for teachings section. Also, Orgyan-'jigs-med-chos-kyi-dbang-po, *Words of My Perfect Teacher*, 2nd ed., (Boston: Shambhala, 1998), pages 317-328. See Lotsawa House, "Seven Branches Serries," https://www.lotsawahouse.org/topics/seven-branches/. For how the Seven Limbs nests within a larger liturgy, see Yeshe, *Becoming Compassion Buddha*, 75-79. Here the Seven Limbs reside within a larger liturgy called *The Inseparability of the Spiritual Master and Avalokiteshvara* written by the 14th Dalai Lama.

Victor Gabriel: A fuller spiritual biography is in Duane R. Bidwell, *When One Religion Isn't Enough: The Lives of Spiritually Fluid People* (Boston: Beacon Press, 2018, p. 92-95).

Women's rituals: Often given short shrift are domestic and women's rituals, see Linda Ho, "Home Altars," in *Oxford Handbook of Buddhist Practice*, edited by Paula Arai and Kevin Trainor, 469-485 (New York: Oxford University, 2022), Jessica Starling, *Guardians of the Buddha's Home: Domestic Religion in Contemporary Jōdo Shinshū*, (Honolulu: University of Hawai'i, 2019), Jeff Wilson, *Mourning the Unborn Dead*, (Oxford: Oxford University, 2009), Neky Cheung, *Women's Ritual in China: Jiezhu* (receiving Buddhist prayer beads) performed by menopausal women in Ninghua, western Fujian, (Lewiston, N.Y.: Edwin Mellen, 2008).

Interreligious prayer in chaplaincy settings

For a discussion of interreligious prayer in chaplaincy settings, see the chapter on "Meaning Making through Ritual and Public Leadership" by Rochelle Robins and Danielle Tumminio Hansen in *Chaplaincy and Spiritual Care in the Twenty-First Century* (Cadge and Rambo, eds., 2022, p. 110-128); the chapter "A Buddhist Chaplain's Prayer" by Anna Gagnon in *Refuge in the Storm* (Michon, ed., 2023, p. 115-122); the article "Buddhists, Get Your Prayer On: Reflections on Christian Spontaneous Prayer by a Buddhist Chaplain" by Hans Gustafson (2018) in *Learning from Other Religious Traditions*; the article "Negotiating Religious Differences: The Strategies of Interfaith Chaplains in Healthcare" by Wendy Cage and Emily Sigalow in *Journal for the Scientific Study of Religion*, March 2013, Vol. 52, No. 1, p. 146-158.

Robins and Hansen write more generally about rituals, in which prayer is incorporated, noting a variety of purposes:
- Steady and support those who are reeling from shock and feeling overwhelmed by a sudden crisis;
- Mark and make meaning from turning points in the life of a community, particularly at times of loss;
- Open and hold space for otherwise unacknowledged or unexpressed emotions, sensations, confusions, thoughts, and hopes, particularly during liminal experiences;
- Engage all of people's senses and their entire being: body, mind, heart, and spirit;
- Create a sense of community, physical and emotional safety, and connection with one's own deeper being, with others, and with the transcendent or ultimate;
- Remember and make meaning of important moments in the past;
- Reveal hopes and dreams for the future.

When developing a ritual, Robins and Hansen recommend following five steps, which can also be used with deciding on or developing a prayer:
1. Assess needs;
2. Draw on wisdom traditions, historic and contemporary, to make meaning;
3. Utilize a clear structure (such as those outlined in the remainder of this chapter);
4. Facilitate connection;
5. Integrate diverse spiritual resources.

Cage and Sigalow found that effective chaplains used two main strategies to negotiate religious difference with interfaith careseekers — neutralize religious difference and code switching. Chaplains neutralize religious differences by using the language of spirituality to seek commonalities with careseekers and their families. Chaplains code switch when they use the language, rituals, and practices of their careseekers.

While various studies of prayer have focused on its structural aspects, literary forms, and theological or Dharmic implications, when chaplains write about prayer, they tend to do so from the heart. For example, Gagnon writes:

> In prayer, I practice manifesting the experience of ultimate truth, the truth of no separation. I practice the outlook of the enlightened mind. I call out to the presence of love and compassion, wisdom and insight that resides in this world. So doing, I connect to that same presence within myself.
>
> Does intercessory prayer work? Can prayer change cause and effect, the results of our karmic actions? If we understand enlightenment as a radical shift in perspective, then I believe it can. I can change the course of my life and the lives of others by working to manifest such divinity here and now. I pray for God's love with my patients, and so doing, I make an aspiration to feel loved, and to bring that love into the hospital room. I call out to God to enter my life and the lives of my patients, and so doing, I begin to make space for God here and now. I begin to connect with the God that is already within me, waiting to bloom and blossom at any moment. As Thich Nhat Hanh tells us: we practice praying both to ourselves and to what is outside of ourselves; there is no distinction.
>
> Christian theologian C.S. Lewis wrote: "I don't pray to change God's mind, I pray to change my mind. I pray because I can't help myself, because I am helpless. I pray because the need just flows out of me all the time — waking and sleeping." In the face of our limits and helplessness, in the face of old age, sickness, and death, we call out in prayer. But it is not God's mind that is changed by such cries; it is our own. It is the God within us blooming with the aspiration to trust and accept life as it is.
>
> Prayer changes life at its very foundation because it changes the way we perceive it.

Rear Admiral Margaret Grun Kibben notes that part of the chaplain's role (Buddhist or otherwise) anywhere they serve is to keep "prayer in the House;" in Kibben's case, the U.S. House of Representatives, which has had its own chaplain since 1789. Part of the chaplain's ministry of presence is to offer to pray with and form those experiencing crisis or distress (Kibben, in Cadge and Rambo, 2022, p. 21). Many books on prayer for Christians (and a growing number of other religious traditions) exist and may be helpful to the Buddhist chaplain when working with interreligious populations. Therefore, the remainder of this chapter focuses on the Buddhist basis of prayer.

9
INTERRELIGIOUS COMPETENCIES
by Nathan Jishin Michon

Cultivating a sense of trust is necessary to provide any decent spiritual care. As Doehring and Kestenbaum describe,

> What makes people spiritually trustworthy? Within secular contexts like healthcare, hospice, long-term care, the military, and educational and prison contexts, people are more likely to trust chaplains who demonstrate respect for their particular practices, values, and beliefs. While all people working in these contexts are expected to respect cultural differences, what makes chaplains unique is their respect for religious, spiritual, and moral differences.[1]

The *CASC/ACSS Policy and Procedure Manual* adds,

> When Spiritual Care Professionals behave in a manner congruent with the [following] values of this code of ethics, they bring greater justice, compassion and healing to our world...respect the right of each faith group to hold its values and traditions...respect the cultural, ethnic, gender, racial, sexual-orientation, and religious diversity of other professionals and those served and strive to eliminate discrimination.[2]

As Buddhist chaplains, especially if we are in non-Asian nations, we will typically be engaging with people from traditions other than our own. Thus, it is critical to consider how we approach such interactions. As the above quotes demonstrate, respect of the careseekers' faith tradition and cultivating a sense of trust come hand in hand to help set the stage for the interactions that take place.

Buddhism has plentiful resources in its traditions that can offer practical and theoretical backbone to the support of those from other faith traditions. The Buddha is said to have prohibited his followers from taking over the religious spaces of other traditions' teachers to prevent situations that might cause ill will toward Buddhist teachings. Buddhist practices like loving-kindness and compassion are stressed as being toward all beings regardless of background. The image of 1000-armed Guan-yin/Avalokiteśvara is depicted with many eyes to see all the diverse needs of the world and many arms to help in the way that each individual needs. Teachings on skillful means emphasize such adaptation in real life situations. Buddhism constantly adapted to the new cultures and traditions it came across through the ages. Kukai founded a multi-faith public school in Japan that taught not just Buddhism, but Confucianism and Daoism (the other major teachings recognized from the time) to ensure that students were well versed in a diverse array of teachings. The resources and examples go on and on.

Although it is impossible to account for all complexities of interactions with people of other religious traditions, this chapter will at

---

1 Doehring and Kestenbaum, 130.

2 Cadge, 131.

least provide additional texture to the considerations we make and tools we can bring into such interactions. I first share some aspects of my own background and aspects of my own formation related to this area before exploring the basic meanings and development of words like interreligious and interfaith. I then explore the interplay of religion and culture, and some considerations around that for spiritual care. Next, the chapter considers how teachings like 'beginner's mind' and 'right mindfulness' can help our interreligious engagements, before emphasizing the value of responsible learning about other religions and traditions. It then discusses different modes of interfaith rituals before discussing the application of both Buddhist and non-Buddhist contemplative practices in our spiritual care with others.

Personal Interreligious Background

As a youth I spent several years living in Dearborn, Michigan, an area that had a fair amount of diversity, albeit a very segregated form of diversity. It was only a few-minutes' drive into Detroit and nearby predominantly black neighborhoods. Closer to my family were the Italian and Polish ghettos (my own family background largely coming from that Polish background). A few minutes in another direction was the Arab area of Dearborn. Dearborn had become the city in the US with the highest percentage of Arab Americans—and along with it, a very high concentration of Muslim Americans. I thus grew up with the experience of religious cultures coming together as well as the conflict and dialog that had to come with such an environment. What does freedom of religion really mean? How do you balance freedom with respectful boundaries? For example, Muslims built mosques and wanted to have the morning *adan* — a call to prayer that is supposed to occur five times per day, including early in the morning on weekends when many surrounding non-Muslim residents may be sleeping. Numerous town hall meetings discussed things like areas and decibel levels that balanced differing groups' needs and decisions. One of the local public high schools at first allowed Muslim students to pray and practice their faith in the hallways, but did not provide a separate prayer space. But could those more devout Muslims properly wash before the prayers? And as the Muslim student population grew, could non-Muslim students navigate around those students in prayer to get their classrooms? Neither group could meet their needs as it was. As with many occurrences when differing cultures come in contact, misunderstandings can lead to animosities, but dialog and exposure can help bring about understanding, trust, mutual resolution, and – ultimately, I believe – more open hearts and minds. In many ways, I was grateful for this exposure from a young age, even if it was just in bits and pieces that I am still reflecting back on, processing, and comprehending.

I was raised Catholic, in a way that I might called dedicated, but loose. My mother and grandparents were very devout, but not to the degree that everything was 'letter of the law.' Both family and teachers at my Catholic school tended to know I was a spiritual child, the one who was always asking priests curious difficult questions...sometimes simply getting the response, "Ummm, good question, maybe go to seminary when you're older and ask that again someday!" Thus, I regularly challenged the tradition, but not in a way that (most) people took as disrespectful. These reflections, challenges, and critiques gradually made my form of Catholicism more and more unique as I began creating what in many ways was a complex personal theology. When I finally came across Buddhism during my late teen years, it was more like a discovery of a name for personal identity than a new thought to transition or "convert" into. "Oh wow, there's a name for what I am!?!"

However, it wasn't a transition without challenges. My mother struggled deeply with it at the very beginning and it took a couple lengthy honest conversations before she felt more comfortable (she soon became very fully accepting and embracing of my Buddhist identity). My grandmother had to be reassured that Buddhism was not a form of Satanism; but eventually I was able to introduce teachings and meditations on topics like loving-kindness which even those devout Catholic family members embraced. I found those interactions and adaptations fascinating in many ways. There were occasionally complementary connections to explore. While Christianity taught people to love unconditionally, there was not as much teaching about how to develop that love. So in some ways, the Buddhist practices I introduced seemed to be welcomed with interest and enthusiasm, a complement to the spirituality they already embraced.

These exchanges and adaptations, though, proved to be very fruitful reference points I reflect on years later as inspirations to participate in various forms of interfaith exchange and dialog. When I began to train and practice as a Buddhist chaplain in the Los Angeles area, I loved the education, but felt my awareness of the diverse religions present in the area was still lacking. Combined with interfaith sensibilities of my youth, I found an interfaith ministry program that trained me in the rituals and views of multiple religious identities, and how to work with different religious and spiritual communities to create ceremonies amenable to all groups involved. The time offered ample reflection on the ways I did this throughout childhood and early adulthood, in a sense gaining early practice with the code-switching as well as the verbal and ritual dances that occur while navigating the faith-based dance floor between old traditions as they shift and flow in each unique present interaction.

Interfaith Consciousness and Definitions

Words for the meetings of and between religions are still relatively new. Although there have been famous events like the World Parliament of Religions dating back to the late 1800s, Christian and general Abrahamic dominance in English-speaking areas limited the drive to create interfaith vocabulary. So the words to represent such interactions didn't come until religious diversity began to grow in the United States. The Immigration Act of 1965 opened up the doors for many people to come to the US from areas that had previously been heavily restricted. The word interfaith itself was still rarely recognized at first. It entered the Oxford English Dictionary in the mid-seventies, but didn't enter most Webster's dictionaries for a couple more decades. Interreligious and multifaith soon entered common use vocabularies as well.

In many cases the words interreligious, interfaith, and multifaith are synonyms with little difference between them. The meanings change more based on the context in which they are used than on differences in definitions themselves. A related word, intra-faith, however, refers to communication, participation, or gathering between two or more people or groups who belong to different traditions within the same religion. An example comprises Pure Land, Zen, and Theravadan Buddhists. Although some aspects of this chapter will touch upon intra-faith issues and practices, this is a large category in itself and most treatment will be found in Volume III of this series.

Although words describing the interactions between religions just came to prevalence within the past several decades, even words for religion itself are still relatively new when considering broader world history. Briefly examining that context can bring important reflections about how culture and religion intertwine and what that means for providing spiritual care to those from other religious backgrounds.

Where Religion and Culture Intertwine

The depth of interplay between culture and religion is fascinating and sometimes disturbing. Many languages never actually had a word for "religion" until their cultures and countries were colonized. In other words, many cultures did not have a way to verbally express "religion" until their own religion was being suppressed. Although Japan was not colonized, its word for religion was not created until the late 1800s, after trade was (rather forcefully) opened with the United States and they needed a word to translate English books that referred to religion. Japanese spoke of "schools" and "teachings" but had no term equivalent to religion before that. In most places, what we consider religion is and has been so deeply infused with local culture that a separate term was never needed to describe it. Even today, culture can be incredibly influential upon religion. A mosque in Beijing can look architecturally far more like a Daoist temple than a mosque from the Middle East. The service of a Catholic church in the USA can more closely resemble the service of Japanese Buddhists in Los Angeles than a Catholic service in West Africa. World religions such as Christianity, Hinduism, Islam, Buddhism, Judaism, and Sikhism can differ greatly in their practices depending where in the world they are happening and depending on the sect or school that adherents practice.

Another related and relevant point is that religious or spiritual culture can impact what we might consider "interreligious." It depends how surveys are constructed, but in general around 90% of the modern Japanese population have considered themselves Shinto. Nearly 80% can consider themselves Buddhist. We would already be at 170% of the population. And yet, only around 30% of Japanese consider themselves religious! For many people from the USA, Europe, and Abrahamic cultures, these numbers or befuddling. Part of the reason lies in the construction of the word for "religion" in Japanese, which combines the character for "sect" or "something separated" with the character meaning "teaching" or "belief." So the word itself can give the sense of adherence to a very particular religion. Yet Japanese religion – and Japanese Buddhism – has historically nearly always been a multifaith type of practice, interwoven with daily Shinto and other native spiritual views and practices. People in Japan often visit a Shinto shrine or Buddhist temple without knowing the difference or sectarian alignment, more because that shrine or temple is known for a particular type of need, like for safe travel, healing from cancer, finding love, or other particular prayers. Similarly open religious boundaries can be found in many Asian cultures, while Abrahamic faiths historically tend to be more strict in defining membership and disallowing multifaith membership. This is known as religious "exclusivism," in which one religion purports a truth that 'excludes' other religions from access to that truth. Exclusivism can be found in some forms of Buddhism, but for the most part, Buddhism has always been more syncretic and "inclusivist." In other words, a religion that 'includes' the truths of other traditions when they align with or do not directly contradict Buddhist teachings.

Those religiously cultural aspects can also impact relevant chaplaincy themes, such as views of afterlife and forms of grieving. Sticking with the above example from Japan, one may think that a Buddhist from a more traditional Buddhist culture might believe in rebirth and that their ancestors are reborn after a certain period of days. But long-term ancestor veneration, along with prayers and communication toward deceased relatives is normal even for Japanese who claim to be "non-religious." One of the most important parts of many households is a family altar which contains *ihai*, standing placards which provide a post-mortem Buddhist name. In many ways people believe these objects to contain remaining earthly spirit or soul of deceased relatives. In some sense, people believe those ancestors and loved ones continue to live on through the *ihai*. This often helps people deeply while coping through the grieving process. Yet there also may be a deep sense of responsibility around them. When major disasters strike, for instance, the family's collection of *ihai* can be far more important to save than a laptop. For some people who lose them in a disaster, it can cause deep despair and a re-grieving process—as if one has lost the soul of a parent to which they were committed to caring for. Awareness of such impacts can help us better understand and be present with those going through the experience.

Thus, these religio-cultural considerations can be incredibly important in how we might care for individuals coming from various cultures. The following chapter will look more broadly and deeply at cultural considerations, but for now we should take it as a point of emphasis just to keep in heart the "beginner's mind" that is so critical to meeting any careseeker where they are in their own spiritual space.

Beginner's Mind and Right Mindfulness

The boundaries of "religion" can be ambiguous. Personal beliefs and values may be quite different from the dogma or doctrine of an individual's ascribed faith. So although we can make educated guesses when hearing a person's religious affiliation, we must always bear in mind that our associated knowledge still brings us nothing more than that regarding the specifics about a person's spiritual views and practices: guesswork.

Ideas like beginner's mind and "not knowing" are common in the Chan/Zen traditions, and similar notions can be found across the spectrum of Buddhist schools. We often speak of trying as much as possible to experience the reality before us just as it is from moment to moment. The more we become aware of various traditions, views, and practices, we must also hold ourselves in check to ensure we still enter every situation with a "beginner's mind." In other words, we still recognize that every individual and situation are unique in their own way. While added awareness can help attune us to certain probabilities about others'

backgrounds, nothing is assured. Of course, our past experience can inform the present, but this does not mean that we should assume that will reflect our new experience.

It is natural for us humans to put others – and sometimes even ourselves – into boxes we categorize. This was an evolutionary necessity so we did not need to waste time re-learning every little new application of previous knowledge. Having eaten a banana before, how do we eat a new banana? How do we drive on a new road we have never been on? Our minds naturally and immediately put things in boxes and draw associations so we can easily navigate daily life. But those boxes that make most parts of our life more convenient can also have a dark side. They can lead to dangerous misjudgments, harmful biases, and prejudices. Increasing awareness of the moment-to-moment formation of thoughts and reactions can lead to the "beginner's mind" and at least help alleviate the negative sides of previously developed associations. We must be very careful not to allow previous education and experience to lead us into assumptions about others' modes of being, remaining open and keeping our minds free to the realities that each moment presents in front of us.

In theory, it may make perfect sense, but sometimes this balance is tricky in practice. For example, say I spend a semester studying Islam to increase my background knowledge and hear time and time again, prayer five times per day is a central practice for Muslims. I read about the history and scriptural background of these daily prayers. I hear stories about the struggles of modern Muslims to maintain that practice in certain modern workplaces. I watch videos of the prayers and visit a local mosque to see prayers in practice. Then, in front of a careseeker I hear they call themselves Muslim and recall all these previous studies. I haven't engaged with many Muslims in my particular workplace and some part of me gets a little excited in recalling those previous efforts finally being applicable. But then one of my questions wrongly assumes they personally try to maintain these prayers in daily life; that may or may not be true depending on any individual's own expression of their spirituality. How do we ensure we are using our background knowledge to properly respect the person in front of us, while also not allowing that knowledge to become a pre-ordained assumption about them?

I think practicing the Buddha's right mindfulness in front of the careseeker is tremendously helpful in protecting that balance. It is important to keep in mind that the Buddha himself taught that there were both skillful and unskillful forms of mindfulness. For a mindset to be "right" mindfulness, it had to include two factors beyond the mindfulness itself: *attapa* and *sampajanna*. Mindfulness, or *sati*, is related to the word for memory and referred to holding something in mind this is what keeps our attention and holds our focus. If we are mindful of breath, we maintain that attention on our breath. *Sampajanna* is the aspect of mind that knows what is happening in body or mind as they are happening. Many definitions of mindfulness include these two aspects. *Attapa*, however, is sometimes ignored or forgotten. The Buddha actually defined this word in the same way he defined right effort, with a fourfold practice: (a) ceasing harmful habits that are present; (b) not allowing new harmful habits to begin; (c) continuing to develop beneficial habits that we already have; and (d) recognizing new beneficial habits we should begin (SN 16:2).

Thus, right mindfulness not only holds certain forms of awareness in mind, but also recognizes from moment-to-moment those patterns of action, speech, and thought which are harmful or beneficial. While asking open-ended questions, holding an openness in our own hearts, and listening to the full individuals in front of us – their words, their actions, their expressions, the subtleties of their reactions – we can also adjust in those moments to what the careseekers are presenting as their own individual needs. By also listening mindfully to ourselves in those moments, we can notice those parts of us that might be turning background knowledge into an assumption and nip it in the bud; shifting to a more open, accepting, compassionate, and wise communication. It may take practice, but that's what our practice is for.

For instance, maybe we have regularly met with devout Christians who adhere strictly to the literal word of the Bible and make sure to go to church every Sunday. But then we meet someone who first identifies themselves as a devout Christian. We find, though, that they go to tarot readings almost as frequently as they go to church, regularly practice meditation and yoga, spent a month on Buddhist retreat, and even include some Hindu devotionalism within their personal Catholic practice. Yet they still fully consider these other outlets aspects of their Christian expression. The number of ways we practice our religiosity is just about as diverse as the number of people themselves. So although it can be useful to have that background information about Christianity when hearing the careseeker is Christian, we must also balance this with a personal awareness to remain fully open to how they themselves manifest that Christianity in their lives.

Responsible Learning and Awareness

With the above in mind about avoiding biases and unfounded assumptions, it is of course still beneficial to engage in responsible learning about other traditions. It is impossible to know the beliefs and practices of every sect and school of all religions of the world. But learning the basics of major traditions, especially those traditions with large populations in our area can at least be helpful in providing care and more deeply identifying with careseekers' needs and concerns. In Buddhism, one of the three poisons at the heart of suffering in the world is ignorance. According to sutras, we overcome ignorance through awareness and discernment. "Abandoning" or "destroying" ignorance completely is listed among the final steps of the Buddha's awakening (see, for example, MN 9;

MN 36; AN 2:29-30). At least in Pali Canon suttas, though, this doesn't mean that we become omniscient – that would be a rather high bar to ask of any chaplain! The kind of awareness spoken of that defeats ignorance is achieved through a constantly well-established mindfulness – we fully know and discern what we are doing and how we are responding moment to moment. Still a high bar, but a path far more manageable and imaginable, in which we can notice graduated improvement through our own experience.

However, I think we can take these basic ideas and also apply them to how awareness and discernment can help overcome the ignorance of other religious and spiritual traditions; this in turn can help us reduce suffering of careseekers. Awareness of not only other traditions, but the limits of our own knowledge, is very helpful while engaging with others, especially those of very different backgrounds from our own. Engaging through book study and personal encounters can both be incredibly effective ways of learning in their own ways. Books and video summaries can help provide broad details that we learn to keep in mind. But personal encounters and visits to places like a mosque or gurdwara can provide the specific texture which helps us truly see that tradition lived in practice within a particular place.

Knowing different parts of other religious theologies can also help. For example, Christianity has many different theological interpretations of "God." God can range from a very person-like, emotional figure in a sky-realm sort of heaven. And God within "process theology" can be a presence of light or goodness existing throughout the cosmos, changing and shifting with the universe's changes and flows.

I find that knowing some of these alternate views helps me in several ways:

1. **Knowledge of what the other might be describing**: just having some basic insight into another person's faith tradition can of course have many benefits. It can provide more thorough spiritual assessments. It can help us ask more specific and intentional questions in response. It might simply bring a subtle yet deeper understanding to that nod and look in our eyes as we acknowledge something they are talking about, helping foster a greater connection.

2. **Helping to provide alternative theologies to another who might be suffering from one particular theological understanding**: For example, if a hospital patient reveals emotional distress associated with their understanding of a fire-and-brimstone version of "God," using directed questions and pointing out various ways of understanding God from within their own tradition can often be like lifting a giant spiritual weight off their heart. They can free themselves from a psychological burden without feeling associated guilt or negative feelings that might otherwise come with denying a part of their faith and tradition. Personally seeing those weights being lifted is a mutually wonderful experience.

3. **In certain situations, when I feel revealing my Buddhist or non-Christian background to a careseeker would be counter-productive, it still allows me to answer honestly "yes, I believe in God" and avoid lying**: I personally try to take the precept on not lying very seriously, but do play with some of the meaning and intent of words in my head as skillful means to avoid creating situations of greater stress and suffering. Along with many other Buddhist chaplains I've talked to, we've all run into situations at some point in time where we had the sense that revealing our Buddhist background might create more harm than good during a visit. It might, for instance, take focus from the careseeker and their needs, while putting the focus on us as chaplains. While I can personally sometimes also use the "ordained as an interfaith minister" card

in my proverbial back pocket, many other Buddhist chaplains lack that option. One way this can come up is a sudden question from the careseeker like, "Do you believe in God?" The context of the question and the needs behind it are important. But there are times where I get the sense that not saying yes will be a big distraction and impediment. Being familiar with some of the multitudinous interpretations of "God," I can simply think in my head of an interpretation that is similar enough to my Buddhist sentiments and answer a brief honest and comforting, "yes." Other times, of course, counter-questions that help them themselves explore that notion of God might be helpful to the situation and concerns they face.

Moreover, engaging with others who come from very different traditions can help shed light on the blind spots of our own views and ways of thinking. I think this is one of the quiet, hidden benefits of engaging with other religions, and even other schools of Buddhism. Many people who live in another nation and culture speak about how they learn more about their own culture through the process. Similarly, when we engage with people of different faith traditions: observing their practices, having open dialog and listening to how and why they do what they do, it can often help us think about our own views and practices—and it helps reveal our blind assumptions to us; it brings forward unconscious thoughts into conscious awareness. We can become aware of previously unconscious biases and be better prepared to root them out. The more we follow through with such engagements, the more we are forced to consider and reconsider who we really are as a Buddhist. In turn, this can help our meetings with people from other traditions become more open, engaged, and authentic interactions.

One important further note related to the fact that we cannot possibly know about (much less represent) all religious and spiritual traditions, is that it is very important to develop a strong interreligious network to refer to when we have questions or to call upon depending on careseeker needs. It is possible and sometimes necessary to find someone and reach out suddenly when we have an important question related to a careseeker need. But, when possible, it is far easier to reach out to an individual who we know personally and have cultivated some relationship with. Other times, say a patient requires last rites or some ceremony that demands the presence of an Imam or Rabbi. Sometimes, there can be little time before you need that clergyperson to come.

Creating an Interreligious Space

Creating an interreligious space that is truly welcoming to people of a broad variety of traditions can be truly challenging. Some traditions require a particular object, symbol, or text, while other traditions may require the lack of imagery. How do we balance making a space welcoming to any and all?

One of the best solutions is a room (or rooms) which balances availability of books and objects with structures or furniture that keep such items out of view when not being used. One way around this is shelves or cupboards that may be opened or closed for use by different individuals and groups. Depending on the room, curtains or other forms of coverings may be convenient. If possible, include a place for washing either directly connected or otherwise nearby such a room/facility; water for various ways of purification can be a common ceremonial need in different ways and at least having a clearly marked source nearby can be incredibly helpful to those with such needs.

Building those networks in advance makes it far easier to call upon those individuals; they know ahead of time that they may be needed by the people you serve and often offer their help in advance.

Interfaith Rituals

Interfaith rituals can take a variety of forms. We will explore two major categories here: those that: (a) combine the traditions of the person or main people involved; and (b) interfaith services that are not specific to any particular view or religion. Following these, the section will also comment on providing rituals for those of traditions other than your own.

The most common time interfaith rituals occur are weddings, when two individuals come together and bring either their own personal or family religious tradition with them. A Hindu family may come together with a Protestant family. A Jewish and Sikh couple may wed. Two individuals from different indigenous traditions might come together for a wedding. A Jewish-Buddhist may wed a Christian-Sikh-Buddhist. The possibilities are almost endless and increasingly common in this globalized world. However, there are many other ritual possibilities as well: birth or coming-of-age celebrations; funerals and memorial services; and so on. Because laws regarding many of these functions differ depending on country, state, and province, it is critical that you first look up your own local laws and regulations regarding the requested ritual. With that being said, rarely will there be laws about more than weddings or funerals, and at least most of those laws deal with paperwork and details outside of the ceremony itself.[3] But because of the diversity, I can only make more general comments within this chapter.

Combining Two or More Traditions

Similar to most chaplaincy meetings, one of the first and most important things to do is listen. In the case of a wedding, we have to speak especially with the couple getting married. It is often important to meet with other key central participants and sometimes representatives from groups that will be participating. Listen to what people's preferences and interests are for the ceremony. You may enter the meeting with a few general outlines of ideas; sometimes people don't have strong preferences to start (or at least are not yet aware of what their strong preferences are). Basic outlines of a service can help start conversations. Watch their reactions closely and see what makes their faces light up or if there are subtle frowns or grimaces at any aspect. These reactions are all issues to explore and may lead to important clarifications or adjustments as time goes on.

In some cases, it may be important to meet with adjacent key people as well. For

---

3 https://theamm.org/marriage-laws/ is a very helpful site for wedding officiants in the USA.

Resources for Working with the Dying and Bereaved

Being with Dying: Cultivating Compassion and Fearlessness in the Presence of Death by Joan Halifax (2008)
Awake at the Bedside: Contemplative Teachings on Palliative and End-of-Life Care edited by Koshin Paley Ellison and Matt Weingast (2016)
Sitting with Death: Buddhist Insights to Help You Face your Fears and Live a Peaceful Life by Margaret Meloni (2021)
The Courage to Care: Being Fully Present with the Dying by Linda Bryce (2021)
At the Time of Death: Symbols and Rituals for Caregivers and Chaplains by David Bieniek (2019)

example, in the case of a wedding, the parents or grandparents might have strong opinions. Depending on the cultural background, they may also be expected to play major roles (maybe even more significant than the couple themselves) in the planning process. It is important to be open to such situations and navigate them with the couple– allowing others to make their voice heard and take some part in the process. Cultural circumstances can change, but the couple is usually the priority; it is their wedding and despite other wishes, we should still ultimately honor the fact that it is their special day.

Funerals and memorials can be more complex if there are differing voices. The passing of a loved one can create particularly strong and sometimes heated emotions, along with very strong opinions. It can also be important to communicate with hospital or hospice staff on rules and regulations around bedside rituals and even to negotiate issues around the disposition of the body. Do the individual's religious requirements fit with the local or facility requirements – and to what degree might there be wiggle room on either side?

When combining elements of rituals from multiple traditions it is especially important to pay attention to both: (a) what are the most critical parts to include from each tradition; and (b) what, if any, are aspects that should be avoided; what might be religiously or culturally offensive (e.g., avoiding pork on the wedding menu if it is a partially Muslim ritual event). It can be helpful to brainstorm and map out these key elements with people involved very early on in the process. Then, the rest of the ceremony can more comfortably be built around that foundation.

No Specified Tradition

Interfaith services without a specified tradition can occur in numerous circumstances. Possibly most common for chaplains are memorial services, such as after a campus tragedy for a university chaplain, and commemorations of key events or large-scale tragedies. Chaplains may also be asked to lead interfaith services in the interest of inclusion and diversity. Likewise, whatever the purpose, inclusion and diversity are critical to such a service. When there is ample time, trying to ensure representation of different traditions through readings, prayers, or focusing on different individuals through ritual acts (e.g., a number of different people called up to each light a candle), having equitable representation is critical. It may take extra effort to find representatives of minority traditions, but whenever possible taking the time to do so is important. This can also be a perfect time to make use of your networks, whether for direct participation, ceremonial recommendations, or for referrals who can provide more appropriate help for the circumstances.

At other times, an institution may simply provide a short period of time (5-10 minutes) for an interfaith or interreligious service that is part of larger ceremony or simply a brief point in time when a team is able to meet (i.e., a brief meeting at a hospital ward at the beginning of a new day's shift). As a general rule of thumb, when you can't properly provide representation of different traditions, using words and ritual actions that can have meaning across religious, spiritual, and non-religious traditions is usually better. We can use our moral authority to speak of commonly valued traits like love and compassion, use phrases that do not favor any specific tradition over another, and speak more to the theme needed or requested for the time.

Rituals of Traditions Other than Your Own

Many chaplains perform prayers for those outside their own tradition. Depending on the type of position as a chaplain, you may have to perform more involved non-Buddhist rituals. For example, Catholic families in a hospital who have a stillbirth or a baby who will not make it can have a non-Catholic perform a baptism if a priest is unavailable at the time. This role typically falls to the chaplain, no matter their denomination. Not only does this require ritual knowledge, but also the willingness, grace, and sincerity to perform it respectfully. Performing rituals from traditions other than your own can be challenging. Yet, as a Buddhist, I think imagining this as one of the thousand-armed bodhisattva Guan-yin's approaches to aiding the cries of suffering in the world or a type of skillful means allows us to more easily adapt than chaplains from certain other traditions. Try to find a mental framework that works for you, because it is then far easier to perform such rituals with sincerity and attentiveness to the careseekers' needs. If you do not feel able to perform a certain ritual, it is sometimes possible to ask a teammate of a different vocation (e.g. nurse or professor) but the same religious tradition as the careseeker or family to actually perform the ritual following the instructions that you have taken the time to research.

Contemplative Practices for Multireligious or Interreligious Care

I sometimes talk to Buddhist chaplains who would love to incorporate more contemplative practices from their own Buddhist traditions into their spiritual care, but are hesitant because they do not want to force their own spiritual tradition onto others. These are valid concerns, so here are a few sample ways to both honor the other in their own space, while also allowing Buddhist chaplains who resonate with such practices to use them when they feel it is appropriate. Buddhist chaplains can then feel genuine to themselves in the Buddhist base of the care they provide, using those practices as tools which may even enhance the quality of care provided.

Learning and Adapting other Faith's Contemplative Practices

Abrahamic traditions have more history of contemplative traditions than people realize and this can offer inroads to those of us with meditative training to adapt our practices readily for careseekers from other traditions. Catholicism, for example, has a long history of "centering prayer" which is remarkably similar to Zen meditation practice, yet with a mantra-like practice. Centering Prayer requires individuals sit quietly and focus on their breath and/or the 'presence' of God. If having trouble with focus, adherents recommend using a repeated word or short phrase like, "Jesus" or "God's love," saying it calmly over and over again either quietly or in one's own head. When calmed and focus becomes strong enough, you can let the word slip away.

I have found it beneficial to know a few facts about the history of centering prayer to legitimize it as a part of Christian and specifically Catholic tradition. But my experience guiding Buddhist meditations felt readily applicable to guiding careseekers in Centering Prayer. There is not space here to cover the hundreds of contemplative practices available from other religious traditions, but there are plenty of resources available when you look. Several titles are included in the breakout box on the next page.

For those who have the interest, I would encourage you to explore and find a few practices for your own chaplaincy toolkit. Reading from a book or watching online videos can be helpful, but if possible, it can add a lot to your experience by contacting experienced practitioners from those traditions. I have found people happy and willing to share their practices even when I tell them I am a Buddhist. Sometimes they are even more enthusiastic when I disclose my religious background – and it leads to wonderful exchanges! Talking to a tradition insider can help you adjust your vocabulary and nuances to more genuinely use the practice with others. As Doehring and Kestenbaum state, "Using calming spiritual practices will help [chaplains] maintain healthy spiritual boundaries and not use their power in spiritually coercive or neglectful ways." (p. 131) So there can be numerous additional benefits for both the giver and recipient.

Non-Buddhist Contemplative Practices

The Experience of Meditation: Experts Introduce the Major Traditions edited by Jonathan Shear (2006)
50 Ways to Pray: Practices from Many Traditions and Times by Teresa Blythe (2006)
Contemplation Nation: How Ancient Practices are Changing the Way We Live by Mirabai Bush (2011)
Contemplative Practices in Action: Spirituality, Meditation, and Health by Thomas Plante (2010)
Thirsty for God by Bradley Holt (2017)
Spiritual Traditions for the Contemporary Church by Robin Maas and Gabriel O'Donnell (1990)
These are the Words: A Vocabulary of Jewish Spiritual Life by Arthur Green (2012)
Be Still and Get Going: A Jewish Medittation Practice for Real Life by Alan Lew (2005)
The Jew in the Lotus: A Poet's Rediscovery of Jewish Identity in Buddhist India by Roger Kamenetz (2007)
Meditation and Judaism: Exploring the Jewish Meditative Paths by DovBar Pinson (2004)
Jewish Meditation: A Practical Guide by Aryeh Kaplan (1995)
The Knowing Heart: A Sufi Path of Transformation by Kabir Helminski (1999)
The Sufi Science of Self-Realization: A Guide to the Seventeen Ruinous Traits, the ten Steps to Discipleship and the Six Realities of the Heart by Shaykh Muhammad Hishan Kabbani (2018)
Japji: Meditation in Sikhism by Swami Rama (1987)
Meditation and its Practices: A Definitive Guide to Meditation in Yoga and Vedanta by Swami Adiswarananda (2007)

10
INTERCULTURAL COMPETENCIES
by Henry C.H. Shiu

Dharmic Basis for Intercultural Competencies

The *Lotus Sūtra* (*Saddharmapuṇḍarīka-sūtra*) is one of the most revered Buddhist scriptures, particularly in China and Japan, where it inspired the formation of the Tiantai and Tendai schools, respectively. Its twenty-fifth chapter, "The Universal Gate of Bodhisattva Avalokiteśvara" (*Avalokiteśvara-vikurvaṇa-nirdeśa*), known in China as the *Pumen pin* (Chapter of Universal Gate) and in Japan as the *Kannon-gyô* (Sūtra of Avalokiteśvara), is particularly celebrated and influential. This chapter contributes to the popularity of Bodhisattva Avalokiteśvara in East Asia as it describes how the Bodhisattva can appear in thirty-three forms that correspond to the spiritual needs of various sentient beings. These emanations include those who follow different paths of Buddhist practice (including the Hearers, Solitary Realizers, and Bodhisattvas) and other forms of Vedic origin. They also include gods and humans, males and females, elders and youngsters, ministers, and householders, the rich and the poor.

For Buddhists, Avalokiteśvara, or Perceiver of the World's Sound, has become the embodiment of "compassion" (*karuṇā*). The magical power of appearing in emanation to liberate sentient beings from the many forms of suffering has firmly established the popularity of the Bodhisattva in Mahāyāna Buddhist practice. All these descriptions of the enlightening activities of Avalokiteśvara echo the theme of "skillful means" (*upāyakauśalya*, more often referred to as *upāya*) of the *Lotus Sūtra*. When read in the light of Buddhist chaplaincy and spiritual care in contemporary society, the chapter of Universal Gate can also inspire Buddhist chaplains to cultivate their intercultural competencies.

Much like Avalokiteśvara in the *Lotus Sūtra*, Buddhist chaplains "manifest" themselves in a role that allows them to serve any community members, regardless of their spiritual affiliation, cultural background, race or ethnicity, and sexual orientation. With only approximately 1.2% of the American population (Pew Forum, 2022) and 1.4% of the Canadian population (Statistic Canada, 2022) identifying as Buddhist, Buddhist chaplains in North America are likely to serve careseekers who practice a religion other than their own or have no affiliation with a religion, including those who identify themselves as "spiritual but not religious." In addition, the world has shrunk into a global village, and both the United States and Canada have become more culturally diverse than ever before. It goes without saying that chaplains have a responsibility to cultivate spiritual and cultural competencies to understand and address the distresses and challenges experienced by individuals of diverse faith communities and cultural groups. The complex role of Buddhist chaplains to non-Buddhist careseekers differs from being a "spiritual friend" (*kalyāṇamitra*) to a fellow practitioner within the Buddhist tradition.

Avalokiteśvara holds a significant position, acting as an emblem of compassion within the Buddhist faith, an interpretation accepted not only by followers of Mahāyāna and Vajrayāna sects but also by practitioners of Theravāda Buddhism. Western perceptions of Theravāda

Buddhism, often filtered through a prism that strips away its multi-dimensional nuances, frequently paints the tradition with broad brushstrokes. These simplified portraits typically trace the silhouette of *vipassanā* meditation techniques and Pāli chants, which ostensibly appear incongruent with the reverential practices towards Bodhisattvas. Yet, this perspective may not fully capture the rich tapestry of this tradition. Although the concept of Bodhisattvahood is more commonly associated with the development of Mahāyāna Buddhism, it is noteworthy that depictions of Avalokiteśvara are regularly discovered within the monastic spaces of Theravāda communities across various South-Asian nations, including Thailand, Sri Lanka, and Cambodia. John Clifford Holt, in his anthropological research, sheds light on the legitimization and significance of beliefs related to Avalokiteśvara within the Theravāda culture of Sri Lanka (Holt, 1991).

Beyond this particular context, the cultivation of compassion is a cornerstone in the broader realm of Theravāda Buddhism. Critiques of early Buddhist schools, which now only encompass Theravāda, are readily found in the oldest Mahāyāna scriptures. These sources, written in a polemical tone, decry the perceived lack of emphasis on compassion within early Buddhism in comparison to Mahāyāna. This characterization, though perhaps intended to foster a greater commitment to the cultivation of *bodhicitta* (the mind of enlightenment) among Mahāyāna followers, stands in stark contrast with the actual practice of Theravāda. Contrary to this criticism, Theravāda Buddhism deeply values and emphasizes the cultivation of the four *brahmavihārās*, also known as the sublime or divine states. These include "compassion" (*karuṇā*), which is one of the central tenets prominently manifested in the practice. Indeed, the representation of Avalokiteśvara in the *Lotus Sūtra* is employed as a symbol that encapsulates compassion. This embodiment transcends ordinary realms to offer a profound source of inspiration for Buddhist chaplains, encouraging them to serve in an increasingly pluralistic society. This symbolic understanding resonates with both Theravāda and Mahāyāna practitioners, revealing the universal significance of compassion in diverse Buddhist traditions.

Many counseling tools have been identified as core competencies for Buddhist spiritual care, including deep listening and appropriate response, being fully present, and witnessing suffering with empathy and compassion, among others. In this regard, as an example, Lee and Oh advocate for integrating the compassion ideal of Mahāyāna Buddhism in the therapeutic stance as a Buddhist chaplain (Lee and Oh, 2019). Given the aforementioned discussions, we can extrapolate this advocacy to embody the spiritual paradigm of Buddhism, encapsulating its various traditions. Similarly, the writers of *The Arts of Contemplative Care*, the first book of its kind to provide a comprehensive overview of Buddhist chaplaincy in North America, emphasize the importance of listening skills, embodied compassion, and attentiveness in the present moment as the foundation of Buddhist contemplative care (Giles and Miller, 2012). Others point out the challenges of performing rituals, prayers or other religious services that are meaningful to careseekers. As with all forms of spiritual caregiving, knowledge in secular psychology, counseling, and modalities of psychotherapy is deemed indispensable. Such areas have been discussed in detail in many recent studies on Buddhist spiritual care. However, "cultural/intercultural competency" seems to be an area that has taken a back seat in chaplaincy training, perhaps because it is viewed as a "soft skill" in comparison.

Principles for Intercultural Competency

Sanford and Michon (2010: 10) define cultural competency as "the awareness and functioning of caregivers in multicultural environments or among populations different from themselves." This definition includes three themes: 1) making no assumptions about other traditions or cultures and being willing to learn about them; 2) educating oneself on other cultural norms, rituals, and practices; and 3) dealing with different forms of oppression and privilege. The first two themes are necessary for a Buddhist chaplain to fulfill the role required by the care-seekers, while the third theme is more related to how "compassion" manifests itself in the socially engaged spiritual practice of contemporary societies. Viewed from another angle, the cultivation of cultural competency by Buddhist chaplains is a modernized expression of *upāya*, or skillful means, to best serve the careseekers in alleviating their suffering.

Upāya deals with the nature of Buddhist teachings and the enlightening activities of Bodhisattvas. Damien Keown proposes a four-stage progressive understanding that helps to comprehend the objectives of each stage of *upāya*. The first stage uses the raft simile to convey that the Dharma is like a raft used to cross over the ocean of *saṃsāra* rather than an object to hold onto. The second stage describes *upāya* as the method of transmitting the Dharma, involving skillfully adapting the audience's terminology to convey the teachings, highlighting the provisional nature of all teachings. The third stage sees *upāya* as an essential component in the spiritual development of the Bodhisattva. The last stage justifies the controversial actions performed by advanced Bodhisattvas. (Keown 1998)

This analysis offers valuable perspectives on the concept of *upāya*, yet it is crucial to acknowledge that this exploration is primarily focused on its interpretation within the framework of Mahāyāna Buddhism. Even though *upāya* enjoys a significant presence in Mahāyāna teachings, this concept is not confined to this tradition and can be traced back to the roots of early Buddhism. Within the Pāli canon, *upāya* assumes the guise of *upāya-kosalla* and its relative adjective, *upāya-kusala*. These terms encapsulate the Buddha's adeptness in tailoring his teachings to match the cognitive capacities and spiritual necessities of his disciples, a trait clearly demonstrated in the *Sigālovadasutta* (DN31) and numerous Jātaka narratives. Therefore, as a paradigm of inspiration for Buddhist chaplains, the scope of *upāya* should not be narrowly confined to the Mahāyāna tradition but should be more universally employed to accommodate even those seeking spiritual guidance from non-Buddhist avenues.

Furthermore, it would be an oversimplification to view Keown's "four-stage evolutionary pattern" of *upāya* as disparate, sequential stages. In reality, these "stages" often coexist and may be manifested concurrently. In many cases, some of these "stages" are conflated, as evidenced in the parables of the *Lotus Sūtra*. For instance, the parable of the burning house tells of a rich man whose house is on fire, but his three children are preoccupied with playing and unaware of the danger. The father then entices them out of the house by claiming that three carts of toys, pulled by a goat, a deer, and an ox, await them outside. However, when the children are safe, they do not find the promised carts but rather a grand carriage draped with precious stones and pulled by white oxen. The rich man represents the Buddha, and the three children represent sentient beings in *saṃsāra*, while the three carts of promised toys refer to the three vehicles of *śrāvakayāna*, *pratyekabuddhayāna*, and *bodhisattvayāna*, and the great oxen carriage represents *buddhayāna*. The parable includes elements of Keown's stage-two explanation, with the father speaking in the language and interests of the children, and the justification of lying in stage-four *upāya*. The parable is further designed to express the concept that the doctrines of *śrāvakayāna*, *pratyekabuddhayāna*, and *bodhisattvayāna* are contingent, pointing towards religious pluralism as opposed to exclusivism or inclusivism. In essence, exclusivists assert that only one faith holds the truth, rendering all other beliefs fallacious; in contrast, inclusivists contend that a single religion contains the absolute truth, while all others merely hold fragments of it.

There are also two distinct paradigms of religious pluralism, each bearing unique implications for interfaith dialogue. One model perceives varying faiths as diverse, localised articulations of a universal essence. Hence, interfaith dialogue is seen as a vital tool for refining the expression of this shared core. Conversely, another model views different religions as fundamentally distinct. In this complex landscape, where does the *Lotus Sūtra's* teaching stand? It appears to hinge heavily on traditional interpretation.[1] Within the Buddhist community, there are advocates for a more inclusivist perspective, highlighting that various vehicles only capture certain aspects of the Buddha's ultimate teachings, and asserting that the absolute truth is exclusively delineated in the *Lotus Sūtra*. Yet, in line with the principle of *upāya*, another perspective posits that all vehicles offer merely provisional depictions of the ultimate truth. This viewpoint suggests that the final reality, described as the buddhayāna, transcends any specific scripture or verbal teaching and lies beyond conceptual comprehension. Thus, the teachings of diverse traditions can all be seen as guiding one toward this personal enlightenment.

Similarly, the aspiration of Avalokiteśvara in chapter 25 of the *Lotus Sūtra* to develop cultural competency as a Buddhist chaplain requires an insightful adoption of *upāya* to suit the needs of the careseekers. This approach maintains that the Dharma is not an object to be attached to, and that appearances in response to the needs of diverse spiritual and cultural backgrounds of care-seekers are a form of spiritual cultivation, and that the occasional need for appropriate responses, such as lying to dementia patients, is justified. In terms of interfaith dialogue, even though it is not necessarily to assert that all religions are equal, one should maintain that at the inception of such dialogues, each participant should acknowledge the parity of all faith adherents in terms of their rights within the conversation.

How to appear in a role that suits the needs of others is not an improvisatory act but rather a result of intentionally cultivating cultural competency. One must learn to be culturally sensitive to become an understanding listener and a better communicator. Below, we will explore the cultivation of cultural sensitivity and competency using Sanford and Michon's definition of the three themes of cultural competency:

1. THE NEED TO REMAIN HUMBLE, MAKE FEW OR NO ASSUMPTIONS, AND BE PREPARED TO LEARN ABOUT OTHER CULTURES AND PEOPLE

First and foremost, the cornerstone of enhancing skills to address the array of distress and challenges, uniquely experienced by individuals from diverse spiritual and cultural backgrounds, lies in fostering the awareness of our preconceptions. It is crucial to handle these assumptions delicately, ensuring they are not utilized to stereotype or diminish a care seeker to mere characteristics of a group they are associated with. More specifically, one should not make assumptions about any individual, culture, ethnicity, age group, gender, or religious or spiritual tradition, nor should one make assumptions about an individual as a representative of a culture, an ethnic group, an age group, a gender, or a religious or spiritual tradition. A person remains an individual in the ethnic or cultural group they are a part of. A culturally sensitive chaplain should never reduce a care-seeker to any perceived stereotypical group. Such assumptions can easily lead to misunderstanding, prejudice, and miscommunication.

Relevant teachings from the Buddhist scripture warn against holding onto any "view" (*diṭṭhi*). The Buddhist notion of "view" is understood as an obstacle to perceiving things just as they are (*yathābhūtadassana*). Although specific examples of "wrong views"

---

[1] Representatives of these two models can be found in John Hick's *God Has Many Names*, 1980, and S. Mark Heim's "The Pluralistic Hypothesis, Realism, and Post-eschatology," *Religious Studies* 25, 1992, p. 207-219.

(*micchā-diṭṭhi*) are given in the Buddhist canon, such as the belief in the existence of self (*attā*) or the denial of the consequences of actions (*kamma*), "wrong views" should also include erroneous opinions we form about someone we do not know, based on generalizations of their cultural, ethnic, sexual, or spiritual backgrounds. Such opinions are obstacles for a spiritual caregiver to perceive careseekers as they are. In the *Abhidhamma*, "wrong views" are explained as:

> Gone over to view (*diṭṭhi-gata*), the thicket of view (*diṭṭhi-gahana*), a wilderness of view (*diṭṭhi-kantāra*), the contrariness of view (*diṭṭhi-visūkāyika*), the turmoil of view (*diṭṭhi-vipphandita*), the fetter of views (*diṭṭhi-saṃyojana*), holding (*gāha*), fixity (*patiṭṭhāha*), adherence (*abhinivesa*), clinging (*parāmāsa*), a bad path (*kumagga*), a false way (*micchā-patha*), falsity (*micchatta*), the realm of (other) systems of crossing over (*titthāyatana*), the hold of the perverted views (*vipariyesa-gāha*). (Fuller, 2005: 79)

These examples of "wrong views" also reflect the different kinds of assumptions we make about other people, based on wilderness, fixation, clinging, falsity, and so on. But "wrong views" are not wrong because they are views from another religious tradition; even "right views" of Buddhist teachings can become "wrong views" if they are held onto with attachment. So "wrong views" are considered "wrong" not because they are different from the Buddhist teachings, but because they can cloud the mind of the person who holds onto them, thus forming unconscious biases, prejudices, and discriminations. They contribute to a fixated perspective of viewing people who do not share the same ethnic, cultural, or spiritual background. Reminding oneself to avoid making wrong assumptions that mistake individuals as the cultures they represent is an important first step in honing cultural competency.

Here, the Buddhist teaching of dependent-origination (*paṭiccasamuppāda*) helps one deepen their understanding that each individual is a sum of many parts, with complex psychological, cultural, religious, societal, economic, and educational histories, as well as beliefs and social location, that shape them into what they are. All these external physical conditions, as well as internal psychological conditions, are the factors which an individual is dependent upon to originate their unique personality. Such identities are fluid but not fixed; however, these fleeting personalities deserve to be respected as they currently are. They all deserve equal access to loving-kindness (*mettā*) and compassion (*karuṇā*).

As Buddhist chaplains or spiritual friends, we should have the insight to recognize and accept that care-seekers are individuals who are different from us and from each other. The goal is not to convert these individuals to our beliefs, judge their worldview or practices, or assimilate them into our culture; instead, it is to embrace them as they are, with loving-kindness and compassion, and to help alleviate their distresses and sufferings. The "right view" here is to have no preconceived notions or hidden agenda.

In other words, the "right view" is to have "no views," much like the teaching in Nāgārjuna's renowned treatise, the *Mūlamādhyamakakārikā* (*Fundamental Verses on the Middle Way*), which demonstrates explicit awareness of the danger of holding onto any view, wrong or right. Practitioners are reminded to keep an open or "empty" (*śūnya*) mind about how things truly are. Such reflection helps free one's mind from the erroneous assumption of "own-being" (*svabhāva*) that may have been imposed onto the perception of the care-seekers. It also directs our attention to see the impermanent nature of the crisis an individual is undergoing, rather than postulating the enduring presence of the situation out of anxiety and fear.

Using the language of Zen Buddhism, this state of mind is known as *shoshin* 初心, or the beginner's mind. Cultivating an attitude of "not knowing," openness, freshness, and being free from prejudices is conducive to avoiding assumptions about care-seekers. The Sōtō Zen concept makes it clear that one cannot merely learn about the concept or stance of making no assumptions about other cultures and people; instead, one needs to cultivate the state of *shoshin* to counter the habitual tendencies of mental formation and unconscious biases by way of meditation. It is the result of a transformed mind. In medical services, for example, the "beginner's mind" can help professionals remain responsive to the individuality of illness. As Louise Younie notes:

> Each patient is a universe of unknowns, presenting with suffering which cannot always be classified with a diagnosis. Improvisation and openness may not just benefit our patients enduring their patient journeys but may also revive and reconnect us with our humanity.
> ...Remaining curious and open ties in with an inductive approach to consulting described as starting where the patient is at and with what they want to say, as opposed to the deductive approach, working to confirm or refute hypotheses in the clinical encounter.
> ...This was deemed good for the patient, as GPs who consulted more inductively had a greater sense of 'knowing' their patient. But the doctors working inductively also seemed to benefit, being found to have greater satisfaction in their practice. (Younie, 2017)

Other qualities, such as deep listening and being fully present, are also "by-products" of this cultivation of *shoshin*. The traditional Buddhist mindfulness meditation that leads to letting go of preconceptions and habitual patterns of perception transforms us by unlearning our belief systems, transports us to a place of curiosity, and transcends us to attain a concentrated state of mind free from distractions. It is not just the foundation of Buddhist spirituality and Buddhist chaplaincy, but also the foundation of the Buddhist approach to cultural competency. Samuel K. Lee points out the importance of having a "theological" basis in the development of cultural competency:

> If, however, the chaplain is lost within his or her ethnocentric theological perspective or worldview and cannot consider the local context...of patients, his or her hermeneutics may result in dogmatic imposition, cultural imperialism, or cultural violence. The ability to engage in interreligious dialogue is another component that should be included in the theological consideration of multicultural competencies. All in all, the basic theological foundation of multicultural competencies must show how who we are theologically shapes what we do as pastoral or spiritual care providers in clinical settings. (Lee, 2004: 48)

The grounding of the *upāya* of cultural competency in the wisdom that frees one from forming "wrong views" about individual care-seekers is how Buddhist theology shapes the approach to cultural competency in providing spiritual care. The emphasis at this stage is on the cultivation of wisdom through contemplative practice. What follows is the development of compassionate skillful means of interacting with care-seekers.

2. EDUCATING THEMSELVES TO A REASONABLE EXTENT ON THE CULTURAL PRACTICES OF DIFFERENT GROUPS

Intercultural competency is generally understood as the ability to interact and communicate effectively with people of different backgrounds, cultures, or religions. Compared to cultural competency, the emphasis of intercultural competency shifts from a passive stance of understanding and listening to an active development of skillful techniques to interact and engage with others meaningfully. The open mind or beginner's mind allows one to develop a sympathetic understanding of differing cultural or religious views, forming the basis of an appreciative orientation toward other value systems, and a genuine curiosity and sincere willingness to learn about them. This learning can include the diversity of other cultures or traditions, culturally sensitive topics, proper gestures, histories and lived experiences, knowledge of rites and rituals performed on particular occasions, meanings of chants and prayers used in other spiritual traditions, how to use the rosary beads, where to place religious images, differences in ethical norms, and more. The list can be endless, and our learning journey is also endless.

While learning is a never-ending journey and one can never be perfect in this endeavor, openness and eagerness transform the practitioner to genuinely appreciate differences in other cultures. Only when equipped with such knowledge and the ability to interact can one best answer the spiritual needs of those being served. There is no presupposition of the Buddhist perspective in relation to others. Grounded in an open mind, Buddhist chaplains can skillfully adapt themselves when engaging with others from different spiritual or cultural backgrounds with respect, deep listening, and complete presence, much like the manifestation of Avalokiteśvara in chapter 25 of the *Lotus Sūtra*. It is with such skillful knowledge and experience supporting interfaith communications that cultural competency becomes intercultural competency. Ringu Tulku Rinpoche wrote a beautiful poem, "It Is a Pleasure to Be a Student," which captures the spirit of "no view" and "beginner's mind" in learning:

I am a student.
I have been a student as long as I remember
And it is a pleasure to be a student.
It is a pleasure to learn that I don't know.
It is a pleasure to learn that I already know.
It is a pleasure to learn that I was mistaken.
It is a pleasure to learn from Great Masters.
It is a joy to learn by sharing what I learnt.
It is a joy to learn how to be what I am.
I seek to learn about the world around me.
I seek to learn about what I actually am.
I seek to learn how to be a proper human being.
Clouds show me the nature of my world.
Rivers show me the nature of myself.
Babies show me how to be more human.
I am a student.
I will be a student as long as I live.
And it is a pleasure to be a student.[2]

The willingness to learn is the key to effective interaction and engagement with others. Showing an interest in learning about others' lived experiences is a signal of genuine care and openness to the careseekers. Successful intercultural competency involves cultural sensitivity and intelligence, both of which result from learning. As Wakoh Shannon Hickey emphasizes in her chapter entitled "Meditation Is Not Enough" (Hickey, 2012), one needs to learn a lot outside of any particular tradition of the Buddha Dharma to gain the competency to serve interculturally. This includes an appreciative knowledge of other religious

---

2 Fisher in Giles and Miller, 2012, p. 173-174.

traditions and cultural practices, the study of contemporary psychology, various modalities of psychotherapy and spiritual counseling, rituals and liturgy used in various Buddhist and non-Buddhist traditions, understanding of ethical norms of different cultures, experiences of working with care-seekers through CPE training, and so on. If the previous stage of the discussion focuses on the use of *upāya*, from scriptural teachings to contemplative practices, to train oneself in the realization of an open mind, this current stage pays attention to the development of compassionate expediency through the acquired wisdom.

Monica Sanford proposes adopting the Three *Prajñās* as the framework for Buddhist spiritual care. She specifically points out that the Three *Prajñās* are not to be confused as being synonymous with the acts of listening, contemplating, and practicing, but as the wisdom derived from those acts and the fruitions of those acts. (Sanford, 2021: 81) This framework provides us with a general guideline for the training of Buddhist spiritual caregivers leading from the stages of self, student, and chaplain, toward that of the *kalyāṇamitra* or spiritual friend. The Buddhist *kalyāṇamitra*-ship is a spiritual friendship that transcends cultural, ethnic, gender, and religious boundaries. While Buddhist wisdom is uncontrived by nature, Buddhist compassion arising from it and manifesting through spiritual friendship needs a lot of knowledge and adaptation. With these interreligious and intercultural competencies as the outcome, it is essential that the Three *Prajñās* framework should not be limited to the knowledge and training within the Buddhist traditions.

In this regard, Mary A. Fukuyama and Todd D. Sevig, both counseling psychologists, propose a five-step multicultural counseling framework that can serve as inspiration to enrich the Buddhist approach to spiritual care in North America. The five-step framework includes: 1) personal awareness of one's own social location and identity; 2) knowledge of the history, formation, and experience of the cultural identities of oneself and the careseekers; 3) skills and abilities to engage in meaningful communication with others to foster mutual respect and understanding; 4) the capacity for empathy and compassion for others; and 5) the actions that are borne out of the foregoing principles. (Anderson, 2004)

The Buddhist Three *Prajñās* framework and Fukuyama and Sevig's five-step framework are complementary, with the former being broader in scope while the latter being more specific in its direction of cultivation. Indeed, the two frameworks can be integrated such that at each of the five steps of the multicultural counseling framework, one can develop the three wisdoms of listening, contemplating, and practicing. The five steps are then reinterpreted not as a linear path of progression, but as a continuous journey of perfecting oneself in the role of chaplaincy. One remains a student, as Ringu Tulku Rinpoche advocates, and finds pleasure in the never-ending journey of learning and perfecting.

Adaptation is an art; adapting traditional Buddhist practices to meet the ever-changing spiritual needs of different societies cannot be strictly defined or bound to an instruction manual. One needs to improvise on the spot when interacting with the care-seekers with full presence, deep listening, careful observation, and authenticity. However, developing improvisational skills is not easy. Oftentimes, it takes years of hard training and learning before one can be good at improvising.

Whichever framework one works with, while the required skills and knowledge can differ with different social environments one works in, at the core of the Buddhist training of intercultural competency is an open mind that is not clung to any attachment of religious identity, sexual orientation, ethnic background, or cultural norm, of both oneself and those of the care-seekers. The effortless manifestation of Avalokiteśvara in the forms of a monk, a nun, a householder, a wife, a wealthy person, a state official, a brahman, one of the Vedic deities, or other nonhumans, etc., is precisely an illustration of the principle of "not-self" (*anattā*). This is the meaning of the "universal gate" of Bodhisattva Avalokiteśvara. Intercultural competency is a universal gate that allows one to effectively interact, understand, communicate, and work with people across all cultural barriers.

3. THE URGENT NECESSITY OF DEALING WITH VARIOUS FORMS OF OPPRESSION AND PRIVILEGE

We can all help to enshrine cultural sensitivity in the workplace, including healthcare units, hospices, schools and colleges, correctional facilities, the military, and so on, to help build a more just and equal society. Unfortunately, systemic racism against Black, Indigenous, and people of colour (BIPOC) and the oppression of women and lesbian, gay, bisexual, transgender, queer or questioning, intersex, asexual/aromantic/agender (LGBTQIA) communities has been pervasive throughout the healthcare and education systems. For example, Tetyana Pylypiv Shippee and others demonstrate that BIPOC users in long-term services and supports (LTSS) "have less access to quality care and report poorer quality of life compared to their white counterparts" (Shippee et al., 2022). It takes courage and bold actions to combat systemic racism. With the cultivation of wisdom and compassion summarized in the first two themes of Sanford's definition of cultural competency, one is naturally led to the third theme, which represents the application of the practice in a socially engaged way. It is to put the embodiment of wisdom and compassion into action to help alleviate suffering on a systemic level.

Taking responsibility for ensuring structures and behaviours do not contribute to xenophobia can help minimize racial prejudice, ethnic hatred, religious intolerance, sexual discrimination, and various forms of violence. Many such practices begin with respecting and protecting others' religious heritage, cultural norms, lived experiences, and native languages. Systemic change begins at the individual level. It is the individual pieces that make up the interrelated whole. Therefore, systemic change is achieved only when change is found in most parts of a system. We all have a role in ensuring a better society is being shaped for everyone. It is important to understand the challenges that oppressed groups are currently facing in our society. Chapter 12 will provide a more detailed treatment of power, privilege, and oppression and what Buddhist chaplains can do to help heal white supremacy, systemic injustice, and individual oppression.

11
PRACTICAL PSYCHOLOGY FOR CHAPLAINS
by Linda Hochstetler

Introduction

I am a Buddhist psychotherapist, trained as a social worker and a long-time practitioner of Vajrayana Buddhism. I think of myself as a spiritual social worker with a special interest in dying and death. My academic studies have been in social work, but I have been a lay Buddhist chaplain (and meditation teacher) for my sangha since 2014. I have studied intensely the many death practices in Vajrayana Buddhism and offered guidance at end of life to many Buddhist and non-Buddhist individuals and their families throughout the dying process and into bereavement.

As a Buddhist chaplain and reader, you may not feel you have had much training in conducting clinical risk assessments. It is not a significant part of many spiritual or pastoral trainings for chaplains. Much training focuses more on spiritual understanding. I realize that while I have trained in psychotherapy and have extensive experience with risk assessments, most Buddhist chaplains do not. Buddhist chaplains generally engage in spiritual counselling and prefer to pass 'harder cases' on to someone else. It is important to work within one's scope of training and to realize one's limits, while also making sure to ask relevant questions and work together on teams to make sure we are not ignoring actual problems.

This chapter on necessary risk assessments by Buddhist chaplains is provided within the context of providing supportive spiritual counselling while also listening for issues outside of your scope. It assumes that as a Buddhist chaplain you have honed the general pragmatic skills covered in earlier chapters. You can provide basic spiritual counselling and feel competent supporting others.

In the midst of a supportive conversation, people regularly go into areas that are really out of the scope of most Buddhist chaplains. These areas are the issues described within a Western framework as 'mental health issues', in the broadest of senses. For Buddhist chaplains delivering services in North America, the Western mental health framework requires them to be competent to screen for any of these issues, and to liaise with other professionals to support the individual through these issues.

Some Buddhist chaplains might think of mental health symptoms as a spiritual crisis. There is a continuum of beliefs in terms of what symptoms might be considered a spiritual crisis and what symptoms might be considered a mental health crisis, and it's not always clear where things fall according to the various people involved. For example, meditation practices often lead to states of deep absorption, which can look a lot like dissociation, a symptom of trauma and emotional dysregulation.

Communication between Eastern teachers and Western Buddhist students can be easily misunderstood, leading to high-risk situations involving abuse. As we've learned from the accusations against several Buddhist teachers, no one is exempt from accountability. Sogyal Rinpoche was a charismatic Tibetan Buddhist teacher and author, and much loved by many students around the globe. In 2017, the senior leaders of his Rigpa organization were forced to publicly apologize for leaving students at risk and failing to address what they knew of

Sogyal Rinpoche's sexual, physical, and emotional abuse. The accountability was not just on Sogyal Rinpoche himself but on the spiritual organization that supported him. There are countless other such examples of ignoring bad behaviour or abuse by spiritual leaders in other religions as well. No religion is above this accountability.

Buddhist chaplains work collaboratively in systems of support which includes organizations and larger governmental bodies. As such, it is important for all chaplains to understand the liability expectations within their jurisdictions. Jurisdictions are determined by the state or province where the chaplain practices or works. These expectations vary greatly and are non-negotiable. In general, the more training one has, the more responsibility one has. A chaplain with a master's degree in counselling has more responsibility than one without this level of training; a chaplain who is also a registered or licensed psychotherapist or social worker may have even greater accountability to a board or college, depending on their state or provincial jurisdiction. While many chaplains also hold mental health clinician licenses (e.g., psycho-spiritual therapist, licensed social worker, marriage and family therapist, and so on), this chapter assumes that the Buddhist chaplain reader has the same basic level of knowledge as a non-clinician.

Liability relates to the expectation of what a trained person ought to know to do in risky situations. A Buddhist chaplain needs to be able to work within their scope of practice for delivering spiritual counselling and support, but also listen in the back of their minds for whisperings or direct mention of issues that might need triaging. This means that that a Buddhist chaplain accepts their role of triage manager for risks beyond their scope of practice.

In order to manage the risk of liability, Buddhist chaplains must document their risk assessment questions, answers, and actions.[1]

At the core of liability risk management is documentation that issues were heard and handled appropriately. This may include a full investigation or simply a further question, as will be described later in this chapter. Regardless of the action, a thorough documentation of the risk and the action taken is a necessary part of the Buddhist chaplain role. This transparency and accountability are necessary for Buddhist chaplains to maintain their respect with other professionals who they work closely with, and also with the Buddhist community at large.

Risk Assessment Protocols

Risk assessments are considered the 'sword' component of Buddhist chaplain work. This involves the radical compassion component of doing what's really necessary for the beings involved rather than allowing suffering to continue. It contrasts with the 'stream' component of chaplaincy that involves the supportive and nurturing counselling role that many chaplains find easier and more comfortable. Being a qualified Buddhist chaplain requires skill in both sword and stream activities.

Risk assessments are made by asking a series of questions about the situation, followed by a determination of the level of risk. The greater the chaplain's skill with risk assessment, the more nuanced the response will be. Levels of risk can include low, medium, and high risk. Urgency to act will be a part of the determination of risk level. Chaplains with less training in risk assessments will generally be distinguishing between low and not urgent risk or higher risk that must be turned over to a supervisor or mental health support that has greater assessment skills.

Suicidal Ideation

It is important to learn to listen for suicidal ideation when providing services to others. Hearing overt and direct statements of intent to harm oneself and act on thoughts makes it

---

1 See chapter 4 for guidance on note-keeping.

easier to determine the risk level, because it is clearer that this situation must be reported to someone. Many situations are a lot more covert and subtle, and it is common for every part of your being to want to ignore the suicidal comments and pretend you didn't hear them. This is normal, even for experienced chaplains.

When a chaplain is trained and knows what to do if there is suicidal ideation, then often it is easier to act. There are many different questions to ask clients to assess the risk of suicide. The following is one common series of questions, as taught by the Centre for Addiction and Mental Health (CAMH). Ask these questions in order, until client is no longer exhibiting risk factors, and then determine level of risk. Allow client to talk about other things as well, and ensure that empathy and counselling are also a part of the suicide risk assessment.

- Have things gotten so bad that you've thought about hurting yourself or ending your life?
- Sometimes when people feel the way you do right now, they start to have thoughts about suicide. Has this ever happened to you?
- Do you have a plan for how you would kill yourself?
- Have you thought about any other methods?
- Do you have any firearms or other weapons at home? Where are they?
- Have you bought or saved pills? Do you have a rope?
- Have you 'rehearsed' or 'gone through the motions' of killing yourself?
- In the next 24–48 hours, how likely is it that you will act on your suicidal plan?
- Would you consider yourself an impulsive person?
- Have you recently felt out of control at times?[2]

Any of these questions can have a rating scale added to them. Ask the client to rate the likelihood of following through on the thought on a scale of 1 to 10, where 1 = very unlikely and 10 = certain.

It helps to remember that just because a client has thoughts of suicide, doesn't mean they will act on them. It is better they are talking about them with you than holding them in, and maybe acting on them in isolation. It is actually quite common for individuals to have passing thoughts of suicide, and with support many suicidal thoughts will pass without ever being acted upon. A client who expresses suicidal ideation but is low risk:

- Has ideas about wanting to end their life, but not a method or action plan;
- The client feels hopeless but can also think of good things in their life;
- The client usually has no history of ever attempting suicide and are able to think of reasons not to attempt suicide;
- The client can imagine things in the future and has supports around in case things change.

When a client presents with low risk for suicide as determined above, encourage the client to talk to their supports. Encourage the client to talk to their family doctor about suicidal thoughts and maybe think about trying a medication like an anti-depressant. Normalize dark thoughts, but encourage not taking action on these thoughts. Encourage counselling and talking about what is going on. Talking about suicidal thoughts doesn't make the client more likely to act on them, and rather provides support and alternatives.

A client who expresses suicidal ideation and is medium risk:

- Has suicidal ideas and a possible method and action plan for ending their life;
- Often the client does not trust themselves not to act on the action plan;

---

2 Suicide Risk: Detecting & Assessing Suicidality. (n.d.). CAMH. https://www.camh.ca/en/professionals/treating-conditions-and-disorders/suicide-risk/suicide---detecting-and-assessing-suicidality

- They may have a history of attempting suicide in the past;
- Despite their own suicidal ideation, the client has an adult around who they trust to help them.

In the case of medium risk, it is important to mitigate the risk. Request the client to remove access to their suicide method (gun, pills, rope, and so on). The responsibility to watch the client must be passed to another adult who is able and willing to accept this responsibility. Ask the client to be watched by another adult until the suicide risk drops to low risk again, or to go to the hospital for assessment if the risk of action increases. It is helpful to contract with the client not to implement the action plan, and ensure the contract seems believable. Within a spiritual care relationship, contracting can draw upon the client's own religious concepts, such as the concept of 'vow' in Buddhism (particularly of non-harming) or 'covenant' (with God) in Judaism or 'surrender' (to the will of God) in Islam. This can be a useful tool for chaplains at this phase. Ask the client to discuss their suicide plan with their family doctor or psychiatrist. Encourage counselling and talking about what is going on.

A client who expresses suicidal ideation and has an action plan that is easily implementable is high risk, and the client:

- Is often isolated and does not have sufficient supports requiring the chaplain to take more responsibility for them;
- Is alone and does not know who to turn to for support;
- Sometimes is using alcohol or drugs when talking about suicide, and this increases the likelihood that they will act on the thoughts;
- Has already implemented some part of the action plan for suicide, but is still alive;
- Requires immediate action on your part if a client reaches out to say they are about to implement an action plan for suicide;
- In many cases, will have a history of attempting suicide in the past;
- May have named a trigger event for a suicide attempt that has now happened (e.g., having access to children denied in a child custody dispute).

The high-risk mitigation plan of action is for the client to agree to take themselves to a doctor within two hours, either a family doctor or emergency room at a hospital; ask the client to let you know when they have done this. Sometimes a better plan is to phone 911 and ask for police to come to take client to hospital, even if they say they don't want to go. Stay on the

---

Suicidality Case Study

Scenario: I received a call from a leader of a local temple. One of his Sangha members had recently stopped attending meditation sits. When he followed up with her, he found she had been hospitalized with suicidal ideation, but had been recently released. He wondered whether he should mention the Buddhist hell realms that one enters into if one chooses to end their life with suicide. He also struggled with allowing this person to sit with the Sangha again, given that they had been sharing their suicidal ideation with other Sangha members and disturbing them. The leader consulted with me, and determined that she had been high risk and getting sufficient support for her mental health crisis from the hospital. Back home she is now low risk and in need of on-going support and monitoring, which she is getting from her psychiatrist. He agreed to contain the conversations to private ones of support with her for the time being, and not mention the Buddhist hells specifically, unless she asked. He also encouraged her to do Lovingkindness practices at home whenever she feels depressed, and to include herself at the centre of the Lovingkindness practice.

phone if you are not in the same place or with the client in person until someone arrives. In some jurisdictions, there are mobile crisis units that will come out on an emergency basis to do mental health risk assessments as alternatives to hospitalization. It is common for clients who have had previous experience with police or hospitals to resist or refuse to go based on past experiences. Buddhist chaplains may need additional support to understand this type of hospitalization trauma, and discussions around alternatives to hospitalizations during mental health crises are often needed.

Homicide Risk Assessments

Homicidal ideation may seem like something for non-spiritual people, but is an extreme form of anger and ill-will, which is experienced by all of us. Buddhist chaplains may like to imagine that they never will need to perform a homicide risk assessment. Risk assessment of homicidal ideation is less common than other risks, and being properly prepared is a good way to reduce stress related to the topic.

The first thing I recommend in possible homicide situations is to start with a thorough suicide risk assessment. In my experience, any person who is contemplating harm to someone else will also be considering harm to themselves. The unsettled mind that is so focussed on harming others includes themselves in the irrational plan of aggressive action. There is no harm in checking for suicide in addition to the specific homicide risk assessment protocol.

After completing the suicide risk assessment questions, add these additional questions for a Homicide Risk Assessment.
- Do you want to take anyone with you?
- Do you have thoughts of harming or killing others?
- Do you have a plan to harm or kill others?
- Do you have access to a gun or other lethal weapons?

With homicide, there is no medium risk. Always move quickly with high-risk action plans to ensure safety of the client and the intended victim(s). Follow the same mitigation plan for homicide as for suicide plans above.

There are some additional steps for homicide assessments.
- Always find someone else to consult with, whether low-risk or high-risk, if the client says anything that makes you think they might be thinking of committing harm of any kind. This person to consult with could be a supervisor, a Sangha member, or any other professional with experience with risk assessments.

Homicidal Ideation Case Study

Scenario: A young man asked to speak to the Buddhist chaplain at his workplace. He reported that his ex-wife had had his wages garnished for child support, but that she had refused to let him see his children. He was so lonely and angry, as well as broke, and was contemplating going to just take the children. He reported to the chaplain that he was willing to "remove" his ex-wife if she gets in his way. The chaplain asked him to clarify what this meant. The man admitted that he had fantasies of killing her, but was willing to stop himself when thinking about the impact on his children. He was able to express sufficient self-restraint and compassion towards his ex-wife, and to promise not to do anything without considering the karma and the consequences. The chaplain consulted with his supervisor at work, and they determined that he appeared to be at high risk with his risk factors, but was actually low risk with his willingness to remember his reasons for not acting on his ill-will. They documented the conversation and encouraged him to attend psychotherapy to address his feelings of loss.

- Ask the client to repeat any homicidal threat you think you might have heard. Be aware of the human instinct to avoid hearing threats and to pretend you didn't hear the words you heard.
- Forward all high-risk homicidal threats to police to determine whether to investigate or not; this is their specialty, not yours. Allow police to notify intended victim(s) if they deem it necessary.
- Focus on suicide risk assessments and accompanying action plans.

Most people have thoughts of anger and ill-will, but most can also imagine reasons not to do so. Remind clients about these reasons – activate their self-restraint and return to calmer mind states that allow the ill-will to pass.

In my experience, there are three situations that trigger people into harming others. Each of these is actually a grief and loss response, and can be powerful if unsupported and the client does not feel that they can handle the strong emotions.
- The ending of a romantic relationship;
- Keeping a parent from seeing their children (custody dispute following separation or divorce);
- Dismissal from the workplace.

Child Abuse

Anyone who hears about child abuse or neglect is obligated by law to report it to the appropriate Children's Aid Society (CAS) or Child Protection Agency (CPA, or sometime CPS). (How such situations are handled in Canada and the USA are very similar, so while this section is written with respect to the Canadian context, the guidelines apply in the U.S. with minor differences noted.) A chaplain, psychotherapist, or social worker in any jurisdiction is expected to have been trained to assess for child abuse, and is held responsible if they do not report it. In Canada, the report to CAS is expected to be done within 24 hours of hearing of the possible abuse of a child who was under the age of 16 at the time of the abuse. In the United States, this applies to any 'minor,' under the age of 18 (19 in Nebraska and Alabama and 21 in Mississippi). In most situations, the professional who hears about the abuse must make the report, and not the professional's supervisor. If the person who hears about the abuse is a volunteer, they are expected to share the information with their supervisor immediately, and the supervisor will make the report. It is considered best practice to encourage any adult to make a report themselves of child abuse or neglect that they either witness or hear about. Follow the directions of your local Children's Aid Society or Child Protection Agency, as they are commonly called in the USA.[3]

CAS does not expect the professional to investigate the alleged abuse or neglect and determine whether it actually happened or how it happened. CAS does the investigation themselves. CAS wants the professional to simply repeat the information told to them and to pass the names and contact information (if available) to them to follow up.

CAS is responsible for investigating all kinds of abuse of children – sexual, physical, and emotional – as well as neglect. Sexual abuse includes all kinds of inappropriate sexual behaviour, and not just sexual intercourse. Physical abuse includes hitting with the hand as well as objects or weapons, and can be a part of discipline, but is still considered abuse. Marks left on the body should be photographed as soon as possible to document severity. Emotional abuse may or may not be investigated by the CAS, but they will determine

---

3 Definitions of Child Abuse and Neglect - Canadian Red Cross. (n.d.). Red Cross Canada. https://www.redcross.ca/how-we-help/violence-bullying-and-abuseprevention/educators/child-abuse-and-neglect-prevention/definitions-of-child-abuse-and-neglect; Definitions of Child Abuse & Neglect, Children's Bureau (n.d.) https://www.childwelfare.gov/topics/can/defining/#:~:text=%22Any%20recent%20act%20or%20failure,imminent%20risk%20of%20serious%20harm.%22

this. Neglect is the failure to provide proper food, clothing, supervision, a clean and safe home, or medical care. It is also the failure to provide emotional support, love, and affection.

CAS discourages the professional from notifying the child or parent that a report is being done. However, to keep the therapeutic alliance intact between the individual and the professional, a professional will likely want to inform the individual or family in advance and to address any upset feelings together. The professional may encourage the individual to make the report themselves if they are over the age of 16 already (or an older teen a legal adult in the USA), or if the reporter is a parent or other adult. In these cases, encourage the adult to report first, and then follow up with a report of your own.

In some jurisdictions there may be a generic CAS, a Catholic CAS, and/or a Jewish CAS. It is helpful to know the religion of the child in determining which one to contact. If in doubt, refer to the generic one. (In the USA, all such agencies are secular and governmental; reports are made without respect to the family's religious tradition.) CAS phone numbers can easily be found through a quick Google search. You must report where the individual is currently located, and not where the abuse happened, or where the abuser currently lives.

In Canada, if a professional hears that a child was abused, they must report it themselves, unless they are convinced that it has already been reported in the past. If there is any question, it is better to report it again. Police officers are obligated to report directly to the CAS in all cases, but if there is any doubt that this has been done, make the report again. In the U.S., if the person who was abused is now a legal adult and no other children are in danger of abuse or neglect, such as younger siblings, the legal responsibility of the chaplain to report has passed. The chaplain may still discuss and support the careseeker to report and potentially prosecute their abuser, if that is the careseeker's wish.

Whether to report something one hears may not be exactly clear, and it's possible that someone might deem it reportable when another person might not think so. Many cases fall in the grey zone. The professional must make a clinical judgment that they can live with and justify regarding the reportability of whatever they hear.

In my experience, many Buddhist chaplains to do not get much training in recognizing signs of child abuse. In the past, much abuse was ignored or had a blind eye turned to it. This is tragic for the children, and has long-standing consequences for the children if they showed up with bruises or told professionals, but there was no action taken. In my opinion, we as a society need to turn this around and take greater efforts to protect children since we now better understand the long-term impact of the child abuse and neglect. Chaplains need to

Child Abuse Case Study

Scenario: A family attended celebrations at their local temple. On several occasions, other families noticed that one of the children had bruises. The chaplain at the temple also noticed. When asked what happened, the child never spoke, and the parents' offered explanations that seemed odd regarding the bruises themselves. The chaplain decided to report the situation to the local CAS. They investigated the situation and the child told them that the bruises were actually discipline for refusing to play the piano pieces well enough. The parents were angry at first, but then agreed to attend support groups on disciplining children respectfully. They expressed appreciation to the chaplain for helping them learn new methods of discipline that were different from their own experiences.

be an active part of protecting and looking out for children.

Distinguishing between discipline and child abuse can be tricky territory. There are many cultural norms regarding discipline and for centuries much abuse occurred under the guise of discipline. We know now that it is possible to discipline in ways that do not demean or harm children. The North American legal definition of physical abuse dictates what is allowed as discipline. Chaplains may feel caught between cultural norms of discipline and local laws, and it is important to know that professionals ignoring laws are held responsible for ignorance. Chaplains must get comfortable talking about the past in ways that doesn't further shame the parents, but also teaches them what is currently acceptable. In general, blame doesn't help the situation, but instead makes everyone feel badly for things that are not changeable in the present. Chaplains can make referrals to other professionals who specialize family therapy, and provide psychoeducation and support to parents to learn better ways of disciplining children that is respectful and follows all laws.

Elder Abuse

I am saddened to report that the abuse of elders by family and caregivers is a worldwide issue across all cultures. Elder abuse was defined by the World Health Organization in 2002 as "a single, or repeated act, or lack of appropriate action, occurring within any relationship where there is an expectation of trust, which causes harm or distress to an older person." This category also includes abuse of a "dependent adult" regardless of age, such as an individual in their twenties or thirties with learning or developmental impairments who cannot care for themselves and has a legal custodial relationship with another adult. (Elders may not be in a legal custodianship when experiencing abuse, as these legal steps are not always formalized as people age.)

Little is known about elder abuse because it is often unclear whether the markers or event that occur are cause by abuse or other issues. Caregivers, senior protective agencies, and doctors are unable to distinguish between abuse and natural events of accident, illness, or aging. In both Canada and the United States, there is still too little training to discern the difference.

Chaplains working with elders may be reluctant to report elder abuse for fear of disturbing family relationships. It may be easier to hold institutions that care for elders to higher standards than families. Markers related to the following easily- observable standards are a place to start:

- Undocumented and untreated injuries and fractures not related to know illnesses;
- Lack of cleanliness in the setting;
- Lack of cleanliness of the elder (unchanged briefs and bed linens, strong bodily odors);
- Suspicious financial statements and money movement;

Elder Abuse Case Study

Scenario: A chaplain was providing support at a residential hospice. One of the dying people who was admitted appeared with bruises all over their body. The chaplain met with the individual separately from their family. She asked about the bruises and the dying person told her that her son was often angry that she was dying, and was often rough with her when moving her into the chair. The chaplain reported this to the nursing staff, and they agreed to monitor the son's visits carefully and make sure that he was offered emotional support for his anger. They agreed to do all the movement for her so family members were relieved of this responsibility. Everyone seemed relieved with the plan, and there were no more new bruises during the dying process.

- Inconsistencies between people in general about what's going on.

In Canada, there is no legal obligation to report elder abuse, as there is with child abuse, and there are no adult protective services. In the USA, state and federal laws mandate reporting of such cases to Adult Protective Services (APS) agencies.[4] Elder abuse that includes financial fraud or physical assault is reportable to the same degree that it is for other adults. However, there is clearly a moral obligation to pass on information to relevant investigative bodies whenever there is the likelihood of elder abuse happening, and to allow them to investigate as needed.

The chaplain is most likely to be involved in the relational aspect of family and professional/institutional caregiving and to ensure that the best possible care is being provided. They are also encouraged to provide support to both individuals and families regarding care of elders, and to work toward improving relationships as a prevention of elder abuse.

Domestic Violence

Domestic violence reporting, unlike child abuse reporting, is not mandatory. The professional is expected to provide supportive counselling to the abused person and to support their decision whether to report it or not. If the individual wants to report the abuse, it is reported to the police. If the abuse is currently happening, it is reported by calling 911. If the abuse is historical, it can be reported at any police station or by non-emergency police phone number.

There are many situations that involve abuse between adults that a chaplain may get involved with. The abuse can take many forms, including emotional, financial, threats against pets or household objects, or controlling conversations. Sometimes the situations are quite clear that there is an abuser and abused person, and other times it is unclear exactly what is going on, and whether abuse is actually happening. A chaplain must exercise good communication skills to listen closely and determine what is really going on in what appears as highly volatile situations.

Much supportive counselling to the abused person focuses on safety planning, to ensure that the abused person believes they have options to end the abuse. Safety planning includes setting boundaries around what will be done if the abuse happens again, planning for a safe place to go to escape or prevent the abuse, and possibly supporting the abused person to separate and move out from the domestic home where the abuse happens.

Support should be offered to whoever is being abused, including children who might be witnessing abuse. If children below the age of 16 in Canada or legal minors in the USA witness domestic abuse (sexual, physical, or emotional), this must be reported to the CAS to investigate. Witnessing domestic abuse has psychological impact for children, and is not just a risk factor for possible impact.

Adults may choose whether to report domestic abuse or not. Some choose not to report it for many years, as they fear the abuse may get worse. Some choose not to report it because there are immigration fears. It is important not to judge the person who does not leave the situation or report it to police. Many people who experience domestic abuse take years to leave their abusers. Many more choose to never criminally charge their abusers, because they also still love them, or maybe fear their abuser will get off anyways.

In Canadian situations when a person calls 911 during a domestic abuse situation and police arrive in time to assess the situation, police are obligated by law to lay charges, while in the USA, it may be left up to the victim to press charges or not. Often this involves police laying double charges on both parties, because it is unclear who is at fault. In my experience in

---

4 State Statues Relevant to Elder Abuse Cases, U.S. Department of Justice, https://www.justice.gov/elderjustice/elder-justice-statutes-0

Canada, this means a larger number of women are now being charged with domestic abuse than ever before, and it is harder for men to recognize the privilege they have in size and gender power in the majority of cases.

Chaplains may not see as much domestic violence as other risk assessment categories if they work in hospitals or prisons. Domestic violence is inherently in the home and might only come out to the chaplain if the abuse is bad enough to warrant medical assistance in a hospital. The chaplain may need to listen well to whisperings or be brave enough to ask questions in any setting if they suspect that they are witnessing the effects of domestic violence.

A chaplain may encounter more domestic abuse when it shows up in the temple or among the sangha in their home lives. This informal witnessing of domestic violence may be more ambiguous and harder to identify and even harder to face and confront. Domestic violence is ultimately about choosing to control someone with whom you are in relationship with. It often begins with a partner who

---

Domestic Violence on U.S. College Campuses *by Monica Sanford*

In the USA, colleges and universities may have responsibilities in relation to domestic violence involving students or staff under a set of regulations referred to collectively as "Title IX." Schools have a responsibility to investigate, adjudicate, and respond to the following situations:
- Discrimination or harassment on the basis of sex or gender;
- Sexual assault and rape;
- Dating violence and stalking.

Every college and university will have a designated Title IX Office or Officer trained to deal with these matters. Almost all school employees are "mandated reporters" who must share information about these concerns with the Title IX Office for investigation.

Chaplains are frequently one of the few designated "confidential resources" on campus, along with counseling centers and health clinics, who do not need to report. Thus, students facing these serious issues will often confide in a chaplain. In addition to providing spiritual care to such students, the chaplain should also be conversant with the Title IX process so they can walk the student through their options. If a student decides to report, the chaplain may accompany them during stages of the process as either a companion or an advocate (depending on school policy).

Schools are legally obligated to become involved when the alleged perpetrator is connected to the school in some way, such as a fellow student, staff member, professor, or volunteer connected to a school program. They are required to investigate even if the alleged victim does not wish to cooperate with the investigation. The school adjudicates the issue using policy guidelines and may take action against the perpetrator up to and including expulsion or termination, but this is not a court of law. It is for the purpose of maintain a safe and welcoming campus. Victims may pursue criminal charges through the local police at any point.

Sadly, these cases often involve students in romantic relationships that have gone wrong. Many of the same guidelines apply as when working with any other situation of domestic violence, though the situation could become complicated by the Title IX process if, for example, a roommate or residence life staff person reports the situation. Moreover, young adults away from home for the first time, may have additional complicating factors of their own due to distance from or lack of supportive social networks beyond the school and general naivety in adult relationships.

If you are a U.S. college chaplain, search your school's name and "Title IX" to find your local office and review their training materials.

insists on limiting what their partner does and who they do things with, and then eventually escalates to violence. As with elder abuse, the chaplain may best approach domestic violence as a break down in relationship between the family members, and one to be remedied with compassion and support.

It is important to remember that abuse rarely just goes away. Abusers seldom, if ever reform, even with support and therapy. And offering loving kindness and compassion to an abuser is not enough to break the conditioned patterns of abuse. It is helpful for a chaplain to be patient as the abused person debates their options, and often returns to the abuser time and again. The chaplain must recognize that abuser recidivism is a massive problem, and an abused person needs time to recognize the patterns themselves.

Addictions

In some situations, chaplains sit down and start the interaction with a formal initial intake assessment. In those situations, they may ask a variety of questions about the client's history, and they may learn naturally about struggles with mental health or addictions. However, for the vast majority of chaplains, they simply walk into rooms and start conversations, and the conversation is much more focused on the present. The chaplain simply follows what is being offered, rather than asking probing questions.

It is easy for a chaplain to miss issues related to addictions and mental health. There can be much shame with these issues, and family members may be more willing to share about the impact of their family member's mental health and addictions than the individual with the issue. That said, it is very helpful to know if there are any drug or alcohol issues with the client and their family.

People are especially reluctant to share their own struggles with addictions when in the thick of them. One strategy for learning more about addictions is to ask open-ended questions about how much use there is, rather than simply asking if there is any use or issue. Ideas about quantity of use varies by user, and most individuals under-report use.

There are many kinds of addictions, and the list seems to be growing. The most common addictions are nicotine, alcohol, recreational drugs (cannabis, cocaine, MDMA, LSD, psilocybin, to name a few), pharmaceutical drugs (Codeine, Oxycontin, various off-label ADHD medications), gambling, sex, and shopping. Our general culture of consumerism and quick fixes makes it hard to fill the shadow of the hungry ghost within ourselves, and addictions are a growing problem for Buddhists and non-Buddhists alike.

The most useful area of addictions for all chaplains to be skilled in handling is drug and alcohol addictions. Drug and alcohol use is all around us with recent legalizations, and particularly with the growing stress of modern life. It is helpful to think about use/abuse/addiction as three levels of impact of drugs/alcohol consumption:

Domestic Violence Case Study

Scenario: A Zen practitioner asked for support from her Buddhist teacher, who was also a chaplain. She was leaving her abusive husband and she feared for her life. Her husband had threatened to take her life if she left, and she was leaving with the children. Her Buddhist teacher recognized that she was being physically abused, and recognized that this could become a high-risk situation. He encouraged her to also connect with a women's shelter who provided them with a place to live and emotional support for transitioning out on their own. He then provided support and monitoring to her during this risky situation.

- Use = limited recreational/functional use;
- Abuse = increased quantity and impact on relationships or work;
- Addiction = reflects a need, either chemical or psychological, to function, and serious impact on relationships, work, and health.

Another way of engaging the individual about their addiction is to ask questions related to the CAGE Questionnaire. Answers to these basic non-clinical questions can guide the chaplain how involved to get with the addiction. The CAGE Questionnaire is not used to diagnose the disease but only to show whether a problem might exist.[5]

- **C** = Have you ever felt you needed to Cut down on your drug/alcohol use?
- **A** = Have people Annoyed you by criticizing your drug/alcohol use?
- **G** = Have you ever felt Guilty about your drug/alcohol use?
- **E** = Have you ever felt you needed an Eye-opener first thing in the morning to steady your nerves or start your day?

Addiction issues do not generally need to be reported anywhere. Even if illicit drugs are in question, it is not the responsibility of the chaplain to report their use to any authority. However, when the client is putting others at risk, the chaplain must keep in mind that they might be required to report child abuse or neglect. Employees who work in safety sensitive positions (i.e. driving of heavy equipment or public transportation) are examples of exceptions. Training in these areas is given to professionals working there, and chaplains are not usually involved in these kinds of situations.

Mental Health

Mental health issues are much more common than addictions. It is generally accepted that one in four persons in North America will experience a mental health crisis throughout their lifetime. These crises may be short or long term, and will often involve a variety of mental health professionals, including doctors, therapists, and even chaplains. For this reason, many professional chaplains are cross-trained as psychotherapists or social workers and specialize in recognizing and even treating mental health issues.

During any initial intake assessment, it really is helpful to know if there are any underlying mental health issues. Intake assessments at the beginning of the relationship with a chaplain require some general risk assessments, along with other intake questions. The intake assessment may include questions related to psychiatric diagnoses, as well as informal self-diagnoses of mental health difficulties. A history of previous psychotherapy, abuse of any kind, as well as suicide attempts or hospitalizations should be noted in your written assessment. Experience with medications and attitudes about these should be noted. Coping strategies, both positive and negative, are important to cover, and can include self-harm and cutting, alcohol/drug use, and isolation strategies. Family history of mental health issues may shed light on family patterns.

Mental health in North America is based on autonomy and personal choice. This means that no one can force treatment on an individual who declines treatment. There are exceptions to this for limited time periods, like immediately following a suicide attempt or other mental health crisis. Medication is the most common treatment, but can also include psychotherapy, complementary therapies (acupuncture, Traditional Chinese Medicine, or homeopathy), or Electroconvulsive Therapy (ECT, colloquially called shock therapy). The client-centred approach includes chaplains who can be limited by what they can offer a client who is unwilling to admit any mental health issue.

The good news is that there is still a great deal that a chaplain can do for a person

---

5 CAGE Questionnaire for Alcohol Problems. (n.d.). https://myhealth.alberta.ca/Health/pages/conditions.aspx?hwid=hw127170

struggling with mental health issues. Listening and just being with someone in a non-judging way goes far to deescalate a crisis and create a safe space for a client to get centred on what they need.

If the chaplain is not a trained mental health clinician, referral is often the best thing they can do for a client. If the client will not accept a referral, chaplains may consult with mental health professionals on how best to continuing caring for someone presenting with the specific mental health issues, while preserving the client's privacy through anonymity.

Effective Referrals

If you've been reading this chapter and worrying a bit about the pressures of hearing these issues and then figuring out what to do with the information you gather, always remember that you are on a team. Sometimes the team is a formal group of professionals, and you know who your immediate supervisor is, and that's who you will report this information to. Consulting is often needed before a referral can be made, and consulting produces the most effective referrals.

In cases where you are a chaplain for a temple, you may initially feel alone. However, I would urge you to think broadly about who else might support you with any of these risky situations and provide another perspective. Two minds are always better than one.

Chaplains may be worried about confidentiality and it's important to remember that in truly risky situations of harm to self or harm to others, confidentiality is inherently waived. Initially, it may be better to consult with identifying information withheld, but in a truly risky situation, safety trumps confidentiality.

Depending on your skills as a chaplain, you may take on lower or higher risk clients yourself. Regardless of your specific comfort level with client complexity, you will want to have a list of professionals to refer to for cases that are beyond your scope of practice or skill set.

As a Buddhist chaplain, you will want to have a Buddhist psychotherapist that you can refer Buddhist clients to for psychotherapy. These may be hard to find in some regions, but on-line psychotherapy has made this much easier to find. That said, most psychotherapists are only qualified to practice in their own province and state in most cases, even when services are virtual.

You will want to refer sometimes to Buddhist psychotherapists that have sliding fee scales to accommodate clients at all levels of financial ability. For those needing free or reduced fee, it may be possible to find a local chaplaincy education program affiliated with a Buddhist agency that uses supervised student chaplain interns to offer free services. The Toronto Center for Applied Buddhism is one such agency that is affiliated with the University of Toronto's Emmanuel College –

Mental Health Case Study

Scenario: A Buddhist chaplain at a mental health hospital met with a client who also identified as Buddhist. She described a recent crisis that included some non-ordinary reality states. Some might have thought she was paranoid and having a psychotic break, but the chaplain normalized her experience, hearing that she had had previous similar experiences when meditating as well. The chaplain included the spiritual background in her risk assessment considerations, and determined that the client did not appear to be at risk at the moment. The chaplain provided support and crisis counselling to the client and she stabilized and returned to her meditation practice. She later reported that the normalization of her non-ordinary states helped her recover faster and she trusted the chaplain, who did not judge her as she'd feared.

Buddhist Stream chaplaincy program.[6]

What distinguishes a Buddhist psychotherapist from a secular one is the appreciation for Buddhist principles, as well as the active encouragement of Buddhist practices. The Buddhist psychotherapist encourages a struggling client to see where they are experiencing greed, ill-will, and delusion or ignorance in ways that increase their struggle. They can also remind the client about suffering, no-self, and impermanence, and how these integrate with the five aggregates that make up a self. In summary, they combine the usual therapeutic modalities with Buddhist principles to help clients understand their mind and situation and help to transform their struggles.

It may also be helpful for chaplains to have access to spiritual psychotherapists other than Buddhist. Most chaplains work in multi-faith settings, and will have clients who practice a wide range of spiritualities. In North America, more and more clients are identifying without a religion, but connected to some form of spirituality, including mindfulness or some form of nature-based spirituality. Most spiritual psychotherapists enjoy bringing in the spiritual aspect into the psychotherapy, and find it can make a deeper transformation for clients.

Regardless of the type of psychotherapist the chaplain refers to, it is hoped that they will have skills and perspectives in understanding spiritual experiences. In some circumstances, spiritual experiences may overlap with Western ideas of psychosis and mental health crisis. For Buddhist practitioners practicing with fasts, sleep deprivation, isolation, or extended periods of silence, the resulting spiritual experiences might look like hallucinations, delusions, separation from self, and even a separation from reality. For the practitioner, it may be considered a deep and powerful experience and even blissful and desirable, but to the untrained or inexperienced chaplain, it may be scary.

---

6 (Toronto Centre for Applied Buddhism (n.d.). www.appliedbuddhism.ca

Non-ordinary Spiritual Experiences

Psychotherapists who pathologize spiritual non-ordinary experiences can traumatize clients, and discourage their further disclosure of these events. It is important that a Buddhist client hears language that relates to their experience and can be encouraged to integrate their experience into everyday life. They decide for themselves whether the experience is helpful or not.

When a chaplain knows that their client engages in a form of spiritual practice and then speaks about any of these experiences, it is important to consider whether the client or anyone else in their life is concerned about the results. One larger consideration is whether the client is able to return to their previous level of functioning , or maybe even higher functioning, on their own. A true Buddhist breakthrough may have some initial challenges, but then ultimately raise a person to a new level of functioning with greater compassion for others. It is common for deep spiritual work to sometimes make a person feel like they have dropped in functioning in the relative world, and it takes a while to stabilize and return to usual functioning.

Sometimes the client may not wish to return (as with the full awakening experience), but in most situations the non-ordinary reality moments are temporary and the person can return to functioning afterwards. This practice of safely realizing the spiritual experience and then returning to the ego world is why most Buddhist teachers encourage students to meditate and practice for set times, such as 50-55 minutes at a time, rather than indefinitely, so as to train to the mind to safely go into the spiritual experience and then safely return again.

Community of Support

Buddhist chaplains will also feel the greatest job satisfaction if they have a community of support for themselves as well. This may be in the form of a clinical or professional supervisor who is also spiritually-oriented, either specifically toward Buddhism or multi-faith. This person is the go-to person for risk assessments, and ideally is open-minded, confident, and supportive, and has greater clinical skills with high-risk situations. Many Buddhist chaplains work in quite isolated situations and are not supervised by clinical supervisors, but rather managers with authority over them, but absolutely no expertise in risk assessment. These arrangements are particularly challenging for new chaplains.

Support for the Buddhist chaplain could also be from peer support. Sometimes this is formal, from a peer support group that meets regularly; sometimes this is informal and as needed. With informal support there is often greater honesty and vulnerability, but not as much accountability. Peer support is especially beneficial for handling the vicarious trauma of dealing with a high-risk situation. It often comes after the event as a way for the chaplain to debrief and reflectively review their actions, and think about different ways of handling the situation in case it arises in the future.

Chaplain support does not need to specifically be related to Buddhists only. Buddhist chaplains tend to feel more included in multi-faith spiritual supports, and tend not to appreciate being the only Buddhist amongst Christians. However, I have supported many Buddhist chaplains who feel left out when all the other chaplains are Christians. This happens most often in rural settings, and in hospitals and prisons with long-standing chaplaincy programs. Hopefully as more Buddhist chaplaincy programs open up in North America this will become less of an issue.

Potential Barriers

There are some barriers to the work of Buddhist chaplains in North America. One issue is that there are so many different forms of Buddhism, including Theravada, Mahayana, and Vajrayana. There are also many different cultures living in North America, including ethnic Buddhists who immigrated from many different countries in Asia and their progeny, as well as convert Buddhists who grew up with other religious or spiritual beliefs but generally identify foremost as Americans or Canadians. These distinctions are even now becoming increasingly permeable, as second-generation-and-beyond children of Asian immigrants who became non-religious or converted to Christianity now reconnect with their Buddhist roots and as the early Buddhist converts of the previous century raise Buddhist children and grandchildren. Non-Buddhists often assume that there are mostly commonalities between all Buddhists, but in my experience most Buddhists have very little experience with other practices. There may even be overt hostility or competition between various forms of Buddhism.

Another issue is that for some forms of Buddhism, mental health crisis is subsumed under the rubric of spiritual crisis. Therefore, some spiritual leaders will discourage their students from seeking out mental health support when in crisis, and try to handle things outside of the health care system. For Buddhist refugees who have fled repressive regimes, there is little trust in government and accompanying mental health supports. One example of this is the situation of Buddhist chaplains not trusting mental health services for refugees of the Khmer Rouge in Cambodia. The chaplains strongly discouraged their members from getting mental health services for psychotic or dissociative issues caused by trauma of the abuse experienced there. They suggested meditative practices alone for handling the trauma.

While not exactly a mental health disconnect, we saw additional examples of this lack of trust during the recent Covid pandemic where various temples and spiritual leaders chose to ask practitioners to ignore government rules regarding gathering and mask wearing. Many encouraged prayers and faith on its own for protecting from the Covid virus.

These contradictory messages from leaders often made individuals experiencing their own crises confused and conflicted about who to trust.

Mental health understanding has grown around the world and has greater support than ever before. However, there is no consensus yet on what treatment is best. Consensus with governments and professionals does not necessarily travel down to individual, families, and caregivers in all cultures.

Another issue is that we now know that spiritual practices can sometimes make mental health crises worse. For example, for people who dissociate to cope with traumatic memories, meditation practices that focus on the breath can bring on panic attacks and actually increase dissociation. In cases of dissociation, practices of loving kindness and grounded practices focusing on the five senses are actually more helpful. For this reason, it is important for chaplains to only suggest spiritual practices that they know are helpful for all people, even if they don't do the practice themselves or know it personally.

It is unfortunate, but most mental health training is limited to academic programs. In other words, it is difficult for chaplains to qualify to take mental health training. Or even if they are allowed entry, it may be too advanced for them and they can't really make good use of it. They need mental health training, but it must be given at the appropriate level. There is a growing need for generic mental health training and public health information for the general public.

One example of this easily-accessed public education is the global movement for 'Last Aid', which centers on end-of-life care.[7] Their virtual presentations provide free training for caregivers (and dying people too) on the dying stages and how to support someone at end of life to have a natural death. This training is geared toward the average citizen and would be a great resource for both non-clincial and professionally-trained chaplains wanting death education. Perhaps there could be more of these trainings on a variety of topics needed for the public, like handling any of the above risk assessment areas.

Continuity of Care

Chaplains are often only one point of contact for people in need. They work collaboratively on teams with a variety of backgrounds. Specifically, they work with both spiritual and non-spiritual professionals and lay people. It is common for each group to have their own language to describe their view of the situation. This is analogous to the story of the Buddhist monk who asked eight blind men to describe an elephant, and each one used different words to describe the tail, trunk, tusks, back, feet, and so on. Clearly the background of the professional working with the client determines how they view the client's problem and how they envision working with that issue.

Spiritual and non-spiritual people have their own language for speaking amongst themselves. These teams work together, but within an explicit or implicit framework. Often doctors and other medical staff or wardens sit at the top, and chaplains find themselves somewhere near the bottom. In some settings, chaplains can do whatever they like so long as they don't interrupt the others doing the 'real' work.

Valuing the role of chaplaincy on teams is an issue that varies setting by setting, but clearly is an ongoing issue for most sites. Regardless of what is done by whom, it is hoped that professionals have a mutual respect for each other's domains. Keeping the client's needs firmly at the centre is the most important way to maintain the respect for all.

General Wholesome Supports

Chaplains have so much to offer clients. Hearing supportive words matters so much to

---

[7] Last Aid | HPCO. (n.d.). https://www.chpca.ca/education/last-aid/

people, and the words matter even more coming from important relationships. Chaplains take the time to listen to their clients and really enjoy hearing what brings meaning to their lives. Risk assessments often focus on the problems, and chaplains balance this with also seeing the parts of the clients' lives that are working well or might make their lives better.

Chaplains are taught all the tools of therapists regarding clients to activate and cultivate wholesome supports. These include the usual encouragements to eat healthy foods in good quantity, exercise regularly either alone or with others, and to practice healthy sleep habits. Following these general practices supports all other guidelines for good mental health.

A new component that many therapists now add for clients and that fits in well Buddhist chaplaincy is to encourage time in nature. Recent studies now show evidence that spending only 20 minutes in nature six days a week or making time for six hours in nature once a month over two consecutive days reduces cholesterol, lowers heart rate, lowers blood pressure, and improves blood circulation.[8] These are many of the same things that mindfulness was proven to affect 40 years ago with studies by Jon Kabat-Zinn.

But the one thing that chaplains can add is the encouragement to lean on a spiritual practice when things get tough. Spirituality is not universally accepted in therapy, but chaplains are allowed to ask and be interested in spiritual practices. They can spend time talking about how the client has used their spiritual practice in the past to support them, and often encourages clients to return to the spiritual practice. Sometime one spiritual practice works better than another, and the individual is the best person to decide this. A chaplain does not want to step into the role of teacher when they aren't in that role for the client, but rather they can invite such conversations and let the client decide what to pursue.

Chaplains can also activate sangha or Buddhist community. If they don't know the sangha of the client personally, they can simply speak about the sangha and remind the client that they have a sangha for support. If they are members of the same sangha, the chaplain can ask whether the client wants them to ask sangha members to help out in any way. Regardless of the method, sangha can be added to the client's group of supporters and combined with practices relating to the Buddha and Dharma.

When Buddhist chaplains are comfortable handling risk assessments well, they can then offer the supportive spiritual counselling that most chaplains say defines their passion for their career.

---

8 *Nature is a Human Right*, edited by Ellen Miles, 2022.

12
PRIVILEGE, OPPRESSION, & POWER

As defined in Chapter 5, power is the sum of one's resources and can be used to achieve one's goals. Different types of status convey or deny power to members of our society on the basis of personal characteristics and group membership. When power is conveyed by a social characteristic that is not something we ourselves have worked to earn, it's called privilege (some forms of privilege, such as education, can be earned, but are generally easier for members of groups with other types of unearned privilege). Being white in the United States conveys unearned power, or white privilege. Likewise, power can and is denied or diminished because of a characteristic or group membership, resulting in oppression. For example, minority racial groups in the United States suffer various forms of oppression that prevent Black, Indigenous, and People of Color (BIPOC) from meeting their basic needs. Privilege and oppression operate through social structures which ensure that the needs (and wants) of members of privileged groups are met at the expense of members of oppressed groups.

Privilege is not free. For one person to have privilege, another person is being harmed. This does not necessarily mean the privileged person is actively or intentionally harming the oppressed person (though this does happen). Rather, privilege and oppression happen largely through systems and structures that require little to no personal interaction between the two. But make no mistake, these systems and structures are not accidental. They have a long chain of historical causation as well as current actors working to uphold them. Social justice is the process of dismantling these systems and structures and redressing and preventing these harms through the creation of a fully egalitarian society. Buddhist chaplains are part of the process of creating a more socially just and egalitarian society as a result of our commitment to reduce suffering.

Power can be both visible and invisible. Being white, male, cisgendered, able-bodied, and of a higher socioeconomic class (which is often made visible through clothing choices) are visible forms of social power. Invisible power consists of knowledge, education, personality, character virtues, and life experience. Power can also be both personal and contextual. Charisma would be an example of personal power useful in a variety of situations. On the other hand, a law degree conveys contextual power in a courtroom, but not necessarily during a football game. Our careseekers are predominantly those within institutions who have the least amount of power: patients, students, inmates, enlisted soldiers, and so on. They can be further disempowered due to racism, sexism, and other forms of oppression. While we also serve those with more relative power, such as staff and leaders, those with less tend to need us more, partly due to this power imbalance.

As chaplains, our experiences of power, privilege, and oppression depend on our positionality and context. These forces affect us, our careseekers, and our coworkers. These forces are even shaping the field of Buddhist chaplaincy, which our 2020/21 survey revealed is close to two-thirds white even though two-thirds of American Buddhists are of Asian descent ("Mapping Survey...," Sanford, et al, 2022). Some forms of privilege and oppression are relatively stable across a lifetime, such as those based on race, gender presentation for cis-gender people, or sexual orientation, while others are more mutable, such as oppressions based on age, education, or socio-economic status.

At a basic level, privilege and oppression are social expressions of the Three Poisons of attachment/greed (*rāga* in Sanskrit or *lobha* in Pali), aversion/hatred (*dveṣa* in Sanskrit or *dosa* in Pali), and delusion (*moha*) that have been codified into structures within our society that operate both within and beyond the level of individual agency. As a source of suffering, they need liberation via wisdom and compassion as much as any other suffering we encounter. Emily McRae also describes how these expressions of the poisons are obscured by the operation of delusion or *avidyā* among the more privileged and powerful members of society, particularly white people (McRae in Buddhism and Whiteness, 2019). Hierarchical power dynamics were not unknown in the Buddha's time, though they took different forms, operating both through systems of patriarchy and caste (among other ways) that were closely tied to socioeconomics.

In any society, privilege and oppression create inequitable and unjust distributions of power and resources by structuring systems that benefit one group at the expense of another. Some scholars have likened these social systems of privilege and oppression to a form of collective karma (Brennan, 2021) that we must work to dismantle as part of our spiritual practice. Once emplaced, these structures and systems perpetuate legacies of inequality even if and when a society begins to reject them. Unfortunately, these structures and systems also operate to reinforce discriminatory ideologies via both explicit and implicit bias. Explicit bias manifests in ideological oppression that codifies which groups are unjustly viewed as superior or inferior to each other. These ideologies are used to structure institutional oppression, or rules and laws that codify who receives what social benefits, rights, and protections, and who does not, creating an unequal distribution of power. Even after ideological oppression is denounced, institutional oppression can and does continue to operate, often through implicit unrecognized biases. Both ideological and institutional oppression fuel interpersonal oppression, when members of the more privileged group speak and act in ways that deny the rights, benefits, needs, and dignity of members of oppressed groups. This is otherwise known as direct discrimination. Finally, members of oppressed groups can even adopt these twisted ideologies through internalized oppression, seeing themselves as inferior to members of privileged groups and acting in ways complicit with their own group's oppression.[1]

To complicate matters further, individuals experience both privilege and oppression in different aspects and contexts. For example, I possess privilege from being white, cis-gender, heteronormative, educated, and middle-class. I also experience oppression as a woman, particularly as a woman working in male-dominated fields, and as a religious minority. In some spaces, my status as a chaplain is given respect and in others it engenders hostility. In relation to my religious identity, I can, if necessary, choose to 'pass,' which is when a member of an oppressed group allows others to assume they belong to a different group (or claims it themselves to maintain safety).[2] Most Buddhist chaplains have some access to privilege in the form of advanced education, though this is not always enough to counteract discrimination faced by chaplains of color, women, queer chaplains, or chaplains living with disabilities,

---

1 See the Chinook Fund's definition of the Four I's of Oppression and other relevant terms, 2015, https://chinookfund.org/wp-content/uploads/2015/10/Supplemental-Information-for-Funding-Guidelines.pdf.

2 See my chapter entitled "Secret Atheist" in the breakout box about Social Justice Readings.

as we shall see from their first-hand reports shared in the last two sections of this chapter.

This chapter explores the experiences of chaplains working with various forms of power, privilege, and oppression as it relates to themselves, their careseekers, and their co-workers. In one section, I use my own life as a case study to illustrate some of the dynamics defined above. The remainder of the chapter draws extensively from the qualitative data collected via interviews and surveys and uses secondary resources to illustrate dynamics being reported by chaplains. Chaplaincy training programs usually include education these topics to enable chaplains to perceive, process, and counteract discrimination both on their own behalf and as an advocate for their careseekers and co-workers.

This chapter is not intended as a complete primer on the definitions and dynamics of power, privilege, and oppression. However, understanding these terms and how they operate in society is essential. The breakout box on the next pages contains vital resources for Buddhist chaplains on these topics. If you are very new to these ideas (and particularly if you possess a high level of privilege), I recommend reviewing some of these resources before continuing with this chapter. You may not agree with all of them, but that, too, is an essential aspect of social justice education.

Likewise, this chapter is written primarily for Buddhist chaplains in North America and may not apply to other settings, particularly Asia. Power, privilege, and oppression operate differently across human societies, though the global reach of Western colonialism, culture, and capitalism has an effect almost everywhere. If you are reading this chapter outside of North America, consider supplementing it with materials related to your social context.

Finally, I must acknowledge my own anxiety and grief around writing this chapter. I do not feel competent to do justice to this topic. Simultaneously, I feel its tremendous importance and that it needs to be done 'right.' Yet I'm going to get it wrong, almost by necessity. I don't know what it is like to be a person of color, disabled, or queer, for example, much as I listen carefully to the experiences reported to me by others. One of the primary dynamics of privilege is to blind us to the experiences of people different from ourselves. Nor can experiences of one type of oppression (i.e., sexism) stand in for another (i.e., racism), though it can help build compassion and solidarity. Thus, my anxiety surfaces. There is grief here as well. Breeshia Wade (2021) and others have pointed out that anti-oppressive work is also grief work. For myself, I experience shame and remorse as I begin to recognize the ways our society has conditioned me to perpetuate harmful behaviors and accept structures that benefit me (a white person) at the expense of those I love. This is compounded by the trauma of being the recipient of discriminatory treatment (mostly sexism) myself.

Systems of oppression are inherently traumatizing for all those caught within them. We are not free from biased thoughts, words, deeds, and systems simply because we begin to see them. And as we begin to see them, our anger, hatred, and shame can come roaring to the forefront. Defensiveness and denial often surface as psychological and interpersonal tactics to avoid dealing with this trauma. The Dharma teaches us a great deal about this dynamic because it is the same dynamic that we uncover as we confront many sources of suffering in our life. Dealing with our own anxiety, fear, loss, grief, and trauma is a major part of working with power, privilege, and oppression. It's hard work, but liberating work for ourselves, others, and our society. As a field, we need more resources to help chaplains with a variety of identities respond effectively to privilege and oppression. I invite all readers to add to that literature.

Kalyāṇamitra: PRAGMATIC SKILLS FOR BUDDHIST SPIRITUAL CARE   VOLUME II

Social Justice Readings

SHORT ARTICLES

Ariel, Courtney. "For Our White Friends Desiring to Be Allies." *Sojourners*, August 16, 2017. https://sojo.net/articles/our-white-friends-desiring-be-allies

Bonner, Tanya Marie. "When Refuge in Another Sangha on MLK Day Was No Longer Enough," *Lion's Roar*, January 16, 2023, https://www.lionsroar.com/when-refuge-in-another-sangha-on-mlk-day-was-no-longer-enough/

Brach, Tara. "Facing My White Privilege," *Lion's Roar*, December 26, 2016. https://www.lionsroar.com/facing-my-white-privilege/

Brennan, Joy. "Deconstructing Whiteness," *Lion's Roar*, June 18, 2021, https://www.lionsroar.com/deconstructing-whiteness/

Collins, Cory. "What is White Privilege, Really?" *Learning for Justice*, Issue 60, Fall 2018. https://www.learningforjustice.org/magazine/fall-2018/what-is-white-privilege-really

Hanada, Julie. "Countercultural Remorse: The Importance of Attending to Grief in Transforming Our Embedded Beliefs," *Reflective Practice: Formation and Supervision in Ministry*, 2021. https://journals.sfu.ca/rpfs/index.php/rpfs/article/view/857/787

Kabat-Zinn, Will. "A Note on Grief and Action," *Medium*, May 29, 2020. https://medium.com/@KabatzinnWill/a-note-on-grief-and-action-8d7a7f150c8d

Koelsch, Patrice Clark. "Adapting the Precepts for Reconciliation," *Lion's Roar*, June 8, 2022. https://www.lionsroar.com/adapting-the-precepts-for-reconciliation/

Kornfield, Jack. "Moral Action and the Dharma," Jack Kornfield Website, October 8, 2020. https://jackkornfield.com/moral-action-and-the-dharma/

Miller, Andrea. "There is a Path that Frees Us from Suffering," *Lion's Roar*, August 7, 2015. https://www.lionsroar.com/path-frees-us-suffering/

Mulay, Tara and Tuere Sala. "Buddhist Justice Versus American Justice," *Tricycle: The Buddhist Reivew*, May 25, 2021.

North-Ellasante, Hilary. "Our Storied Bodies: The Interweavings of Coming In," *Lion's Roar*, September 15, 2022. https://www.lionsroar.com/our-storied-bodies-the-interweavings-of-coming-in/

Salzberg, Sharon and angle Kyodo Williams. "Love Everyone: A Guide for Spiritual Activists," *Lion's Roar*, November 8, 2020. https://www.lionsroar.com/love-everyone-a-guide-for-spiritual-activists/

Sofer, Oren Jay. "10 Things White People Can Do to Work for Racial Justice," Oren Jay Sofer Blog, May 31, 2020. https://www.orenjaysofer.com/blog/racial-justice

Wade, Breeshia. "How Buddhism shaped my understanding of anti-racist work as grief work," Personal blog for Breeshia Wade, October 22, 2023. https://www.breeshiawade.com/post/how-buddhism-shaped-my-understanding-of-racism-and-fear-of-loss-as-grief

Yetunde, Pamela Ayo. "Beginning a Buddhist Pedagogy for the Privileged Oppressed." *Lion's Roar*, November 2, 2022. https://www.lionsroar.com/beginning-a-buddhist-pedagogy-for-the-privileged-oppressed/

Books & Chapters

Blackburn, Anne. "Colonialism and Postcolonialism." 2010. In *Buddhism*. Oxford University Press.

Cheah, Joseph. 2011. *Race and Religion in American Buddhism*. United Kingdom: Oxford University Press.

Joshi, Khyati Y. 2020. *White Christian Privilege: The Illusion of Religious Equality in America*. New York: New York University Press.

Gross, Rita M. 2009. *A Garland of Feminist Reflections*. 1st ed. Berkeley: University of California Press.

Han, Chenxing, and ProQuest. 2021. *Be the Refuge: Raising the Voices of Asian American Buddhists*. Berkeley, California: North Atlantic Books.

King, Ruth. 2018. *Mindful of Race: Transforming Racism from the Inside Out*. Boulder, Colorado: Sounds True, Inc.

Kujawa-Holbrook, Sheryl A., and Karen Brown Montagno. 2023. *Injustice and the Care of Souls: Taking Oppression Seriously in Pastoral Care*. 2nd ed. Minneapolis: Fortress Press.

McMahan, David L. 2008. *The Making of Buddhist Modernism*. United Kingdom: Oxford University Press.

Mitchell, Scott A. 2023. *The Making of American Buddhism*. United Kingdom: Oxford University Press.

Owens, Lama Rod. 2020. *Love and Rage: The Path of Liberation through Anger*. Berkeley, California: North Atlantic Books.

Williams, Angel Kyodo, Rod Owens, and Jasmine Syedullah. 2016. *Radical Dharma: Talking Race, Love, and Liberation*. Berkeley, California: North Atlantic Books.

Rattansi, Ali. 2007. *Racism: A Very Short Introduction*. Oxford: Oxford University Press.

Rothberg, Donald Jay. 2006. *The Engaged Spiritual Life: A Buddhist Approach to Transforming Ourselves and the World*. Boston, Mass.: Beacon Press.

Selassie, Sebene. 2020. *You Belong: A Call for Connection*. New York, NY: HarperOne, an imprint of HarperCollins Publishers.

Vesely-Flad, Rima. 2022. *Black Buddhists and the Black Radical Tradition: The Practice of Stillness in the Movement for Liberation*. New York: New York University Press.

Wade, Breeshia. 2021. *Grieving While Black: An Antiracist Take on Oppression and Sorrow*. North Atlantic Books.

Ward, Larry. 2020. *America's Racial Karma: An Invitation to Heal*. Berkeley, California: Parallax Press.

Williams, Duncan Ryūken. 2019. *American Sutra: A Story of Faith and Freedom in the Second World War*. Cambridge, MA: Harvard University Press.

Yancy, George, and Emily McRae. 2019. *Buddhism and Whiteness: Critical Reflections*. Lanham: Lexington Books.

Yang, Larry. 2017. *Awakening Together: The Spiritual Practice of Inclusivity and Community*. Wisdom Publications.

Yeng, Sokthan. 2020. *Buddhist Feminism: Transforming Anger Against Patriarchy*. 2020. Cham: Palgrave Macmillan.

Yetunde, Pamela Ayo, and Cheryl A. Giles. 2020. *Black & Buddhist: What Buddhism Can Teach Us About Race, Resilience, Transformation & Freedom*. Boulder, Colorado: Shambhala Publications, Inc.

Yoo, David K. and Khyati Y. Joshi, et al. 2020. *Envisioning Religion, Race, and Asian Americans*. Honolulu: University of Hawaii Press.

Reckoning With the Positionality

One need seems to be for greater diversity – including ethnic, racial, linguistic, and socioeconomic diversity – in the field of Buddhist chaplaincy. When I was a CPE resident, I was the only Asian American Buddhist chaplain in the 10+ person spiritual care team and the only person who could speak Mandarin.[1]

As chaplains, we begin exploring the effects of our social positionality during our training. This includes understanding the effects race, sex, gender presentation, sexual orientation, education, socioeconomic status, class, nationality, native language, appearance, age, ordination status, ability, and various other cultural and personal factors have had on us throughout our life.

How have these factors shaped the person you have become? What habitual patterns have you developed to survive in a world where various identity factors are valued differently and result in differential treatment? How have you experienced oppression and privilege and how have you responded to these experiences? This reckoning goes far beyond simply recognizing differences, though that is one aspect. Chaplains with unearned privilege, particularly white and male privilege, must learn to see their privilege as well as the oppression of other groups that it obscures. Chaplains subject to oppression learn to navigate obstacles to achieve their goals. Most chaplains experience both, in some way, though not equally.

When different aspects of privilege and oppression overlap, this is called "intersectionality," a term attributed to Kimberlé Crenshaw, a law professor at UCLA who investigated cases of discrimination against, for example, black women within organizations that otherwise hired both black men and white women.[2] While Crenshaw coined the term we now use, the experiences of people facing "interlocking oppressions" or those who are "multiply marginalized" have been highlighted by feminist and BIPOC activists for decades.[3] Our positionality as chaplains likewise involves understanding our intersectionality in relation to both privilege and oppression. The *Responding to Spiritual Leader Misconduct Handbook* includes the diagram on the opposite page (adapted for clergy from a STEM equity organization; used with permission). Take a moment to place a star on each line where you believe you fall on each spectrum and then note how many stars are above and how many are below the black line labelled "Domination." For Buddhist chaplains, a line for monastic and lay-person or a line for language proficiency might be appropriate. Then take some time to consider your results (see question 8 in Chapter 13) and how your different forms of power or vulnerability affect your behavior.

In her book, *Mindful of Race*, Ruth King offers mindfulness exercises to help Buddhist practitioners explore racial privilege and oppression. Her book includes a chapter on "What White People Can Do with Privilege" and "What People of Color Must Do Together." Notice the difference in the verb 'can' versus 'must,' which eloquently illustrates the distinction between privilege and oppression. Members of privileged groups possess the "privilege" of not needing to address systemic oppression to go about our daily lives, while members of oppressed groups are obliged to deal with it every day. Therefore, the first

---

1 *Mapping Buddhist Chaplains in North America* Survey Response to the question 41 "What do you think is the biggest challenge or need for the field of Buddhist Chaplaincy?", 2020-21.

2 Crenshaw describes this particular case in her 2016 TED Talk "The Urgency of Intersectionality," https://youtu.be/akOe5-UsQ2o?si=aGEt_ZXFsj5z30GC)

3 A short history is available at "The Roots of Intersectionality" from the University of Rochester, SON Council for Diversity, Equity, and Inclusion, https://son.rochester.edu/newsroom/2022/intersectionality.html.)

PRIVILEGE, OPPRESSION & POWER

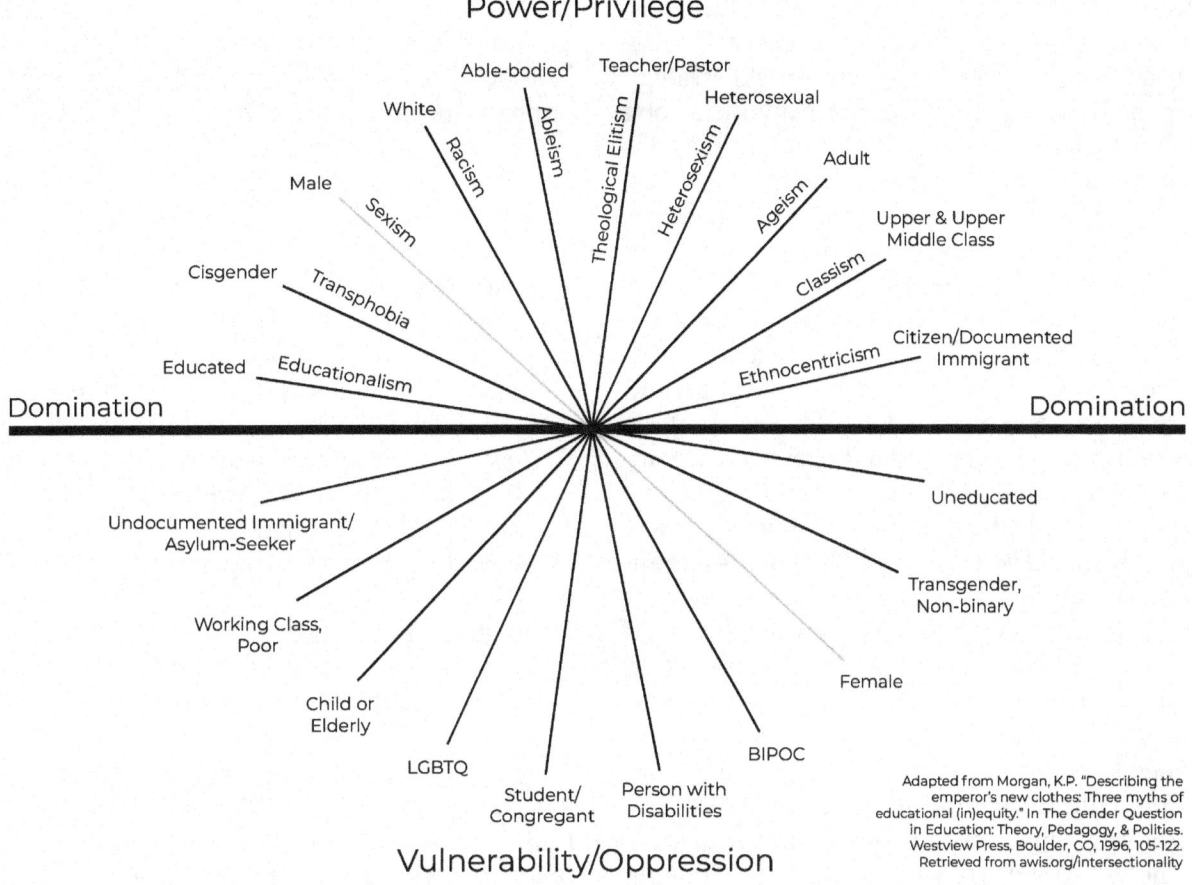

task for white people, according to King, is "owning their racial group identity and exploring what that means," for themselves without asking people of color (POC) to explain it to them (King, p. 189). We (white people) need to wake up to the ways we benefit from whiteness. We must overcome the delusion (*moha* or *avidyā*) that says we deserve these benefits, that these benefits are "normal" and "the same" for everyone when they are not, or that no one is being harmed (they are) because we personally aren't behaving in explicitly racist ways. King (p. 190) reminds us that "The racial crime is in disowning whiteness while still benefiting from whiteness."

In her subsequent chapter for POC, King shares her perspective that "The harsh reality of racial life for POC is that there are no guarantees from ignorance or harm, no safety net. Hearts will be broken, and bodies will be harmed. But we are not victims. We are works of art," much like the Japanese art of *kintsukuroi* or mending broken pottery with gold (King, p. 213). POC must also examine "assumptions we have made about what the term people of color means to us as individuals and as members of racial groups" and then "inquire into how we have been impacted as individuals and as racial groups – and herein lies the diversity among us. Each racial group has its own stories about and experiences of oppression, even if they don't use the term people of color." (King, p. 214) For example, some Asians and Asian-Americans have shared experiences of not associating with the POC term or feeling welcome in BIPOC affinity groups. Likewise, some South Asians have felt unwelcome in affinity groups that are predominantly East

Asian. This is not accidental; dividing different oppressed groups and encouraging racism between oppressed groups is an explicit strategy for maintaining racial hegemony with a long history. Therefore, King reminds us "There is much we can learn and offer each other when we begin to rely on our capacity to wake up, heal, and suffer well." (King, p. 2014)

For POC and other oppressed groups (e.g., women, queer folx, religious minorities) this can begin by attending to internalized oppression. According to King "the programing of internalized oppression is to distress each other, to believe in scarcity, and to believe we are unworthy as individuals and as a body of color." (King, p. 216) Chenxing Han has written poignantly in *Be The Refuge* (2021) about the experiences of internalized oppression among young Asian American Buddhists who felt ashamed of their inherited traditions as somehow "old fashioned" or "superstitious," labels advanced mostly by white Buddhists to legitimate so-called "modernized" (read: conforming with white cultural values and norms) Buddhism. Exploring internalized oppression must be done with love and support because "Talking about internalized oppression can be difficult. It activates old wounds we would like to think were healed, and it can feel like oppression on top of oppression." (King, p. 214) One way that internalized oppression appears when oppressed people come together is through a "hierarchy of oppression" in which different groups claim "We suffer the most." Another way is through ignorance about the experiences of oppressed others, such as black men failing to acknowledge that black women experience oppression differently, or groups not knowing how the distinct history of oppression in America shapes other groups' responses to social conditions. Combined, this can result in some oppressed groups feeling unseen both by privileged people and other oppressed people, making it hard to build solidarity. "Such squabbling is exploited through structural racism." (King, p. 215)

Yet both Han and King sound messages of hope that people of color can overcome the heartache and division created by internalized oppression. King writes:

> I have faith in our ability to recover. It may not always be as quickly as we would like, but most of us have the capacity to recover. And we can help each other to do this. We can move through our hurt together by shifting into mindfulness and away from fixation on who or what is wrong. What supports recovery in such moments is to turn inward toward the bruising and to care tenderly for the hurt we are experiencing. (King, p. 221)

King eloquently describes her own journey through this process in her chapter "Wholeness is No Trifling Matter: Race, Faith, and Refuge" in the anthology *Black & Buddhist* (eds. Giles and Yetunde, 2020). Lama Rod Owens writes in *Love and Rage* (2020) about how deep, painful hurt underlie lifelong experiences of anger, rage, and depression. Only by looking at and tending to the hurt did Owens start to address and understand the anger. King provides various contemplative exercises in *Mindful of Race* to help people through this "practice of 'golden repair,'" (King, p. 222) many of which include the use of mindfulness to become aware of our experience and choose our responses in the same way as described above. In the autobiographical chapter from *Black & Buddhist*, King described the power of this journey through mindfulness on her own reckoning with her racial identity through the framework of the Four Noble Truths, concluding with this:

> My advice: Practice the dharma, then do your best. Grieve, rest, keep hate at bay, and join with others for contemplation and refuge. Don't get too far ahead of now. This moment is enough to digest. Sit, breathe, open.

Don't be a stranger to moments of freedom that may be flirting with you. Allow distress to teach you how to be more human. Sit in the heat of it until your heart is both warmed and informed, then make a conscious choice to be a light." (King, in *Black & Buddhist*, p. 174)

I find this is good advice for anyone, though the experience of doing it will necessarily be shaped by our social location. Thus, reckoning with that positionality is the place we all begin.

At some level, Buddhist chaplains will all experience oppression, simply from being a religious minority, if nothing else. And at some level, Buddhist chaplains will all experience privilege, such as from being educated and having the role of chaplain within the institutions where we serve. This privilege gives us power, which we must use skillfully. The *Responding the Spiritual Leader Misconduct Handbook* defines power as "the sum of one's resources. Someone with access to money, education, authority, and social privileges has more power than someone who lacks access to any or all of those resources." (p. 61) Whereas "Vulnerability is a lack of resources." (p. 62) Oppression occurs when someone is actively prevented from accumulating and maintaining the resources they need to survive or when unearned power is unequally distributed within a society. Those with more power have the responsibility to help those with less, but many fail to use their power in this way. Buddhism provides helpful guides to using power responsibly, such as examining our motivations (Right Intention), behaving skillfully (Right Action), and understanding the effects of our actions clearly (Right View). Vows and precepts place constraints on our behavior to ameliorate misuses of power, but they are not in themselves sufficient. We must bring vigilance (Right Mindfulness and Right Effort) to determine if our actions are consistent with guiding Buddhist virtues such as loving-kindness, compassion, equanimity, and sympathetic joy in both their motivation and effect. This will not always be easy, given the challenges faced by Buddhist chaplains.

Case Study: A White Suburban Bubble

I find many lessons about power, privilege, and oppression by reflecting on my own life using the concepts described above. We can consider this as a case study to illustrate some dynamics of how privilege and oppression are embedded in our society and passed on to each subsequent generation. I was raised in a white suburban bubble in the Midwest. We knew racism and sexism were wrong; this was accepted. I was also taught that racism and sexism were things of the past, solved by the Civil Rights Movement of the 1960s and the feminism of the 1970s, respectively. Yet, there were many inconsistencies that undermined this explicit message.

My mother always had a job, so women were clearly accepted in the workplace. Never mind that she always complained of being cold but would not wear slacks to the office for fear of being perceived as "unprofessional." Segregation was now illegal, as it should be, everyone agreed. Never mind that our suburb had no black families. That could be easily brushed away with the word 'minority,' leading to the belief that people of color were simply scarce. Never mind the existence of urban African American and Hispanic-majority neighborhoods nearby that we were also clearly told were "unsafe." We all knew Native American words because they were used to name our cities, counties, and rivers. Never mind that none of us knew any actual Native Americans. As a girl, I was encouraged to be whatever I wanted to be when I grew up. Never mind that most of what I wanted was the freedom that seemed to come from being a tomboy. There was no prayer in school. Never mind that the schools never planned after-school practices on Wednesday (but they did on Friday) so the local churches could hold youth classes. These inconsistencies were only visible in hindsight. At the time, they were all known to me, but I was not cognizant of how the "Never mind…" conditions illustrated the operation of ideological, institutional, interpersonal, or internalized oppression (or a combination of all four). Rather I absorbed both the explicit messages (e.g., racism = bad) and implicit conditioning (e.g., people of color = avoid) of my environment.

Only in college did I have sustained encounters with people different from myself in race, sexual orientation, national origin, or religion. My undergraduate degree required a single "diversity" elective and the university somehow managed to find a Black professor from Africa who was more critical of African Americans than I had ever heard any white teacher be. The largest university in the state (26,000 students) didn't offer a single course that covered Buddhism, not even in the so-called 'World Religions' class (this has changed). Only in graduate school did I begin noticing the dynamics of unearned privilege, implicit bias, and systemic oppression, largely through the experiences of classmates and coworkers. Disappointingly, much of what I had been taught as "history" was still very much in the present.

I made a lot of mistakes. I experienced sexism and misogyny as a woman and religious discrimination as an atheist and, later, Buddhist. While distinct from other forms of oppression like racism and able-ism, these experiences engendered a sense of solidarity with other oppressed groups. Nevertheless, during this time I said and did discriminatory things, perpetuated harm and oppression, because I didn't know any better. And my white privilege insulated me from learning any better for a long time. In fact, white privilege continues to blind me to certain things right up to the present day.

Strangely, homophobia was the first kind of direct oppression on my radar, while also being the least visible in my immediate environment. I recall a conversation in the car with my mother when I was about 10 years old. I had overheard her talking with my grandmother and wanted to know what they meant by "gay," which, based on their tone, clearly was not good. She told me it was when a man loves another man rather than a woman, or vice versa. I then asked, "What's wrong with that?" to which she replied, "Well you wouldn't want them teaching your kids, would you?" This made absolutely no sense to my adolescent brain, but it was clear that it was not a topic my mother wanted to discuss. I only became conscious of the struggle for LGBTQIA+ rights as an adult, when legalizing gay marriage was on the national stage. Given that most of the opposition to gay marriage was rooted in the Christianity I had already left behind, it seemed a natural thing to support. The lesson I take from this is that discriminatory ideology must be learned. Because homosexual identities and issues were not visible or discussed within my childhood environment, I did not learn to be prejudiced against homosexual people. Unfortunately, since I was exposed to negative media portrayals of "transvestites" growing up, I did need some remedial education on the topic of transgender identity and trans rights. Gender identity was a real learning curve that only arrived in my late twenties, by which time I had already done unwitting harm. Though I never opposed being transgender or breaking out of the gender binary, I simply did not know how to recognize what was going on and be a good ally.

Sexism was the most visible form of privilege and oppression. I knew it when it was applied to me, from childhood onward, though it took years for me to begin to recognize how much of it I had subconsciously internalized and subsequently weaponized against other women. This "internalized oppression" manifests when a member of the oppressed group either tacitly or consciously accepts the narrative of inferiority to the supposedly superior (male) group. Many of the women in my life have explicitly expressed sexist ideologies and stereotypes against other women. While I overtly opposed such ideas, it took me a long time to reckon with the judgmental narratives I constructed in my mind around "femininity" in general and other women in particular. Essentially, I rejected expressions of femininity as "weak," "silly," or "vain," thus subconsciously reinforcing a patriarchal narrative. Learning to embrace and celebrate femininity as an adult has been liberating. Oppression, whether external or internal, is a barrier to joy and thriving.

Racism was harder to learn to see because I had been actively fed disinformation by my family, schools, and popular culture. As noted, some of these messages were incoherent. On the one hand, racism was bad, illegal, and also something our society had overcome. On the other hand, depictions of Black, Indigenous, and People of Color (BIPOC) in popular media were often very negative and I should be careful when visiting certain neighborhoods in the city where BIPOC folks lived. Because they didn't live in my neighborhood due to the generational effects of institutional racism, I was insulated from witnessing active forms of interpersonal racism. Sadly, functional segregation is just as pervasive today as when it was mandated by law. Privilege also insulated me from many stereotypically racist dynamics.

The very same words or behaviors directed towards me were not perceived as racist, but reinforce racist dynamics when directed at a others, particularly BIPOC folks. Take, for example, the question of "Where are you from?" I have been asked the question countless times in my life. It is a standard ice-breaker question used in white American conversation patterns, often combined with "What do you do (for work)?" Both are subtly intended to reinforce in-group/out-group and classist hierarchies. For me, the question "Where are you from?" is innocuous, because my answers are within the customary categories. I can say "I'm from Gretna" or Omaha (the bigger city next door) or Nebraska or the Midwest or America and all of that will be readily accepted. Because I've been asked this question since childhood, I've also been subtly trained to ask this question of other people. This demonstrates that even explicitly non-racist people can learn and then unthinkingly practice racist behaviors as part of the broader culture. And when hearing others object to the "Where are you from?" question, it can seem baffling at first, but a close examination of my own experiences provided a glimpse into the more nefarious dynamic BIPOC folks are pointing out.

As an adult college student, I did some projects in small town Nebraska. Folks from rural areas are often suspicious of folks from the city. Many don't really think city folk can understand their way of life or make decisions in the best interests of rural communities. I learned to overcome this suspicion by adding, "But my Mom is from Ainsworth and my Dad is from Valentine," two recognizable small towns in Nebraska. This immediately made me one of the "in-group" by proxy and people became more relaxed, helpful, and informative. Now I could imagine this dynamic on a much larger scale, with stronger embedded forms of prejudice and no recourse (due to ideological and institutional racism) to becoming a "in-group" member by proxy. Thus, a question like "Where are you from?" exchanged between two white people trains racist behaviors and we don't see those behaviors as racist because we are insulated by white privilege. Our answer will not be followed up with "Where are you really from?" or "Where are your people from?" or other such questions that insinuate the person doesn't really "belong" here. (Although white people asking other white people about their assumed European ancestry is not uncommon.)

I take two lessons from this example. First, I can't use my own experience alone as the basis for judging if a behavior is oppressive or not. I need to believe others when they tell me something is harmful to them. And yet, when I carefully reflect on the social purposes behind particular behaviors, I can often find questionable practices. I can learn to understand the full range of effects of a certain behavior or social structure. Second, I cannot always determine if a behavior is oppressive by hypothetically applying it to myself to see if I would be harmed or offended by it. Some oppressive behaviors are overtly discriminatory and would be harmful to anyone. Yet many oppressive behaviors target only certain groups while being harmless to those with sufficient privilege.

I still have work to do to become a better ally to those experiencing various forms of oppression. For example, when originally considering this chapter, I felt it would be important to find an author who has written before on this topic so the work would have more "credibility." I have never written explicitly about privilege and oppression (other than on Christian hegemony in the field of chaplaincy), though I do try to reference it when such dynamics affect other aspects of chaplaincy. Finding a co-author would also be an opportunity to bring more voices of color to this project. Yet, when I approached potential chapter authors (all POC), I was encouraged to take on the chapter myself as a white ally. "White people need to do their own work," I was told, since white people are most directly responsible for and benefit from the systemic oppression of people of color. This is true, even among actively anti-racist white allies.

I also realized that I, personally, had never written directly about privilege and oppression, particularly regarding race, because I never had to. As an educated, able-bodied, cis-hetero white woman, my social position, financial stability, physical safety, and credibility have never depended on dismantling oppression (other than Christian hegemony). Like the *devas* of the heavenly realms, where life is too easy to motivate practice, I had never been sufficiently motivated to write a on this topic – which is, itself, a form of privilege. Likewise, asking chaplains of color to do all the hard work of dismantling oppressive systems while also being subject to those systems is, in itself, a further form of oppression. I see this as both a product of my white privilege and a failure of Right View and lack of compassion, which, in Chapter 3 we learned means actively doing something to alleviate the suffering of others. My compassion often fell short in predictable ways when viewed in light of the dynamics of power that create privileged groups and oppressed groups within our society. When I my ego couldn't tolerate the fear of getting this chapter wrong, I looked for a way out by asking chaplains of color to shoulder that burden. I'm still reckoning with my own positionality. Thankfully, the Dharma and the chaplains I do research with have a lot of wisdom on this topic, so, as it turns out, I may actually be suitably positioned to write this chapter.

Dealing with Discrimination

Just as I have used my own case study above to illustrate many of the dynamics of power, privilege, and oppression, I shall use data collected from Buddhist chaplains to illustrate other dynamics in the following sections. The quotes come from a variety of sources collected between 2017 and 2022 and, taken at their word, demonstrate what Buddhist chaplains deal with in the field, Buddhist communities, and personal lives on a regular basis.

First, Buddhist chaplains report experiencing direct discrimination in their work due to their personal characteristics and the groups to which they belong. This includes ideological, institutional, and interpersonal forms of oppression.[1] "In the world that I work, as a female ordained Buddhist Chaplain, the majority of individuals are Christian, and mostly male Christians. This is the biggest challenge," one chaplain told us in response to a question about the biggest challenge they face (*Mapping Survey Response*, 2020/21). Another said "I am Asian female-presenting, first generation immigrant. As such, my voice don't carry weight in Asian

---

[1] I also assume the presence of internalized oppression, though this is not generally reported in my data and may be ameliorated by chaplaincy training or Buddhist practice.

Buddhist communities as men are considered above. In Western communities, I'm seen as not a competent practitioner, either for many different reasons, but perhaps mostly because I belong to margins in the society [sic]," in response to the question about their greatest personal need (*Mapping Survey Response*, 2020/21). Racism, sexism, homophobia, classism, ableism, and many other forms of discrimination create hardships in chaplains' personal lives, religious practice, and spiritual care work.

Chaplains report prejudices from careseekers, families, colleagues, educators, supervisors, and even fellow chaplains as well as from within their own Buddhist communities. One chaplain wrote about the multiple sources of discrimination they face:

> Sometimes it's also challenging for me at the intersection of gender, religion and culture. Some patients are surprised and a little resistant to me being a woman chaplain, and so I feel even more uneasy about revealing that I am also Buddhist...it feels like enough to navigate that I am female and Asian. Many Asian Buddhists I meet do not know what a chaplain is, and prefer monastic visits. Some of the Asian patients I meet would prefer male monastics over female. So, there are overlapping areas of resistance to explore around gender, religion and race...just to let me in the door. (*Mapping Survey Response*, 2020/21)

It is not only Asian chaplains who face these challenges. Another chaplain told us, "I'm a minority as a Mexican-American and a non-Christian…. I've had a patient say, 'I don't need to talk to you, you're a Mexican.' I live and work in a part of the country where this kind of behavior is not uncommon." (*Mapping Survey Response*, 2020/21) Black chaplains and queer chaplains have reported similar experiences.

Despite the relatively positive perception Americans as a whole tend to have towards Buddhism (Pew Research Center, 2017), Buddhist chaplains report experiencing discrimination due to religious identity. This often begins during their education and training and continues into their professional lives. Chaplains regularly report that the very structure of the profession, including the expected learning outcomes for educational programs as set by groups such as the Association of Theological Schools (ats.edu), Association for Professional Chaplains (apchaplains.org), Association for Clinical Pastoral Education (acpe.edu), and Canadian Association for Spiritual Care (spiritualcare.ca) are all normatively Christian, making them ill-suited for Buddhists. (This Christian normativity can even infiltrate Buddhist schools and programs, as they must tailor their curricula to meet external expectations in the job market.) Many chaplains shared sentiments such as "I also found some aspects of CPE learning too ill-informed in regards to trauma, privilege, difference, Buddhism, and non-Theistic traditions in general." (*Mapping Survey Response*, 2020/21) I have written about the effects of Christian hegemony extensively elsewhere, so I will not reprise those writings here (see listing in the breakout box on the next page).

A recent survey by the Association of Professional Chaplains found that chaplains experience discrimination from chaplain educators, fellow chaplains, careseekers, and multi-disciplinary colleagues.[2] While levels of discrimination from careseekers were the highest, chaplains appeared to have effective strategies for dealing with such incidents. Whereas levels of

---

2 See the "Chaplaincy Diversity and Sensitivity Study" convened by the Religious and Spiritual Diversity Task Force, a collaboration between NAJC, NACC, ACPE, APC, AMC and CASC, in 2022; preliminary findings were given in the presentation "Gauging Feelings of Acceptance Among Chaplaincy Students, Staff, and Educators: Perceptions of Bias and Discrimination," prepared by Barry E. Pitegoff and presented on June 9, 2023; survey n = 422.

Resources About the Effects of Christian Hegemony on Buddhist Chaplains

Edwards, Sachi. 2024. "Creating Welcoming and Supportive Campus Climates for Buddhist Students: Barriers and Opportunities." *New Directions for Higher Education 2024* (206): 53–63. https://doi.org/10.1002/he.20499.

Sanford, Monica and Francis Lee. *Brightly Shining Jewel: How Sanghas can Care for Their Buddhist Chaplains*. Self-published as a freely distributed handbook. 2024.

_____. "Can One Care for a Soul that Doesn't Exist? and Other Koans from Buddhist Chaplains." *Injustice and the Care of Souls]: Taking Oppression Seriously in Pastoral Care*. 2nd ed. Edited by Sheryl A. Kujawa-Holbrook and Karen B. Montagno. Augsburg Fortress Publishers, 2023.

_____. "Suffering, Self, & Structures: Remarks for Buddhist-Christian Thought and Spiritual Care," *Journal of Buddhist-Christian Studies*, 2024.

_____. *Kalyāṇamitra: A Model for Buddhist Spiritual Care, Volume I*. Nepean, ON: Sumeru Press, 2021.

_____. "Secret Atheist: Internal and External Tensions affecting Buddhists as Inter-Religious Professionals." *Navigating Religious Pluralism in Spiritual Care and Counseling: Essays in Honor of Kathleen J. Greider*. Edited by Jill Snodgrass. Claremont School of Theology Press, 2019.

_____. "Theological Reflection Without 'Theo:' Transcendent Connections for Buddhist Chaplains in Inter-Religious Settings." Presented at the American Academy of Religions Annual Conference, Theology and Religious Reflection Unit, November 17, 2018. Available at hds.academia.edu/monicasanford

Various chapters in *The Arts of Contemplative Care* edited by Giles & Miller, Wisdom Publications (2012) reference dealing with Christian normativity, including
- Berlin, Chris, "Widening the Circle: Engaged Bodhicitta in Hospital Chaplaincy," p. 81-92
- Brooks, Ginger, "A Little Nowness," p. 265-272
- Jensen, Lin, "Wrong Speech: Knowing When It Is Best to Lie," p. 291-300
- Power, Mark, "Buddhist Chaplaincy in a Christian Context: A Personal Story," p. 63-72
- Ruhl, Steven Kanji, "Report from the Field: Being an American Zen Buddhist Minister," p. 301-308

---

discrimination from chaplaincy educators were the lowest, "the [open-ended] responses [asking chaplains to elaborate] were the most detailed and most abundant" on this topic (slide 10), demonstrating the deep concern that chaplains have for the shortcomings of those from whom they have higher expectations. The report stated that "Chaplaincy education environments were expected to be safe spaces and to those commenting, they were not" (slide 41). The report makes clear that all chaplains, including Christian chaplains, reported experiences of bias and discrimination both from those of other traditions ("inter-faith") as well as those within their own traditions ("intra-faith").[3] Comments within our own data from Buddhist chaplains corroborate these experiences.

Buddhist chaplains in the joint discrimination survey were grouped together with Hindu and other chaplains in a category labelled "Eastern" (n=19 or 4.5%). Eastern chaplains were far more likely to perceive bias or discrimination from careseekers than Protestant chaplains, with three-quarters (74%) reporting these experiences. The draft survey report available

---

3 It is not clear how much of this was attributable to religious identity and how much to other factors such as race and gender.

at the time of this writing did not disaggregate for the other sources of bias or discrimination, though it did provide a summary of representative comments from chaplains of the different identity groups. One shared comment read: "Yes, many colleagues have the same assumptions about chaplaincy as I mentioned above: 1) that our work is inspired by a divine power and if you don't believe in that divine power or connect to it you can't do the work; 2) that Buddhism is basically Protestantism + meditation; 3) that Buddhist chaplains can't serve non-Buddhist or theistic care-seekers because we're too different; etc." (Pitegoff, slide 29). My own research with Buddhist chaplains has uncovered similar sentiments.

Careseekers may reject their services as a result of the chaplain's religious identity. "As a chaplain there have been times where I have been rejected after disclosing my practice as a Buddhist." This experience can be echoed by co-workers who fail to call the chaplain or make offhanded comments demonstrating ignorance and assumptions about, or prejudice against, Buddhism. The same chaplain continued, "I have been tokenized in department settings and then looked at quizzically when hedging to speak on behalf of all of Buddhism," (*Mapping Survey Response*, 2020/21). Other chaplains described being "called the devil," (*Mapping Survey Response*, 2020/21) experiencing religious bullying, being proselytized to by patients, staff, and other chaplains. This discrimination prevents careseekers from receiving care from which they would otherwise benefit, especially when other chaplains may not be readily available for a referral.

As a result, many chaplains have developed strategies for introducing themselves that do not immediately disclose their own religious identity, preferring to refer to themselves as an "interfaith chaplain," "spiritual care provider," or just "chaplain." Sometimes this leads others to assume the chaplain is Christian (related to a commonly reported assumption that all chaplains are Christian) and leaves the Buddhist chaplain feeling conflicted around questions of appropriate self-disclosure, informed consent, and Right Speech. In the parlance of privilege and oppression, this phenomenon is known as "passing," wherein a member of an oppressed group allows others to assume they are members of the privileged group to avoid difficulty. When asked directly about their religious "denomination" or tradition, Buddhist chaplains have developed answers to that question based on the needs of the situation and their own person background. There is no single approach, but here are some examples that have been shared with me:

"Have you experienced bias or discrimination from a…"	Yes	No
Chaplain educator	34%	66%
Another chaplain	48%	52%
Somone receiving your care	59%	41%
A colleague from a different discipline	43%	57%

Chaplain Tradition	"…experienced bias or discrimination from someone receiving your care"
Eastern (including Buddhist)	74%
Other	71%
Jewish	68%
Muslim	68%
Catholic	56%
Protestant	55%

Source: Pitegoff, Barry E., "Gauging Feelings of Acceptance Among Chaplaincy Students, Staff, and Educators: (Perceptions of Bias and Discrimination)" slides presented to the Religious and Spirituality Diversity Task Force on June 9, 2023.

- "I'm a Buddhist, though I was raised as a Christian and received an interreligious education, so I respect all religions and understand your tradition."
- "I'm a spiritual person and I practice many kinds of meditation and prayer from a variety of traditions."
- "I'm happy to share my tradition with you, if you like, but I'm more interested in what kind of spiritual or religious practices help you in times like this. Is

religion or spirituality important to you?"
- "Oh, I'm not here to proselytize. I understand you're Baptist, right? I want to support you to draw strength from your tradition. What would help most right now?"
- "I'm a Korean Buddhist monk and my tradition teaches me to respect all other religions. I would love to learn more about how your religion helps you when things like this happen."
- "It's okay. I'm a Buddhist chaplain. I don't know a lot about Paganism, but I know what it's like to be a religious minority and I'm not going to try to 'save' you. Why don't you tell me more about the Pagan beliefs and practices that are important to you?"

In some cases, it can help alleviate tension to share one's Buddhist identity early in a caring encounter if the careseekers is of another religious minority tradition or non-religious. The assumption that all chaplains are Christian is pervasive and connected to the assumption that all Christians proselytize. Some religious minority careseekers may refuse chaplaincy services from anyone on that basis. Likewise, in my time working as a college chaplain, letting Hindu or Jewish or non-religious students know that I was a Buddhist chaplain often created a sense of solidarity and reduced the time they felt they needed to spend explaining how their religious needs were different from normatively Christian beliefs and practices. In education, corrections, or the military, chaplains may work closely with their own designated religious communities, while still navigating normatively Christian administrative structures. However, in health care settings where most chaplains are employed, they will work most commonly with Christian or post-Christian (e.g., with a Christian family background but now identifying as "non-religious" or "Spiritual-but-not-religious," and so on) careseekers, family, and staff.

Many chaplains were keenly aware of socioeconomic privilege. Careseekers experiencing trauma and crisis often find themselves in their situations because of a lack of power due to the uneven distribution of resources in our society. This is particularly visible for chaplains who serve in corrections and health care. When asked if their education was effective, one chaplain said that "Weaknesses in my training for myself and my peers would be around religious literacy issues and social determinants of health, including diversity and equity matters," (*Mapping Survey Response*, 2020/21) referencing the intersectional nature of socioeconomics with race/ethnicity, gender, and other characteristics. Another chaplain called for more research in this area based on their experiences:

> As a chaplain in a safety-net, public hospital [with a] Level One trauma center, the need is so clear that dialogues that truly examine the facts and realities of the economic and social-justice cause-and-effect impact of the United States' rampant economic inequality/Western medicine system paradigm through the lens of Buddhist dharmic texts and bearing-witness practice is not only needed, but would be illuminating and fascinating. (*Mapping Survey Response*, 2020/21)

These socioeconomic barriers affect both careseekers and chaplains. In some cases, chaplains with differing abilities reported having to pay higher fees (a "disability tax") to access the same community resources and education available to able-bodied chaplains. Chaplaincy education is often high-cost and high-commitment (up to three-years of full-time graduate education and up to one-year of full-time hospital residency) for a relatively modest salary if one should achieve full-time employment thereafter. Many Christian denominations provide support for their members and clergy to pursue this kind of education, but few Buddhist communities are able to do so at this time, creating socioeconomic barriers to Buddhists who wish to enter the profession.

Many Buddhist communities support their chaplains in non-economic ways, such as through direct Buddhist teachings and practice. However, sadly, Buddhist chaplains also experience oppression within their own Buddhist communities. One chaplain explained that "The biggest challenge I continue to face is in how often Buddhist communities I'm involved with continue to perpetuate systems of harm and do little to truly commit to liberation," and another said that they have "[overcome] the challenges I've had to face in a community that is white-dominated and lacks strong class, able-ism, and gender analysis." (*Mapping Survey Response*, 2020/21). Buddhist communities can likewise perpetuate ideological, institutional, interpersonal, and even internalized oppression on the basis of race, gender, hetero-normativity, able-ism, classism, and in various other ways. A 2023 study on the relationships between Buddhist chaplains and their Buddhist communities revealed that some chaplains prefer not to affiliate with a Buddhist community for these reasons, despite recognizing how supportive it can be to be part of a religious community.[4] The more committed action our Buddhist communities take to support social justice, understand privilege, and dismantle oppression, the more it benefits all members, including chaplains. There are many useful resources for communities who want to do this kind of work.[5]

Finally, sometimes Buddhist chaplains report experiencing discrimination from other oppressed groups. For example, cis-gender women can fail to support transgender women, colleagues who fight age-ism may perpetuate able-ism, or racial minority affinity groups that exclude other racial minority people. One chaplain shared that "For myself as an Asian American in a convert Buddhist center. It's a little bit... frustrating in some aspects, since when it comes to affinity groups, and like BIPOC, Asians are not exactly always considered BIPOC for some odd reason," (*Buddhist Community Interview* 2022). Several Asian American chaplains have reported this phenomenon. These forms of interpersonal oppression are based on internalized ideologies inculcated by dominant norms. In all cases, they benefit the privileged group by preventing members of oppressed groups from forming alliances in solidarity with one another, as Ruth King addressed in the previous section. Buddhist practices to witness suffering and generate compassion and loving-kindness towards others, balanced with an equanimous attitude that treats all suffering as worthy of a response, can serve as a powerful antidote. While chaplains reported experiencing many types of oppression, they also reported many effective ways of responding to it.

Working Towards Social Justice

On a positive note, many chaplains (of all religions) are actively working to support social justice. Through our training in spiritual care, we become sensitive to power dynamics, learn how to recognize privilege, and respond effectively to instances of oppression. This includes addressing the explicit and implicit biases and stereotypes with which we have been conditioned by society. Buddhist teachings, particularly Buddhist psychology and practices for the cultivation of non-attachment and equanimity can be very useful in this process. One chaplain told us:

> It is continually a challenge to drop all the ideas I have about a person or situation or what I believe might be helpful to the person or situation. I believe the greatest gift I can provide

---

4 See *Brightly Shining Jewel* by Sanford and Lee, in the breakout box on page 188.

5 See the breakout box on page 192.

is lovingkindness in the presence of full-hearted attention, and sometimes a fear or insecurity about "am I doing enough?" or "am I doing it right?" interferes with this. In addition, there are many challenges a person with white privilege desiring to support those who are most vulnerable in our society; I have continuous work to do to grow my awareness of the harm caused by white supremacy, and to actively work to resist the dominant systems of oppression. (*Mapping Survey Response*, 2020/21)

Most of the Buddhist chaplains who responded to our survey in 2020 and 2021 identified their race as "White/Caucasian" (about 67%) and many said that white privilege was one of their greatest challenges. Some also listed other forms of privilege, such as based on gender or age. Chaplains saw these challenges as rich ground for their own spiritual work, "My [biggest challenge is] culturally deeply engrained privilege and biases as a white man will provide important and challenging inner work for the rest of my life, I expect." (*Mapping Survey Response*, 2020/21) Overcoming the delusion (*avidyā*) of privilege benefits both society and the spiritual life of the practitioner.

While "white people need to do their own work," is a common refrain I heard when researching this chapter, Buddhist chaplains of color, those who are female, queer, and so on, have paved the way with important insights and useful strategies. This includes building solidarity across lines of difference. "People in the most marginalized, when they realized I had come from similar back ground and/or suffering, their eyes sparkled and there was a surprise in a positive way [sic]," (*Mapping Survey Response*, 2020/21) one chaplain told us.

Those we care for need to know that we truly understands the hardships they have experienced, that we are prepared to believe them, and will work together as allies. "As someone who is a double minority in this country, racially and religiously, I draw on my experiences to support and advocate for those who feel marginalized in a way that is sensitive to power dynamics," (*Mapping Survey Response*, 2020/21) another chaplain said.

Drawing more chaplains from diverse backgrounds into the profession (especially to redress the racial imbalance) and ensuring that

---

What is Implicit Bias or Implicit Association?

Implicit biases or associations are those we carry subconsciously and may act on, even when we hold explicit views and intentions to the contrary. Theories about implicit bias were developed in the 1990s by psychologists Mahzarin Banaji and Anthony Greenwald. The American Psychological Association defines implicit as "a negative attitude, of which one is not consciously aware, against a specific social group"[1] and describes it as a learned set of thought patterns that affect both our perceptions and behaviors. For example, we may perceive the behavior of one person as malicious and another person as accidental based on implicit biases about their respective social groups. These biases are often inculcated through media representations of group stereotypes and messages absorbed in childhood, such as those described in the case study above. Researchers at Harvard have developed the Implicit Association Test[2] to help people learn what implicit biases they may hold and how to correct associated behavior.

---

1 https://www.apa.org/topics/implicit-bias
2 https://implicit.harvard.edu/implicit/takeatest.html

they are welcomed and supported will have a positive effect on so many careseekers.

Chaplains report how rewarding this work can be. Chaplains advocate for careseekers in need and serve as a bridge between the careseeker and institution in which they are receiving care by drawing their needs (and sometimes neglect or mistreatment) to the attention other staff. They also serve on boards and committees working towards tangible institutional change. When we asked our survey respondents what they most celebrated about their work, one chaplain told us how they "Collaborated with colleagues to initiate a process to address racism in our chaplaincy department that has resulted in an ongoing space for chaplains to gather, learn and discuss how racism affects them personally and how we respond to racism in our hospitals." (*Mapping Survey Response*, 2020/21) Chaplains often serve as the ethical voice of an institution, both in regular meetings and committees, and as part of groups convened specifically to address diversity, inclusion, and belonging. "I care a lot about justice in my institutional workplaces, often serving on committees or workgroups to address racial equity and advocate for those marginalized in our systems (including myself)," (*Mapping Survey Response*, 2020/21). Sometimes they convene such groups where none existed before, or they bring the intersectional lens of religious identity to the conversation.

The most satisfying work I did as a college chaplain and leader of an interfaith center revolved around diversity, inclusion, and belonging. This includes reviving an African American-led Christian group on campus (as the prior one had died out a few years before) in collaboration with a local church, negotiating with Dining Services to win a commitment to build a kosher kitchen and food service venue on campus, formally recognizing the Pagan chaplain and student group and ending years of marginalization that allowed the now visible group to grow and thrive, and adding a Hindu chaplain who had just begun to work with south Asian students (a large and visible minority on that campus) when I departed for my next position. It has trained me to look around any room I am in and ask "Who is here? Who is not here? Why is that? And what can I/we do about it?" This is especially important in rooms where decisions are being made and budgets allocated. (Remember, a budget is a moral document. A financial statement literally shows what an institution values or doesn't value.)

I can and do use the power I have to center diverse voices and concerns, in consultation with other staff, faculty, and (most importantly) students. In my academic setting, exposing students to Buddhists from a variety of traditions and backgrounds, ensuring that every student has multiple opportunities to become aware of the work of or connect with a Buddhist who is like them in an important respect (e.g., race, gender, queer identity, language, culture, and so on) as well as those who are different from them across various spectrums, is an important goal of education. Other Buddhist chaplains report similar strategies within their sanghas. One told us "Lama [Name Redacted] who is our spiritual director, you know he's a middle-aged white dude, but he's very aware of it, and so he really is constantly seeking ways to center other peoples and other communities, and not just people that look and sound like him. So I would say, that's the change that it's very intentional," (*Buddhist Community Interview* 2023). This work is deliberate and should not be undertaken without the consultation of members of the communities and groups involved. "Nothing about us without us," is important to remember. Buddhist chaplains often encounter tokenism (i.e., symbolic inclusion devoid of real change) in their workplaces (by being the only Buddhist, only non-theist, only POC, or across multiple dimensions). We should not replicate this tokenism in our own work. Some chaplains are encouraged by the success of such efforts, while recognizing there is more work to do. "Oftentimes I do look around, and I think oh, there's not a lot of brown people around here. But I think that even that is changing, because our leadership is very aware of that, and they really look for ways to become more inclusive and representative. And I think that's changing." (*Buddhist Community Interview* 2023) one told us recently.

Nevertheless, chaplains have repeatedly said they see more work that needs to be done. "I also think whiteness and systemic racism is a major challenge in the field, we need more focus on collective liberation through dismantling systems of oppression." (*Mapping Survey Response*, 2020/21) This work needs to be a central focus of both our formal chaplaincy education (and more integrated into CPE training) as well as part of our personal spiritual practices. One chaplain said, "Like to me all this is really obvious, like if you're practicing Buddhism, you should be noticing how all these systems of repression serve each other." (*Buddhist Community Interview* 2023) Chaplains can be at the forefront of this work, both within their institutions and their Buddhist sanghas. "I think I would like to help my community become more conscious of how power privilege and oppression function within the community. I'd like to hold abbots/teachers accountable if they sleep with a young student within a month of arriving at their monastery." (*Buddhist Community Interview* 2023) Systems of accountability are crucial to this process. This chaplain continued, "I'd like to help communities discern between a privileged aloofness and actual equanimity when meeting social justice issues. I would like to dismantle classist, racist, and patriarchal norms that are perpetuated within these communities under the guise of spiritual practice or spiritual attainment." (*Buddhist Community Interview* 2023)

Unfortunately, communities have not always lived up to these principles of accountability. In Chapter 5 we discussed the importance of personal and professional boundaries and creating a community of accountability for oneself. Communities also need to step forward and create accountability processes to handle both the violation of professional boundaries by members of their leadership and grievances on account of discrimination and oppression (these two are often intertwined). The *Responding to Spiritual Leader Misconduct Handbook* has important guidance on how to create an accountable community, including:

- Prioritizing protection of the vulnerable party (e.g., those with less power or privilege);
- Prioritizing truth, transparency, and accountability over reputation (e.g., who are you protecting? the institution, the leader, or the vulnerable party?);
- Evaluating boundary violations separately, rather than weighing harms against benefits (e.g., amazing teacher, great fundraiser, etc.);
- Creating pathways towards reconciliation, if possible;
- Creating community cultures of prevention through education;
- Having clear and available ethical codes, grievance procedures, and designated people to report violations to or hold others accountable.

The Buddhist tradition of *Patimokkha*, or ritual confession of misdeeds and communal response, can provide important guidance even to non-monastic Buddhist communities.[6] The *Patimokkha* embodies the principles listed above. Buddhist communities that have engaged in social justice and accountability work have developed modern ethical codes and policies that can also serve as examples. A small sample of these are listed in the breakout box on the next page.

One of the most important ways to work towards social justice is to continually build cultural competency. This is a lifelong project,

---

[6] See Thanissaro Bhikkhu's *Introduction to the Patimokkha Rules* as a good starting place, https://www.vipassana.com/canon/vinaya/bhikkhu-pati-intro.html

Resources for Creating Inclusive Buddhist Communities

"5 Ways Buddhist Communities can Take Part in Social Change" by Colin Beavan, June 12, 2018 article in *Lion's Roar* https://www.lionsroar.com/221913-2/

"Buddhists and Racial Justice: A History" by Ann Gleig, July 24, 2020, in *Tricycle* https://tricycle.org/article/buddhists-racial-justice/

Heartwood Center for Integrative Health & Healing Survivors Program to connect survivors of guru and teacher abuse, https://www.heartwoodcenter.com/meditation/survivorsprogram/

Resources On Disability and Ableism For Everyone (Disabled And Non-Disabled Alike) from the East Bay Meditation Center https://eastbaymeditation.org/about/radical-inclusivity/resources-on-disability-and-ableism/

"Sangha Sutra: Ethical Guidelines" for the Zen Center of Los Angeles including "ZCLA Statement of Right Conduct," "ZCLA Grievance Policy," and "ZCLA Teachers Ethics Statement" https://zcla.org/about/governance/sangha-sutra/

"Sexual Abuse, Whiteness and Patriarchy" panel with Lama Rod Owens, Dr. Shante Paradigm Smalls, moderated by Dr. Nalika Gahaweera, posted by Ann Gleig, October 5, 2021 https://youtu.be/yDY6sgMIi9s

"Sexual Misconduct and Legal Liability Issues in the Sangha" webinar by Carol Merchasin, moderated and posted by Ann Gleig, October 5, 2021 https://youtu.be/rzoMdW8GEVI

On Engaged Buddhism and Social Justice from the Atlanta Buddhism and Meditation Blog https://georgiameditation.org/buddhistblacklivesmatter.html

On Equity, Diversity, Justice, and Inclusion (EDJI) from the San Francisco Buddhist Center https://sfbuddhistcenter.org/edji-equity-diversity-justiceinclusion

On Social Justice from the Spirit Rock Meditation Center https://www.spiritrock.org/resources/social-justiceresources

On Social Justice from Access to Zen https://accesstozen.org/social-justice-resources

---

but a very fulfilling one that helps us question our assumptions and expand our horizons. Chaplains have reported that "I suspect many white and cis-gendered Buddhist chaplains lack the cultural competency, as well as the understanding of structural racism, required to serve BIPOC and Trans folks in the United States. Relatedly, I believe we must dedicate more time and effort to uncovering and transforming our sexist and racist conditioning, as well as de-centering whiteness in Buddhist sanghas and Buddhist chaplaincy training programs," (*Mapping Survey Response*, 2020/21). Many white chaplains concur, one writing "As a white (non-professional) Buddhist chaplain, I need to develop greater cultural competency to serve BIPOC, non-binary and transgender, and disabled folks. Although I am committed to uncovering and transforming my racist conditioning as a white-bodied woman, I have a long way to go on this path. I would appreciate opportunities to discuss and do this important work with other white Buddhist chaplains," (*Mapping Survey Response*, 2020/21) demonstrating that privileged chaplains are aware that they need to both learn from diverse others and do their own work, as individuals and a group, to construct a more just society.

This can and should begin with chaplaincy education programs and CPE training. When we asked if they received effective training, one chaplain told us "Yes in many regards but needed to do more regarding systemic racism, White privilege, and cultural competency [sic]. The students and faculty were mostly white and did not adequately prepare chaplains to serve a diverse patient population. This deep work and awareness is critical in being an effective chaplain." (*Mapping Survey Response*, 2020/21) This is not always easy work and needs the support of faculty educators (and others with power) because, as another responses shared, "Many of my fellow-students were not only deeply unaware of their privilege in the world, as straight white Christian cis men; they were also deeply defensive. Working in an institution where issues of power and oppression play out with sometimes deadly consequences, this is a huge gap." (*Mapping Survey Response*, 2020/21) Recall that the definition of oppression is when social groups are prevented from attaining the resources necessary to sustain their basic needs, often for the benefit of a more privileged group. Thus, social justice is an urgent life or death issue, especially in healthcare settings, where disparities in medical outcomes based on race, gender, and so on, are well documented. Chaplains can and do have a role to play in addressing these disparities.

One concern perhaps unique to Buddhists is the need to develop pan-Buddhist cultural competency. Because health care is the largest employment sector for Buddhist chaplains (46%), a great deal of chaplaincy training is geared towards meeting the needs of this sector, in which chaplains will mostly care for Christian and post-Christian careseekers and staff. For example, we spent more time in my three-year Buddhist chaplaincy training program addressing Abrahamic religious diversity than Buddhist religious diversity. There was a required course on interreligious spiritual care, largely focused on the Abrahamic religions. Courses on Buddhism were chosen from among many electives and often focused on a single practice (e.g., meditation), scripture, tradition, or even a narrow historical time period of a single tradition. No pan-Buddhist survey course coving the living traditions of Buddhism was even offered. As a result, much of my knowledge of Buddhist diversity is self-taught or acquired through my personal relationships with fellow Buddhists (which I suspect are broader than most chaplains due to my research). Thus, it does not surprise me that many other chaplains point out that one of the largest challenges is "Cultural differences and language barriers of the first generation Asian Buddhists in the US and Western (White) Buddhists [sic]. Cultural competency in general [is needed]." (*Mapping Survey Response*, 2020/21)

While Buddhist chaplains are often a minority in the field, working in isolated pockets where they are expected to be able to know and respond to the breadth of Buddhist careseekers they may encounter, they frequently report how inadequate they feel to this task. One chaplain told us that "Depending on the demographics of where a chaplain works, one challenge would be for white European American Buddhists to minister to ethnic Buddhists. I have encountered it a little with Buddhists from southeast Asia. The people I encountered practice very differently from how I was taught." (*Mapping Survey Response*, 2020/21)

When the Buddhism they rely on as their own spiritual tradition is the only, or one of only a few traditions they know, they struggle to aid their fellow Buddhists, who could represent the full diversity of global Buddhism. Another saw clearly that "There are different emphases in different lineages," but admitted "I only practice in one particular lineage. Although I know these different emphases exist, I personally don't know what they are. Can a Buddhist Chaplain know all these differences, and is it necessary, or is the understanding of karma and emptiness and love and compassion enough? I don't know." While they found their personal practice of Buddhism a great support in their work, they worried if it was sufficient. Others offered more concrete situations, "For example, hospital chaplains from Theravada tradition may not have the proper resources to address the needs of a Chinese Buddhist," (*Mapping Survey Response*, 2020/21). Since most Buddhist chaplains (67%) are white, Asian and Asian American Buddhists (who make up roughly 67% of Buddhists in America, according to the Pew Research Center, 2014), probably receive the least effective spiritual care services. Chaplains are aware of this: "Also as a western trained Buddhist I often was called on by Asian patients who had a completely different perspective and I was probably least helpful to that group," (*Mapping Survey Response*, 2020/21).

Nor is it sufficient to be versed in diverse forms of Buddhism. Cultural competency in this area involves understanding the Asian cultures in question as well as the Asian diaspora and immigration experience. These experiences are quite distinct for many cultural groups.

For example, Chinese immigrants began arriving in the 19th century and faced decades of persecution (Chinatowns were burned and Chinese people lynched), whereas Chinese arriving in the 20th century are part of a broader Chinese diaspora that began after World War II and the Communist revolution in mainland China. Since then, Chinese Buddhism has largely flourished outside of mainland China (e.g., Taiwan, Malaysia, America). Chinese Buddhist temples in the U.S. also serve as hubs for preserving Chinese culture and language.

Japanese Buddhists likewise began to arrive in the U.S. in the 19th Century and early 20th Century, but experienced a very different type of persecution and imprisonment in the mid-20th Century during World War II.[7] During this period, Japanese Buddhism underwent changes to help it seem more assimilated and "American," including the largest Jodo Shinshu organization changing its name to the "Buddhist Churches of America." While there are useful recent publications about these and other communities, many books on "Buddhism in America" (or Canada), both historical surveys and "lived religion" studies, have focused on white Buddhists because these English-fluent communities are more accessible to researchers. Multiple generations of Asian-Americans have complex relationships with their Buddhist cultural heritage, which Chenxing Han is exploring in her books (*Be the Refuge*, 2021, and *One Long Listening*, 2023). I could not possibly recount all of the historic dynamics or the cultural competencies Buddhist chaplains could benefit from learning even if I dedicated this entire chapter to the task (nor am I qualified to do so). This is just a brief illustration of the distinctions. The books listed in this chapter and in the bibliography provide a good place to start self-educating.

Pan-Buddhist cultural competency is important, in part, because of the expectations and ignorance reported among many of our professional colleagues. As one chaplain noted,

> Buddhism in its diversity isn't particularly well understood by my colleagues. I've made it a priority to learn about and have conversations with other Buddhist communities so that I have a better understanding of different rituals, practices, and beliefs, but the Buddhist world is so huge! I feel pressure to be "the Buddhist chaplain" (which feels being expected to be "the Abrahamic faith chaplain"). This last issue also connects into the divides between Western convert Buddhists and Asian Buddhists. The three Buddhist chaplains that I'm aware of in my region are all western convert Buddhists. Are we the best people to be supporting the large community of (mostly) Pure Land Chinese Buddhists in our communities? (*Mapping Survey Response*, 2020/21)

Another chaplain shared that "staff look to me to answer the question of death rites for anyone who is Buddhist despite their tradition. I am very new and will learn more as I go, but I am not the Buddhist encyclopedia," (*Mapping*

---

7 See Duncan Ryuken Williams book *American Sutra*, 2019.

Survey Response, 2020/21). Nevertheless, who will look after the needs of these Buddhist care-seekers and families? Our non-Buddhist colleagues will do their best and provide the listening, witnessing, and compassion in which all chaplains are trained, but Buddhist chaplains consistently report that, however well-meaning these colleagues are, their actual knowledge of Buddhism is very limited and often plagued with blanket assumptions based on the one or two traditions they may have encountered.

Finally, some Buddhist chaplains report a need to overcome intra-Buddhist sectarian preferences, noting that there are "Still some disparaging comments between Buddhist practitioners," (*Mapping Survey Response*, 2020/21). This is not surprising, given that Buddhist history and literature is rife with sectarian rhetoric extolling the virtues of one tradition over the failings of another. In trying to teach pan-Buddhist courses at Harvard Divinity School, I often find myself dealing with papers or Dharma talks that give a very good outline of a particular concept or practice, but then also include a paragraph or three disparaging differing practices or understandings. For a teacher, this is a challenge because it is accurate to say that the different traditions hold such views, but in a classroom with a variety of students from across the Buddhist traditions (and non-Buddhists), such rhetoric is of little educational value and can often do harm (and obliterate from memory any other useful thing the author may have said). This experience makes clear to me that sectarian differences can serve as a barrier to pan-Buddhist cultural competency if we are not careful to watch for them and active in our efforts to overcome them.

In summary, despite the challenges of social injustice, Buddhist chaplains cultivate ways to thrive and use their power to more towards a more just society. These strategies include:

1. Becoming knowledgeable about the dynamics of power, privilege, and oppression during one's education and proactively considering one's positionality and how to cope with such working conditions in advance;
2. Using one's personal spiritual practice to cultivate resilience in the face of these forms of suffering, such as via the exercises developed by Ruth King, above, and including understanding oppression through the lens of Dharma, such as the Three Poisons (attachment, aversion, delusion), and how to be liberated from it;
3. Cultivating strong connections with other Buddhist chaplains, Buddhist caregivers in other professions, or minority identity caregivers from across the caregiving professions to find solidarity and support;
4. Continually and skillfully advocating for oneself and others of minority identity within the profession of chaplaincy, particularly through ongoing education about and reduction in Christian hegemony.

While the quotes shared throughout this section are those of individual chaplains, they are chosen because they are broadly representative of a wider sentiment within the data collected from interviews and surveys between 2017 and 2023. They demonstrate that Buddhist chaplains are keenly aware of power, privilege, and oppression and agree that more work needs to be done to improve social justice. In all datasets collected so far, no chaplains expressed contrary views (e.g., discounting oppression or disparaging social justice efforts). While the challenges are great, I am encouraged that this profession is on the right track.

13
PART II CONCLUSION & REFLECTION

When reviewing the chapters in this section, a classical Buddhist theme stands out to me: suffering and liberation from suffering. Each chapter illustrates ways that different groups of humans respond to suffering, whether through ritual, different religious traditions, a variety of cultural practices, various responses to mental and emotional anguish and wellbeing, and by using (and often misusing) social power. The teaching of the Buddha, throughout his long career, covered many subjects, but as far as I am aware, all of them can be directly related to this central theme of suffering and the cessation of suffering. Likewise, each of the authors in this section offer they own perspective on this theme through the lens of the topics of their chapters.

Victor Gabriel provides us with a wonderful chapter on Ritual and Prayer from the Buddhist perspective. I also highly recommend to readers the resources for inter-religious ritual provided in the breakout box at the beginning of Chapter 8. Gabriel's chapter prompted me to reflect on the many times I have used ritual and prayer in my own work as a chaplain. The prayers I offered and rituals that I organized were inter-religious or multi-religious, often developed on short notice, and each almost entirely unique. Chaplaincy students are naturally anxious about the process of designing rituals or providing prayers for others, especially for those who do not share the same religious tradition. They often want tidy formulas or "off the shelf" solutions that they can just pull out and follow the instructions. Rituals and prayers provided by chaplains are, in my experience, never as simple as making macaroni and cheese (there are no instructions on the box). This is stressful for new chaplains, so the first step in offering a prayer or designing a ritual is managing our own anxiety about it!

Familiarity with a wide variety of rituals and prayers (and their component parts) can be your best tool, just as a good chef knows what all the different spices in her cupboard smell and taste like. It is good to observe and participate in a variety of prayers and rituals and to talk to others about how they experience them.

My greatest challenge in providing ritual and prayer is that the elements they incorporate rarely resonate with me the way they do with the careseekers I serve. For example, I clearly don't direct my prayers to a deity (though some Buddhists do), but that is an important aspect of prayer for most of the people I serve. On a personal level, I don't have a strong emotional response to ritual and incorporate very little of it in my personal life. However, in speaking with and observing others, I have developed a vicarious appreciation for ritual and prayer by understanding the power it has for them. I am constantly curious how different people can experience the same ritual in very different (but often equally meaningful) ways. It is not lost on me that my current chaplaincy position, which I shall describe further in the final section of this conclusion, is almost entirely ritual in nature. So it's a good thing that I learned from wonderful friends and teachers like Dr. Gabriel and Rabbi Rochelle Robins, whose work he references. Regardless of your own relationship to ritual, you will be called upon to offer prayers and rituals that feel unfamiliar to you, as well as those in which you have been immersed your entire life. This is an area where chaplains can fully develop their flexibility and creativity. Ritual design can be a source of comfort and joy, even when those rituals are in response to some of the darkest tragedies we face.

Nathan Jishin Michon's chapter on Interreligious Competencies (Chapter 9) begins with a description of the respect and trust we must develop to work across interreligious lines with careseekers who are very different from ourselves. He then describes some of the many Dharma concepts that aid Buddhist chaplains in doing this work. This chapter prompts me to reflect on my own understanding of religious diversity and how I hold respect for diverse careseekers, even when I don't believe what they believe or practice as they practice. As part of my commitment to Buddhism, I cultivate respect for others based on their capacity for buddhanature. I can think of buddhanature in two ways, both as the actualized wisdom they always and already carry within them and as their potential to become fully enlightened buddhas in the future. Either way means that I could be sitting in the presence of a buddha or bodhisattva at any moment, so I had better behave accordingly! In situations of individual spiritual care, this has served me well.

As a college chaplain, director of an interreligious center, instructor, and administrator of multireligious programs, I have often found myself working at the edges of my interreligious competencies. I would find myself thinking "I don't know enough about [X religion] to be doing this job!" but there was no one else available to do it. If I didn't step up, no one would. (Of course, if there is someone else, then always defer to these experts. But in the field of mutli-religious education, I have learned that no professor can be an expert in all the religions in the room. It is nevertheless valuable to have the diversity of religions in the same room together.) In these situations, I was keenly aware of the imbalance between my level of competency and my level of responsibility.

I would occasionally send a joking (not joking) email to my former professors demanding "Why didn't you teach me how to interview a rabbi?" or whatever the latest bizarre thing for which I suddenly discovered I was responsible. Of course, they could not teach me everything I needed to know about other religions (or even about other Buddhisms!). That is a (multi-) lifelong project.

The interreligious skills they did teach me were far more important – how to acknowledge my limitations, do my homework, surface my own assumptions and ignorance, reach out for help, listen carefully, collaborate with others, put myself in their shoes, defer to experts, and be willing to take on responsibilities that outstripped my competency when necessary. Thus, the answer to the question of "How do you interview a rabbi?" (as a Buddhist chaplain) turns out to be: 1) first you spend a lot of time talking to the network of Jewish colleagues you've hopefully developed relationships with so you can ask them all your naïve questions you're afraid sound stupid; 2) then you have long conversations with your Jewish students about what they want for their High Holy Days services and what they expect from a rabbi; and 3) finally, you trust the rabbis you're interviewing to know more than you do and look for someone who wants to work with the expectations of your Jewish students.

Most interreligious competencies are grounded in or grow from strong interpersonal competencies. Of course, concrete knowledge also helps, so that when said rabbi asks "What *machzor* [Jewish prayer book for the High Holy Days] will you use?" you at least know what a *machzor* is, even if you don't have an answer as to which one would be best (trust the students and the rabbi to have opinions). I have discovered that I will learn these things as I need them and I will not forget them once so learned. I have never been good at memorizing facts and terms before I know why they are important. But after being improbably responsible for organizing High Holy Day services during a gap in our Jewish campus staff, I will never forget what a machzor is! Trust your ability to learn as you go, stay humble, and ask for help – these are life competencies as much as interreligious ones.

Henry C.H. Shiu provides an important chapter on Intercultural Competencies (Chapter 10), which has significant overlap with Michon's chapter as culture and religious are explicably intertwined. In this chapter he reviews Fukuyama and Sevig's five-step multicultural counseling technique which "includes: 1) personal awareness of one's own social location and identity; 2) knowledge of the history, formation, and experience of the cultural identities of oneself and the care-seekers; 3) skills and abilities to engage in meaningful communication with others to foster mutual respect and understanding; 4) the capacity for empathy and compassion for others; and 5) the actions that are borne out of the foregoing principles."

I believe Buddhist chaplains need to spend more time in step 2, learning the history, formation and experience of cultural identities. To some extent, chaplains must become students of history, particularly recent (post-1800) and contemporary (post-1940) history.

In North America, this includes being conversant with the history of Asian immigration as two-thirds of Buddhists are of Asian heredity (Pew Research Center, 2012, p. 36). The Asian immigration experience is one marked by diaspora and multiple dislocations. Some Asian cultural groups left countries ravaged by colonialism, war, and famine to try to build a better life in North America only to be uprooted again by the discrimination of Euro-American settlers. Various waves of Asian immigrants have very different stories, based on time period and country of origin. These distinct stories are almost entirely unknown to the American public, including among other Asian immigrant communities. Asian immigrants and their descendants have also faced distinct forms of racism, sexism, and religious discrimination compared to other groups. Added to this is the marginalization of Asian experiences within Buddhism and the dominance of white Buddhists as the representatives of Buddhism to America more broadly.

This history and present context prompted Funie Hsu's article entitled "We've Been Here All Along," in *Lion's Roar*,[1] among other publications. Despite backlash from certain sectors (and in response to it), we are now benefiting from an increase in publications related to Asian American Buddhism, some of which I referenced in Chapter 12. This includes the recent creation of "Bodhi Leaves," by *Lion's Roar* (https://www.lionsroar.com/bodhi-leaves/), which they describe as "The Asian American Buddhist Monthly" online magazine. These publications help Buddhist chaplains of all backgrounds become more conversant with one another's cultures.

As we learn about other cultures, we also become more aware of our own culture. For those with cultural privilege, this can include the recognition that we have a culture rather than just a default "norm." What is "normal" for us is quite different for others. For example, it never occurred to me that not everyone organizes a schedule by starting events on the hour, half hour, or fifteen-minute mark (e.g., 12:00, 12:15, 12:30, 12:45, etc.) until I attended a program in Taiwan where the schedule was arranged on the ten-minute mark (e.g., 12:00, 12:10, 12:20, and so on). Nor did I realize that how far in advance events are planned and advertised is also culturally determined. Thus, American students often missed out on opportunities to attend Buddhist programs in Asia by setting their schedules too far in advance, even months before program announcements were issued, and finding themselves locked into other plans. Neither way of doing things is good or bad, just different. However, psychologists have demonstrated that human beings often conflate "different" with "wrong" (as in mor-

---

[1] https://www.lionsroar.com/weve-been-here-all-along/

ally wrong and/or dangerous). Think about walking into a room that has always had a certain chair on the left side but suddenly now has that chair on the right side. Our initial reaction might be to say the chair is in the "wrong" place (and we probably feel immediate aversion to the change), but there's no moral right or wrong to the position of the chair (interior design principles notwithstanding in this hypothetical). Part of cultural competence is learning to be aware of this instinctual reaction to difference and correct for it. For example, I was raised in a culture were wearing a hat indoors was considered rude. Yet criticizing a student for "disrespecting" me by wearing a head covering in class would, in turn, be disrespectful to their culture, which may normalize, prioritize, or even require a head covering. These are only a few small examples.

Linda Hochstetler's Chapter 11 focuses on guiding chaplains to conduct psychological risk assessments for those in their care and making appropriate referrals. Social and mental health crises often have a spiritual component, and spiritual crises can be precipitated by social crises or mental health concerns. Both are affected by other kinds of distress and crisis, such as sudden injury, illness, disaster, or the loss of a loved one, job, or relationship. Thus, it can often be tricky to distinguish just what kind of help a careseeker needs and, in fact, they may benefit from multiple kinds of support. Yet there are also clearly situations beyond the chaplain's scope of practice which, for the safety of the careseeker and our own wellbeing, we must learn to recognize.

Hochstetler's chapter reviews suicidal ideation, homicide risk assessment, child abuse, elder abuse, domestic violence, addiction, and other mental health concerns. It is useful to roleplay some of these situations using the listening and responding exercises provided in Chapter 7. During this roleplaying, you can receive feedback from peer as well as multidisciplinary colleagues, if available, on your response to the situation. Moreover, roleplaying will enable you to assess your own immediate affective and internal response to hearing someone say something as drastic as "I want to kill myself" or "My boyfriend said that if I try to leave him, he'll kill me and my daughter" or "I'm sure someone is coming into my room and moving my things no matter how many times I check the door lock" (all real examples). These are shocking things to hear, whether for the first or the hundredth time. However, what careseekers need in that moment is to be heard and taken seriously. They may have decided to confide in you because they are convinced no one else will believe them. That demonstrates a great deal of trust. And yet, chaplains should not grapple with any of these issues alone.

That is when we reach out to make referrals and find a community of support both for the careseeker and for myself. As a campus chaplain, I have personally called the counseling center to make appointments for students, walked them there, and sat with them until they could be seen. Likewise, I have been called by the counseling center when a student with spiritual concerns needs to be referred to a chaplain, or when they'd like a chaplain there to support and pray with the student who is experiencing a sudden bereavement. Yet, I have also worked with students who refused any referral and insisted they would only talk to me. While I am honored by their trust, in order to be the trustworthy person they need, it was also my responsibility to reach out to my professional network for anonymous consultation. By explaining the student's situation and presentation without identity details to trusted colleagues in psychology, medicine, and other fields, I was able to gather critical advice on how best to support them (and myself) if I was the only kind of support they would accept. It was also important for me to be honest with the student when their situation was beyond the scope of my ability to support.

Finally, it has occasionally been important for me to seek spiritual care for myself in response to the stress such situations can generate.

It is natural to feel a high level of anxiety at the prospect of suicide or after witnessing a psychotic episode. Yet there are also other, less obvious, situations that can throw us for a loop. I experienced one when providing spiritual care to a student seeking an abortion. I have always supported the reproductive right to choose, so I was surprised by how disturbed I was following that encounter and immediately reached out to my then CPE supervisor for support. Together, we were able to talk things through and reach the source of my disturbance so that I could remain a healthy supportive presence for that student at our next meeting. Recall the thesis of the first volume: *kalyāṇamitra* need *kalyāṇamitra*. In addition to referring others to different or further care, sometimes you must be ready to refer yourself.

The final chapter of this section is my own (Chapter 12: Power, Privilege, and Oppression). I hope this chapter gives anyone reading it food for thought and also encourages them to write more about their own experiences in this area. The chaplains I interview all see social justice as a critical component of their work because it directly addresses suffering due to social inequities rooted in the three poisons of greed, hatred, and delusion. Not all Buddhists are committed to this vision of social justice (or accept its root causes or structural/systemic supports), but among chaplains who work directly with people who are suffering, there seems to be a broad consensus. Nevertheless, chaplains feel discouraged when their own Buddhist communities don't affirm what they are witnessing on a daily basis or commit to helping them address systems of privilege and oppression that undergird this suffering. We may not immediately realize that, Buddhist chaplains as a profession, are in such solidarity with one another due to our relative isolation from one another. Many Buddhist chaplains are the only one at their clinical site. Yet it heartens me to know that this solidarity exists and that there are so many glorious bodhisattvas out there already doing the work. I hope it likewise heartens you. May all beings be swiftly and completely liberated from both the social and the spiritual sources of suffering within this lifetime! *Sadhu, sadhu, sadhu.*

Reflection Questions for Chapters 8 through 12

1. How were prayer and ritual introduced to your life? For example, were they a family activity or were you explicitly taught to do or something you observed others doing? Consider both religious and secular settings, including school rituals (e.g., pledge of allegiance, school songs, graduation ceremonies). What are your earliest memories of engaging in ritual or prayer? How do similar rituals or prayers resonate with you now (or not)?

2. What role does ritual or prayer play in your life today, if any? What communal rituals or prayers do you regularly engage with? What individual personal rituals and prayers have you adopted or developed over your life? Think about the meaning, emotional valence, symbolism, and manner of each. Consider both formal (e.g., religious services, prescribed practices) and informal rituals (e.g., always eating the same food on your birthday, greeting particular trees on your daily walk), and both collective and individual prayer. Why have you continued to do them?

3. What does your Buddhist tradition teach about members of other religious or spiritual traditions, either implicitly or explicitly? Why do other religions exist? How does this understanding affect the way we think about, feel towards, and treat members of other religious traditions (or people of no religion)? What does your tradition teach about the history of its interactions with other religious groups and what messages are conveyed in this history? What does your tradition

say about how to interact with others in the present day? Does your tradition engage in intra-Buddhist or inter-religious dialogue or cooperation with other groups? If so or if not, what message does that convey about religious others? What is your own understanding of how to relate to those different from yourself?

4. Consider the following questions:
   a. How favorable is your opinion of members of other religious groups? On a five-point scale, do you have a very favorable (5) or very unfavorable (1) opinion of the following groups: Evangelical Christians, Catholics, Mormons, Jews, Muslims, Atheists, Mainline Protestants, Confucians, Taoists, Hindus, Pagans, Buddhists of your own tradition, and Buddhists of other traditions. Mark as 0 any group that you feel you don't know enough about to have an opinion. You may add other groups to this list that you have opinions about.
   b. Do you know someone who belongs to that group? Place a check mark next to any group where you personally know at least one person who is a member of that group, such as a friend, family member, colleague, or neighbor. Place a second check mark next to groups where you personally know several people. Place a star next to groups that you are familiar with because you have attended their religious services or events.
   c. Is there any difference in the favorability ratings you gave to groups to whom you have a stronger personal connection (checks and stars) compared to those you do not know as well or at all? What affects these different favorability ratings, if anything?
   d. How do your responses compare to those of Americans more generally? Why might they be similar or different?[2]
5. Can you describe a time when you were surprised to discover something you took for granted as "normal" for everyone was not shared by other cultural groups? What was your immediate reaction to it? How did you come to understand the difference over time? Where you able to gain an appreciation for it or not?
6. Consider the issues covered in Chapter 11 under Risk Assessment Protocols. Most people's lives are affected by these situations, either that they experience or are experienced by someone close to them. We often absorb messages about these situations from an early age. What were some of the earliest messages you can recall about these kinds of situations and mental health issues? Reflect on how these messages influenced your perspectives on and behavior relating to these issues, including if and how they still do.
7. Take one of the following quizzes and reflect on your results. Did any of the questions surprise you? Why was that? Did your result surprise you or did it feel relatively accurate? Why was that? What reflection does this prompt? Are you motivated to take any particular action as a result?
   a. Anxiety Test: https://www.healthcentral.com/quiz/anxiety-test
   b. Happiness Test: https://www.healthcentral.com/quiz/happiness-test
   c. Depression Test: https://www.healthcentral.com/quiz/depression-test

---

2 These questions are modeled on the Pew Research Center's survey on American's attitudes towards religious groups last conducted in 2022, which can be found here: https://www.pewresearch.org/religion/2023/03/15/americans-feel-more-positive-than-negative-about-jews-mainline-protestants-catholics/.

8. Complete the diagram in Chapter 12 mapping different aspects of Power/Privilege and Vulnerability/Oppression. Then consider, which aspects do you identify with most strongly? Which have the greatest impact on your daily life and your work as a chaplain? How do they affect your daily behavior? Which are the most noticeable/noticed by other people in your various life contexts? Are there any aspects that are missing and, if so, which ones? How does this affect your relationship with those on the opposite side of that spectrum, if at all?
9. Take one of the tests at the Harvard Implicit Association test website (https://implicit.harvard.edu/implicit/takeatest.html) and reflect on your results using the following questions: Which test did you take first and why did you choose that one? Did your results surprise you and, if so, why is that? If you assume the test is correct, reflect on your life and consider where, from whom, and what messages you might have absorbed that contributed to that result? If you think the test is incorrect, consider what you might write to the test designers, including questions you could ask, about the test. Repeat this process for a variety of tests as appropriate.

Ritual Design Exercises

This exercise can be done alone, but it tends to be more powerful when done with a partner. Find a classmate or friend who is willing to do this exercise with you. Consider that rituals often take place in "liminal" contexts, according to Rochelle Robins and Danielle Tumminio Hansen chapter on ritual in *Chaplaincy and Spiritual Care in the Twenty-First Century* (eds. Cadge and Rambo, 2022):

> Chaplains often meet careseekers in "high stakes" moments, in life-and-death and boundary situations, or in times of transition. Liminality or liminal spaces are terms that capture the "in-betweenness" of these moments. Liminal spaces are points on the map of life that are in between normalcy as we have known it and what life will become. Sometimes liminal spaces are physical spaces – like a hospital room – and sometimes they are spaces of time, as in the case of the time between the death of a loved one and the funeral. Either way, they can lead to transition, changing boundaries, and new thresholds and meanings. They have the potential to allow us to acknowledge circumstances from which might emerge new possibilities that can simultaneously feel promising and out of our control. (p. 114)

1. What kind of liminal spaces have you experienced in the past year or are experiencing now? Which of these have been marked by ritual and which have not? Why or why not? Are there any you have not marked by ritual that you would like to? Let's design that ritual. (Suggestion: Do not select a highly emotional event for this exercise, such as a recent death. Rather, consider simple but significant moment, such as moving to a new home, celebrating an anniversary, or starting or ending a new project, and so on.) Either:
    a. Do a little reflective writing about your chosen liminal space to help start your ritual design process; OR
    b. Tell a classmate about your liminal space and ask them to design a ritual for and with you.
2. Review Robins and Hansen's list of purposes for prayer and ritual and five steps for designing a ritual provided at the beginning of Chater 8. Consider that rituals often stabilize and support, honor meanings, facilitate sacred turning

points, mark important moments, open space for emotions and sensations, engage the whole person (often including forgotten parts), create a sense of safety or community or relationship, express lament, envision individual or communal hope, remember and reveal, hold the past, and many other things. What is your ritual's purpose?
3. Draw on meaningful symbols, objects, songs, spaces, places, people, and other resources. What, who, when, and where do you need for your ritual? How and what connections will be forged, strengthened, or severed?
4. Structure the ritual according to existing traditions, new needs, or adapt to both. What are the sequence, actors, audience participation (if any), leader (if any), connection, and community (if any)? Does this ritual involve others or is it solitary and involve only yourself? Take a few minutes to write out a brief plan for the ritual.
5. Optional: Share your ritual plan with a classmate (either the ritual you have designed for yourself or the one you have designed for them). Ask each other clarifying questions. Offer each other something to consider including in the ritual. Be sure to thank you partner.
6. If you are able, carry out the ritual at a suitable time and write a reflection journal about the experience. How did you feel before, during, and after the ritual? How did your expectations compare to doing the ritual? Did anything surprise you and, if so, why? What would you change if you were ever to do this ritual (or one like it) again? What is the spiritual, religious, cultural, or personal significance of the ritual?

When the students in my "Meaning Making" course participated in this exercise, I asked them if they preferred to design their own ritual or work with a classmate to design rituals for one another. They overwhelmingly chose the latter and designed rituals for one another, even though each student was paired with a classmate of a different religion from themselves, often one they had limited knowledge about. At the conclusion of the exercise, they verbally reflected on the experience of having someone else design a ritual for them as an act of care, in and of itself. They were surprised and gratified by how seen they felt, especially in relation to previously unacknowledged liminal moments in their lives. The elements of the ritual were meaningful to them because they felt their partner deeply listened and understood their emotional and spiritual needs, even when some of the ritual aspects were entirely new to them. A few students even carried out their gifted rituals and reported back positively in written reflections. The only caveat I will add to this report is that these students, while very diverse, had already built a community of knowledge and trust over eight weeks of being in class together. It may, therefore, be advisable to only engage in this exercise with a partner or group that you already know somewhat and have a sense of trust with.

The next ritual exercise involves designing a multi-religious ritual. We can distinguish between interreligious rituals and multi-religious rituals in a few basic ways.

Following are some sample texts for prefaces I have used for multi-religious services in response to crises and tragedies. You may repurpose them as you see fit.

The theme of the service is established in advance and the readings, prayers, songs, chants, and so on, from all religions reflect that theme. When the service is in response to an event that affects one religious tradition or cultural community more than others, then that group selects the theme for the service and provides the first and last offering within the program, and possibly the homily in the middle as well.

PART II CONCLUSION & REFLECTION

Interreligious Rituals	Multi-Religious Rituals
Both take place with a diverse multi-religious audience	
Designed to serve a specific purpose (e.g., celebration, mourning) or theme (e.g., love, forgiveness, hope)	
Usually does not begin with a preface other than a general welcome	Begins with a preface inviting the audience to participate or observe as they prefer and letting them know that some aspects may be unfamiliar
Selects ritual elements that are broadly recognizable and acceptable to all members of the audience	Selects ritual elements that are appropriate to the ritual purpose or theme according to their religion of origin, even if unfamiliar to the audience
May alter some language so as to broaden the applicability (e.g., "God" instead of "Jesus")	Does not alter language or presentation
May omit some language that would be objectionable or would not be recognizable to some audience members	Does not omit unfamiliar or even objectionable language
Usually performed by one or a small number of leaders who may not represent all the traditions being drawn upon	Usually performed by a team of leaders who each represent the traditions being drawn upon
May limit audience participation to the most universal or unobjectionable aspects	Invites audience to decide to participate in all, some, or none of the aspects, with reminders throughout

Welcome. We are here today in response to [purpose of gathering in 2-3 sentences]. This service is an opportunity for members of the community, of all religious traditions and none, to come together and share messages of [theme: support, healing, and peace] from within our diverse traditions. We have asked each tradition to share what is authentic and healing for them. You are invited to participate where you feel comfortable and simply listen where you prefer. Thank you for choosing to spend this time with us. To open this service, I would like to introduce [first speaker].

A shorter version:

We have asked those who join us today and speak the truth from their traditions as they know it. You are welcome to join in where you feel comfortable and listen in solidarity where you prefer. Thank you.

As an alternative example, below are the Opening Sentences from the Harvard Divinity School Noon Service, which is hosted each Wednesday by a different campus group.[3] This call and response sets the stage for a service that is not only very different from week to week, but may also be very different from the traditions of the audience members. The call and response prompts the community to remain open as the host group offers what is authentic to their tradition without modification. Please use only with attribution.

One: Welcome to the Harvard Divinity School Noon Service. Each week, we aspire anew to be welcoming and

---

3 https://hds.harvard.edu/news/2023/11/17/beloved-tradition-noon-service-hds

vulnerable with ourselves and one another.
All: In this hour, may we find ourselves in a space of truth and openness.
Host Group: As leaders, may we share our traditions in a spirit of hospitality with those who may not understand what we do or why, having the courage to be true to our traditions with an open heart.
Participants: As participants, may we be open and present with our peers in their own context. May we be willing to experience the unknown.
All: In this time and in this assembly, may we embrace each responsibility with earnestness and compassion for our companions. Though we may travel different paths, may we find solidarity, comfort, and hope in our common purpose as a community of seekers, working towards collective liberation from white supremacy and other forms of oppression.

Using these tools, work together in a small group to design a multi-religious ritual addressing one of the following scenarios. Decide on a clear order of service, date, time, and location, and list of materials and implements you will need. Write your ritual as a script, with who says what in what order, from the preface or opening, listing all the readings from scripture or poetry, songs lyrics, meditations, and compose a homily as appropriate. Consider the flow from one offering to the next. For example, you may want to intersperse readings in between songs, rather than grouping like elements. Write the conclusion, considering what you want your audience to take away from the experience or do as a result (e.g., support a cause, donate, volunteer, and so on) or what further resources you can remind them of (e.g., counseling services, food pantry, and so on). This may become a long document once everyone's contributions are added. Example scenarios:

1. There has been a shooting at a religious community in a major city about a hundred miles away. While no members of your community were directly harmed, many know people involved with that community. They are also rightly fearful that such events may be repeated and concerned with supporting the community through this difficult time.
2. A natural disaster has occurred in an international city that many members of your community are from. Some have lost friends and family members, but they cannot go home due to the nature of the disaster. This city is in a country with one predominant religion, though it has a mixture of smaller traditions. The members of your community are mourning, worried about their loved ones, and want to help, even from so far away.
3. A beloved member of the community has died suddenly in tragic circumstances. Everyone is shocked and grieving. The family members would like to hold a memorial in the community. They represent at least two distinct religious traditions and are very open-minded in spiritual matters. Everyone in the multireligious community wants to honor this person in some way, while also respecting the wishes of the family.

When complete, read through your document in full, with each person reading (or singing, chanting, and so on) their own contribution. Then share feedback and reflect on how the different elements worked or could work better.

New Explorations in Buddhist Chaplaincy

About seventy students stood as the opening bell rang, each holding a stem with a handful of flowers. It is unlikely that any of them had ever experienced a ritual such as this before (I hadn't) or would again. Such rituals usually happened only a handful of times in the life of any Buddhist community. Together we read the opening words and bowed to the altar, where a large picture frame was draped with a white cloth. I explained our purpose and thanked the school's head chaplain (Protestant) and Muslim faith leader, both standing just to my left, for attending this event. The students then circled the room, each laying their spray of flowers before the shrouded image and bowing. After all offerings had been made, several of the senior students helped me tie white strings to the still hidden image and then carried those strings around the room until each and every person present was grasping the string between the thumbs and index fingers of their joined palms. Then we exhorted the Buddhas and Bodhisattvas of the ten directions to give us their attention, bestow their blessings, and remain firmly to help us suffering beings. We recited the *Mantra of Dependent Origination*, the *Mangala Sutta*, and the *Karaniya Metta Sutta*. Then I invited the students to stand once more and taught the *Mantra Requesting to Remain* in the Tibetan, and invited them to recite it three times, each louder than the last, until the room was filled with shouts of "Om Supra-Tishta Vajra Ye Svaha!"

I cut the string on each side of the frame and the senior students aided me in cutting between each student still holding their string, now charged with blessings, that they were invited to tie around their wrists. Finally, I removed the white cloth, revealing the image in the golden frame, and jumped just a little as the students broke out in applause (that wasn't in my ritual program). With the image now revealed, I explained how it had been made especially for them and how no other Buddhist community in the world had an image like this. This was their Buddha, sitting on a lotus thrown, smiling over the *Dharmachakra mudra*, which symbolizes teaching (i.e., turning the wheel of Dharma). He was flanked on the one side by a bodhi tree and a deer and on the other side by a maple tree and a moose, symbolizing Buddhism's origin in India and its current home in New England. After the closing words and closing bell, many students took the invitation to come up and look at the image more closely, taking pictures with their phones and pointing at this or that detail. Then they stacked their cushions and chairs along the edges of the room and put their boots on before departing into a light February snow.

Despite my research and consultations with Buddhist colleagues, it was, no doubt, an unorthodox consecration ceremony, combining elements from many different Buddhist traditions and making do with what materials we had on hand. The image being consecrated was itself unique, commissioned from an artist in Canada[4] who makes sacred images as part of her spiritual practice. The location of the service was also unprecedented, a Christian boarding school in New England, which enrolled students from the age of 13 to 18. While the student body was globally diverse, barely a handful had any family background in Buddhism or even a personal interest. They attended daily Christian chapel services, but on the weekends could choose from among six different religious services. Most of those who had offered flowers, shouted the mantra, and applauded so enthusiastically (much to my gratification) had only selected the Buddhist service to avoid the more theocentric ones. This was likely their first ongoing exposure to Buddhism (aside from reading about it in a world history textbook in the 9th grade curriculum). As the Buddhist Life Leader for that school year, I tried to make it a good experience, but I'll admit that I was mostly making it up as I went along. I didn't know anyone who had done this before, and that's the refrain of many Buddhist chaplains these days.

Chaplaincy is growing in unexpected places. While the largest percentage of Buddhist

---

4 Kaitlyn S.C. Hatch, https://www.kaitlynschatch.com/

chaplains work in the healthcare system (42% according to our *Mapping Buddhist Chaplains in North America* survey; Sanford, et al., 2022), the number of chaplains serving prisons and jails, universities and colleges (and now high schools), and the miliary are growing. Many chaplains provide spiritual care within their religious community, as traditional monastics or Dharma teachers. Yet, a growing number of chaplains do work that defies easy categorization into these traditional sectors. They write and publish, create art, found their own non-profit organizations, or work as self-employed spiritual counselors and life coaches. They create unique curricula focused on issues dear to them, such as anti-racism, climate change, grief and bereavement, or addiction recovery. Many have shown a distinct flair for spiritual innovation and entrepreneurship, crafting un-conventional careers. Some make ends meet my continuing existing careers as nurses or lawyers, while offering spiritual care in ways the world desperately needs but hasn't yet figured out how to pay for (and to those who receive it who maybe shouldn't need to pay for such care).

In the United States, the historical forms of religion, spirituality, and social relations in general is changing. Over two hundred years ago, this country shifted from a pattern in which religious institutions were established and funded by the state (through taxes) to a pattern that relied on the voluntary associations of individuals to form and fund not only churches but religiously inspired organization of all kinds, including hospitals, homeless shelters, publication groups, and even schools such as the one where I recently consecrated an image of the Buddha. When Buddhism came to the United States, it adapted to this pattern. It had little choice; the laws are written in such a way as to support or even require incorporation as a non-profit to enable a group to receive, hold, and pay out money. Temples, Dharma centers, schools, and publishing groups were founded based on the model of voluntary association and financial donations of members. In some, the traditional monastic or priestly leadership continued to wield considerable authority while in others, the members themselves make most decisions, even when a guiding teacher is present. Some organizations have chosen to support chaplains by creating educational programs, ordination pathways, and endorsement models. However, some don't really know what a chaplain is or remain suspicious if it is worthy of support. Buddhists in the latter type of community nevertheless find pathways into chaplaincy. However, where a Buddhist community falls on this spectrum is increasingly becoming a moot point for those Buddhists who prefer not to affiliate at all. This pattern of disaffiliation is an echo of stronger social forces.

The entire social and religious landscape in America is changing. The share of Americans who seldom or never attend religious services reached a majority (54%) in 2023, compared to 43% in 2013. Most Americans (58%) do not donate to religious organizations. Even among those who self-identify with a particular religious tradition, only around a quarter make weekly donations and this number dwindles to only 7% for Americans under the age of 30. This social trend is not confined to religion but affects all voluntary organizations. After peaking in the 1970s, even the membership of Boy Scouts of America had lost half its members by 2019 and numbers have continued to plumet in the way of scandals and controversies. The same is true of almost all social and civic clubs (e.g., Elks, Shriners, Lions, Rotary, and so on). Ted Smith provides a good overview of these social trends in his book *The End of Theological Education* (2023). Though written from a Christian perspective, Smith is summarizing a great deal of sociological research that affects the society at large, Christian theological institutions included. See Chapter 2 "Individualization," for a particularly enlightening summary.

As formal membership dwindles, Americans no longer claim religion as an aspect of their identity. The only religious identity category that is growing is "unaffiliated," which rose from 21% in 2013 to 26% in 2023. ("Religious Change in America," PRRI, March 2024) The Pew Research Center projects that religious "nones" will approach a majority by 2070 if recent trends continue. ("Modeling the Future of Religion in America," Pew Research Center, September 2022) Demographers of religion don't have enough data to project what this may mean for American Buddhists, but I tend to assume that many of the same cultural trends that affect the dominant Christian and Jewish traditions (about which we have data) also affect the smaller groups (e.g., Buddhists, Hindus, Muslims, Indigenous Religions, and so on). While religion no longer defines identity, belief and spiritual practice continue, though without the orienting framework a religious tradition can provide. While religious "none" are more skeptical than religious adherents, 69% maintain believe in God or a higher power and 49% say that spirituality is "very important" to them. ("Religious 'Nones' in America: Who They Are and What They Believe," Pew Research Center, 2024)

Despite lingering belief and spiritual practices among many "nones," they still find compelling reasons to leave organized religion – and with it their religious identity – behind. According the Pew Research Center:

> There are many theories on why disaffiliation sped up so much in the 1990s and how long this trend might continue. For example, some scholars contend that secularization is the result of increasing "existential security" – as societal conditions improve and scientific advances allow people to live longer lives with fewer worries about meeting basic needs, they have less need for religion to cope with insecurity (or so the theory goes). Others say that in the U.S., an association of Christianity with conservative politics has driven many liberals away from the faith. Still other theories involve declining trust in religious institutions, clergy scandals, rising rates of religious intermarriage, smaller families, and so on. When asked, Americans give a wide range of reasons for leaving religion behind, Pew Research Center has found. ("Modeling the Future of Religion in America," Pew Research Center, September 2022, p. 20)

Some of these reasons include that they simply "don't believe" or "don't need religion," they dislike organized religion or institutions altogether, believe but don't care to practice their religion, or are unsure or undecided about religious or spiritual matters. This latter group may dabble in many different religious traditions and may be contributing to the rise in the number of people who identify themselves as "Buddhish" rather than Buddhist.

Growing disaffiliation from organized religion, institutions, and voluntary associations of all kinds is a large part of what is leading so many people, including chaplains, away from the traditional sectors of chaplaincy employment and driving the rise of spiritual innovation. Some chaplains may themselves have good reason to disaffiliate (or may never have affiliated to begin with), while others are simply following those in need of spiritual care. The latter see people in need of spiritual care who they could never reach through the traditional institutions. Disaffiliating with religion, it seems clear, does not make one immune to existential, philosophical, ethical, or spiritual crises.

As a college chaplain, this was my motivation behind creating a program known as Department 42 (a Douglas Adams reference). The purpose of this program was to use popular culture to explore big existential questions. What young adults may lack in a shared religious vocabulary they often make up for in a thorough understanding of the Force, wizards' and witches' spells, superpower taxonomies, and starship technobabble. Moreover, the stories that accompany these vocabularies are emotionally moving, ethically complex, and widely discussed. One may try to avoid "religion and politics" at the dinner table, but the latest Marvel or Star Wars movie is fair game. Thus, students were eager to attend events entitled "How to Be Good in The Good Place," "Harry Potter and How We Deal with Death," and "Knowledge and Power in the Chronicles of Narnia." Nor did conversation remain at the level of the pop culture in question. Many students were willing, even eager, to share how the death of their difficult grandfather reminded them of aspects of the Harry Potter story, or about the time they had to consider telling their dear friend a painful truth. Lacking spiritual communities of their own, they had few safe outlets for such "deep" conversations. The use of a particular pop culture niche created a shared vocabulary with which to explore and develop complex ethical and existential issues that had been neglected in an (perhaps misguided) effort to respect religious diversity by not imposing any one tradition's language on a religiously plural group. While the program was led by (the geekier) members of the Spiritual Life department staff, the department's logo was deliberately absent from flyers and emails, so as to invite the widest possible assortment of community members. Nevertheless, students quickly caught on to who was hosting the event, and (with no proselytization in sight) brought their even less religious friends to subsequent gatherings.

While I offer this as an example of spiritual innovation, it is only a partial response to the trends I highlighted above. After all, Department 42 did take place within and through an institution – a university – even as it sought to reach students who were disaffiliated from and distrustful of organized religion. Many chaplains are developing even more meaningful spiritually innovative programs, despite the lack of an institutional "home" in which to situate them or a funding model through which they can continue to pay rent while launching their visionary response to the suffering they see in the world. There are grants aplenty, but often for a narrow range of issues that the existing institutions have already recognized. Whereas these entrepreneurial chaplains are witnessing and responding to new challenges on a daily basis that haven't yet been recognized, researched, or quantified by the powers that be. Chaplains go where the suffering is happening and that leads them into places that grant administrators and boards of trustees, however well-meaning, have not reached. In many of these places – collections of unhoused people, addiction recovery groups, online support forums – the people the chaplain wishes to serve are those least able to provide any kind of financial support, nor should they be asked to.

Some groups have found funding and created programs along the traditional pathways. Organizations like Chaplains on the Way in Waltham, MA, and the Night Ministry in San Francisco, CA, serve people who are unhoused. Authors like Breeshia Wade, Pamela Ayo Yetunde and Chenxing Han publish books and turn them into anti-racist curricula to be offered through schools and Dharma centers. Still others convince institutions that have never had a chaplain before, like private companies, pet home-hospice veterinary services, and, in at least one instance, a marine mammal rehabilitation facility, that they could benefit from spiritual care. Yet other chaplains are still looking for their niche, where they can offer spiritual care in the innovative ways they see are needed and buy groceries at the same time. It will take all our skills and ingenuity to figure out how to do this. I have no clear answers (nor does anyone I know – yet). For while suffering beings are limitless, Dharma gates are endless, and spiritual care is infinitely adaptable.

Appendices

APPENDIX

BUDDHIST CHAPLAINCY PROGRAMS

Institution	Required Coursework	Recommended Coursework / Electives	Co-Curricular Requirements
University of the West		Buddhist Meditation Practicum, Topics in Buddhist Meditation, Topics in Contemplative Practice	Weekly hours of contemplative practice = semester credit hours (typically 9 or 12)
Naropa University	Meditation Practicum I, II, and III, Buddhist Meditation Intensive	Meditation Practicum IV, Contemplative Practice Intensive, Contemplative Christianity, Contemplative Judaism, Contemplative Islam, Breeze of Simplicity: Meditation Weekend, Zen Buddhism, Opening the Heart: Meditation Weekend, Mindfulness Instructor Training I, II, and III, Hindu Tantra, Shambhala Training Levels I-V, Taijiquan, Yoga, Ikebana/Kado	
Institute of Buddhist Studies		Introduction to Buddhist Meditation, Meditation in the Theravada Tradition	
Harvard Divinity School Buddhist Ministry Initiative		Buddhist Meditations: Principles and Practices	
Maitripa College	10 credits in the Meditation Pillar course group, options include: Introduction to Buddhist Meditation, Techniques of Buddhist Meditation: The Medium and Great Scope, Techniques of Buddhist Meditation: Madhyamaka, Madhyamaka Meditation, Meditations on Emptiness, Insight Dialogue: Interpersonal Meditation		
Emmanuel College at the University of Toronto (Master of Psychospiritual Studies)	Foundational core courses that include Multi-Religious Theological Education and Leadership, Introduction to Counselling and Spiritual Care, and five courses from the following list: Foundational Tenets and Practices of Buddhism, History of Buddhist Traditions, Buddhist Meditative Traditions, Classic Buddhist Texts, Buddhist Ethics, and Buddhist Contemplative Care	Designated Elective Courses in the areas of Coloniality and Power, Life Stage Ministry, Religious Diversity and Pluralism, and Spiritual Care, Counselling and Mental Health	

Case Studies

Buddhist Spiritual Assessment for Charlie

Background

Clinical Site: VA center in a large metropolitan area in California
Chaplain: Chaplain C, a half-Korean-American lesbian, cisgender woman in her late 40's, who practices Seon (Korean Zen) Buddhism and works as a chaplain for the Veteran's Administration
Dates and Length of Contact: almost weekly contact via AA and PTSD groups for six months followed by formal pastoral care every 2-8 weeks (varies) for the past year and a half as well as continued support group meetings
Careseeker: Charlie (not his name)
Age: 30
Religion: Vajrayana (Tibetan) Buddhist with supernatural beliefs (i.e., astrology, clairvoyance)
Ethnicity: white European-American ancestry
Gender: cis-male
Relationship status: currently single, heterosexual
Occupation: undergraduate student, works part-time

(Note: Chaplain C and Charlie were also featured in vignette 3 in chapter 1 of Kalyāṇamitra Vol. I.)

1. Describe the nature of suffering (*dukkha*)

Charlie is a healthy white male of medium height, medium build, with brown hair and brown eyes. He is fit and has no known medical complaints. He is preparing to graduate from college with a bachelor's degree in May. He works part-time at his college and occasionally expresses dissatisfaction due to normal job stresses. He is active in a campus martial arts club. He attends two weekly support group meetings at the VA for AA and PTSD and also meets with Chaplain C for spiritual care.

Charlie has a very 'forceful' personality. He stands tall, speaks loudly and clearly, walks into a room with purpose, and is assertive. He recognizes that he can sometimes be aggressive. Some these qualities have been reinforced through military training; others have been moderated, providing him with a level of self-control necessary for military service. He has strong opinions and is not shy about voicing them; he is open and up-front about personal topics both in the pastoral relationship and more public settings. He feels emotions strongly, ranging from excitement to anger to sadness; his affect is rarely flat or difficult to read.

Two themes characterize the nature of Charlie's suffering over the past few years: 1) uncertainty; and 2) alienation. In early interactions, the first theme was paramount. He was just starting college, living in a new state, with different people, and on a very different career trajectory than he had been in the military. Uncertainty, although uncomfortable for Charlie, was something he accepted as necessary and even, at times, beneficial. Charlie recognizes that he is a very all-or-nothing person; he sees things in black and white and makes strong, swift judgments about right and wrong. He dislikes ambiguity, or what Buddhists call 'groundlessness.' However, he also recognized the value in learning to see 'the gray' and live in groundlessness (i.e., possibility, flexibility) some of the time. Charlie struggled to actualize this wisdom, often reverting to black-and-white thinking unconsciously, especially in response to an emotional trigger. His quick judgments have sometimes harmed himself and the people around him. His awareness of this has grown.

The second theme of alienation took longer to unearth. As with uncertainty, some disconnection was expected when Charlie left the military and moved to California to attend college, but it has intensified over time due to new and old wounds. Charlie carries suffering with him from his parents' relationships. First, he hates his biological father for being abusive. On the one hand, he looks up to his mother for being brave enough to leave him. On the other hand, he resents his mother for 'settling' for a relationship with his step-father that Charlie views as deeply dissatisfying. He is determined not to have relationships like his parents' relationships.

He has admitted to not being a good past relationship partner, "using" women, and having the relationship be "all about me." He now describes a desire for a relationship that is deeper and more respectful, for someone to be his "queen." However, his most recent relationship was very volatile and ended with anger and resentment. Charlie admits to crossing a physical line during an argument when he "grabbed" his ex-girlfriend and has expressed remorse. In the aftermath of their breakup, he got a DUI, which he describes as "poor judgment." Since then, he has only dated sporadically, as his schedule has been very full with school, work, volunteering, VA meetings, and temple services.

He attends PTSD support and AA meetings, has been sober for over a year, and expresses the desire to remain sober. He "hates" being single and "coming home alone." He misses being in a relationship even as he acknowledges that his last relationship was "dysfunctional" and "not good." He wants to start a family and worries as he enters his thirties that this will become more difficult. Charlie appears to be seeking a relational 'home' and expresses anger, frustration, and sadness when possibilities don't pan out.

This anger (hate/frustration/sadness) is the most frequent and intense form of suffering Charlie experiences. He worries that women are afraid of him as a result and do not perceive him as a 'safe' person. On the one hand, Charlie takes pride in not being a 'safe' person, that is, being able to handle himself in combat or a fight due to his military and martial arts training. He wants women to perceive him as a protector. However, he also acknowledges that his anger can become volatile and is not always easy for him to control, so his potential partners "may be right to be scared." This source of pride is thus also a source of shame.

Charlie is a Vajrayana Buddhist practicing in a Tibetan tradition. His home temple is in Virginia, where he was stationed during his military career, but with Chaplain C's help, he also connected with a local Tibetan group that his visits about once a month. He appreciates the more mystical and metaphysical aspects of the tradition as well as the practical wisdom. Charlie believes in astrology, clairvoyance, and other supernatural phenomena. He practices breath meditation, deity meditation, and mantra meditation. He also practices martial arts and appreciates the spiritual aspects of physical exercise. Charlie accepts (intellectually) the general Buddhist view of suffering as born from desire or craving, often centered in human expectations for the world to work out the way we want it to. He also believes that suffering is rooted in ego attachment and has stated "I have a huge ego!" When loving-kindness meditation to cultivate self-compassion has been suggested, he admits that he has a hard time with that.

Charlie has Christian roots, now set aside, and tends towards quasi-pantheistic views. He draws strength, purpose, and comfort from his spiritual practices on a daily basis while also occasionally expressing anger, frustration, negativity, or disappointment as they challenge him to grow as a person. Charlie occasionally expresses transactional thinking in relation to his spiritual path (see section 2c).

Charlie regularly seeks spiritual guidance and care from several spiritual mentors and teachers, including Chaplain C. Charlie refers to Chaplain C as his "big sister" and frequently comes to her office saying "I need a chaplain" or "I need to process [emotionally] something that's been bothering me." He is willing to accept reframing, challenges, and even direct advice, although he often maintains his strong views on particular subjects. He can articulate his own boundaries while accepting input from others. Charlie and Chaplain C have occasionally had confrontational interactions, sometimes based around work or school, sometimes of a more spiritual nature. Charlie seems to bounce back from these instances quickly and continues to seek spiritual support.

2. Determine the immediate causes (*samudaya*) of the suffering, using the three roots as guides

a. Attachment (*lobha/raga*)

Charlie passionately pursues objectives he believes are important and defends his ideals. Attachment to his identity as a protector and leader means he takes his responsibilities seriously, making him someone others can count on, but also someone who desires to have control over a situation and who expects to see clear positive results from his hard work. In the long run, Charlie is strongly attached to a vision of the future in which he is happily married, with children, the dominant figure in his household, part of a deeply bonded group of friends/co-workers, healthy and fit, and well respected at work that he believes to be important. He expects that he should be closer to this goal than he currently sees himself. Charlie tends to focus on one goal at a time and changes his focus only when exhausted from trying to achieve that goal.

b. Aversion (*dosa/dveṣa*)

Charlie expresses his aversion most commonly as frustration, outrage, and anger, rarely as fear or anxiety. When dissatisfied with a situation, he will stand up to express himself and try to correct things. However, his attachment to 'correct' ways often develops into strong aversion for things that are 'wrong.' This causes friction in his working relationships and sometimes the breakdown of those relationships when he perceives the person involved to be what is 'wrong.' This aversive response is rooted in a tendency for black-and-white thinking. When Charlie can be coached to see the 'grey,' or complexity of a situation, sometimes his anger will ease.

c. Ignorance/Delusion (*moha*)

Charlie occasionally expresses transactional thinking, i.e., "I'm working so hard on myself spiritually and just waiting for the right woman to show up, but the universe isn't cooperating." This kind of thinking can be either reinforced or mitigated by how Charlie interprets his Buddhist tradition. On the one hand, Tibetan Buddhism does emphasize karma – that good deeds bring good outcomes and vice versa. On the other hand, it also emphasizes the mystical and multi-lifetime nature of karma – that only an enlightened master understands what deeds will lead to what outcomes and when. In the meantime, karma from previous lives continues to ripen in this one and what we do now sows seeds that may not bear fruit for many lifetimes to come. When challenged, Charlie admits that he knows the universe is not transactional in that sense (it doesn't "owe me"), but this does not appear to mitigate his feelings of impatience, frustration, unfairness, and anger.

Charlie struggles to internalize many of the teachings that he intellectually values: loving-kindness towards others including enemies, non-judgment, compassion for self and others, patience, non-attachment/non-aversion or equanimity. It appears that part of him, his non-intellectual self, may not truly believe that these qualities are worthwhile and/or may perceive them as threats to his existing ego-narrative.

3. Discover what it would look to reduce suffering and, if possible, bring about joy (*nirodha*)

In the Buddhist tradition that Charlie practices, reducing the three unwholesome roots and the cultivation of their opposites – non-attachment/equanimity, non-aversion/loving-kindness, and wisdom – alleviates suffering. These require cultivation of internal qualities and practice of moral precepts that preserve/promote harmonious relationships and prevent further negative karmic outcomes. In the Tibetan tradition, this is often accomplished through dedication to teachers, deity meditation (in which one identifies oneself with the ideal qualities of the deity), and moral behavior. Charlie has a clear spiritual goal, the enlightened bodhisattva, although the path to this outcome is not always clear.

Charlie interprets this goal in a way that matches his military identity, for which the Tibetan tradition leaves ample room, in the form of wrathful protector deities. The metaphor of spiritual warfare can be found in the Tibetan tradition. Charlie tends to identify more with the bodhisattvas of flaming swords than falling flowers, which gives him a strong sense of home in the Tibetan tradition. These bodhisattvas are often used as psychological metaphors for cutting through one's own attachments and delusions to free inner wisdom; on the other hand, Tibetans have classically believed them to also be very real beings, which also matches Charlie's mystical and metaphysical beliefs. Charlie is pursuing a path to free himself from his own afflictions and, in the bodhisattva ideal, to then work to free others from suffering.

In a more mundane sense, Charlie has also internalized the classic 'American dream' of home, wife, family, and fulfilling career. His spiritual path is interwoven with his domestic ideals, which have been seen as a hindrance to spiritual attainment in some forms of Buddhism. Tibetan Buddhism both affirms and contradicts this tendency, providing ample examples of spiritual masters with a full family life while most monks remain celibate. Monasticism is seen as the best path for most spiritual seekers, but not exclusively necessary for enlightenment, which is also available to exceptional laypeople. Charlie identifies with these worldly masters and seeks to follow in their footsteps within the American context, a modern bodhisattva warrior, respected professional, and secure family man.

4. Co-create a path (*magga/marga*) to that place relying on…

In addition to the words, action, livelihood, and relationships below, Buddhism offers concrete guidance in the form of antidotes to the three poisons of attachment, aversion, and ignorance. Those struggling with attachment should practice generosity; in Charlie's case generosity of spirit, extending the benefit of the doubt to others, may be more fruitful than material generosity. He needs and accepts encouragement and reminders of this direction from his spiritual mentors and friends. Those struggling with aversion, particularly manifest as anger, should practice patience. Charlie can sometimes experience patience as helplessness or resort to apathy rather than patience, therefore it is also important for him to recognize concrete steps or long-term changes of which he may have lost sight. Finally, the antidote for ignorance/delusion is two-fold. First, through the cultivation of steadiness/concentration through meditation and second, by the reliance on learned teachers. Charlie should continue his meditation practice and his relationships with mentors and teachers.

a. Words that encourage joy, consolation, or healing (*sammā-vācā/samyag-vāc*)
Extensive Buddhist literature on the bodhisattva path serves as an inspiration to Charlie. *The Way of the Bodhisattva* by Shantideva is one of the most widely known of these. The 10 chapters of

The Way balance humility with heroic responsibility. Texts such as these both inspire Charlie and help cultivate non-attachment to ego. He draws comfort from his faith in the buddhas and bodhisattvas who've come before, who are protecting him now, and who he aspires to join. They strengthen his sense of calling.

b. Actions that relieve suffering and increase happiness
(sammā-kammanta/samyak-karamānta)
Charlie continues to practice self-care through physical fitness, which helps him cope with stress. His continued sobriety is also a source of pride; he sometimes seems worried about his ability to maintain his sobriety, which leads to vigilance. He meditates regularly, which he finds helpful though challenging.

It may be beneficial for Charlie to take a break from his normal workload of full-time student, part-time worker, and student leader. His graduation in May will be a good opportunity to let go of some of the stress of school and leadership and deliberately craft a life at a more sustainable pace.

c. A renewed sense of life purpose or meaning
(sammā-ājīva/samyag-ājīva)
Charlie is approaching an important transition in his life. He is about to graduate college and is considering next steps. He no longer intends to rejoin the military and is considering graduate programs. He applied for but was not accepted to one program. His tendency to focus on one opportunity at a time amplifies his risk for either reward of disappointment. Charlie has resisted advice from several people to pursue more than one opportunity (i.e., apply to multiple programs) at a time. Disappointment tends to manifest as a threat to Charlie's ego-identity. He will need steady support through this transition and reassurance that there are many ways to help others and live a meaningful life. No single disappointment will change that.

d. Supportive social networks and resources
(sangha)
Charlie wants a supportive social network similar to what he had in the military, but this is unlikely to be recreated in civilian life. This could be a time for Charlie to 'count his blessings' in the social relationships he already has and take steps to preserve and strengthen those relationships. Graduation also means leaving many of his friends from his college social circle. However, his connections at the VA and the local Tibetan temple will remain and those relationships are supportive and stable. With his newfound flexibility, Charlie may choose to invest in his social support system in other ways. Charlie may want to consider spending more time with his local sangha. Likewise, he could invest in friendships, dedicate more time to dating, or travel to see his family. Given the strength he derives from strong social bonds and the alienation he has lately recognized, relationships may be one of the most helpful investments Charlie can make in the immediate future.

Buddhist Spiritual Assessment for Edith

Background

Clinical Site: small, private college in the Northeast
Chaplain: Chaplain E, a white, cisgender, heterosexual man from a Soto Zen Buddhist tradition who teaches mindfulness workshops for the college wellness center
Dates and Length of Contact: Met in mid-August; monthly counseling sessions through December
Date of Spiritual Assessment: January
Careseeker: Edith (not her name)
Age: 26
Religion: indeterminant, unaffiliated; secular psychological worldview
Ethnicity: white European-American ancestry
Gender: cis-female
Relationship status: single (assumed, never stated), orientation unknown
Student status: graduate student in social sciences

1. Describe the nature of suffering (*dukkha*)

Edith is a twenty-six-year-old graduate student who is suffering from loneliness and acculturative stress caused by the move from Georgia to the Northeast to attend graduate school, including some insomnia and adaptation stress of new living arrangements. Edith appears healthy otherwise. Edith has experienced some frustration and conflict within her peers, particularly directed at one individual who she perceives as "ignorant and selfish." She may also suffer from some emotional and cognitive dysregulation. A diagnosis has been alluded to (referenced a past support group for emotionally disturbed young adults) but not confirmed. Issues of insecurity, self-worth, and perceived treatment/value by others appear to play a role. In conversation, Edith often seems scattered and may present several issues at once.

Chaplain E first met Edith during the new student orientation activities on campus. She seemed quiet and somewhat withdrawn and had just arrived from Georgia and lives on campus. She visited Chaplain E in their office in the wellness center about a month later and has dropped by about once a month since then. Chaplain E made notes after each conversation and has drawn on them for this assessment. Chaplain E has also seen Edith at activities on campus.

From their first conversation, Chaplain E began to wonder if Edith was on the autism spectrum. She enters and exits his office abruptly. She usually speaks with a flat tone and little facial affect, although it is clear she feels strongly and uses emotional terms. She rarely makes eye contact, especially when she is speaking (more when listening, especially when listening to something that gets through to her). Her monologues are often disorganized, wandering, vague, and sometimes contradictory. She answers questions obliquely rather than directly. This had made discerning details about her background somewhat difficult, so it has been hard to interpret how past experiences have bearing on present circumstances.

Their first conversation related to Edith's transition to campus life. After about 45 minutes, Edith focused on anxiety due to a letter from a friend she believes is in a dysfunctional/abusive relationship and who expressed an interest in visiting Edith. It seemed that while Edith did not necessarily want to resume that relationship, her lack of connections here made it difficult to relinquish the friendship. The pattern of avoiding what she wants to talk about or coming to it from a circuitous route repeated in later conversations.

In their second conversation, a few days later, Edith seemed more anxious, possibly due to lack of sleep and social pressures of dorm life and a new program. The structure of her program brings her into frequent contact with a classmate whom she describes as narrow-minded, an ignorant "know-it-all," and attention-seeking. During this conversation, Edith made several contradictory statements that seem to indicate internal conflicts due to self-esteem and ego-attachment. ("I feel invisible. / I don't want attention. / I'm a big deal. / I felt like a dirt bag. / If I died, I would be famous. / If I died, no one would even notice.") Further questioning did not reveal suicidal ideation. On the one hand, Edith seemed to feel superior to her annoying classmate and used this to justify her aversion to him. On the other hand, Edith seemed to feel insignificant, ignored, and uncared for by her teachers and classmates. She was also still concerned about the letter from her friend, but seemed less inclined to resume the relationship.

About six weeks later, Edith came by to again vent frustration regarding the classmate she finds annoying. She seemed to appreciate attentive listening and the experience of cathartic relief; however, when Chaplain E asked if they had talked about what Edith wanted to talk about today, Edith said no, but then declined to bring up what she wanted to talk about describing it as "mundane." Chaplain E told Edith it was "her agenda." Twice, when asked direct questions, Edith provided long, rambling indirect answers that didn't seem related to the question. Edith can name emotional responses, but often minimizes them with cognitive language ("not rational," "it's logical," "I know that..."). Her communication patterns are hard to interpret and may lead to her feeling misunderstood by or disconnected from others.

During their last conversation, in early December, Edith was very upset, experiencing shame, frustration, and anger, over the way she perceived she had been mistreated by some campus staff, causing her to cry. She believed their behavior was evidence that they did not value her or she was not a worthy person. She questioned her self-worth, disliked the inability to control outcomes through correct behavior, and disliked perceived misjudgment by others. Edith has repeatedly demonstrated an ability to accept reframing of situations, especially to take on a more 'big picture' view. In this instance, reframing the situation as more about them ("they may have had a bad day") than her seemed to help. She can cognitively bring herself to a state of intellectual empathy for others via reframing, but does not appear to exhibit empathy or an ability to reframe ('not all about her') in the moment to understand others.

Edith has not mentioned parents, siblings, family of origin, or her childhood. She does talk about how life in Georgia was different from the Northeast. She has mentioned past friends and old professors, but does not seem to have any existing close relationships. She has not mentioned a romantic partner and her sexual orientation is unknown.

2. Determine the immediate causes (*samudaya*) of the suffering, using the three roots as guides

a. Attachment (*lobha/raga*)

Edith studied social sciences while she was in college in Georgia. She is attached to her psychological knowledge, though her understanding appears intellectual and academic, rather than integrated. She ties her academic abilities to her self-worth, particularly to her superiority over the 'annoying' classmate. They 'justify' her right to be in her present graduate program, but this leads to self-doubt when she considers that the classmate she looks down on is in the same program as her. Edith is attached to her judgements of other people. She is attached to a desire that people should know and value her, and wants to connect with others and receive praise for her academic and intellectual abilities. However, her emoting and communication styles may hinder these connections and frustrate her desires, leading to further self-doubts.

b. Aversion (*dosa/dveṣa*)

Edith has strong aversion to people she considers to be ignorant or somehow inferior ("who think they're somebody when they're nobody"). Presently, there is one classmate in this category whom she interacts with regularly and believes should not be in the same graduate program with her. Her aversion led her to initially avoid confrontation. Later in the semester, repressed irritation caused an in-class outburst (second-hand information, not reported by Edith). Her aversion for certain individuals seems to limit her ability to experience concern, compassion, or empathy for that person. Instead, she expresses pity, frustration, or anger towards them.

Edith is also extremely averse to words or deeds from others that she perceives as evidence of a low opinion of her. In other words, she is "somebody," not "nobody," and should be treated as "somebody." Lack of the desired level of attention, concern, interest, and/or patience from others leads her to feel shame and anger. These emotions can become overwhelming and tend to dictate an ego-centric interpretation of the behavior of others, leading to a pervasive fear for her own worth and value. This creates an aversion to conflict or to bringing up any issue or topic of conversation Edith fears may be too "mundane," not worth her listener's attention, or may reduce the listener's opinion of her.

c. Ignorance/Delusion (*moha*)

Edith has never identified herself as belonging to any religious, spiritual, or social community, friend group, or club, which leads Chaplain E to believe she may have a very academic and idiosyncratic understanding of other people. Her knowledge of psychology has given her ample examples of human mental illness and pathology, but little practical understanding or emotional intelligence. In the absence of supportive social ties, her views of others have the potential to become confused, as conflicts between academic theories mix. Edith's understanding of psychology also seems somewhat muddled with other disciplines (e.g. medicine, neuroscience). At the same time, her academic knowledge can be used to form narrow judgements of/against others ("They're a narcissist…") based on limited interactions.

Edith appears, at least part of the time, to operate under the idea of a formulaic or mechanistic social structure, in which proper behavior will lead to the desired result (i.e., study and good grades will lead to academic success, which will lead to other people valuing her, and vice versa, those who don't then have little/no value). This may be exacerbated by her study of psychological pathology and does not take the full complexity of human nature into account. It places all responsibility for outcomes, good or bad, either onto herself as the agent without due credit for the agency of others, or shifts all the blame to others for their failure to follow the implied rules and value/treat her accordingly, possibly as a result of their immutable psychological pathology. She interprets the results through an ego-centric lens related to her own self-worth and experiences shame and anger over perceived mistreatment.

3. Discover what it would look to reduce suffering and, if possible, bring about joy (*nirodha*)

In addition to the words, action, livelihood, and relationships below, Buddhism offers concrete guidance in the form of 'antidotes' to the 'three poisons' of attachment, aversion, and ignorance. In Edith's case, ignorance/delusion seems to be the strongest root of suffering, as it propels her attachment and aversion. The antidotes for ignorance are steadiness or equanimity and reliance on teachers. Edith does not appear to have found an academic or professional mentor or teacher here on whom she can rely for guidance. She has strongly resisted all attempted mental health referrals suggested by Chaplain E and will not seek therapy. She has not referenced any practice that might cultivate equanimity (instead she uses cognitive minimization, which is a limited-use strategy). The antidote for attachment is generosity; in Edith's case, if she had a mentor or a therapist, they could encourage a generosity of spirit necessary to see things from other people's points-of-view and cultivate compassion and empathy. Loving-kindness meditation may be useful here, but it is not clear if Edith would engage in that practice reliably without external prompting. The antidote for aversion is patience; Edith may already be misinterpreting patience as non-confrontation and could benefit from learning and practicing constructive confrontation, active listening to others, and non-violent communication strategies.

4. Co-create a path (*magga/marga*) to that place relying on…

a. Words that encourage joy, consolation, or healing (*sammā-vācā/samyag-vāc*)

Edith could benefit from two kinds of words: 1) reframing from trusted teachers, counselors, and friends to establish a more 'big picture' view and calm ego-triggered shame attacks; and 2) studying human psychology in a less academic and more self-reflective way. Edith may benefit from directed reading followed by contemplative reflection on emotional intelligence, positive psychology, and humanistic philosophy to balance her knowledge of psychological pathology. Edith should not study medicine or mental illness without the guidance of someone against whom she can check her understanding.

b. Actions that relieve suffering and increase happiness (*sammā-kammanta/samyak-karamānta*)

Edith desires connection and affirmation. She could benefit from finding a social community and working with a mentor and/or therapist who has comprehensive psychological knowledge and appreciation of academic study, and a strong foundation in neurodivergence. A therapist or mentor would be in a stronger position to confront delusions and mistaken views, but would run the risk of rejection and alienation if they did so insensitively. A therapist might be able to form a strong relational alliance to help co-uncover Edith's emotional and mental processes and their roots, but may not have the perceived authority necessary to correct damaging misunderstandings. Edith places more authority on the perceptions of her academic professors, but they may not be able to form the therapeutic alliance Edith needs. If Edith does have an autism-spectrum or mental health diagnosis, a therapist may also be able to provide care in the best way for her circumstances. Edith may wish to seek out both when she can. In the meantime, she should determine what activities help relieve stress and promote self-care. This may be a good topic for her next conversation with Chaplain E.

c. A renewed sense of life purpose or meaning (*sammā-ājīva/samyag-ājīva*)

It is unclear to what extent Edith sees herself in the role to which she aspires at the conclusion of her program (i.e., clinical mental health care provider). She may or may not ultimately be comfortable in this role. Now is a good time to self-reflect on what her ideal life may look like in 5-10 years and reverse engineer the path to that outcome.

d. Supportive social networks and resources (*sangha*)

Edith may find her own shame and anger decreasing in a community where she felt held, accepted, and valued, but was still strong enough to challenge and correct her in a gentle and open way. She has worked to fit in by volunteering for leadership of a student club, but may benefit more from receiving than giving care at this stage. Edith could flourish in a safe, supportive environment that recognizes her gifts but also insists she do the difficult self-reflective work to grow beyond damaging interpretations of others. Edith may be able to find this environment within her program if she could: a) be more open about herself with trusted teachers and classmates; and b) remain open to direct feedback about her communication style, gentle confrontation, and continued reframing.

Bibliography

84000 Translation Editors. "Sūtras for Well-Being." https://84000.co/resources/sutras-for-well-being.

Access to Insight. "Threefold Refuge." https://www.accesstoinsight.org/ptf/tisarana.html.

Ameling, Ann. 2000. "Prayer: An Ancient Healing Practice Becomes New Again." In *Holistic Nursing Practice* 14(3), April 2000: 40-48.

Analayo, Bhikkhu. 2003. *Satipaṭṭhāna : The Direct Path to Realization*. Cambridge MA: Windhorse Publications.

Anderson, Robert G, and Mary A Fukuyama. 2004. *Ministry in the Spiritual and Cultural Diversity of Health Care : Increasing the Competency of Chaplains*. New York: Routledge Taylor & Francis Group.

Arai, Paula and Kevin Trainor. 2022. "Introduction: Embodiment and Sense Experience." In *Oxford Handbook of Buddhist Practice*, edited by Paula Arai and Kevin Trainor, 1-18. New York: Oxford University.

———. 2022. "Introduction to Part VI: Domestic and Monastic Practices." In *Oxford Handbook of Buddhist Practice*, edited by Paula Arai and Kevin Trainor, 403-404. New York: Oxford University.

Association of Theological Schools. 2020. *Standards of Accreditation 2020*, iii. https://www.ats.edu/files/galleries/standards-of-accreditation.pdf.

Australian Broadcasting Corporation, "Operation Golden Ord," https://youtu.be/6X-Gfwxsdzg time mark 0:19.

Barbuto, John E., and Daniel W. Wheeler. 2006. "Scale Development and Construct Clarification of Servant Leadership." *Group & Organization Management* 31 (3): 300–326.

Barnard, Laura K., and John F. Curry. 2011. "The Relationship of Clergy Burnout to Self-Compassion and Other Personality Dimensions." *Pastoral Psychology* 61 (2): 149–63. https://doi.org/10.1007/s11089-011-0377-0.

Barr, Adam T, and Ron Citlau. 2014. *Compassion without Compromise*. Bloomington, MN: Bethany House Publishers .

Bell, Catherine. 2009. *Ritual Perspectives and Dimensions* (Revised Edition). Cary Oxford University Press Ann Arbor, Michigan Proquest.

Berzin, Alexander. 2010. *Wise Teacher, Wise Student*. Shambhala Publications.

Berzin, Alexander and Matt Lindén. "What is Prayer in Buddhism?" https://studybuddhism.com/en/essentials/what-is/what-is-prayer-in-buddhism.

Beyer, Stephen. 1973. *Cult of Tārā: Magic and Ritual in Tibet*. Berkeley: University of California.

Bidwell, Duane R. 2018. *When One Religion Isn't Enough: The Lives of Spiritually Fluid People*. Boston: Beacon Press, 92-95

Blofeld, John. 1977. *Mantras: Sacred Words of Power*. New York: E.P. Dutton.

Bodhi, Bhikkhu. 2012. *The Numerical Discourses of the Buddha: A Translation of the Aṅguttara Nikāya*. Boston: Wisdom Publications.

———. 2005. *In the Buddha's Words: An Anthology of Discourses from the Pāli Canon*. Boston, MA: Wisdom Publications.

———. 2000. *The Connected Discourses of the Buddha*. Boston, MA: Wisdom Publications.

———. "Going for Refuge and Taking Precepts." https://www.accesstoinsight.org/lib/authors/bodhi/wheel282.html.

Brennan, Joy. 2021. "Out of the Abyss." In *Augustine and Time*. Rowman & Littlefield.

Bstan-pa'i-ñi-ma, and Zhe-chen Rgyal-tshab Padma-'gyur-med-rnam-rgyal. 2013. *Vajra Wisdom: Deity Practice in Tibetan Buddhism*. Boston: Snow Lion.

Buddho editors. "Dhajagga-paritta Chant." https://buddho.org/the-dhajagga-paritta-chant-iti-pi-so/.

Buswell, Robert E. 1990. *Chinese Buddhist Apocrypha*. Honolulu, HI: University of Hawaii Press.

Buswell, Robert E, and Donald S Lopez. 2014. *The Princeton Dictionary of Buddhism*. Princeton, NJ: Princeton University Press.

Cadge, Wendy, and Shelly Rambo. 2022. *Chaplaincy and Spiritual Care in the Twenty-First Century: An Introduction*. Chapel Hill: The University Of North Carolina Press.

Cadge, Wendy, and Emily Sigalow. 2013. "Negotiating Religious Differences: The Strategies of Interfaith Chaplains in Healthcare." *Journal for the Scientific Study of Religion* 52 (1): 146–58.

Cheah, Joseph. 2011. *Race and Religion in American Buddhism: White Supremacy and Immigrant Adaptation*. Oxford: Oxford University Press.

Cheung, Neky. 2008. *Women's Ritual in China: Jiezhu (receiving Buddhist prayer beads) performed by Menopausal Women in Ninghua, Western Fujian*. Lewiston, N.Y.: Edwin Mellen.

Chodron, Thubten. 2019. "Importance of Motivation." "https://thubtenchodron.org/2019/05/significance-intention/.

Clinebell, Howard John, and Bridget Clare Mckeever. 2011. *Basic Types of Pastoral Care & Counseling Resources for the Ministry of Healing and Growth*. Nashville Abingdon Press.

Clinebell, Howard, and Bridget Clare McKeever. 2011. *Basic Types of Pastoral Care and Counseling: Resources for the Ministry of Healing and Growth*. Nashville, TN: Abingdon Press.

Condon, Paul, and John Makransky. 2020. "Recovering the Relational Starting Point of Compassion Training: A Foundation for Sustainable and Inclusive Care." *Perspectives on Psychological Science* 15 (6): 1346–62. https://doi.org/10.1177/1745691620922200.

Conze, Edward. 1994. *The Perfection of Wisdom in Eight Thousand Lines & Its Verse Summary*. South Asia Books.

Copp, Paul. 2014. *Body Incantatory: Spells and the Ritual Imagination in Medieval Chinese Buddhism*. New York: Columbia University.

Crossman, Brian, and Joanna Crossman. 2011. "Conceptualising Followership – a Review of the Literature." *Leadership* 7 (4): 481–97. https://doi.org/10.1177/1742715011416891.

Dhiman, Satinder, Gary E Roberts, and Joanna Crossman. 2018. *The Palgrave Handbook of Workplace Spirituality and Fulfillment*. Cham, Switzerland: Palgrave Macmillan.

Doehring, Carrie. 2015. The Practice of *Pastoral Care, Revised and Expanded Edition*. Louisville, KY: Westminster John Knox Press.

Doolittle, Benjamin R. 2015. "Burnout, Compassion Fatigue, and Job Satisfaction among Hospital Chaplains: A Systematic Review." *Research in the Social Scientific Study of Religion*, vol. 26. BRILL, p. 180-197.

Dudjom Rinpoche. 2017. *Activity Ritual of the Extremely Black Hayagriva*. Lasing, IA: Saraswati Bhawan.

Duncan Ryūken Williams. 2019. *American Sutra: A Story of Faith and Freedom in the Second World War*. Cambridge, Massachusetts: The Belknap Press of Harvard University Press.

Dzongsar Jamyang Khyentse. 2017. "King of Aspirations." https://dharmatranscripts.wordpress.com/2017/02/19/the-king-of-aspiration-prayer-transcript-of-talk-given-by-dzongsar-khyentse-rinpoche/.

_____. 2007. *What Makes You Not a Buddhist*. Shambhala Publications.

_____. 2012. *Not for Happiness*. Shambhala Publications.

Ellison, Koshin Paley. 2016. *Awake at the Bedside : Contemplative Teachings on Palliative and End-of-Life Care*. Somerville, MA: Wisdom Publications.

Ellison, Koshin Paley. 2022. *Untangled*. Balance.

Emmanuel Yartekwei Lartey. 2003. *In Living Color : An Intercultural Approach to Pastoral Care and Counseling*. New York, NY: Jessica Kingsley Publishers.

FaithTrust Institute . 2022. *Responding to Spiritual Leader Misconduct*. Amazon Digital Services LLC - Kdp.

Flannelly, K. J., Roberts, R. S. B., & Weaver, A. J. (2005). Correlates of Compassion Fatigue and Burnout in Chaplains and Other Clergy who Responded to the September 11th Attacks in New York City. *Journal of Pastoral Care & Counseling*, 59(3), 213-224.

Fitchett, George. 2002. *Assessing Spiritual Needs : A Guide for Caregivers*. Lima OH: Academic Renewal Press.

Fuller, Paul. *The Notion of Diṭṭhi in Theravada Buddhism: The Point of View*. London and New York: Routledge-Curzon, 2005.

Friedmann, Dayle A. 2013. *Jewish Pastoral Care a Practical Handbook from Traditional and Contemporary Sources*. Woodstock, VT: Jewish Lights.

Gabriel, Victor. 2014. "Embodying Generosity: A Comparison of Buddhist and Feminist Views of the Body in the Chöd Ritual," PhD diss. University of the West.

Galek, Kathleen, Kevin J. Flannelly, Paul B. Greene, and Taryn Kudler. 2011. "Burnout, Secondary Traumatic Stress, and Social Support." *Pastoral Psychology* 60 (5): 633–49. https://doi.org/10.1007/s11089-011-0346-7.

Gilbert, Paul. 2017. *Compassion: Concepts, Research and Applications*. New York, NY: Routledge.

Giles, Cheryl A, and Willa Miller. 2012. *The Arts of Contemplative Care : Pioneering Voices in Buddhist Chaplaincy and Pastoral Work*. Boston, MA: Wisdom Publications.

Goetz, J. L., & Simon-Thomas, E. (2017). The landscape of compassion: Definitions and scientific approaches. In E. M. Seppälä, E. Simon-Thomas, S. L. Brown, M. C. Worline, C. D. Cameron, & J. R. Doty (Eds.), *The Oxford handbook of compassion science* (pp. 3–15). Oxford University Press.

Graves, Joel C. 2007. *Leadership Paradigms in Chaplaincy*. Boca Raton, FL: Dissertation.com.

Greene, Gordon. 2019. *Facing Suffering*. Water Margin Press.

Gustafson, Hans. 2018. *Learning from Other Religious Traditions : Leaving Room for Holy Envy*. Palgrave Macmillan US.

Gyamtso, Rinpoche Khenpo Tsultrim. 2001. *Progressive Stages of Meditation on Emptiness*. Zhyisil Chokyi Publications.

Han, Chenxing. 2021. *Be the Refuge : Raising the Voices of Asian American Buddhists*. Berkeley, California: North Atlantic Books.

_____. 2023. *One Long Listening*. North Atlantic Books.

Hickey, Wakoh Shannon. 2010. "Two Buddhisms, Three Buddhisms, and Racism." *Journal of Global Buddhism* 11 (11): 1–25. https://doi.org/10.5281/zenodo.1306702.

Ho, Linda. 2022. "Home Altars," in *Oxford Handbook of Buddhist Practice*, edited by Paula Arai and Kevin Trainor. New York: Oxford University, p. 469-485

Holt, John. 1991. *Buddha in the Crown: Avalokiteśvara in the Buddhist Traditions of Sri Lanka*. Oxford University Press.

Hookham, Shenpen K. 2021. *The Guru Principle: A Guide to the Teacher-Student Relationship in Buddhism*. Boulder, CO: Shambhala.

'Jigs-med-gling-pa, R.-byung-rdo-rje, O-rgyan-'jigs-med-chos-kyi-dbang-po, and 'Gyur-med-tshe-dbaṅ-mchog-grub. 2006. *Deity, Mantra, and Wisdom: Development Stage Meditation in Tibetan Buddhist Tantra*. Boston: Snow Lion.

Justes, Emma J. 2014. *Please Don't Tell*. Abingdon Press.

Kalupahana, David J. 1991. *Buddhist Thought and Ritual*. Paragon House Publishers.

Keown, Damien. 1998. *Buddhism and Abortion*. Springer.

King, Ruth. 2018. *Mindful of Race*. Sounds True.

Kong-sprul, B.-gros-mtha'-yas and Sarah Harding. 2002. *Creation and Completion: Essential points of Tantric Meditation*. Boston: Wisdom.

Kornfield, Jack. 2009. *A Path with Heart*. New York, NY: Random House Publishing Group.

Lee, Kin Cheung. 2023. *The Guide to Buddhist Counseling*. Taylor & Francis.

Lee, Kin Cheung, & Oh, A. 2019. Introduction to human view intervention: A Buddhist counseling technique based on Mahayana Buddhist teachings. *Journal of Spirituality in Mental Health*, 21(2), 132-151. Web.

Lee, Samuel K. 2008. "Toward Multicultural Competencies for Pastoral/Spiritual Care Providers in Clinical Settings." In *Ministry in the Spiritual and Cultural Diversity of Health Care: Increasing the Competency of Chaplains*. New York: Routledge Taylor & Francis Group.

Loden, Geshe Acharya Thubten. 1996. *Fundamental Potential for Enlightenment in Tibetan Buddhism*. Tushita Publications.

Loden, Geshe Acharya Thubten. 1996. *Meditations on the Path to Enlightenment in Tibetan Buddhism*. Melbourne: Tushita, p. 159-192

Lotsawa House. "Seven Branches Series." https://www.lotsawahouse.org/topics/seven-branches/.

Lozang Trinlae, Bhikshuni. 2018. *Kun-Mkhyen Pad-Ma DKar-Po's Amitāyus Tradition of Vajrayāna Buddhism*. Vajra Books.

Mahinda Deegalle. 2022. "Aural Practices of Chanting and Protection." *Oxford University Press EBooks*, May, 301–19. https://doi.org/10.1093/oxfordhb/9780190632922.013.17.

McSherry, Wilfred, and Linda Ross. 2010. *Spiritual Assessment in Healthcare Practice*. Keswick, England: M & K.

Michon, Nathan Jishin. 2023. *Refuge in the Storm*. North Atlantic Books.

Miller, Jean Baker, and Irene Pierce Stiver. 1997. *The Healing Connection*. Boston, MA: Beacon Press.

Miller, William R., and Kathleen A. Jackson. 1995. *Practical Psychology for Pastors*. Hoboken, NJ: Prentice Hall.

Ñāṇamoli, and Bodhi. 2001. *The middle length discourses of the Buddha: a new translation of the Majjhima Nikaya*. 2nd ed. Boston: Wisdom Publications in association with the Barre Center for Buddhist Studies.

Neff, Kristin. 2015. *Self-Compassion: The Proven Power of Being Kind to Yourself*. New York, NY: William Morrow Paperbacks.

Nhât Hạnh, Thích, and Rachel Neumann. 2006. *The Energy of Prayer: How to Deepen Your Spiritual Practice*. Berkeley, Ca: Parallax Press.

Nivitigala, Sumitta. 2016. *Vandanā: A Book for Buddhist Chanting*. El Monte, CA: AK Digital Printing.

Ng, S. man, Chow, K. W., Lau, H. P., & Wang, Q. (2017). Awareness Versus Un-Clinging: Which Matters in Mindfulness? *Contemporary Buddhism*, 18(2), 277–291. https://doi.org/10.1080/14639947.2017.1374326

Nouwen, Henri J. M. 1972. *The Wounded Healer*. New York Doubleday.

Nyanaponika, Thera. "Four Sublime States." https://www.accesstoinsight.org/lib/authors/nyanaponika/wheel006.html.

Oliver, Ronald, Brian Hughes, and Geoffrey Weiss. 2018. "A Study of the Self-Reported Resilience of APC Chaplains." *The Journal of Pastoral Care & Counseling* 72 (2): 99–103. https://doi.org/10.1177/1542305018773698.

O-rgyan-'jigs-med-chos-kyi-dbang-po. 2018. *Words of My Perfect Teacher*, 2nd ed. Boston: Shambhala.

O-Rgyan-'jigs-Med-Chos-Kyi-Dbang-Po, Dpal-Sprul, and Rab-Gsal-Zla-Ba, Dil-Mgo Mkhyen-Brtse. 1992. *The Heart Treasure of the Enlightened Ones: The Practice of View, Meditation, and Action: A Discourse Virtuous in the Beginning, Middle, and End*. Boston, MA: Shambhala Publications.

Owens, Lama Rod. 2020. *Love and Rage: The Path of Liberation through Anger*. Berkeley: North Atlantic Books.

Padmasambhava and Chokgyur Lingpa. 2016. *Dzogchen Deity Practice: Meeting your True Nature*. Leggett, CA: Rangjung Yeshe.

Pamela Ayo Yetunde, and Cheryl A Giles. 2021. *Black and Buddhist: What Buddhism Can Teach Us about Race, Resilience, Transformation, and Freedom*. Boulder, Colorado: Shambhala.

Pema, Dragpa. "Four Immeasurables." https://www.padmasambhava.org/sermon/four-immesurables/ (sic).

Peterson, Marilyn R. 1992. *At Personal Risk: Boundary Violations in Professional-Client Relationships*. New York, NY: Norton.

Phabongka Rinpoche. 2006. *Liberation in the Palm of Your Hand: A Concise Discourse on the Path to Enlightenment*. Boston, MA: Wisdom Publications.

Piyadassi, Thera. "Book of Protection." https://www.accesstoinsight.org/lib/authors/piyadassi/protection.html.

Potprecha, Cholvijarn. "Sammā Araham Meditation, Self and Nibbāna." https://buddhanature.tsadra.org/index.php/Articles/Samm%C4%81_Araha%E1%B9%83_Meditation_Self_and_Nibb%C4%81na:_Equivalents_of_Buddha-Nature_Discourse_in_Thai_Buddhist_Traditions_by_Potprecha_Cholvijarn.

Ramsay, Nancy J. 2004. *Pastoral Care and Counseling*. Nashville, TN: Abingdon Press.

Ray, Reginald. 2004. *In the Presence of Masters*. Boston: Shambhala.

Rigpa Shedra Wiki. s.v. "Dharmakaya." https://www.rigpawiki.org/index.php?title=Dharmakaya

Robbin, Mckayla. 2016. *We Carry the Sky*. North Charleston, SC: Createspace Independent Publishing Platform.

Roberts, Stephen. 2012. *Professional Spiritual & Pastoral Care : A Practical Clergy and Chaplain's Handbook*. Woodstock, VT: Skylight Paths Pub.

Roberts, Stephen B. 2012. *Professional Spiritual & Pastoral Care*. Readhowyouwant Com Ltd.

Roukema, Richard W. 2003. "Pastoral Ethics: A Psychiatrist's View." In *Counseling for the Soul in Distress*, 1st ed., 223–36. United Kingdom: Routledge. https://doi.org/10.4324/9781315809021-15.

Sanford, M., Yuen, E., Giles, C., Ostlund, H.J. and Baskin, A., 2022. *Mapping Buddhist chaplains in North America*. Waltham, MA: Chaplaincy Innovation Lab.

Sanford, Monica. 2021. *Kalyāṇamitra*. Ottawa, ON: Sumeru Press Inc.

Śāntideva, Bstan-'dzin-Rgya-Mtsho, Dalai Lama Xiv, and Padmakara Translation Committee. 2008. *The Way of the Bodhisattva: A Translation of the Bodhicharyāvatāra*. Boston, MA: Shambhala; Enfield.

Saddhatissa, Hammalawa. 1991. "Significance of Paritta and its Application in the Theravada Tradition." In *Buddhist Thought and Ritual*, edited by David Kalupahana. New York: Paragon.

Salguero, Pierce. 2022. *A Global History of Buddhism and Medicine*. New York: Columbia University.

Seppala, Emma, Stephanie L Brown, Monica C Worline, James R Doty, Emiliana Simon-Thomas, and C Daryl Cameron. 2017. *The Oxford Handbook of Compassion Science*. New York, Ny: Oxford University Press.

Shambhala Publications. "Resource Guide to The Way of the Bodhisattva." https://www.shambhala.com/way-of-the-bodhisattva-resource-page/

Shaw, Miranda. 2022. "Buddhist Practice in South Asia." In *Oxford Handbook of Buddhist Practice*, eds. Paula Arai and Kevin Trainor. New York: Oxford University, p. 29-33.

———. 2006. *Buddhist Goddesses of India*. Princeton: Princeton University.

Shippee, Tetyana Pylypiv, Chanee D. Fabius, Shekinah Fashaw-Walters, John R. Bowblis, Manka Nkimbeng, Taylor I. Bucy, Yinfei Duan, Weiwen Ng, Odichinma Akosionu, and Jasmine L. Travers. 2022. "Evidence for Action: Addressing Systemic Racism across Long-Term Services and Supports." *Journal of the American Medical Directors Association* 23 (2): 214–19. https://doi.org/10.1016/j.jamda.2021.12.018.

Smith, Ted A. *The End of Theological Education*. United Kingdom: Wm. B. Eerdmans Publishing Company, 2023.

Sopa, Geshe Lhundup . 2004. *Steps on the Path to Enlightenment*. New York, NY: Simon and Schuster.

Sonam, Thakchoe. 2022. "Theory of Two Truths in India," *Stanford Encyclopedia of Philosophy* (Summer 2022 Edition), Edward N. Zalta (ed.), https://plato.stanford.edu/archives/sum2022/entries/twotruths-india/

Stamm, Beth H. (2005). *The Pro-QOL Manual: The Professional Quality of Life Scale: Compassion Satisfaction, Burnout & Compassion Fatigue/Secondary Trauma Scales*. Baltimore, MD: Sidran Press.

Starling, Jessica. 2019. *Guardians of the Buddha's Home: Domestic Religion in Contemporary Jōdo Shinshū*. Honolulu: University of Hawai'i.

Thanissaro, Phra Nicholas. 2018. "Beyond Precepts in Conceptualizing Buddhist Leadership." *Journal of Buddhist Ethics* 25.

Thanissaro Bhikkhu. "Refuge." https://www.accesstoinsight.org/lib/authors/thanissaro/refuge.html.

Tibetan Buddhism. "Refuge and Bodhicitta." https://youtu.be/nc5rTIgQ5AE.

Trainor, Kevin, and Paula Kane. 2022. *The Oxford Handbook of Buddhist Practice*. Oxford University Press.

Tricycle editors. 2000. "Prayer: A look at prayer for Buddhists in the West," in Tricycle, Spring 2000. https://tricycle.org/magazine/prayer/.

Trungpa, Chogyam. 1992. *Transcending Madness*. Shambhala Publications.

Tsadra Foundation. "Buddha Nature." https://buddhanature.tsadra.org/index.php/Main_Page.

Tsering, Tashi. 2009. *Foundation of Buddhist Thought*, V. 5. Boston: Wisdom.

_____. 2008. *Awakening Mind*. Boston: Wisdom.

Tsong-Kha-Pa Blo-Bzang-Grags-Pa, Joshua W C Cutler, Guy Newland, and Lamrim Chenmo Translation Committee. 2015. *The Great Treatise on the Stages of the Path to Enlightenment*. Ithaca: Snow Lion.

Tsultrim Gyamtso. 2001. *Meditation on Emptiness*. Seattle: Nalandabodhi, p. 15-17.

Van Gennep, Arnold. 1961. *Rites of Passage*. Chicago: Chicago University.

Van Schiak, Sam. 2020. *Buddhist Magic: Divination, Healing, and Enchantment through the Ages*. Boulder: Shambhala.

Vrtička, Pascal, Pauline Favre, and Tania Singer. 2017. "Compassion and the Brain." In *Compassion: Concepts, Research and Applications*. New York, NY: Routledge.

Wade, Breeshia. 2021. Grieving While Black: An Antiracist Take on Oppression and Sorrow. Berkeley, California: North Atlantic Books.

Wangdu, Lobsang. "Tibetan Dedication of Merit Prayers." https://www.yowangdu.com/tibetan-buddhism/dedication-of-merit-prayers.html#:~:text=By%20this%20merit%20may%20all,may%20I%20free%20all%20beings!

Wiens, Jesse. 2016. *In A Thousand Hands: A Guidebook for Caring for Your Buddhist Community*. Ottawa, ON: Sumeru Press Inc.

Williams, Paul. 1989. *Mahāyāna Buddhism*. 2nd ed. New York: Routledge.

Wilson, Jeff. 2009. *Mourning the Unborn Dead*. Oxford: Oxford University.

Wilson, Martin. 1996. *In Praise of Tara: Songs to the Saviouress*. Boston: Wisdom.

Yancy, George, and Emily Mcrae. 2019. *Buddhism and Whiteness: Critical Reflections*. Lanham: Lexington Books.

Yeshe, Thubten. 2012. *Becoming the Compassion Buddha*. Simon and Schuster.

_____. 1987. *Introduction to Tantra: Transformation of Desire*. Boston: Wisdom.

Younie, Louise. 2017. "Beginner's Mind." *London Journal of Primary Care* 9 (6): 83–85. https://doi.org/10.1080/17571472.2017.1370768.

Yun, Hsing. 2003. *Pearls of Wisdom*. Buddha's Light Publishing.

Zoogah, David B. 2014. *Strategic Followership*. Palgrave Macmillan US EBooks. New York, NY: Palgrave Macmillan. https://doi.org/10.1057/9781137354426.

Zopa, Lama Thubten. 2018. *The Four Noble Truths*. Simon and Schuster.

———. 2018. Meditations on Rejoicing, 2018. https://www.lamayeshe.com/article/meditations-rejoicing.

———. 2002. *The Direct and Unmistaken Method*. Lama Yeshe Wisdom Archive.

INDEX

A

Accountability, 5, 92-97, 122, 167-168, 181, 204
Addiction, 129, 169, 178, 212, 220, 222
Assessment
    Assessment model, 71-72, 122
    Assessment tool, 63, 68-71
Association of Professional Chaplains, 95
Atheist, 186, 194, 198
Attachment, 13, 31, 50-51, 56-57, 68-71, 139, 164, 201, 208, 228-231, 233-235
Authenticity, 27-28, 164

B

Beginner's mind, 5, 146, 149, 162-163
Board Certification, 94
Bodhicaryāvatāra, 11, 30
Bodhicitta, 120, 134, 136-137, 139, 158, 198
Bodhisattva, 11-13, 30, 50, 92, 100, 116, 133, 139, 155, 157, 210, 230
Boundaries, 5, 16, 19, 22, 26-27, 37, 54, 77, 79, 81, 83-91, 93, 95, 97, 121-122, 146, 148-149, 155, 164, 175, 204, 215, 229
Buddha-nature, 30, 35
Buddhaghosa, 51, 116
Buddhist Churches of America, 207
Buddhist Practice 13, 15, 27, 94, 96, 134, 138-139, 141-142, 145, 147, 157, 164, 180, 196, 201
Burnout, 5, 22, 27, 34, 37, 51-56, 61, 81, 237

C

Chaplaincy Program, 180
Charting, 5, 65, 74
Child abuse, 6, 172-173, 175, 178, 212

Christianity, 16, 24, 27-28, 35, 38-39, 43, 56, 61, 64, 68, 75, 105, 107-110, 112, 132, 143, 147-148, 150-151, 155, 189, 194, 196-200, 203, 206, 208, 219-221, 225, 228
Clinging, 50, 70-71
Code of Ethics, 95
Colleges, 165, 176, 220
Community, 51, 75, 77, 81, 93-97, 113, 125, 131, 143, 160, 168, 180, 189, 212, 216, 220, 222
    Buddhist Community (see *Sangha*) 36, 55-57, 64, 69-70, 89, 93-94, 99, 104, 107, 108, 115, 117, 120, 130, 138-139, 170 171, 176, 183, 188, 196, 197, 201, 204, 205, 207, 213, 231, 235
    Christian Community 112
    Community of Accountability 92-95, 204
    Community Building 113
    Healthcare Community 58
    Leadership of Community 99, 101-104,
    Local Community 75, 116-117, 231
    Monastic Community 108
    Religious and Faith Community 77, 81, 94, 95, 112, 157, 163, 200, 201, 218, 220
Compassion, 5, 13-14, 19, 26-27, 34, 36-37, 48-62, 89, 94, 105, 109, 112-113, 130, 134-137, 139-140, 142-143, 145, 153-154, 157-159, 164-165, 168, 171, 177, 180, 186-187, 193, 196, 201, 206, 208, 211, 228-229, 234-235, 237
    Self-Compassion 29, 58, 61, 89, 90, 122, 228
Concentration, 19, 25, 33, 36, 73, 116-117, 146, 230
Confidentiality, 5, 74, 79-82, 87, 94, 179
Connection, 5, 24, 27-28, 36, 57, 59-60, 79, 83, 86-87, 117, 122, 126, 133-135, 138, 143, 151, 189, 214, 216, 235
Contagion, 5, 26, 52-54

Contemplation, 15, 23, 116, 156
Contemplative Care, 22-23, 33, 35, 38, 58,158, 198, 225
Contemplative Practice 23-26, 28-29, 57, 115, 132-134, 146, 155-156, 162, 164, 225
Conventional, 30, 138-140, 220
Countertransference, 5, 75, 82-83

D

Dalai Lama, 107
Death, 11-12, 26-27, 47, 87, 106, 109, 112, 126, 129-130, 143, 153, 167, 182, 206-207, 215, 222
Dependent origination, 219
Dharma, 11-12, 19, 41, 58-59, 63, 66, 69, 72, 93, 96,105, 108, 113-114, 117-120, 133, 135, 138, 159-160, 183, 187-189, 192, 196, 210, 219, 222
   Buddhadharma 36, 68, 163
   Dharma Protector 131
   Dharma Talk 16, 30, 208
   Dharma Teacher 36, 85, 89, 99, 112, 220
   Dharmakaya 139
Discrimination, 6, 35, 111, 145, 176, 186-187, 190, 194, 196-199, 201, 204, 211
Distraction 22, 26, 33, 36, 152, 162
Domestic violence, 6, 175-177, 212
Dukkha (see also Suffering), 52, 69, 122, 227, 232

E

Eightfold Path, 38, 69, 116-117
   Right Action, 193
   Right Effort, 150, 193
   Right Intention, 16, 193
   Right Mindfulness, 5, 116, 146, 149-150, 193
   Right Speech, 38-39, 46, 199
   Right View, 16, 40, 45, 106, 116, 196
Elder abuse, 6, 174-175, 177, 212
Emotion, 13, 21, 50, 52, 59, 209
Emotional intelligence, 234
Empathy, 5, 16, 19, 26-27, 35-36, 41, 44, 49-53, 55-57, 59-61, 66-67, 82, 126, 158, 164, 169, 211, 233-234
Emptiness, 16, 30, 59, 130, 133, 137, 206, 225
End-of-life care, 153, 182
Equanimity (see Upekkhā), 14, 23, 26, 36, 50-51, 56, 58-59, 62, 73, 89, 130, 139, 193, 201, 229-230, 235
Ethics, 14, 43, 90, 95, 101, 105, 145, 205, 225

F

Fatigue, 5, 27, 37, 52-55, 59, 61, 237
Family 11, 22-23, 29-30, 47, 55-56, 61, 64, 66,71-72, 75, 77, 79, 81-82, 87, 91, 105-107, 126, 130-131, 146-149, 153, 155, 168-170, 173-175, 177-178, 195, 200, 213-214, 218-219, 228, 230-231, 233
Feminism, 189, 193
Four Divine Abodes, 5, 56
Four Noble Truths, 7, 69, 192
Friendship, 7, 88, 96, 164, 232

G

God, 39, 47, 59, 63, 66, 68, 77, 85, 105-107, 110, 143, 151-152, 155, 157, 170, 217, 221
Good follower, 5, 99

H

Harvard Divinity School, 9, 115, 208, 225
Healthcare, 12, 44, 47, 55, 58, 63, 73-74, 83, 103, 113, 143, 145, 165, 181, 200, 206, 220, 225, 235, 237
Hermeneutics, 162
History, 54, 63-64, 71, 75, 121, 155, 164, 169-170, 177-178, 190, 205, 213,
   Buddhist History 23, 107, 208
   World History 147, 149, 155, 192, 194, 211, 219, 225
Hospital, 12, 15, 22, 37, 44, 47, 55, 80, 129, 133, 143, 151, 154, 170, 179, 198, 200, 206, 215

I

Illness, 26, 92, 106, 126, 129, 174, 212, 234-235
Impermanence, 140, 180
Intention, 16, 19, 26, 28, 35, 37, 39, 45, 50-52, 87, 132, 141, 193
Intercultural competency, 6, 158, 162-164
Interdependence, 16, 59-60, 136

Interreligious, 5, 16, 67-68, 129, 131, 145-149, 151-155, 160, 162, 164, 199, 203, 206, 210-211
    Interreligious Chaplains 94
    Interreligious Prayers 143
    Interreligious Rituals 129, 146, 153, 216-217
    Multireligious, 5, 16, 210, 218
Islam, 148-149, 170, 225

J

Jewish, 16, 35, 38, 48, 111, 153, 156, 173, 199-200, 210-211, 221
Judaism, 148, 156, 170, 225

K

Karma, 2, 14-15, 17, 46, 105, 171, 186, 189, 206, 229

L

Laypeople, 93, 99-100, 108, 230
Leadership, 5, 16, 19, 89, 101-107, 109, 111-114, 124-125, 143, 204, 220, 225, 231, 235
    Leadership Studies 99, 104-105
    Servant Leadership 105, 112-114, 124
Liberation, 11-12, 26, 46, 51, 63, 67, 69, 100, 116, 119, 121, 134, 141, 186, 189, 201, 204, 218
Limits, 86-87, 93, 143, 151, 167
Listening, 5, 15-16, 19, 25, 28, 30, 33-41, 43-45, 47, 60, 69, 100, 105, 113, 121, 150, 152, 167, 179, 207, 212, 232-233
    Active Listening 27, 31, 36-38, 40, 77, 235
    Deep Listening 158, 162-164
    Listening Exercises 12
    Not-Listening 19, 22, 33-343
Loving-kindness (see *Maitrī* and *Mettā*), 26, 29, 38-39, 44, 56, 58, 62, 89, 109, 113, 145, 147, 193, 201, 228-229, 235

M

Mahayana 13, 16, 51, 120, 181
Maitrī (see Loving-Kindness), 56, 139
Meaning, 16, 23, 25, 40, 61, 65-66, 69, 72, 96, 100-101, 117, 126, 137, 148, 151, 154, 165, 208, 213, 222
    Meaning Making 31, 77, 143, 216
    Meaning of Life 109-110, 183, 231, 235
Meditation, 5, 23-25, 29, 33-34, 40-41, 44, 51, 56, 70, 73, 94, 115-116, 119, 132-133, 136-138, 141, 150, 155-156, 158, 162, 170, 179, 182, 199, 205-206, 225, 230, 235
    Deity Meditation/Practice 51, 137, 140 141, 209, 228, 230
    Guided Meditation 58, 122
    Mantra 23, 45, 137, 141, 155, 219 228
    Meditation Exercises 134
    Meditation Teacher, 19, 21, 167
    Mindfulness Meditation (see Mindfulness)
    Samadhi 117
    Vipassanā 114, 204
    Zen Meditation 115, 155
Mental health, 6, 35, 55, 61, 65, 68, 80, 88, 130, 167-168, 170-171, 177-183, 212, 214, 225, 234-235
Mettā (see Loving-Kindness), 56, 139
Military, 74-75, 82, 103, 114, 145, 165, 200, 227-228, 230-231
Mind Training, 136
Mindfulness, 5, 19, 25, 30, 40, 52, 59, 70-71, 73, 116-117, 134, 136, 146, 149-150, 162, 180, 183, 190, 192-193, 225, 232
    Mindfulness-Based Stress Reduction (MBSR), 41, 58, 126
Monasticism, 93, 100, 105, 107, 118, 197, 220, 230
Muditā (see Sympathetic joy), 56
Mundane, 11, 15, 30, 88, 230, 233-234
Muslim, 111, 146, 149, 154, 199

N

Nirvana, 68, 136, 138
Non-Self, 27, 30-31, 59, 130, 137
Not-knowing, 59
Note-keeping, 5, 31, 39, 45, 74-76, 106, 168

O

Open-heartedness, 5, 36, 49
Oppression, 6, 17, 79, 92, 130, 159, 165, 185-187, 189-199, 201-208, 213, 215, 218

Outcomes, 15, 24, 26, 28, 74, 102-103, 137, 197, 206, 229-230, 233-234

P

Pastoral Care, 16, 23, 35, 43-44, 65, 189, 198, 227
    Pastoral acts, 66
    Pastoral authority, 107
    Pastoral caregiving, 35
    Pastoral relationship, 227
    Pastoral stances, 66
    Pastoral theology, 26, 67
    Pastoral training, 167
Pedagogy, 188
Personal boundaries, 84-86, 88, 90
Positionality, 6, 190, 193, 196, 208
Power, 6, 12, 29, 33, 84-91, 93, 101, 104, 109-110, 112-114, 129-130, 133, 135, 141, 155, 157, 165, 176, 185-187, 189-193, 195-209, 213, 215, 221-222, 225
    Healing Power, 134
    Social Power, 185, 209
    Spiritual Power, 85
    Symbolic Power, 103
Prajñā (see Wisdom), 15, 45, 60, 117
Prajñāpāramitā, 136
Praxis, 1-2, 5, 12, 138
Prayer, 5, 16, 39, 61, 66, 70, 74, 77, 81, 111, 116, 129, 131-143, 146, 149, 155, 193, 199, 209-210, 213, 215
Presence, 5, 14, 16, 19, 21-29, 31, 47, 59-60, 70-71, 77, 79, 109-112, 114, 129, 133, 140, 143, 151-153, 155, 159, 163-164, 196, 202, 210, 213
Prison, 47, 80, 145
Privilege, 6, 17, 84, 130, 159, 165, 176, 185-191, 193-197, 199-208, 211, 213, 215
Professional boundaries, 5, 16, 79, 81, 83-87, 89-91, 93, 95, 97, 122, 204
Projection, 5, 37, 60, 82-84
Psychology, 6, 26, 53, 57-60, 94, 158, 164, 169, 171, 173, 175, 177, 179, 181, 183, 212, 234-235
    Buddhist Psychology, 67, 70, 201,
    Positive Psychology, 58-59, 235
    Practical Psychology, 33, 167

Q

Questionnaire, 5, 113, 124-125, 178

R

Race, 33, 35, 85, 157, 186, 189-190, 192, 194, 196-198, 200-203, 206
Racism, 58, 92, 111, 130, 165, 187-189, 192-195, 203-205, 211, 220
Rebirth, 136, 148
Reflection, 5-7, 15, 19, 26, 30-31, 37, 70, 79, 94, 96, 115, 117, 119, 121, 123, 125, 147, 198, 209, 211, 214-217, 219, 221, 235
    Reflection questions, 6, 16-17, 213
    Reflexivity, 5, 19, 23, 28-31, 34
    Self-reflection 77, 83
Relationships, 7, 21, 37-38, 41, 53-55, 60-61, 64-65, 75, 77, 81-84, 86-90, 93, 97, 99, 102-103, 107, 109-111, 115, 117-118, 121, 126, 174, 176, 178, 183, 201, 228-231, 233-234, 237
    Personal Relationship 22, 47, 57, 89, 111, 206
Responding, 5, 16, 33, 35, 37-39, 41, 43, 45-47, 105, 123, 151, 190, 193, 201, 212, 222
    Responding exercises, 5, 123, 212
Risk Assessment, 6, 72, 129, 168-169, 171, 176, 179, 181, 212, 214
Ritual, 5-6, 16, 57, 66, 77, 106, 108, 129,131-133, 135-137, 139-143, 147,153-155, 204, 209-210, 213, 215-219
    Buddhist Ritual 137, 140, 141
    Interfaith/Interreligious Ritual 129, 146, 153, 216, 217
    Public Ritual 132, 134
    Women's Ritual 142
Romantism, 81-82, 88-89, 172, 176, 233

S

Sangha, 36, 56-57, 64, 69-70, 93-94, 99, 120, 138-139, 170-171, 176, 183, 188, 205, 231, 235
Śāntideva, 11, 30, 102, 116, 135
Satisfaction, 5, 27, 29, 48, 55, 57, 59, 61-62, 69, 162, 180
Servant leadership, 5, 99, 112-114, 124-125
Skillful Means (see *Upāya*), 105, 145, 159, 162

Social Justice, 6, 111, 130, 185-188, 201, 204-206, 208, 213
Spiritual Assessment, 5-6, 45, 63-73, 75, 77, 122, 227, 232, 237
Spiritual Authority, 5, 41, 107-111, 115, 126
Spiritual Formation, 29, 31, 54, 61, 105-106, 115-117, 121
Spiritual Friend, 11, 34, 83, 94, 105, 157
Spiritual Leadership, 5, 16, 19, 99, 101, 103-105, 107, 109, 111, 113
Standards, 13, 71, 95, 104, 131, 174
Suffering (see *Dukkha*), 11-17, 19, 26-27, 36, 38, 44, 46-53, 56-57, 59-61, 63, 68-72, 74, 89, 92, 106, 109-110, 112, 115, 120, 126, 129, 136, 138-140, 150-151, 155, 159, 162, 165, 168, 180, 185-188, 196, 198, 201-202, 208-209, 213, 219, 222, 227-235
Sympathetic joy (see *Muditā*), 50-51, 56, 62, 133, 193

T

Teacher-Student, 99
Theological, 24, 96, 131, 143, 151, 162, 197-198, 220, 225
Theology, 26, 28, 41, 66-67, 146, 151, 162, 198
Theravada, 51, 134-135, 141, 181, 206, 225
Three Jewels, 138-139
Three *Prajñās*, 7, 15, 25, 164
Tibetan, 5, 13, 33, 75, 96, 108, 118, 129, 131, 133-136, 138-141, 167, 219, 227-228, 230-231
Transference, 5, 37, 75, 82-83, 103, 136
Trauma, 5, 21, 51-54, 61, 79-81, 110, 115, 124, 167, 171, 181, 187, 197, 200
Two Truths, 37, 137

U

Ultimate, 30, 103, 124, 137-140, 143, 160
Universities, 176, 220
University of the West, 16, 225
Upāya (see Skillful Means), 157, 159-160, 162, 164
Upekkhā (see Equanimity), 56

V

Vajrayana, 13, 16, 35, 51, 141, 167, 227-228
Vinaya, 93, 204
Virtue, 12, 50, 133-135
Visuddhimagga, 51
Vows, 13, 85, 92, 100, 139, 193

W

Wisdom, 14-16, 25, 29-31, 46, 48, 50-51, 57, 59-60, 66, 72, 85, 94, 105-106, 109, 112-113, 115, 117, 120, 124, 134, 139-141, 143, 162, 164-165, 186, 189, 196, 198, 210, 227-228, 230
Writing, 9, 17, 25, 30-31, 65, 67, 70, 75-76, 111, 118, 140, 187, 199, 205, 215

Z

Zen, 22, 35, 37-38, 43, 115-116, 147, 149, 155, 162, 177, 198, 205, 225, 227, 232